Stanford Studies in Jewish History and Culture

EDITED BY *Aron Rodrigue and Steven J. Zipperstein*

Rhinestones, Religion, and the Republic
Fashioning Jewishness in France

Kimberly A. Arkin

STANFORD UNIVERSITY PRESS

STANFORD, CALIFORNIA

Stanford University Press
Stanford, California

©2014 by the Board of Trustees of the Leland Stanford Junior University.
All rights reserved.

Printed in the United States of America on acid-free, archival-quality paper

Library of Congress Cataloging-in-Publication Data

Arkin, Kimberly A., author.
Rhinestones, religion, and the Republic : fashioning Jewishness in France / Kimberly A. Arkin.
pages cm
Includes bibliographical references and index.
ISBN 978-0-8047-8600-3 (cloth : alk. paper)
1. Jews, North African--France. 2. Sephardim--France. 3. Jews--France--Identity.
4. Nationalism--France. 5. France--Ethnic relations. I. Title.
DS135.F84A75 2013
305.892'4044--dc23
2013013481

ISBN 978-0-8047-8790-1 (electronic)

Typeset by Bruce Lundquist in 10.5/14 Galliard.

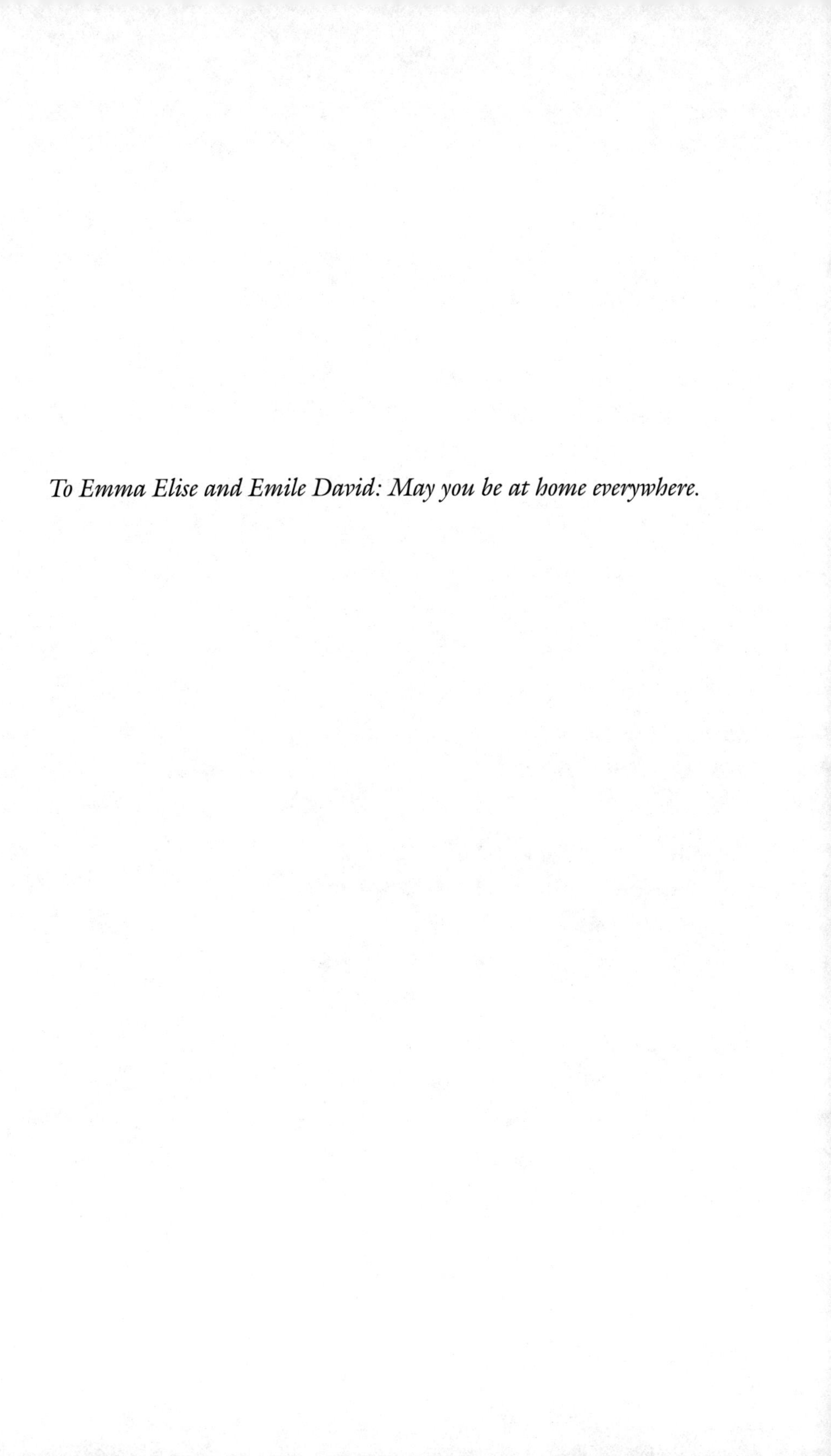

To Emma Elise and Emile David: May you be at home everywhere.

Contents

Acknowledgments

This project would not have been possible without the time, help, and energy of scores of Parisians who generously let me into their lives. I would like to thank the teachers in the three day schools I attended, many of whom graciously dealt with the frustrations and inconveniences of having a foreign researcher in their classrooms, and some of whom confided in and befriended me. I would also like to thank the adolescents I got to know; they often chose to talk to a researcher about their world and how they saw it rather than chat or play with friends. While neither of these groups of generous people will agree with everything I have to say here, I have tried to do justice to the very real difficulties they face being Jews in contemporary Paris. In addition, the men and women of the Union des Etudiants Juifs de France's executive committee went out of their way to find a use for me and to share their experiences and insights. I cannot thank them enough for giving me access to an entirely different world of Parisian Jewishness.

Academic books do not get written without extensive scholarly support, both intellectual and financial. Mine came from both sides of the Atlantic. In the United States, faculty at the University of Chicago always provided challenging and invaluable advice. In response to a confused question, John Comaroff lit the torch that ultimately illuminated the path to this manuscript and my thinking about belonging in France. "Kimberly," he explained, "race is about effacement; ethnicity is about claim!" This book is the result of years spent pondering that sentence. Leora Auslander continuously pushed me to think more deeply about the classed, gendered, and national dimensions of my story. Claudio Lomnitz was a fabulous skeptic, asking hard questions about complexity and evidence. Without friends and Boston University colleagues who commented on all or part of this manuscript, my arguments would be far less interesting, coherent, and sophisticated. Naomi Davidson, Rob Weller, and Jenny White, all immensely busy people, read and reread, helping me figure out what I was trying to say and how I could say it better. Adam Seligman called me on all of my shortcuts, pushing me to be more precise in my terminology and sharper in my theoretical claims. Along the way, Matti Bunzl, Noah Coburn, Joanna Davidson, Andrew Gilbert, Ethan Katz, Andrea Muehlebach, and Justine Quijada offered insight and new directions. Many thanks to my external reviewer at Stanford University Press, whose comments and intellectual generosity helped me rethink certain assumptions and clarify crucial arguments. And many thanks to my editors at Stanford—Norris Pope, Judith Hibbard, Aron Rodrigue, and Steven Zipperstein—who took a chance on a book that falls between many disciplinary cracks. On the other side of the Atlantic, I had the privilege to work and think with a number of scholars and students at the Ecole Normale Supérieure, including Eric Fassin, Michel Feher, and Béatrice de Gasquet. Thank you for helping me better understand the French context. All errors, whether factual or analytical, are entirely my own.

Financial support for the project also came from two continents. The fieldwork for this manuscript was funded by the Institut d'études politiques in Paris and the French government's Chateaubriand fellowship. The writing was partially supported by a Charlotte Newcombe fellowship and by a postdoctoral fellowship at Boston University. The publication of the text was underwritten by a much-appreciated grant from Boston University (BU), just one of the many ways that BU's College of Arts and Sciences and the Department of Anthropology have gone out of their way to support junior faculty and their research.

And last but not least, I could not have done this without my family. Long before I ever thought of becoming an anthropologist or an academic, my parents were certain I would end up teaching in a university. They taught me to be intellectually curious, encouraged me to love writing and reading, and supported my wanderlust—no easy feat given an extended family that thinks France is as far away and as foreign as the Antipodes. Adrien, first as friend, then as boyfriend, and finally as husband, helped make France a second home and a continuous object of study. Our life together has been a constant (albeit inadvertent) illustration of how strange and analytically interesting French Republicanism and secularism actually are; and our cultural, disciplinary, and perspectival differences have made me a better anthropologist.

Significant portions of chapter 6 were previously published under the title "Rhinestone Aesthetics and Religious Essence: Looking Jewish in Paris," *American Ethnologist* 36, no. 4 (2009): 722–734.

*Rhinestones, Religion,
and the Republic*

Introduction

Margot and I stepped off the Parisian public bus and began speed-walking past barely opened shops and roses nodding in well-groomed yards.[1] Neither of us wanted to miss the school bell; I needed permission to sit in on a new class, and she dreaded another impatient note home to her parents. Although only 15 years old and tiny for her age, her red Converse sneakers set a merciless pace I had trouble matching. As usual, she had coordinated her sneakers with a form-fitting hooded sweatshirt, tight jeans, large hoop earrings, and a giant Jewish star pendant—a modest version of the "uniform" worn by many of the students at her Jewish day school.

Margot and I had gotten to know each other over the previous few months. Her government-funded suburban religious school was one of several in which I was doing fieldwork in and around Paris. She was a friendly and voluble, if somewhat socially marginalized, high school student. In the hallways between classes, in the lunchroom, and on the bus we sometimes shared when returning to Paris, she dished out school gossip, complained about teachers and the administration, recounted past vacations, and shared her fears and aspirations.

That morning I was doing the talking. The weekend before, I had attended a well-publicized, if controversial, demonstration against anti-Semitism in Paris. Newspapers had reported a relatively low turnout; I had been surprised by the preponderance of middle-aged adults, particularly given the disproportionate impact anti-Semitism seemed to have on Jewish teenagers and young adults.[2] So I breathlessly asked Margot questions while we ran. Had she gone to the demonstration? What did she think about it?

"No, I didn't go," she said with a laugh. "I'm a racist, so I can't go to an antiracist rally, can I?"

"What do you mean," I stuttered. "I mean what do you mean when you say you are a racist?"

"It means I hate Arabs."

For a number of reasons, this conversation should have been surprising, even paradoxical. In the first place, why was Margot so ready to proclaim her "hatred" for an entire ethno-religious minority? To a considerable extent, French Jewish politics after World War II emphasized the indivisibility of racism and anti-Semitism (Mandel forthcoming). In the 1970s and 1980s, even when Jews were not directly affected by racist, often anti-Arab violence, Jewish newspapers and magazines reminded their readers of Jews' moral obligation to oppose any and all forms of exclusion (e.g., Grunewald 1980c, 1983, 1985b; Smolarski 1986; chapter 2).[3] Any form of racism, so the argument went, was motivated by the same nefarious nationalist logic and would—sooner or later—negatively impact Jews. Even when it became clear that French Muslims and Jews did not see eye-to-eye on Israeli or French foreign politics, some very visible Jewish pundits continued to insist on combating the shared ideology behind racism and anti-Semitism. In a March 1980 editorial titled "La nécessaire solidarité avec les travailleurs immigrés" (The necessity of solidarity with immigrant workers), the editor of the major Jewish weekly *Tribune Juive* upbraided Jewish organizations that were not respecting the biblical injunction to remember the stranger. He wrote:

> I know that the overwhelming majority of immigrant workers . . . are Arabs, Maghrebi citizens who support the Arab Umma and have a perspective on Israel that is, for us, untenable. But . . . is it not possible for French Jews, who are assimilated to Israeli Jews, to open a dialogue . . . with these men, women, and children who are in such difficult straits? Can we not show that the aberrant image of Zionists sketched by Arab propagandists and even often by Jews does not correspond to reality? In addition, is it not our mission here in France, when faced with hundreds of thousands of workers from the Maghreb, who are in constant contact with their families and friends on the other side of the Mediterranean, to build bridges and begin a dialogue? (Grunewald 1980c:4)

Similarly, in 1983, Eric Ghebali, the newly elected president of the largest Jewish students' union Union des Etudiants Juifs de France (UEJF), noted: "Even if it has become standard to unconditionally support the democratically elected government of Israel, the UEJF will show its commitment to Israel and peace through a Jewish-Arab *rapprochement*, particularly through cultural activities that will bring Jewish and Arab students together" (Ghebali 1983:16). Given this history, why did Margot sever anti-Arab racism from anti-Semitism? And why did she openly and unabashedly call herself a "racist"?

Second, although Margot clearly distinguished herself from those she called "Arabs," a blanket term often used to refer to anyone presumed to be Muslim or of North African origin, her position in France's schema of categorical identities—Frenchness, Jewishness, Arabness—was hardly clear. Like the vast majority of her day school classmates, Margot was what French Jews call *Sephardi*, the daughter and granddaughter of North African immigrants. Between the 1950s and the 1980s, approximately 55,000 Tunisian, 50,000 Moroccan, and 125,000 Algerian Jews immigrated to France (Bensimon 1972:2; Laskier 1983a:342; Taieb 1989:57).[4] Again like her classmates, Margot hailed from an upwardly mobile family, but she lived in a mixed-income, geographically peripheral Parisian neighborhood. As a result, unlike most *Ashkenazim*, or long-established European Jews, she shared street corners, apartment buildings, and bus lines with the children and grandchildren of other relatively recent immigrants, particularly Arab Muslims. With grandparents and even parents who still spoke Arabic at home, she was also far more likely to share cultural practices, culinary habits, musical repertoires, and even aesthetics with other North Africans than with Ashkenazim or other bourgeois Parisians.

For many French Jews and non-Jews, Margot was thus not only a Jew, she was also an Arab Jew, a subject position that both bifurcated Jewishness and blurred the boundaries between Arabness and Jewishness. As a result, she, like many of her classmates, had been taken for "Arab," insulted as a "dirty Jew," and dismissed by some of her (not always Ashkenazi) Jewish teachers as ignorant, low-class, and materialistic. If the French generally presumed that Jewishness and Arabness were mutually exclusive, categorical identities, such a neat separation was not so obvious from Margot's vantage point. So why, given the ambiguity of Margot's position in France and her obvious physical, social, and cultural proximity to Arab Muslims, did she reject any association with "Arabs"?

Margot's refusal to demonstrate against anti-Semitism was a third surprise. In the first place, she was hardly indifferent to the problem of anti-Semitism. She told me early in our relationship about an anti-Semitic encounter witnessed on a Parisian bus: a Jewish boy who had accidentally shoved an "Arab" passenger had been threatened and even hit by the passenger's friends, despite repeated attempts to apologize. She also readily recounted the anti-Semitic experiences of friends and friends of friends. Like many of her classmates and their parents, she worried about what the state's slow response to the post-2000 growth of anti-Semitism meant for a Jewish future in France. Over the past 30 years, similar concerns about post-Holocaust anti-Semitism in France have driven both Jews (and non-Jews) into the streets in large numbers. In the early to mid-1980s, when French Jews feared a resurgence of deadly anti-Semitic attacks tied both to neo-Nazis and events in the Middle East,[5] a series of demonstrations against anti-Semitism mobilized large swaths of the French Jewish community interested in defending Jews' "rightful" place in the Republic. In 1980, after the bombing of a Parisian reform synagogue on rue Copérnic and then French Prime Minister Raymond Barre's famous gaffe about Jewishness and Frenchness,[6] more than 200,000 people marched in Paris against anti-Semitism and for Republican values, the French flag in hand. After the 1985 bombing of a movie theater showing a film about Adolph Eichmann, the Jewish press reported a demonstration in which Jewish and non-Jewish protesters chanted, "Arabs in Meton, Jews in Paris, it's my buddy who's being assassinated," thus confounding distinctions among ethno-religious minorities (Haymann 1985:11; Lewer 1985:17). And in 1990, after the desecration of a Jewish grave in Carpentras, 200,000 people again responded to Jewish institutions' calls for a massive protest in favor of French Republicanism.[7]

Margot's refusal to demonstrate can thus be read as a rejection of the post-Holocaust French Jewish tradition of publicly arguing for the inclusion of Jews (and others) in French national imaginaries. Indeed, many of her classmates claimed that such demonstrations were pointless or that Jews should not be responsible for demanding Jewish rights in France. Some even went so far as to insist on the fundamental incompatibility between Frenchness and Jewishness, or to insist that Jews had no future in France (see chapters 3 and 5). Given this history of Jewish public engagement and the pride many teachers and parents felt in their dual identity as Jewish *and* French, Margot's seeming disinterest in a Jewish future in France was new.

And finally, there was Margot's outfit. I called it part of a Jewish day school "uniform" because I found similar forms of dress in all the Jewish schools in which I worked, regardless of geographical location and religious orientation. Whether in the relatively wealthy, leafy suburbs to the east of Paris or the gritty, heavily minority neighborhoods to the north, I easily identified Jews by looking at sneakers, jean brands, necklaces, and earrings. This in and of itself was hardly surprising. Like many of her teenage counterparts all over the developed world, Margot consciously constructed identities through the tools of the global market (Dolby 2001; Gopinath 2005; Hall 2002). Her clothing brands, colors, and cuts; hairstyle; jewelry preferences; and hangout locations proclaimed a particularly ethnicized and classed form of Jewishness, one known by her peers as *chalalah* (see chapter 6). In other words, Margot's red Converse sneakers, matching hooded sweatshirt, tight jeans, and hoop earrings were as much a part of her Jewishness as the day school she attended and her family's abbreviated Sabbath rituals.

But Margot was enrolled in Brith Abraham, an orthodox Jewish day school dedicated to relatively strict observance of Jewish law and to encouraging students to dress "Jewish," meaning in accordance with the precepts of *tzniout*, or modesty. Although girls were allowed to wear pants, they were not supposed to cultivate sex appeal and were forbidden to show their shoulders, collarbones, or knees. For those who respected tzniout, a Jewish star was hardly a necessary or sufficient mark of Jewishness; simplicity, modesty, and gender distinction were. Margot, however, was heavily invested in a sartorial style—those form-fitting clothes and large earrings—that violated the spirit (if not the letter) of tzniout. In the eyes of observant Jews, her skin-tight jeans blurred gender lines, the low-cut T-shirt revealed far too much skin, and the flashy colors and jewelry called inappropriate attention to her body and material means. So why was Margot dressed this way? More importantly, why did Margot—like many of her classmates—think of this combination of jeans, sneakers, earrings, sweatshirt, and T-shirt as a "Jewish" style when she learned something very different in school?

Racializing Religion

These paradoxes do not apply uniquely to Margot. Many of her classmates from similar socioeconomic and historical backgrounds both articulated and embodied these ruptures and discontinuities. Why? What motivated Margot and many other day schoolers to refuse to recognize "Arab" and "Jewish" structural similarities in France *and* to openly embrace "racist" forms of discourse? What produced the seeming rupture between Frenchness and Jewishness that led to Margot's disinterest in protesting anti-Semitism? Why did Margot work to visibly mark her Jewishness in ways that were not religious, if not irreligious? What, if anything, might these questions have to do with the ways in which young Jews were rethinking national, religious, and ethnic identities? And how might answers help us understand the relationship between and among religion, race, and identity in the post-modern, post-colonial context of contemporary France?

This book explores the puzzles and paradoxes raised by Margot and her Jewish day school classmates. It does so by outlining the construction, reconstruction, and contestation of Jewishness, Arabness, and Frenchness as primordialized categories of belonging in Metropolitan France. I will suggest that for historical reasons tied to the particularities of French colonialism in North Africa and decolonization in the Metropole (chapters 1 and 2), Sephardi Jews like Margot blurred the boundaries between and among these three categories. In other words, Margot and her friends were liminal in France's postcolonial triptych of identity categories, threatened with exile from Frenchness both as Arabs and as Jews. Despite a powerful theoretical tradition that links this kind of experience of liminality—and particularly the liminality associated with youth—to antiessentialism and antiracism (Bauman 1991; Bhabha 1993, 1994; Bucholtz 2002; Dolby 2001; Gilroy 1990; Gopinath 1995; Hall 1990; Hebdige 1979; Park 1928; Wulff 1995; also see chapter 6), I argue that the categorical uncertainties around Margot's identity underwrote both her racist and racializing tendencies. In other words, the lived experience of Sephardi liminality in France produced the opposite of what social science theory has so often predicted. Within the structural and material constraints of postcolonial France, imagining identity in the naturalized terms of race became one of the few ways to negotiate both anti-Arab racism and bourgeois (sometimes Ashkenazi Jewish) hostility toward ethno-religiously marked practice. Racializing Jewishness helped distinguish Arab Jews from Arab Muslims, who were imagined as a heteronomous population, too fully saturated by embodied religious obligations to embrace French secularism and liberal democracy (Davidson 2012). It also shored up strained Sephardi ties to Ashkenazim and therefore to "European" values, whiteness, and (at least in theory) Frenchness (see chapter 3).

As a result, Margot and her friends were far more likely than their parents or teachers to attempt to construct and understand Jewishness as inevitably visible and legible (see chapter 6). They were also more likely than their elders to reject hybrid identities, refusing the possibility of being Jewish and French, or of being Jewish and Arab. Instead, they insisted on the absolute ontological as well as expressive differences between and among all these categories. The more liminal their structural position—if they were Moroccan rather than Algerian, struggling to remain middle class rather than well established, living in immigrant neighborhoods rather than the heart of Paris—the less tolerable any form of identitarian ambiguity seemed to be. The less inherently natural and exclusive their Jewishness appeared, the more likely it was to be primordialized through appeals to race. Race, in other words, became the grounds on which some young Sephardim tried to reconstruct lost or endangered organic communities within the context of multiethnic, multiclassed peripheral Parisian neighborhoods. In the process, as we will see, they ironically fashioned and biologized themselves out of the French nation.

Writing Jewish Racism

Margot's racializing tendencies may have been relatively new, but they were certainly not news to the institutionalized French Jewish community. Eight months into my fieldwork, I agreed to write an abstract of my early results for a graduate student conference at the Ecole Normale Superièure, a prestigious French university. My abstract, which highlighted adolescent racism and racialization, ended up circulating well beyond the world of conference participants. It landed in the inbox of a bureaucrat in the central administration of a Jewish school network in which I worked. From there it was ultimately circulated to the principals of every day school in Paris.

Within a week after the circulation of the abstract, I was removed from all three of the schools in which I had been working: a coeducational school that I will call "Brith Abraham," an all-girls school that I will call "Beit Sarah," and an all-boys school that I will call "Beit Ya'acov."[8] All three schools were located in the semiurban zones that ring Paris to the north, east, and south, and accessing them from Paris often required a combination of metro, regional train, and bus rides. They were all part of larger educational networks that historically educated Jews in North Africa. And all three first started educating French Jews in the years following decolonization and massive North African Jewish migration. From March 2004 until December 2004, with a two-month break in July and August during summer recess, I spent two days of every week at Brith Abraham, two days at Beit Sarah, and one day at Beit Ya'acov.[9]

By the time I was removed from both Brith Abraham and Beit Sarah, I had become part of the landscape. My strange accent and syntax, non–North African roots, and ambiguous position within school hierarchies had faded from view. Students had stopped treating me like a cross between an alien and a rock star. Most teachers seemed comfortable with my constant presence, even in their classrooms. And administrators were happy to use me as a substitute teacher, a hall monitor, or an exam proctor when they found themselves shorthanded. In both schools I taught English (very badly) to upper-level middle- and high-school students. In exchange, I was given the opportunity to explore official national and school-based narratives of self and belonging by sitting in on what school officials called *khol* (secular) classes taught by state-paid and educated teachers as well as *kodesh* (religious) classes provided by privately trained and financed instructors. I talked extensively with secular and religious teachers, administrators, and parents about the identitarian goals of Jewish education, the effects they hoped it would have on students, their aspirations for students and French Jewry more generally, and their fears for the future. We also talked about their Jewishness and Frenchness, how Jewishness should be institutionally defined, why it had become so important to separate Jewish kids from other French children, and what this meant for thinking about national moral and political community.

I compared these formal and informal narratives with the kinds of stories adolescents told about themselves, about "Jews" more generally, and about a whole range of "others"—"the French," "the Arabs," "the blacks," and so on. To do so, I followed students through average days, attended assemblies, watched students interact with school officials and each other, and participated in school-based community activities. I informally interviewed students at lunch and recess; accompanied them into public spaces that forced interaction with non-Jews; and participated in lively group discussions about racism, national politics, identity, and school. I also recorded a number of formal interviews with students outside of school, mostly individually, but sometimes in groups.

Within days, all of this came to an end. And for a few months, even my physical removal hardly satisfied school officials, one of whom hoped to prevent me from ever doing fieldwork with Jews in France again. I had gone from being a relatively trusted insider—one administrator had even asked for my help with the American consulate over a visa problem—to an enemy.

In many ways, my removal was part of a larger struggle over the politics of representation, which is in turn tied to the paradoxes that produced Jewish racism in France. French Jews—and most particularly Sephardim—are both relatively powerful and impotent. Historically, Jews have been highly upwardly mobile and are, on average, more educated than the French population as a whole (Cohen 2002:17–18).[10] Over 40 percent of Jews work in jobs with considerable cultural or economic capital in France; they are upper-level state employees, liberal professionals, writers, and academics (ibid.:20). As part of the dominant class, French Jews have the resources to produce their own representations of Jews. There are Jewish listservs, websites, and documentaries devoted to re-presenting French anti-Semitism, Israel, and the Israeli-Palestinian conflict. The Conseil Représentatif des Institutions Juives de France (hereafter known as the CRIF), one of the most powerful Jewish organizations in France, sends out a daily electronic newsletter with a press review and commentary. Its president regularly writes editorials for national newspapers, agrees to written and oral interviews, and meets with government officials. Community centers, synagogues, day schools, Jewish student unions, and youth groups host their own public debates about a whole range of issues—religion in the Republic, anti-Semitism, foreign policy, and, of course, Israel. Paris boasts at least a score of Jewish magazines, newspapers, analytical reviews, and scholarly series, many of which are advertised and sold at regular newspaper kiosks. There is a full-time Jewish radio station as well as a number of television programs. And demonstrations led by Jewish organizations are regular occurrences on Parisian streets. In other words, Jews have constructed a (partially visible) parallel public sphere with Jewish accounts of what are perceived to be Jewish issues (Werbner 2002). A good part of my fieldwork, particularly after my "excommunication" from Jewish schools, involved exploring these representations and the way they have changed over the last two decades.

But this highly developed representational apparatus does not mean that Jews have the power to shape public perception. "Jewish" interests are hardly hegemonic. At least since the Six Day War in 1967—which followed hard on the heels of the French decolonization of North Africa—French foreign policy and public discourse has long favored what many call "Arab" interests. As many Jews note with anger, both print and televised media tend to be sympathetic to the plight of Palestinians and quick to denounce Israeli actions. When "Jewish" opinions are solicited for the national press, the writers and scholars asked usually confirm mainstream representations. As a result, they are seldom viewed favorably within the parallel Jewish public sphere. For example, *Le Monde* and *Libération*, two major national dailies, regularly publish Esther Benbassa's commentaries on the Israeli-Palestinian conflict and French Jewish identity (see, e.g., Benbassa 2002, 2004a, 2004b, 2004c, 2006, 2010; Benbassa and Attias 2001). However, Benbassa, a left-wing Sephardi historian based at the Ecole des Hautes Etudes en Sciences Sociales,[11] is reviled by many with a voice in the Jewish press. She has been accused of everything from self-hatred and being a useful idiot for rabid and racist pro-Palestinians to shoddy scholarship and ignorance (Kurtz 2007; Lévy 2001; Trigano 2007).[12]

This inability to decisively impact public opinion, particularly on issues related to Israel, is evidence of Jews' dominated status within the dominant class. Whatever the intent of state policy and media depictions, they seem to align mainstream French politics with socio-economically and culturally dominated Muslim groups who have been called by French government practice, national discourse, and increasingly their own social and religious networks to identify with "Arab" causes. If these representations (fleetingly) turn Muslims into part of the French political mainstream, they also presuppose and entail Jewish alienation from some normative social values. This, in turn, symbolically reverses relations of domination between Arab Muslims and Jews. This dynamic has been particularly noticeable since the beginning of the second Palestinian Intifada in 2000, when the French press blamed Israel for precipitating the violent upheaval and France's then-socialist government was slow to respond to the resulting wave of anti-Semitism in France.

If Jewish exclusion from the mainstream consensus on Israel and Palestine is proof of relative Jewish marginality, Jews often understood it as a sign of their absolute domination. During my fieldwork, a number of French Jews did not (perhaps could not) understand or experience themselves as part of the dominant class. Some, particularly Sephardim, imagined themselves as the only truly dominated population in France. Faced with a rise in anti-Semitism often attributed to "Arabs," many Jews argued that a complacent (post-)Catholic French majority was in league with a bloodthirsty Arab minority to persecute Jews. At a Jewish community center conference on the French media, anti-Semitism, and Israel, one evidently panicked Sephardi audience member screamed: "They are all out to get us!"[13] This sense of powerlessness and victimization made the question of Jewish representation crucial.

The "charge" of Jewish racism fueled this sense of panic because it seemingly placed Jews on the wrong side of history. On a variety of discursive levels, an accusation of "racism" entails exile from post-Holocaust European modernity and even civilization. As a result, human rights groups, French newspapers, the occasional government official, and a whole range of pro-Palestinian groups condemn Israel by accusing the Jewish state of systemic racism.[14] At the same time, some French Jews and non-Jews accuse "Arabs" of anti-Semitism as a way of arguing for their exclusion from both European and French citizenship (Brenner et al. 2002; Brenner 2004; Finkielkraut 2003; Taguieff 2005). For some teachers and administrators, this context meant that it was just as important to combat student racism as to conceal its existence. The principal at Beit Sarah told me that he tried to correct every "wrong" word his students uttered. A handful of teachers at Brith Abraham devoted entire lessons to dismantling student stereotypes (see chapters 4 and 6). But in some cases the desire to conceal any potential parallels between Jewish and "Arab" children trumped any pedagogical mission. One important administrator at Brith Abraham instructed teachers not to challenge racist student remarks, noting that teachers just needed to "understand" where students were coming from. From this kind of perspective, highlighting the racializing tendencies of Jewish youth was clearly perceived as arming the enemy—as comforting those in the white Catholic majority and the Arab Muslim minority who traded consciously or unconsciously in anti-Semitism. As one school director noted: "Why would I bring someone into my school who can then be used as a weapon against me?"

The high school principal who saw me as a loose cannon certainly had a point. My story about shifting conceptions of Parisian Jewishness is not always flattering, and it could be misread. There is growing propensity in France and Europe more generally to reduce social behaviors to a kind of cultural biology; through this lens, my work could be read as "proof" of anti-Semitic stereotypes about Jewish materialism, clannishness, and imagined superiority. Is this a reason not to write about the racialization of identity going on among some French Jews, or at least to write about it very differently? For some of my informants, the answer is clearly yes. But that anxiety echoes the same reductionist and essentializing tendencies that this book rejects. This book is not about the essence of any group, Jewish or otherwise. Quite the contrary. It is an attempt to illustrate the ways in which a particular set of actors navigated social conditions that were of neither their own choice nor their own making. As we will see, the tensions and structural binds with which the Jews in this story—parents and children, teachers and administrators, self-identified Sephardim and Ashkenazim, struggling middle-class salespeople and relatively privileged academics—were regularly confronted led to attitudes, arguments, and actions that challenge the platitudes of liberal multiculturalism. In many ways, this was overdetermined, called into being by the conceptions of identity, nation, and religion that structure belonging and exclusion in postcolonial Europe. Ignoring the practices of some young Jews would hardly do justice to the very difficult social tightrope many Jews (and Muslims) are forced to walk in France. It also would reproduce the very logic that underwrites both anti-Semitism and racism, reducing structurally conditioned behaviors to culturally determined, if not racial, traits.

There is a second reason why I have not shied away from a story that might raise eyebrows in France. My tale is deeply historical and thus specific to a particularly classed and ethnicized group of French Sephardim. But it nonetheless has implications for some of the larger questions animating contemporary political debate and scholarship about national identity, minority identity politics, and secularism, particularly in Europe. My story historicizes and deconstructs the supposedly primordial conflict that pits "Jews" against "Arabs" all over Europe and the Middle East (Taguieff 2002; Weinstock 2004; Ye'or 1980, 1985, 1999), insisting instead that the two categories are dialectically tied and therefore mutually constitutive (see chapter 1). I also challenge the facile conflation of European Muslims with practices of self-exclusion, including racism (Brenner et al. 2002; Taguieff 2002; Trigano 2003; also see Fernando 2009, 2010). Rather than presume that Islam itself is atavistic and incompatible with Western values (Bensoussan 2004; Brenner et al. 2002; Hirsi Ali 2007; Tagueiff 2002, 2005; Trigano 2003; Ye'or 2005),[15] or that economic exclusion has led to the alienation of Muslim youth (Cesari et al. 2001; Kepel 1987; Wihtol de Wenden 1999), I call attention to contradictions within national logics that place a variety of ethno-religious minorities, including Jews and Muslims, in impossible structural binds (see chapters 2 and 6). And finally, I question whether illiberal religious traditions themselves pose the most intractable problems in contemporary Europe (Bowen 2007; Fourest 2005; Huntington 1996; Roy 2004). It may in fact be nonreligious expressions and enactments of ethno-religious identities that fuel some of the major ruptures between minority and majority populations (see chapter 4). In other words, as France and Europe continue to wrestle with 21st-century versions of the "Jewish question," my work offers new ways of thinking about the production of national community, intolerance, race, and racism within the postcolonial nation-state.

One French "Natives" and Native Jews

> [W]e insist on declaring that we were born French, that we are
> French, and that we shall always remain French. We form neither
> a race nor a people, but an integral part of the nation from which
> nothing could separate us. . . . Frenchmen, not through adoption,
> but from the beginning. Frenchmen not in name only but with all
> our hearts and all our ardent convictions. The great majority of the
> Jews of France . . . ask you with confidence not to let the gesture
> [the new anti-Jewish law] that has been announced be carried out
> and to save once more French unity.
> —Letter to Marshal Pétain signed "Parisian Jews," April 14, 1941
> (cited in Birnbaum 1996:350)

> I know the colonizer from the inside almost as well as I know the
> colonized. But I must explain: I said that I was a Tunisian national.
> Like all other Tunisians I was treated as a second-class citizen,
> deprived of political rights, refused admission to most civil service
> departments, etc. But I was not a Moslem. In a country where so
> many groups, each jealous of its own physiognomy, lived side by
> side, this was of considerable importance. The Jewish population
> identified as much with the colonizers as with the colonized. They
> were undeniably "natives," as they were then called, as near as
> possible to Moslems in poverty, language, sensibilities, customs, taste
> in music, odors and cooking. However, unlike the Moslems, they
> passionately endeavored to identify themselves with the French. . . .
> For better or for worse, the Jew found himself one small notch above
> the Moslem on the pyramid which is the basis of all colonial societies.
> His privileges were laughable, but they were enough to make him
> proud and to make him hope that he was not part of the mass of
> Moslems which constituted the base of the pyramid.
> —Memmi 1991:xiii–xiv

A central claim of this book is that young Sephardi Jews are multiply
liminal in France and that they respond to that liminality by racializing Jewishness. Understanding this claim requires an exploration
of the historical forces that produced French Jews, and particularly
North African Jews, as liminal beings uncomfortably situated between
Frenchness and foreignness, Europeanness and Arabness, religious

particularity and secular universality. It also requires exploring how and why primordial difference has, at least for some young Jews, become an overdetermined mode of both understanding and constructing Jewishness, Frenchness, and Arabness. In this chapter, I will argue that, in different ways, the construction of Jewishness in post-Revolutionary France and under French colonialism in North Africa created the conditions of possibility for understanding Jewishness as ontological difference and race. In the Metropole, this was driven by the impossibility of advocating for Jewish "nativeness" to France, or what the Parisian Jews quoted above called being "Frenchmen, not through adoption, but from the beginning," without simultaneously constructing and reifying the essentialized category of "Jew."[1] However inadvertent, this reification elided vast differences in history, religious practice, language, and social class among various populations of Metropolitan French Jews. While the specter of homogenized, essential Jewish difference haunted the post-Revolutionary French Metropolitan project, it was one of the foundations for colonial practice in North Africa. In the colonies, as Albert Memmi suggests in the epigraph above, Jewishness became a privileged way of at least partially escaping "nativeness," which was assimilated to Arabness, primitivism, and the impossibility of Frenchness. But in making Jewishness one of the few roads to Frenchness in all three North African colonies, French colonial officials, Metropolitan Jewish organizations, and indigenous Jews themselves turned Jewishness into an inescapable essence. I thus argue that the very practices that allowed for the (endlessly deferred) possibility of Jewish Frenchness in the colonies also may have ultimately made Frenchness impossible, with considerable implications for postcolonial French Jewish practice.[2]

From Nations to Nation:
Constructing a Metropolitan Jewish "Community"

In a literal sense, Jews might be considered "native" to the French nation-state. There have been Jews living in the territory we now call "France" since the Roman period, when they formed part of the avant-garde of merchants and colonizers seeking profit in their newly acquired lands (Bourdrel 2004:13). Despite a series of never-completed, always short-lived expulsions that occurred in the medieval and early modern periods,[3] there have always been Jews living in the *Hexagone*. But as a number of writers have noted, claiming nativeness has only a tangential relationship to the gross materiality of geography and birth (Ceuppens and Geschiere 2005; Comaroff and Comaroff 2000; Geschiere and Nyamnjoh 2000). It is a deeply ideological claim that rests on particular assumptions about the nature of society and community.

In the French context, national "nativeness" had little meaning prior to the Revolution.[4] Relations between subject and state in pre-modern France were hardly based on notions of national belonging in which firmly bounded territorial units coincided with the limits of state practices and subjective imaginaries. As Benedict Anderson has written: "It is characteristic that there has not been an 'English' dynasty ruling in London since the eleventh century (if then); and what 'nationality' are we to assign to the Bourbons?" (1991:21). Well into the 17th century, members of a single generation living in the borderlands of what we would now call "France" might find themselves sequential subjects to a "French" king, a "Spanish" (or "German") king, and a local lord with his own army, all without changing lifeways, languages, or practices (Sahlins 1990:1427–1428). At that time one belonged to a locality, a lord, and, perhaps most abstractly, to the "Christian nation," a global ecumene of the baptized incarnated in local forms of power and authority legitimated through relations with the Church (Anderson 1991).

The Revolution proposed abolishing these uneven, hierarchical linkages between various categories of subject and ruler, replacing them with a "flat" vision of the nation as a limited, predominantly political community whose general will expressed itself through state policy. Within orthodox interpretations of such an imaginary, origins were irrelevant. Worse, they were anti-Revolutionary, vitiating the idea of national unity as a conscious political contract uniting individuals whose differences of birth were to be invisible or meaningless (Noiriel 1996:39). Thus the aristocratic émigrés who fled territorial France during the Revolution, members of a class that had literally and symbolically embodied the French state prior to 1789, were denied French nationality and citizenship rights under the Revolutionary constitution on the grounds of their political and ideological unfitness. But while political ideology often trumped birth or "rootedness" in determining who could claim Revolutionary "Frenchness," it did not always do so. As members of the National Assembly debated designing uniforms for French citizens, established a public deistic religion, and proposed a school system that would eliminate local dialects and superstitions, it became clear that even Revolutionary "Frenchness" had (or needed) a cultural content (Ozouf 1988). This, in turn, implied that certain kinds of people by virtue of birth had privileged access to French national culture while others did not. Some people were naturally French (native) while others were irredeemably foreign. These contradictory principles ultimately created an impossible structural bind for Jews. While theoretically abolishing corporate groups that might mediate between the state and its citizens, Revolutionary debates and post-Revolutionary government actions turned Jews living in France into a legal and potentially ideological "community" for the first time.

Prior to the Revolution, Jews lived in more or less autonomous communities run by governing coalitions of religious and wealthy lay leaders. In addition to regulating daily life—access to ritually slaughtered meat, life-cycle rituals, and education—rabbinical courts adjudicated civil matters involving Jews. Although criminal cases, even those involving only Jews, were within the crown's jurisdiction, rabbis and *dayanim* (religious judges) often (but not always) prevented Jews from having recourse to "Christian" courts (Hertzberg 1990:58).[5] In other words, a Jew was born into a community that took responsibility for him or her from birth until death, "assuring his or her security and representation vis-à-vis various powers" (Benbassa 1997:54). Under these circumstances, the idea of the Jew as an individual who could be abstracted from the practices and structures associated with his or her collectivity made little sense. According to Simon Schwarzfuchs: "This mode of organization, which lasted until the emancipation period, assumed that Jews did not exist as individuals, but as organized collectivities, communities whose territorial definition was often variable. The isolated, independent Jew did not exist: he always was part of a group" (1989:33).

As a result of this fragmented, local mode of communal organization, there was no national French Jewish community prior to the Revolution. By the time the French crown finished annexing territories in the 18th century, there were at least four geographically, culturally, and judicially distinct groups of Jews in France, all clustered near literal borderlands: a small but influential community of "Portuguese or Spanish" Marranos, or crypto-Jews, settled in southwestern France, particularly in and around Bordeaux; the papal Jews of Avignon, Carpentras, Cavaillon, and Isle-sur-Sorgue who lived under Vatican protection until the Revolution; a tiny, diverse, illegal, and therefore largely unstructured group of Parisian Jews; and "German" Jews living in Alsace and Lorraine, northeastern provinces recently captured from the Prussians (Hyman 1998).

With an estimated population of twenty to thirty thousand, the "German," or Ashkenazi, Jews made up the overwhelming majority of the Jewish population living within what would become modern France (Hyman 1998:21). But most of the wealth and all of the cultural capital lay in the hands of the Bordeaux Jews, also called Sephardim, who were often merchants, French-speaking, and highly assimilated.[6] Ashkenazim, on the other hand, were poor and socially and physically isolated from non-Jews. In addition, unlike most Bordeaux Jews, Ashkenazim observed Jewish laws governing the most minute details of everyday life. In the years leading up to and even following the Revolution, Bordeaux's Jewish elites worked rather tirelessly to maintain this highly unequal status quo, protesting in the 1780s that any attempt to regulate Jews qua Jews "would be creating an incoherent and monstrous hodge-podge of people who are fundamentally [*essentiellement*] different in their mores, their language, their occupations, their prejudices, and a mass [*foule*] of other nuances that separate them" (cited in Schwarzfuchs 1989:92). As the National Assembly began debates in 1789 about which, if any, Jews should be made into French citizens, Sephardi representatives continued arguing that, in contrast to the barbaric "German" Jewish masses, they were uniquely fit for Frenchness.[7]

When all Jews living in France were emancipated by the Revolutionary National Assembly in 1791—almost two full years after that body issued the seeming universal Declaration of the Rights of Man and the Citizen—they were simultaneously individualized as potentially full and equal citizens and collectivized as a national Jewish community for the first time (Hertzberg 1990). While being exhorted to dissolve all subnational loyalties and attachments, they were also made to swear allegiance to the Republic as a group—a measure that had not been required of any other minority. Although the Revolutionary state assumed the debt of almost all newly dissolved corporations, including the Catholic Church, it refused to do so for the traditional local organizations that managed Jewish political and religious life (Hyman 1998:34). Instead, individual Jews were held responsible for their collective past, a move that served to recreate collectivity in the present.

"Only Paradoxes to Offer"

This tension around Jewishness—individual religious conviction versus inescapable collective identity—persisted throughout the 19th and 20th centuries, often leaving French Jews in the impossible position of denying their collective difference by invoking it (Fernando 2009; Scott 1996). Not only had the old, local Jewish collectivities been abolished, there had never been a "French" Jewish community into which Jews could retreat. Yet as indivudals, Jews' capacity for "native" Frenchness was always questioned and often dismissed as impossible because ties of kinship and culture were presumed to bind Jews to one another within and across national boundaries.

Napoléon's *Consistoire*, the central religious authority designed to regulate Jewish conduct, illustrates this dynamic. It ultimately had a paradoxical effect, promoting a certain kind of assimilation while simultaneously insisting on the necessity of collective regulation of French Jewish conduct. From 1808 until the separation of church and state under the Third Republic in 1905, the Consistoire attempted to control the form and content of French Jewishness. Every department with more than 2,000 residents was to be provided with a synagogue, rabbi, and local consistory, an elected board whose electors were named by the government (Albert 1977:58-60). Under the impetus of the reform-minded laymen who controlled the consistorial board, religious practice was changed to more closely resemble Christianity, thus lessening the appearance of Jewish difference even in the "private" realm of organized worship (Albert 1977; Graetz 1996:56–63). By the mid-19th century, consistorial rabbis wore uniforms—a black robe, long white lace collar, and black hat—that had been inspired by priestly dress. Baby-naming ceremonies were initiated for boys and girls as a structural equivalent to baptism. French became the language for sermons and synagogue business, replacing Hebrew and Yiddish. Weddings—which traditionally took place in the home, without officiating clergy—were transformed into synagogue ceremonies celebrated by consistorial rabbis. Undermining traditional Jewish orthopraxis, a standardized "catechism"—a set of belief statements to which students were expected to consent—was even introduced as the foundation for bar mitzvah preparation.

It is not that these attempts to control both public and private Jewish practice worked. They did not. Observant Jews, many of whom still lived in Alsace-Lorraine, created small, independent prayer groups that bypassed the Consistoire entirely. The Consistoire fought these attempts tooth and nail. Throughout the 19th century, central and local consistory officials solicited police assistance in hunting down and rooting out unauthorized prayer groups, small orthodox synagogues (*shuls*), and renegade rabbis (Albert 1977:52).[8] Later in the century, as the observant Eastern European immigrant population grew, the Consistoire changed tactics, forcing members of "illegal" *minyanim* (plural for *minyan*, or religious quorum) to become dues-paying members; in return, Consistoire leaders occasionally proposed subsidizing the salaries of (presumably appropriate) rabbis (Green 1986:81–83). After the 1905 law separating church and state, when the Consistoire lost both its exclusive standing and its state subsidies, efforts to co-opt all Jews were redoubled.

Despite these failures, the effort and elite imaginaries that inspired Consistoire practices had a dramatic impact on the kinds of identity narratives available to French Jews more generally, creating what historians now call "Franco-Judaism" (Birnbaum 1996; Landau 1990; Nicault 1990). This impact could be felt from the pulpit, in the classroom, and on the pages of the new national Jewish press.[9] Franco-Judaism did not mean abandoning a notion of distinctive Jewish identity, but rather reframing Jewishness so that it overlapped with the post-Revolutionary

French nation. As many Jewish elites suggested, Judaism and French nationalism seemed to share a common project and tension—that of a supposedly universal message carried and incarnated by a particularly defined group of people. Throughout the 19th century, and increasingly after the establishment of the Third Republic in the 1870s, consistorial rabbis, community periodicals, and Jewish elites rewrote the messianic strain of traditional Judaism as a foreshadowing of the Revolution and the construction of the French nation-state. The messiah was in fact the emancipation and Paris the new Jerusalem. Jews, chosen by God to be a "light among the nations," were simply the forerunners of French citizens, who would spread the universal message of liberty, fraternity, and equality throughout the world. Being a good Jew meant being a good Frenchman, and vice versa.[10]

Even when Jewish ethno-religious sensibilities and French national interests ostensibly clashed, belying the seamless fusion proclaimed from the pulpit, consistorial rabbis routinely downplayed the conflict and/or sided with national interest. But they did so without necessarily denying the ethno-religious ties that bound them to non-French Jews. In the 1880s, for example, French Jews began mobilizing in support of Russian Jews who were victims of violent, state-sanctioned pogroms. Some Jewish groups called for pressure to be put on the tsar to stop the killing and thus stem the mass exodus of Eastern European Jews (Marrus 1971:154–155). This position changed dramatically, however, as French and Russian relations warmed up in the 1890s. The French chief rabbi Zadoc Kahn articulated this shift in an 1891 pastoral letter:

> On coming to the aid of our brothers in Russia, we are obeying one of the most legitimate of sentiments, we are accomplishing a work of pious solidarity which should not lend itself to any misinterpretation. As French Jews, we are pleased with recent events [the Franco-Russian *entente*] which have so brilliantly raised the prestige of our country and have crowned twenty years of efforts, of moderation, of wise and fruitful negotiation. (cited in Marrus 1971:158)

By the end of the 19th and beginning of the 20th centuries, material measures suggested that Jews had indeed become "native" French. They had done so in the same ways and at the same time as many lower-class provincials. As Eugen Weber (1976) has argued, it was only at the end of the 19th century that the French government began a concerted effort to fully homogenize the nation, while integrating it into the state. The war the Revolution had declared on dialects, superstitions, and local cultural practices was largely fought by the Third Republic (1871–1940), in part through the creation of a network of public, secular schools staffed by teachers who had received standardized training from the state. Mandatory universal military service complemented schooling practices, separating boys from their parents and villages and placing them with recruits from different geographical areas to literally show them "France." At the same time, a greatly expanded bureaucracy based on competitive examination brought hundreds of thousands of people into public service for the first time (Noiriel 1999). Jews benefited socially and economically from this étatization of nation. While they had been systematically excluded from government councils and upper-level civil service positions until the end of the Second Empire in 1871, the Third Republic created what historian Pierre Birnbaum has called "state Jews," Jews whose career and life horizons were closely entwined with the bureaucratic machinery of the French state (Birnbaum 1996:60). At the same time, the remaining formal obstacles to Jewish participation in French bourgeois society fell. The local autonomy that made separate Jewish taxation regimes or militias possible in some cities well into the 19th century became unthinkable.[11] Jews were accepted into France's most elite educational institutions, became commanding officers in the army, and taught non-Jewish children in schools all over the country. They were journalists in mainstream newspapers, recognized artists, and chaired academics. If intermarriage rates were still low, social interaction between religious groups was high, most Jews having long abandoned the dietary restrictions and rabbinical laws that tightly regulated contact with the non-Jewish world. In addition, Jews had proven their commitment to French identity and French nationalism with their lives (Landau 1990). Thousands of Jews enlisted immediately and fought valiantly to keep Alsace and Lorraine French during the 1870–1871 Franco-Prussian war. When that effort failed, 15,000 Jews moved west into French-controlled areas, breaking up family and communal ties that had long bound Jews on both sides of the border into transnational communities. To a large extent, by the early 20th century, French Jewish social and economic horizons had come to overlap with those of the rest of the French middle class, thus creating common material and political interests (Birnbaum 1996; Schuker 1985:154).

But this was only one part of the story. The establishment of full legal equality under the Third Republic did not eliminate the sense that Jews comprised a foreign corporate body at the heart of the nation.[12] The series of coups d'état and failed revolutions that wracked French political life in the early part of the 19th century were systematically accompanied by anti-Semitic violence. Jews were targeted in 1830 as the Restoration government fell and again in 1848 as the July Monarchy gave way to the Second Republic. In 1848, people protesting in the streets of Paris screamed, "Long live the Republic" and "Death to Jews" in the same breath. The economic, social, and political upheaval that accompanied the creation of the Third Republic proved no exception (Noiriel 1999). Anti-Semitic leagues, political parties, and pamphlets flourished, uniting elements on both the Catholic right and radical left who saw the new state as morally dangerous for the nation. On the right, Catholics used anti-Semitism to mobilize the masses against parliamentary democracy's "betrayal" of the nation's rural, Christian values—a betrayal that was best symbolized by both the real increase in Jews occupying important state positions and the perception that the state had become a Jewish cabal. The slogan the Catholic National Union used for a meeting held in Paris in 1900 was "France for the French! Death to the Jews!" (Birnbaum 2000:121). On the left, socialists adopted arguments first made by the physiocrats in the 18th century, conflating Jews with the murky world of financial capital and therefore with "unproductive" economic endeavors that sapped the country of vital resources and workers of their power. Socialists, Blanquists, and Boulangists, on the one hand, and pro-clerical, often monarchical Catholics, on the other, became active in the same kinds of anti-Semitic leagues (ibid.:121–122).

Both these renewed forms of anti-Semitism and Jewish reactions to them indicate that Jews still inhabited a paradoxical position in France, stuck between being an embodied corporate community and individualized members of a religious faith. This is particularly evident in relation to the two most dramatic (and oft-rehearsed) periods of anti-Semitism in 19th and 20th century France: the Dreyfus Affair and Vichy.

In 1894, in the midst of an economic depression and public calls for revenge against Germany, a French spy employed as a maid in the German embassy found evidence that a French officer was sharing secret military information with the enemy. Captain Alfred Dreyfus, a graduate of the Republic's elite engineering and military schools and an assimilated Alsatian Jew whose family had moved to Paris in the wake of the French defeat at Sedan, was quickly associated with the crime. He was tried and found guilty by a military tribunal using "secret" evidence that was never presented to the defense. In January 1895, before a Parisian crowd screaming, "Death to the Jews," Dreyfus was stripped of his military honors and sent to a prison on Devil's Island. Despite a series of retrials that made the military's dearth of evidence and conspiratorial cover-up apparent, Dreyfus's conviction was not voided until 1906.[13]

The "Dreyfus Affair," as well as the anti-Semitism it encapsulated and encouraged, powerfully illustrated the extent to which many in the French public still imagined Jews as a transnational, corporate community. In the context of dramatically increased Jewish immigration from Eastern Europe,[14] Dreyfus's Alsatian Jewishness sufficed to make him a plausible German spy and traitor, even in the absence of supporting evidence (Weber 1985:20).[15] Similarly, Jewish reactions to the Affair were driven by the necessity of combating the specter of Jewish corporatism. At the time, many Jews believed firmly in Dreyfus's guilt, in part because it was simply unimaginable that the Republican regime would falsely convict an innocent man. For those who believed Dreyfus innocent, however, it was virtually impossible to defend him without confirming the specter of Jewish corporate identity raised by anti-Semitic accusations. As many Dreyfus supporters recognized, any *Jewish* opposition to the *chose jugée* (literally "the already judged thing") would make the affair look like a "Jewish" issue; they therefore remained silent (Birnbaum 1998:80; Marrus 1971:203). At the same time, Jewish institutions and elites quietly encouraged non-Jews to speak out. Just after a series of anti-Semitic riots in 1898, when a group of Dreyfus supporters formed the Ligue pour les droits de l'homme (League for the Rights of Man), a Jewish newspaper noted with satisfaction that only three of the group's thirty-four executive members were Jewish, implying that support for

Dreyfus had nothing to do with Jewishness (Marrus 1971:227). The academic Silvain Lévi put it somewhat differently in 1898: "As long as it had to do with Dreyfus alone, I thought that it was my duty to remain silent. The cause of an innocent man had nothing to gain before public opinion by the adhesion of a Jew; it risked [rather] to lose by it" (cited in ibid.). In other words, any Jewish support for a Jew reeked of Jewish corporate separatism. But at the same time, avoiding that specter required Jews to remember their Jewishness in every political context while acting like it was irrelevant. Ensuring that the public face of the Dreyfusard cause was not "Jewish" required that Jews simultaneously deny and inhabit Jewish difference.

A similar story can be told about Vichy's infamous statut des juifs. First enacted on October 7, 1940, the *statut* defined Jews as a racial group and banned all those so classified from major civil-service positions (Birnbaum 1996:339). Less than a year later, the Vichy government passed a second statut des juifs, this time stripping French Jews of their remaining civil rights and authorizing internment of anyone who met the first law's racial criteria (ibid.:167). With a stroke of the pen, this second series of "Jewish laws" abolished legal distinctions between French Jews and the rapidly growing population of Jewish immigrants living in France, in effect insisting that "a Jew was a Jew was a Jew."[16] Clearly undermining the individualizing Republican impulse, this move insisted that French Jews had more in common with Russian Jews than they did with their non-Jewish neighbors (Birnbaum 1996; Marrus and Paxton 1981). But at the same time, in contrast to German officials, members of the Vichy government did in fact distinguish between what Admiral François Jean Louis Darland called "good old French Jews" and foreign Jews (cited in Marrus and Paxton 1981:85). Although infrequently used, the Vichy government created official procedures that would allow highly assimilated, long-established Jews to escape the punitive, humiliating, and ultimately deadly statut des juifs.[17] In addition, almost all Vichy officials eventually sought exemptions for individual French Jews—friends, former colleagues, decorated generals, and important artists (ibid.:85–91).

In the end, for a number of reasons, being a French Jew rather than a foreign Jew, and being an assimilated French Jew rather than an unassimilated one, made a difference.[18] In 1942 Vichy responded to German demands for the massive deportation of Jews from France by rounding up foreign and stateless Jews, thereby at least delaying the deportation of French citizens (Marrus and Paxton 1981:249). The distinction between "Jews" as a blanket racial category and French Jewish citizens also carried weight at the popular level. Throughout the war, even as the Vichy government increasingly participated in the Final Solution, officials worried about French public opinion. For good reason; Vichy's unpopularity was evident by 1941 (Munholland 1994; Sweets 1988). Although there was certainly no massive uprising to protect Jews, fear of a public backlash led Vichy officials to reject some extremely public forms of anti-Semitism. The regime thus resisted German pressure to introduce the yellow star into unoccupied portions of France (Marrus and Paxton 1981). In addition, thousands of French citizens worked quietly and behind the scenes to protect French Jews who were their friends and neighbors by hiding them or procuring false papers.[19]

These admittedly small exceptions and measures had real material consequences. Between 1942 and 1944, 75,000 Jews were deported from France. Of those 75,000, 51,000 were foreigners or recently naturalized immigrants who had been stripped of their citizenship in the 1930s (Conan and Rousso 1994:36). Of the remaining 24,000 deportees, about 8,000 were the French-born children of immigrants; another 8,000 were French, but had been denaturalized for various reasons under Vichy (ibid.). It is thus likely that long-established French Jews—the "good old French Jews" mentioned by Darlan—comprised at most 21 percent of total deportees. Assuming with Michael Marrus and Robert Paxton (1981:364) that, at the time, about half of the Jewish population in France was French and half was foreign, foreign Jews were over four times more likely to have been deported than French Jews. There are similar discrepancies in the number of casualties. At Liberation, 10 percent of French Jews and 40 percent of foreign Jews living in France had been killed (Birnbaum 1996:368). In other words, even state and public anti-Semitism under Vichy helped construct and (to a lesser extent) disaggregate "Jew" as a universal ethno-racial category.

The letter from "Parisian Jews" to Marshal Pétain with which this chapter began shows how many French Jews reacted to Vichy and the

German Occupation They did so with the outrage of French citizens raised to believe that national belonging was a political and cultural commitment that transcended origins. Scores of Jews wrote unanswered letters to Pétain protesting their treatment on the grounds of their citizenship status and national allegiances. Some went so far as to deny that they were "Jewish" on any grounds, let alone the racial grounds laid out in the statuts des juifs. Just after the creation of the Union Générale des Israélites de France (General Union of Israelites in France; hereafter UGIF), the Vichy equivalent of the German Judenrat, a former member of the Conseil d'état wrote to Pétain:

> Having Jewish ancestry, having never dreamed of dissimulating or denying [that] fact. . . . I categorically refuse to consider myself a French Israelite, a French Jew. I am a Frenchman who is not Jewish by race—for there is no Jewish race; all anthropologists and other scientists who have concerned themselves with these questions have recognized this. . . . It is therefore in an arbitrary manner that the texts calling for legal measures of anti-Jewish persecution, signed by the marshal of France, head of state, have classified me as a Jew. (cited in Birnbaum 1996:355–356)

But like those who called themselves "Parisian Jews" in their letter to Pétain, most French Jews who wrote protest letters did not deny their "Jewishness," however defined. Instead, they reproached Vichy's failure to live by the Franco-Jewish compact in which they continued to believe. Whatever the government thought of foreign Jews, French Jews were French citizens first and foremost, meaning they enjoyed equal rights with all other French citizens. A general who was stripped of his post in November 1940 wrote rather sarcastically to the War Department:

> I have the honor . . . of declaring that, according to you, I am a "Jew" and, according to my numerous friends and comrades, my superiors and my equals and my subordinates in the army, a French Jew. . . . I do not claim and do not desire to accept the benefit of article 8 of the *statut des juifs* [the section that accorded exemptions] even though I belong to a French family that is at least two centuries old and that has numbered many honorable and honored officers. That would mean implicitly recognizing that my status as a French citizen with the same rights as other Frenchmen was up for discus-

sion, and that is something my reason and my heart refuse to do.
(cited in Birnbaum 1996:345)

The Consistoire itself seems to have largely followed this line of reasoning, emphasizing the Frenchness of French Jews and protesting Vichy's failure to distinguish between French and foreign Jews. Jacques Helbronner, a former member of the Conseil d'état and the lay head of the Consistoire in the early 1940s (he was ultimately deported and gassed), noted: "The law does not target the Jews as Frenchmen or foreigners, but, in servile imitation of the occupying authority, no longer knows or recognizes anything but a Jewish herd where nationality, even French nationality, is no longer more than an accessory without value or importance" (cited in Birnbaum 1996:363). After the creation of the UGIF and its designation as the sole legal agency representing Jews vis-à-vis state authorities, the Consistoire spent much of its time and energy decrying the way in which the organization undermined the terms of Franco-Judaism. Although some members of the Consistoire ultimately worked for and with the UGIF (Vichy had threatened to appoint someone to oversee the UGIF if no Jewish leaders agreed to accept the responsibility), they angrily protested the formulation of the organization. For these men, being a Jew meant being a member of a religious group; the UGIF, a "secular" organization with no religious mission, presumed Jewishness was an ethnic or racial category. As Consistoire member René Meyer noted, it was impossible to accept an institution "where French Jews are, through the application of racial principles entirely foreign to the genius of our country, treated by the government of the marshal exactly on the same footing as foreigners or stateless peoples. . . . Frenchmen and foreigners would be intermingled" (cited in ibid.:367). Considerably less was said in this correspondence about the awful daily business of the UGIF: extorting money from the "Jewish community" for payment to the German Occupiers, the liquidation of Jewish businesses, and the redistribution of liquidated assets to keep Jews who were barred from virtually every occupation fed and clothed.

Just as in the letter from "Parisian Jews," in all of these arguments there is an implied rejection of transnational or diasporic conceptions of Jewish identity that would tie persecuted French Jews to similarly threatened Jewish foreign nationals. There is a concomitant insistence on Frenchness as the only meaningful foundation for moral and political community. But the very form of these pleas works against this insistence. Signing a letter on behalf of "Parisian Jews" or writing in the name of French Jewish interests implies the existence of a national *Jewish* community. It suggests that certain writers stand as tokens of a definable and recognizable type, and it is only as tokens of that collective and definable type that they are allowed to deny the difference between Jewish and non-Jewish French people, while insisting on the difference between French and non-French Jews. In other words, while trying to dissolve Jewishness as the foundation for a distinctive identity, the writers were forced to invoke it.

I have briefly recounted stories told in greater length and detail by others in order to illustrate the ways in which Metropolitan French Jews never escaped the paradox of individuality and collectivity established by the Revolution's reformulation of social and political community.[20] In some cases, French Jews insisted on an elective affinity between Jewishness and Frenchness, attempting to turn Jewishness into a privileged mode of acquiring "native" Frenchness. But in many other instances, French Jews denied the relevance of Jewish collectivity, insisting on their adherence to a Franco-Jewish compact that dissolved Jewish corporatism into privatized belief. But they did so from a position of collectivity—the Consistoire, Jewish newspapers, letters signed on behalf of anonymous groups of French Jews—that undermined Republican claims about individualized identities and beliefs.

If most Metropolitan attempts to negotiate Jewish Frenchness relied on at least a partial erasure of Jewish corporate identity, in many ways the opposite was true in the North African colonies. In different ways in Algeria, on the one hand, and Morocco and Tunisia, on the other, access to Frenchness—whether in the form of citizenship, French-language education, or even social proximity to the colonizer—depended on Jewish collectivity and distinction, particularly from Muslims. As a result, to an even greater extent than in the Metropole, perpetuating imagined Jewish collectivity was built into the very terms of acquiring Frenchness. Not surprisingly, the centrality of Jewishness varied inversely with the proximity of native North African Jews to Frenchness.

Neither *Indigène* nor French:
North African Jews in a Colonial Context

Unlike Metropolitan Jews, who struggled to become French "natives," North African Jews fought to resist being conflated with *indigènes*, the French category for subjugated colonial subjects, particularly Muslims. There were in fact many good reasons to conflate North African Muslims and Jews. The term currently used in France to refer to North African Jews—Sephardim—evokes Spain and establishes a putative link between the presence of Jews in North Africa and the Spanish expulsion orders in the late 15th century. However, most North African Jews may be more "native" to the region than Arab Muslims. The earliest evidence of Jewish settlement in North Africa considerably predates the Arab conquest.[21] Although there were waves of Jewish immigration from continental Europe in the 15th century and again in the 17th (primarily Italian Jewish merchants, often called the *Livournais*), these populations often jealously guarded their customs and their lineages from intermixture with native Jews (Abitbol 1985:50; Allouche-Benayoun and Bensimon 1998:19; Chouraqui 1998a:193). Even as late as the 1960s, Spanish was still viewed as a marker of elite status among Moroccan Jews (Allouche-Benayoun and 1998:24).

If for centuries prior to colonization distinctions between and among native and European Jews were sometimes carefully maintained, the differences between Jews and Muslims could be quite blurry. *Dhimmi* laws introduced after the Muslim conquest under the Caliph Omar were premised on absolute distinction between Muslims and other "protected minorities," including Christians and Jews (Allouche-Benayoun and Bensimon 1998:25–26; Cohen 1996; Corcos 1964; Stillman 1980). Although dhimmitude did not imply a single status across time and space, it did typically guarantee the right to self-governance and tolerance in exchange for a series of religious and political concessions, including acknowledgment of the supremacy of the Muslim faith (Chouraqui 1998a:91).[22] This seems to suggest that dhimmi were imagined as distinctive corporate groups that could not be confused with Muslims. But law and lived practice may have been quite different things. Mark Cohen (1996) has suggested that dhimmi laws were often enforced only in the breach, and, unlike in Europe, Jews were not necessarily considered a "corporate" group (58). Thus the lines between Jew and Muslim were often ambiguous. For example, Jews living in the Atlas Mountains apparently remained largely indistinguishable from their Muslim Arab and Berber counterparts, riding forbidden horses, wearing forbidden clothing, carrying forbidden weapons, and escaping discriminatory taxes that Jews closer to the coast were required to pay (Allouche-Benayoun and Bensimon 1998:25–26). If some Jews could "pass" as Muslims, the opposite also seems to have been true. After the conquest period, some Jewish converts to Islam were still taxed as if they had remained Jews, a highly ambiguous legal response to the converts' apparently equally ambiguous religious practices (Corcos 1964:274). In other contexts, Jews rose to some of the highest political positions in the land (Corcos 1964:271; Stillman 1980:11).[23]

Even in cases when the lines separating Jewish dhimmi from Muslims hardened, communities were never hermetically sealed. Unlike in Europe, where Jews often did not speak the same language as their gentile neighbors, North African Jews and Muslims lived and worked in the same tongue, often with only minor differences in pronunciation and vocabulary (Allouche-Benayoun and Bensimon 1998:102; Chouraqui 1998a:139; Tapia 1986:32–33). Jews were never universally banned from particular economic spheres and were not restricted in their commercial dealings with Muslims (although they were, at times, forbidden to own land). This meant that while Jews were, on the one hand, heavily concentrated in some trades and, on the other, underrepresented in most agricultural activities, their economic activities were closely intertwined with those of Muslims (Chouraqui 1998a:100; Cohen 1996:54; Tapia 1986:49–50). Jews and Muslims also regularly interacted outside of purely professional contexts. Muslims ate in Jewish homes, and Jews were often overnight guests of Muslims (Allouche-Benayoun and Bensimon 1998:103–104).[24] Although there were often Jewish quarters, or *mellah*, in North African cities,[25] there was no formal residential segregation; wealthier Jews and Muslims tended to live in close proximity to one another (Abitbol 1985:172). Key social markers like names were shared. More than half of North African "Jewish" family names also exist among Muslim Arabs and Berbers (Chouraqui 1998a:203). Jews gave newborns Arabic names often used by Muslims, for example, Yahya, Khalifa, or Sa'doun for men and Aïcha, Messaouda, or Meleha for women (ibid.). Even religious practices—the domain imagined as most clearly separating Jews and Muslims under Islamic rule—sometimes overlapped or had symbiotic elements. Anthropologist Harvey Goldberg's (1978) analysis of the role of Muslims in the Mimouna, the traditional North African Jewish festival marking the end of Passover, powerfully illustrates the (at least) subjunctive world of Muslim-Jewish complementarity present in religious ritual (Seligman et al. 2008).[26]

These legally, economically, socially, and even religiously fluid boundaries between Muslims and Jews hardened under the social and economic turmoil that preceded formal colonization.[27] But they were fully reified by colonial practice, which turned Muslimness and Jewishness into quasi-racial categories associated with very different imagined capacities for assimilation and Frenchification (Lorcin 1995). In all three North African French colonies, Jewishness was invoked by Metropolitan Jews, government officials, and Jewish natives as proof of greater potential or actual proximity to Europeans. As we shall see, in Algeria, Jewishness provided the most obvious and direct path to Frenchness through the naturalization en masse of all Algerian Jews living in territories controlled by the French colonial state. But it was in Morocco and Tunisia, where Jews were never legally assimilated to European or French colonialists, that Jewishness both created the possibility for Frenchification and became an exclusive, terminal identity category in and of itself.

Algeria

France began its formal military conquest of Algeria in 1830. Arab and Berber Muslims mounted fierce and sustained opposition to the French invasion. Some Jews joined them, viewing the European invasion as a repeat of medieval Spanish incursions and thus a harbinger of dire political and social consequences (Ayoun 2003:40–41). Many others did not. Familiar with the story of the French Revolution and Jewish emancipation, many of Algeria's 25,000 Jews viewed the French military presence as an opportunity to escape dhimmitude (Ayoun 2003:41; Bensimon 1998:33–34; Chouraqui 1952:100).[28] By 1833, local Jews were active in the defense of French-ruled cities against attempts at Muslim reconquest (Ayoun 2003:41).

Over the following thirty years, as Algeria became legally and ideologically part of France,[29] French colonial officials, Metropolitan legislators, and French Jewish elites lobbied for and introduced a series of legal and social changes that institutionalized Jewish association with and Muslim alienation from European rule.[30] In October 1830, a military decree recognized two legally distinct, but formally equivalent, "nations" in Algeria: Muslim and *Israélite*, each with a separate body of customary law overseen by a government-appointed official (Shepard 2006:25). These, it should be noted, were racial categories: legal communal affiliations could not be changed by marriage or conversion, they were acquired through "blood" (ibid.:24). But shortly after creating these legally recognized ethno-racial groups, Algeria's military rulers undermined their structural equivalence. They fired the new head of the Jewish "nation," depriving Jews of their parallel legal system and forcing them to rely on French courts that had otherwise been reserved for European colonists (Sussman 2002:49). By 1842, this de facto arrangement had been formalized: autonomous rabbinical courts were abolished. Although Jews, like Muslim indigènes, were to be judged according to religious law, they were tried in French courts in front of French judges assisted by rabbinical consultants.

Metropolitan Jewish institutions argued for and supported any legal changes that separated native Jews from Muslims and helped close the gap between Jews and European colonists (see Abitbol 1990; Ayoun 2003; Schwarzfuchs 1980; Sussman 2002). As early as 1833, the Consistoire Central in Paris began pressuring the National Assembly and War Department to create a replica of the French consistorial system in Algeria, a move Metropolitan Jews imagined as a precursor to annexation and therefore assimilation.[31] In the 1840s, a considerable stream of correspondence between the Consistoire and government representatives emphasized the strategic role Frenchified Jews might play in the ongoing colonial struggle. The Altras-Cohen Report, an internal consistorial study written in the 1840s, noted: "The Consistoire Central must promote and assure the assimilation of the Jewish population of Algeria to the European population, and more particularly the French population. We must, in the more-or-less long term, turn Jewish Algerians into European Jews, which really means French Jews; this will allow them to become an important part of the French colonial mission" (cited in

Schwarzfuchs 1980:44). Arab Muslims, it was continually implied, were a threat to the colonial project. But French Jewish organizations noted that the large urban Jewish populations concentrated in coastal cities could be used—if appropriately treated—to counterbalance this threat. In 1860, Consistoire board member Adolphe Crémieux (who would later become a minister of justice under the Third Republic) told an appellate court in Oran:

> The land of Egypt is Algiers; for my unfortunate brothers, Algiers is the land of servitude that they left barely 30 years ago. And since that time, look at the progress they have made. It is a real wrong to attack the Jews of Algeria; between them and the Arabs the intellectual distance is enormous. . . . If you knew how much they love those who delivered them. . . . They want to be French; they are worthy of being French and will soon become French. (cited in Abitbol 1990:203–204)

In some ways, it was a replay of the Revolutionary argument: Jews treated as Frenchmen were culturally predisposed to behave as such.

The Consistoire occasionally took its arguments one step further, insisting that Algerian Jews were better suited to Frenchness than many European colonialists. The Altras-Cohen Report questioned the government's willingness to accept Spanish, Maltese, English, and even German settlers in Algeria given their well-known antipathy to French moral and political values (Sussman 2002: 57). In addition, the report stressed that these Europeans were known to have mere mercenary motives; they were looking for economic opportunities, not for ways to increase the power and glory of the French nation. Algerian Jews, on the other hand, had illustrated their commitment to French national principles and values by their willingness to assimilate (ibid.:57–58). France's national interests, the report implied, were thus better served by Algerian Jews than European settlers.

This did not, however, mean that Metropolitan Jewish elites embraced what were then contemporary Algerian Jewish practices and mores. Internal Jewish correspondence was replete with condemnations of the superstitious and primitive beliefs and actions of "native" Jews. In the late 1830s, a French Jewish physician attached to the colonial hospital at Bône offered the Consistoire a proposal for the improvement of Algerian Jews: Algerian children should be removed from their families, sent to the Metropole to be educated, and then returned to North Africa as healthy examples to be emulated (Schwarzfuchs 1980:38). In 1855 the chief rabbi of Algiers, the Metropolitan Michel Weill, told his superiors that "native" Jews needed to be ruled with a firm hand because they only respect "what glitters and strikes the imagination" (cited in Abitbol 1985:42). Even as late as 1902, French rabbis stationed in Algeria were still criticizing their native congregants. The Metropolitan rabbi for the town of Tlemcen in Algeria published a book in which he questioned Algerian Jewish fitness for Frenchness, dwelling on the "Arab characteristics" and "barabarism" he found among his own flock (Abitbol 1985:47).

Publicly, however, Metropolitan Jewish organizations worked to eliminate these "barbarisms," helping transform the imagined elective affinity between Jewishness and Frenchness into a tangible reality. As part of this Jewish civilizing mission, the Consistoire immediately and repeatedly proposed eliminating all the signs and supports of traditional Jewish corporate life, including disbanding rabbinical courts, outlawing traditional dress, closing *midrashim* (religious schools), imposing mandatory military service, establishing French schools that offered both religious and secular curricula, and subjecting Jews to French civil law (Schwarzfuchs 1980:45). These suggestions proved convincing to Metropolitan legislators. In 1832, the first French school for Jews opened in Algiers. This was soon followed by considerable governmental financing of French-language Jewish education that included religious instruction (Chouraqui 1998b:109; Chouraqui 1952:211).

The separate (and sometimes contradictory) efforts of the War Ministry, French Metropolitan legislators, and French Jewish institutions reached their climax in 1870, just after the fall of the Second Empire. In 1865, both Jews and Muslims had been granted French nationality and given the option of renouncing their "local civil status," that is, submission to local religious law, in exchange for French citizenship (Friedman 1988:9; Shepard 2006:26). Few had done so.[32] Five years later, that option became a legal requirement for Jews and Jews alone. Called the Crémieux Decree, after its author, the first Jewish Minister of Justice Adolphe Crémieux, the new law turned the 37,000 Algerian Jews residing in areas already under French occupation into French citizens whether they desired citizenship or not (Chouraqui 1998b:20;

Stora 2003:20). Algerian Muslims would not be given French citizenship until 1944 or equivalent political rights until 1958 (Shepard 2006:31–32).

In some ways, the Crémieux Decree can be seen as inverting the Revolutionary predicament of Metropolitan Jews. During the Revolution, the National Assembly had argued about whether Jews might be French *in spite of* their Jewishness. The opposite was the case in Algeria. The Decree granted Frenchness *because* of a particular ethno-religious affiliation.[33] Prior to the passage of the law, the Consistoire and elite Metropolitan Jews had lobbied intensely for the dissolution of Jewish "national" life in Algeria, just as their predecessors had during the years following the Revolution. But the singling out of Jews, even for assimilatory purposes, reinforced Jews' corporate status and made that group identity into a privileged path to Frenchness.[34] While Muslims could be *considered* for citizenship after renouncing their "personal status," that is, subjugation to religious law and courts, only Jews had a guaranteed path to Frenchness. For some Moroccan and Tunisian Jews, this proved too enticing a lure to pass up; some moved to Algeria and/or claimed Algerian ties in an effort to gain citizenship (Bensimon 1971:16).

The material effects of the Decree cannot be underestimated. In addition to legally transforming formally native Jews into Europeans, naturalization accelerated the rapprochement between Jewish and "French" practices, often in domains that emphasized distinction from native Muslims. French or Frenchified names gradually came to replace traditional Arabic ones altogether: Oureida became Rose, Beida became Blanche (white), and Sultana became Reine (queen); Rahmim became Raymond, and Maklouf became Maurice (Friedman 1988:62). Jews also quickly abandoned religious schools as soon as they gained the legal right to enroll in public, secular institutions with European colonists.[35] French-educated Jews then flocked to liberal professions favored for their prestige and independence, particularly law and medicine, abandoning the traditional artisanal occupations that brought them into close and sustained proximity to native Muslims. At the same time, the Crémieux Decree opened all civil service and military positions to Jews, allowing for the emergence of a solid middle-class. As they moved up the socioeconomic ladder, many Jews moved out of traditionally Jewish or "native" districts and into neighborhoods built for and inhabited by European colonists (Tapia 1986:38). They also began taking vacations in Europe and sending their children to complete their studies in France.

Jewishness thus became the foundation on which native "Frenchness" was built in Algeria, gradually separating Jews culturally and politically from the Muslim population. But this does not mean European colonists perceived Jews as fully "French."[36] From the very beginning of the colonial occupation, French military commanders sometimes cited Jewishness as a reason *not* to accept Algerian Jews' pretensions to Frenchness. When serving as governor general of Algeria from 1841 to 1847, General Thomas-Robert Bugeaud encouraged the War Ministry to expel all the Jews in Algeria, arguing that their status as intermediaries and translators prevented vital contact between French officials and Muslims. He also believed that Jewish access to civil service positions in civilian-controlled coastal cities incited Muslim resentment (Schwarzfuchs 1980:42). Far from viewing them as potential Frenchmen, Bugeaud described Jews as potential double-traitors: they were too slippery a category, too close to everyone for anyone's safety. He described Jews as quick to lord their new French privileges over their Muslim former rulers and as «willing to reveal French military movements to local Muslim insurgents (ibid.).

Colonists, who avidly sought the expansion of civilian rule, disagreed with French military commanders on just about every aspect of the colonial project. But they came to echo Bugeaud's hostility toward Algerian Jews. Although some deportees from the 1848 Revolution supported the Crémieux Decree, most colonists joined the military in (falsely) attributing ongoing Muslim military resistance to resentment over Jewish emancipation. They made the repeal of the Crémieux Decree one of the centerpieces of Algerian politics until the close of World War II (Marrus and Paxton 1981:192). Colonists argued that Jews were unfit for French voting rights, which required an independence of thought and conviction impossible to achieve in a group still imagined in corporate terms. The Consistoire, in particular, was continuously accused of rigging local elections through vote-buying and clientelism.[37] Given the significant proportion of naturalized Jews within the French voting population—in 1886 more than 16 percent of the eligible "European" population was Jewish—these accusations were both politically motivated and seemingly credible (Abitbol 1990:208; Friedman 1988:16). In addition to arguing that Jews could not respect the form or principle of universal suffrage, colonists also argued that "native" Jews were in fact "Arabs." By this they meant Jews had no "natural" connections either to Europe or to France and therefore no business being French citizens. Just after the passage of the Crémieux Decree, the former prefect of Oran wrote to the French parliament demanding the abrogation of the act:

> The indigenous *Israélites* are not French but Arabs who are Jewish in religious terms. Their mother tongue is Arabic, which they speak badly and write in Hebrew letters. A small number speak French fluently; far fewer can write our language. The immense majority has learned, through relations with us, an unformed jargon that is indispensable for their commercial activities. Their mores are Oriental and almost all of them wear Oriental dress. . . . Strangers to the traditions of French nationality, outside of European civilization, these Orientals do not have a homeland. (cited in Dermenjian 2003:61)

Strictly speaking, a large plurality of European colonists also included "strangers to the traditions of French nationality." In 1886, almost half of the non-Muslim Algerian population consisted of people without French citizenship (Friedman 1988:16; Shepard 2006:29). Many were from Spain, Italy, or Malta and had never set foot in Metropolitan France (Allouche-Benayoun and Bensimon 1998:45). And herein lay the problem. Many colonists had also been naturalized, rendering their claims to "native" Frenchness no more secure than those of Algerian Jews. As a result, settlers attempted to construct European Frenchness as qualitatively different from Algerian Jewishness with racist arguments that ran counter to Revolutionary ideology. For many colonists, Frenchness was racially determined, just like every other social category in colonial society. Being French meant (often nominal) Catholicism and what was referred to as "Latin origins," a reference to the *northern* shores of the Mediterranean (Abitbol 1990). Jewish inclusion challenged this racial definition of Frenchness and dangerously blurred the lines between "naturally" naturalizable "Europeans" and "natives," the distinction on which colonial social and economic privileges depended (Memmi 1991:72–74). If a legal act could render a "native" as "European," on what immutable cultural or racial grounds could colonists base their claims to social dominance? And furthermore, if Jewish "natives" could become Frenchmen, what about the millions of Muslims still considered "subjects" of the French colonial authorities? The Crémieux Decree thus hinted at the fragile, constructed nature of colonial privileges, inevitably raising the specter of the end of European social and economic hegemony (Dermenjian 2003:50).

Such arguments about Jewish Arabness and non-Frenchness fueled a strain of virulent anti-Semitism in North Africa that dwarfed anything that occurred in the Metropole (Sussman 2002:77). This was particularly notable during the Dreyfus Affair and again under Vichy. In the 1890s, candidates running on anti-Semitic platforms and calling for Jewish disenfranchisement were elected to executive and legislative positions in major cities, including Constantine, Oran, and Algiers (Allouche-Benayoun and Bensimon 1998:267–268). As mayor of Constantine in the late 1890s, Emile Morinaud fired Jews from all local civil service positions, ordered hospitals to refuse them treatment, and even threatened to exclude them from public schools (Cole 2010). Anti-Semitic mayors in Oran and Algiers quickly followed suit. And in these two cities, anti-Jewish persecution extended beyond legal measures. European colonists planned and executed deadly pogroms in Oran in 1897 and in Algiers in 1898. In both cases, colonists blamed the violence on Muslims outraged by the Crémieux Decree (Allouche-Benayoun and Bensimon 1998:268–269). In 1934, accusations by European anti-Semites that Algerian Jews benefited materially and politically from the subjugation of Algerian Muslims helped produce a deadly explosion of Muslim anti-Jewish violence in Constantine (Cole 2010; Katz 2010).[38]

In 1940, Vichy would seem a godsend to the politicians lobbying ceaselessly for the denaturalization of Algerian Jews. Almost immediately, the Algiers government petitioned Pétain to abrogate the Crémieux Decree; the request was quickly granted (Stora 2003:23). Algerian Jews whose families had voted in regional and national elections for three generations were suddenly stripped of their nationality and citizenship rights. Children and university students whose parents and grandparents had attended French public schools were expelled, consigned to religious institutions long derided and abandoned. With the stroke of a pen, they returned to "indigenous" status but did not regain any of the communal religious institutions that still regulated Muslim life. They occupied a kind of no-man's-land, subject to French law but deprived of any protections under it.[39] And even when Republican institutions were finally restored in March 1943, the head of the Algerian government, General Henri Giraud, refused to reinstate the Crémieux Decree on the grounds that "all racial discrimination" should be eliminated between Jews and Muslims (cited in Abitbol 1990:213). Only under considerable pressure from the American government and various Jewish organizations did Charles de Gaulle reestablish the citizenship rights of Algerian Jews in October 1943 (ibid.).

Thus the racial logics that animated virtually every aspect of colonial life underwrote and reinforced Jewish corporate difference. French policies used religious affiliation as one of the central axes along which to divide the Algerian indigenous population, turning Jewishness into a privileged means of claiming proximity to European colonists.[40] Over the long run, this separated Jews materially, culturally, and politically from Muslims, who were deprived of rights for almost the entire colonial period. It also gave Algerian Jews deep cultural affinities with Europeans, many of whose practices were eagerly adopted even before the Crémieux Decree made Frenchification quasi-obligatory for all Algerian Jews. In an attempt to undermine the foundation of Jewish privilege, European settlers constantly attempted to have Jews racially recategorized as "Arabs," a demand that would have eliminated the possibility of Jewish claims to Frenchness. But even without that reclassification, the racialization of Jewishness that made possible a neat distinction between native Jews and Muslims problematized Jewish Frenchness. Jews could never be accepted by European settlers as an indistinguishable part of the "French" nation.

The ambiguity and ambivalence of Algerian Jews' position vis-à-vis European colonists and native Muslims became painfully apparent during the Algerian war for independence in the 1950s and early 1960s. Courted by both sides on the grounds of cultural and political affinity,[41] Jewish institutions seem to have done everything they could *not* to take an official position on the escalating conflict, insisting on the internal diversity of Jewish opinions (Sussman 2002:111). Jacques Lazares, the founder and editor of the major Algerian Jewish journal *Information Juive*, typically noted in 1960:

> The Jewish community of Algeria is not a political entity; it has never been one; it neither wishes nor pretends to be one. At its heart, it contains a wide range of opinions. The Jews of Algeria, as a collectivity, do not have to take a stand on a political juncture that emerges from the conscience of each person. As free citizens, enjoying full rights, it is the responsibility of each person to act where he or she wishes and how he or she understands. (cited in Sussman 2002:111)

In a sense, this denied the existence of a corporate Jewish identity, arguing that Jews only had individual opinions on the subject, which had nothing to do with their Jewishness. But there is a way in which this deafening silence nonetheless suggests a unique Jewish position vis-à-vis the conflict. Sympathy for Muslim dissatisfaction with an obviously discriminatory system, political and material ties to French rule, and the social fragility of Jews' structural position made this silence both necessary and prudent. In addition, Jewish elites regularly proclaimed themselves the only "liberal" population in Algeria—meaning that while they identified as French, they also cherished universal human rights and thus a reformed colonial system (Sussman 2002:125). In the midst of extreme social and political upheaval, even the silence itself suggests a sense of distance from both French and Algerian nationalist concerns.

Algerian Jews could not remain in their own separate world forever. Some joined the Algerian independence movement; others joined paramilitary organizations dedicated to keeping Algeria French (Abitbol 1990:214–215; Sussman 2002). But the overwhelming majority threw their lot in with 815,000 *pieds-noirs*, or European colonists, who abandoned Algeria just before and after the signing of the Evian Accords that conceded Algerian independence (Bensimon 1971:2). Many Algerian Jews fled because they imagined themselves as French, could not imagine living their Frenchness outside of French national territory, and presumed they would be as unwelcome in newly independent Algeria as any other European colonist (Bensimon 1971:36; Shepard 2006). Others, however, saw escalating nationalist violence against Jews and the increasingly Muslim content of nationalist identity claims as evidence that their *Jewishness* posed a particular problem in a non-French Algeria (Friedman 1988:95). Whichever permutation of the relationship between Jewishness, Algerianness, and Frenchness they adopted, the overwhelming majority of Algerian Jews did not immigrate to Israel (Shepard 2006:182).

Jewish "choices" at the end of the French colonial period thus encapsulate the larger argument I am trying to make. By virtue of their Jewishness, Algerian Jews were expected and encouraged to identify more closely with the French colonizers than with their Muslim neighbors. At the same time, both their Jewishness and their indigeneity made full assimilation to Algerian pieds-noirs impossible.[42] As one of Sarah Sussman's Jewish Algerian informants noted, "we were sitting between two chairs" (2002:87). So despite significant assimilation and widespread Jewish identification as French, Algerian *Jewishness* had the potential to remain a defining identity in and of itself.

The Protectorates: Tunisia and Morocco

Algeria was unique among France's North African colonies; it was the only colony to be formally annexed to the Metropole. Neither Tunisia nor Morocco were ever considered settlers' colonies, and they both remained at least nominally under indigenous Muslim control throughout the colonial period. In addition, the Crémieux Decree proved to be an exception in the history of French colonization of North Africa. No second decree was ever issued for Tunisia or Morocco, even after the French finally gained more or less exclusive influence in, respectively, 1881 and 1912. On an individual level, French naturalization remained extremely difficult if not illegal for Muslims and Jews in both colonies (Chouraqui 1952:117–119; Cohen-Hadria 1980:53–54; Sebag 1991:154–162).[43] Thus Jewishness did not provide an exclusive legal path to Frenchness in either of these contexts. Nonetheless, I will suggest that Jewishness played a significant role in access to agents of Frenchification (or Europeanization) and in the perception of shared European sensibilities. Two discursive practices of very different orders—European strong-arm tactics and the educational efforts of the Alliance Israélite Universelle (hereafter AIU)—were central in making "Jewishness" an important means of claiming French political and cultural sensibilities.

During the 19th century, the growing European presence in both Tunisia and Morocco helped reify "Jews" as a social category, thus generalizing otherwise very limited ties between Jews and the would-be colonizers.[44] In both Tunisia and Morocco, European consuls and foreign ministers often invoked Muslim treatment of Jews to justify military or diplomatic interventions. The Muslim populace and its rulers, it was argued, did not and would not sufficiently protect the human rights of non-Muslim subjects, almost all of whom were Jews in Morocco and Tunisia (Abitbol 1998b:167–168). As Norman Stillman notes, these moral concerns both cloaked and bolstered imperial interests, leaving the two "inextricably joined" (1991:6). But such arguments also did real social work. Insisting that Jews needed protection from Muslims in North Africa suggested that ethno-religious distinctions were the most significant axes of difference within North African societies. This, in turn, helped make such an assumption into a social reality.

Vying for influence and valuable trade relations, Spain, England, and France offered relatively assimilated Jews a way of extracting themselves from local social relations and power hierarchies. From the mid-18th century on, the "protégé system," so-called because of the protection it was thought to offer eligible non-Muslims living in Muslim lands, allowed European consuls to create human spheres of influence among merchants and middlemen who remained Tunisian or Moroccan subjects. Although not created specifically for Jews, a small Jewish elite—typically consular employees and Jews involved in colonial trade—benefited enormously from the system, making its maintenance one of the top priorities for European Jewish organizations, including the English Board of Deputies and the AIU (Chouraqui 1998b:38). Once granted protégé status, Jews were exempt from military service, from the required non-Muslim tax, and perhaps most significantly, from local legal regimes (Laskier 1983b:148). This meant they could flout any remaining dhimmi provisions, including restrictions on dress and behavior. In Tunisia, for example, Jews with European citizenship and those who were protégés wore European pants and jackets with wigs and hats; their wives walked around the streets unveiled.

In addition, the European powers pressed for structural changes that would entirely eliminate dhimmitude. Norman Stillman suggests:

"From the European point of view, religious tolerance in the Islamic world was one of the necessary first steps toward progress in the region" (1991:6–7). In Morocco from the mid-19th century on, the sultan was visited and pressured by European, particularly English, representatives demanding greater respect for Jewish rights (Laskier 1983a:34). Between 1870 and 1880, Michel Abitbol suggests, fully one-quarter of all European consular correspondence about Morocco dealt with treatment of Jews, who made up less than 3 percent of the population (1998b:164–168). When the cumbersome and confusing protégé system seemed endangered in the early 1880s, English Jews petitioned the British foreign ministry to continue to support it in Morocco. They noted that Jews not only played an important economic role in favor of European trade, they

> are also a great civilizing factor, and if consular protection is withdrawn they will be left entirely at the mercies of the ignorant, fanatic, and barbarous Moors. . . . We ask your Lordship, as the representative of her Majesty's Government, to consider the necessity and importance of retaining at least, and, if possible, of extending this protection of Moorish subjects to the Jews and non-Mahommedans generally in Morocco. We ask, as regards the Jews, that this should be done, and we say it would be best done by treaty. (cited in Laskier 1983a:50)

The government agreed, at least to a certain extent. It saved the protégé system but did not grant the wholesale extension of protections that the board seems to have envisioned.

In Tunisia, the French also used Jews as an excuse for ever-greater incursions against the bey's sovereignty. In one of the most famous incidents of the precolonial period, French diplomatic and then military forces used a harsh legal ruling against a Jew as an excuse for intervention, expressing their displeasure by conducting menacing military exercises off the Tunisian coast.[45] The display of force resulted in a concession: a decree that separated citizenship rights and religious affiliation (Abitbol 1998b:169; Chouraqui 1998b:26–27; Rodrigue 1990:189). Just a few years later, this decree became the foundation for a new Tunisian constitution and a uniform code of civil and criminal laws, neither of which made any distinction between Muslim and non-Muslim Tunisians (Sebag 1991:118).

European diplomats and Jewish organizations justified their support for the protégé system and/or more systemic legal reforms by citing Jewish life conditions. Jews were cut off entirely from the political process in both Tunisia and Morocco. By the beginning of the colonial period, they were barred from most governmental positions, and their security depended largely on the goodwill of national and local leaders. In addition, perhaps in part *because* of the protégé system, they often became scapegoats as European economic and political power weakened local rulers.[46] Jews, however, were not the only victims of precolonial legal systems and/or the political and economic shifts encouraged by colonial incursions (Laskier 1983a). Nomadic tribesmen, local notables, and even central governments often roughly treated Muslims, particularly the poor. But the European powers had a tendency to ignore Muslim ill-treatment at the hands of other Muslims; to European eyes such harassment appeared to be less a human rights issue than evidence of cultural barbarism. As a result, Muslims were never eligible for European protection, a status reserved for non-Muslims—and thus primarily Jews in Morocco and Tunisia—who were imagined as inevitably oppressed by Islamic rule.

For some Muslims, the particular attention to Jews made growing European influence indissociable from "Jewish" interests. Natives attempting to thwart or influence European powers often took local Jews hostage along with European nationals. In 1907 when the French invaded Casablanca—ostensibly to restore order after a series of anti-European riots—Muslims in Oujda, Casablanca, and Fez, all cities closely associated with French economic and military penetration, attacked Jews (Chouraqui 1998b:45; Laskier 1983a:42). Similarly, on the eve of the creation of the Protectorate, mutinous Moroccan troops sacked the mellah in Fez (Laskier 1983a:22).[47]

If European diplomacy and the protégé system offered elite Jews a way out of traditional power relations and customs, the AIU offered the Jewish masses access to European languages and dispositions (Laskier 1983b:148). Immediately after its creation in Paris in the 1860s, the AIU established permanent observation bases in Morocco and then Tunisia, thereby facilitating the monitoring of Jewish treatment. At the same time, the organization began building what would become an extensive network of Jewish schools in both countries (Chouraqui 1952:216–218). These institutions were often staffed with European Jews who doubled as human rights observers; they did everything possible to attract attention to the plight of native Jews. After the beginning of the Protectorate periods in Tunisia and then Morocco, the AIU joined the Consistoire in lobbying the French foreign ministry to legally conflate Tunisian and Moroccan Jews with their French counterparts (Abitbol 1985:50). The AIU thus backed petitions to organize Consistoires in Tunisia and Morocco and constantly advocated for the wholesale naturalization of Jews in both colonies, even long after it had become abundantly clear that the French government had no intention of issuing a second (let alone third) Crémieux Decree (Laskier 1983a:165).

Despite these largely failed attempts at legal reform, the AIU was extremely successful in promoting its vision of Jews as particularly well suited to European civilization and thus as potential colonial allies. This happened primarily through schooling. At its founding in 1860, the organization identified its mission as

> saving and encouraging *Israélites* who suffer for their faith and are damaged in their life chances, interests, and dignity; rehabilitate the word Jew; apply the principles of 1789 and proselytize in favor of liberty of conscience; resuscitate intellectual life among Oriental Jews; create schools; incite youth to overcome their materialist inclinations with the help of morality and religious sentiments. (cited in Tapia 1986:59)

As early as 1862 in Morocco and 1878 in Tunisia, the AIU had evidence that it was accomplishing its mission. In those years, the AIU opened its first schools in each colony, and they immediately filled to capacity. Over the next 50 years the network would expand rapidly in both places. Often opposed by local religious leaders, the schools offered a hybrid program that managed to appeal to unassimilated Jews from modest economic backgrounds. Designed as a means of "regenerating" traditional North African Jews, the curriculum offered a combination of basic secular education, technical training geared toward "productive" employment, and religious studies, including biblical Hebrew instruction, Jewish history, and biblical exegesis (Chouraqui 1952:215–218). All secular subjects were taught in European languages, primarily French, but also Spanish and English. And initially, all secular instructors were European Jews.[48]

To keep the peace with native religious leaders, teachers for Hebrew and kodesh classes were recruited locally and received almost no formal European training. But despite this concession to local mores, the schools sought to thoroughly reform student dispositions. Those with biblical- or Arabic-sounding names were given new, often Frenchified ones (Allali et al. 1989:48; Cohen-Hadria 1980:51). Children were stripped, bathed, deloused, and redressed in simple European-style clothes before being allowed to enter school. After AIU boys' schools had proved capable of surviving conservative religious opposition, the organization began promoting education for girls, thus defying centuries of custom in Arabic-speaking Jewish communities. This revolutionized assumptions about Jewish womanhood and ensured that European languages would literally become Jews' mother tongue (Sebag 1991:140; 143). Even religious practices were to be reformed. Pure moral principles were to be distilled from the wealth of native "superstitions," most of which were imagined as "Arab" rather than Jewish. Judaism was thus to be reimagined in universal, moral terms, making many distinctive public practices irrelevant to observance and creating the conditions of possibility for the privatization of remaining religious practices (Cohen-Hadria 1980:51).

Given the relative importance of the Jewish population in both Tunisia and Morocco (about 50,000 and 100,000, respectively), the European powers quickly recognized the potential power of AIU's endeavors to create loyal (if small minority) native populations. As a result, once the Protectorates had been established, the French government moved relatively rapidly to fund AIU schools. In 1889 it began supporting AIU schools in Tunisia (Chouraqui 1952:216; Sebag 1991:263). And in 1915, almost a decade after the formal separation of church and state in the Metropole, the same kind of support became available in Morocco (Laskier 1983a:151–161). In 1903, partially as a result of this increasingly close relationship with formal French colonialism, the AIU agreed to standardize its secular curriculum, basing it largely off the Department of Education's program for Metropolitan elementary schools. This meant Tunisian and Moroccan Jews, just like their coreligionists in the Metropole, learned about "our ancestors the Gaullois" (ibid.:104–107).

It is hard to overestimate the impact of AIU schools on late 19th- and early 20th-century Tunisian and Moroccan Jews. In both Tunisia and Morocco, large numbers of Jewish children were socialized in these semipublic Jewish schools. Until the end of World War I, the vast majority of Tunisian Jews enrolled in schools with secular curricula went to AIU institutions (Tapia 1986:59).[49] After the war, Jews were given greater access to the public institutions attended by European colonists. But a large plurality of school-aged Jewish Tunisians continued to attend AIU schools for some part of their education. In 1931, for example, more than 22 percent of Tunisian Jews enrolled in school attended one of the AIU's five Tunisian institutions (Sebag 1991:192). Just before independence, that number had risen to 28 percent (ibid.:263). In Morocco, AIU's monopoly over Jewish education was even more pronounced. Although there were several semisecular schooling options for Jewish parents in the pre-Protectorate period, the hybrid Jewish-secular character of AIU's instruction gave it a privileged place on the Moroccan educational scene. By the time Morocco became a Protectorate in 1912, the AIU operated 15 schools that served about 5,500 elementary-aged girls and boys (Bensimon 1978:96). That number increased dramatically under General Hubert Lyautey's rule from 1912 to 1925, when the AIU became the most popular educational institution for Jews of all social classes (Laskier 1983a:74). After World War II, the AIU began to have some competition from far more orthodox Jewish groups, like the New York–based Eastern European Hasidic Lubavitchers and the Sephardi network Ozar Hatorah (lit., "Treasure of the Torah") (Laskier 1983a:247). In particular, Ozar Hatorah, flush with funds provided by the American Joint Distribution Committee, made rapid inroads into Morocco's observant communities. But it never achieved the scope of the AIU network. In 1956 AIU ran 83 schools responsible for the education of 33,605 students, including a very small number of children of Muslim notables (Bensimon 1971:21). The contrast with Moroccan public schools, which targeted European families, is striking. Between 1945 and 1950, such schools educated only 2,000 Moroccan Jews (Laskier 1983a:305).

The cultural impact of AIU schooling was just as striking. If the AIU was explicitly interested in creating cultural and intellectual distance between native Jews and Muslims by eliminating cultural commonalities, it was also interested in collapsing the distance between North African and French Jews. The use of French public schools' secular curriculum was one way of doing this. And, to some limited extent, its effects can be measured by the hysteria it provoked among local religious leaders, who saw it as alienating Jews from their own traditions and milieu. In 1900 a group of Jews from Tunis sent French Chief Rabbi Zadoc Kahn a letter decrying the AIU's work in Tunisia. They noted:

> Each nation has a national education system that is the product of its national life, is imbued with its spirit and national traditions, proceeds from its historic past, and answers the present-day needs of its national life. . . . The Alliance Israelite . . . in violation of the most basic rules of conduct, is seeking to impose the French spirit, embodied by the French national educational system, on the Jewish population of Tunisia. While the Jews of France can still pride themselves on partaking to a certain degree in the national life of the French, they will surely not venture to believe that the same is true of Tunisian Jews, whose past has nothing to do with France or the French, and whose traditions and mores have nothing to do with French civilization—a civilization, moreover, that appeared in Tunisia only yesterday. (cited in Abitbol 1985:53)

And indeed, many Jews educated in AIU schools abandoned the ways of life common in their families for generations. They moved out of Jewish neighborhoods and took apartments in districts primarily inhabited by Europeans. At the same time AIU-educated women began having fewer children, and family structure shifted to a nuclear model. European dress became common, first for men and boys and then for women. Even rituals that structured traditional Jewish life fell into disuse, leaving annual observances in the place of the prayers and religious gestures that had previously accompanied every routine act. And, most concretely, Tunisian and Moroccan Jews learned to speak French. Except for a few AIU establishments, Arabic was largely shunned as a language of instruction until the very end of the Protectorate period, when AIU officials realized that postcolonial survival meant adapting to new circumstances (Laskier 1983a:254; Sebag 1991, 140). This focus on French allowed thousands of Jews to gain access to new occupations, including positions in the Tunisian and Moroccan colonial administrations that required French reading and writing skills (Chouraqui 1998, vol. 2:133; Laskier 1983a:289; Tapia 1986:54–55). By the end of the colonial period, almost 60 percent of Moroccan Jews and 90 percent of Tunisian Jews were functionally literate in French. The comparison with Muslims is instructive: only about 13 percent of the Muslim population in either country spoke and wrote French (Abitbol 1998a:289).

But while AIU schools helped divide Jews from Muslims by Frenchifying or at least Europeanizing their sensibilities, they also (in part inadvertently) maintained distinctions between Jews and Europeans, helping establish the centrality and salience of Jewishness as a separate ontological category. In keeping with the French colonial agenda in both Tunisia and Morocco, AIU schools ensured that most Jewish children would not even try to attend Protectorate schools designed for European children (Abitbol 1998b). And despite AIU's push for the naturalization of both Moroccan and Tunisian Jews, colonial officials hoped that this segregation, in turn, would temper or even eliminate Jewish demands for naturalization.

In addition, although AIU aspired to turn young Tunisian and Moroccan Jews into French men and women, the impact of exclusively Jewish schooling did not necessarily line up with that intent. The AIU never sought to eliminate Jewishness entirely, but it did try to avoid creating an ethno-racially defined "Jewish community" that stood apart from European colonialists. This meant that if AIU officials looked with pride on the "Jewish solidarity" created through an emphasis on the religious links among Diasporic populations, they opposed the ethno-national imaginary that underwrote emergent Zionism.[50] But the experience of Jewish schooling often led AIU students to embrace various forms of ethnicized chauvinism, including Zionism. Moïse Nahon, an inspector for AIU schools in Morocco, found himself unpleasantly surprised by students during a routine visit to a Tétuan school. The students told him that they "must be proud of being Jews because their Sabbath is more important than the Catholic Sunday; that God prefers Jews over all people, and the Messiah will appear to redeem the Jews and only the Jews" (Laskier 1983a:115). Similarly, Samuel Daniel Lévy, an AIU graduate who then trained in

Paris to be an AIU teacher, believed that Muslim and Christian societies were jealous of Jews' inherent superiority and thus did everything in their power to hold them in inferior positions. This conviction led him to Zionism, but not away from the AIU. He defended the AIU's mission as a means to an end: it exposed Jews to Hebrew and taught them about the global Jewish community, thus unintentionally preparing them for Jewish national life. Despite the AIU's efforts to combat Zionism, hundreds of AIU graduates and a number of teachers came to similar conclusions, leading to considerable financial support for the Zionist cause and in some cases to emigration (Laskier 1994).

The relatively wide appeal of political Zionism despite official AIU opposition is significant: it speaks to the profound liminality Jews experienced as a result of colonial rule. Alienated from Muslim natives *and* refused admission to full legal Frenchness, Jews seemed to fit nowhere but among themselves. To a greater extent than in Algeria, Jewish reactions to Moroccan and Tunisian independence movements suggest that Jews were living in a kind of limbo, unwilling to fully ally with any side of the political equation. Throughout the early 20th century, a thin trickle of relatively wealthy Moroccans and Tunisians had settled in the Metropole. The increasing militancy of the nationalist movements in the 1940s and the political instability of the 1950s encouraged small numbers of poorer Jews to head to France for the first time (Bensimon 1971:30). The creation of Israel in 1948, along with growing hostility within Muslim nationalist circles to the Jewish state, increased Jewish emigration and changed its destination.[51]

But despite violence tied to nationalist unrest, some of it directed against Jews, about two-thirds of Tunisian and Moroccan Jews did not emigrate either prior to or immediately after decolonization (Tapia 1986:62). Unlike Algerian Jews, whose material and social position was inextricably tied to French rule, many Moroccan and Tunisian Jews stayed to give the new nationalist governments a chance. This was not, however, necessarily motivated by ideological or existential solidarity with Muslim fellow nationals. As in Algeria, the nationalist parties in both countries had long worked to encourage Jews to imagine themselves as potentially active parts of the nascent nation.[52] But most Jews were unmoved by these pleas. Taught by colonial experience to imagine themselves as first and foremost an ethno-religious community whose interests diverged from those of native Muslims *and* the French, the vast majority of Tunisian and Moroccan Jews remained neutral during the innumerable strikes, rallies, and military actions that punctuated the end of the Protectorates. After the French departure, they stayed, but only as long as economic circumstances were reasonably favorable. And for many, that period proved rather short. The definitive rupture with France in the early 1960s led to structural adjustments that particularly impacted Jews, who could no longer maintain their lucrative European contacts and did not have the Arabic language skills to participate in the new national economy (Memmi 1974:54).

On top of these economic difficulties, Jews often abhorred the move to ally independent North African governments with the Arab League, which had attacked Israel in 1948, 1952, and 1967. During the Six Day and Yom Kippur wars, enraged Muslims attacked Jewish homes and stores in both Tunisia and Morocco. While the violence was often strongly repressed, Jews believed it occurred with the tacit approval of government authorities (Bensimon 1971:35; Memmi 1974). One hundred years of carefully cultivated alienation from native Muslims had made it impossible to believe that governments run by Muslims, let alone Muslim governments, would safeguard Jewish interests and rights (Bensimon 1971). Over the two decades following independence, the vast majority of Jews left both Tunisia and Morocco. And, unlike Algerian Jews who overwhelmingly chose France, most Moroccan and Tunisian Jews fled to Israel. Of the 250,000 Jews who left Morocco in the decades after independence, 145,000–175,000 of them made aliyah (Laskier 1983a:342). About half of the 115,000 Jews who left Tunisia went to Israel (Taieb 1989:57). This is hardly a surprise. European tactics and AIU schools made Jewishness a privileged way of escaping "native" society and gaining access to French dispositions and culture. But they also ensured that many Jews would imagine themselves first and foremost as Jews. Choosing to live in the "Jewish state" thus looked like an obvious solution for a group that defined itself ethnically, religiously, and even nationally as "Jewish." Far more so than in Algeria or the Metropole, many Moroccan and Tunisian Jews thought of themselves as part of a transnational Jewish community increasingly incarnated in Israel.

Conclusion

As the quotes at the beginning of this chapter suggest, nativeness posed mirror-image problems for Jews in the Metropole and the colonies. In post-Revolutionary Metropolitan France, nativeness depended on effacing Jewishness as a subnational and transnational collectivity. For some Metropolitan Jews, this meant emphasizing the isomorphism and elective affinity between Jewishness and Frenchness. For most others, it meant embracing and enacting Franco-Judaism by reducing Jewishness to privatized and individualized belief. In colonial North Africa nativeness, which was synonymous with subjugation as well as inferiority and irrationality, needed to be escaped rather than embraced. Doing so depended on emphasizing Jewishness as a potentially homogeneous, transnational identity that united French Ashkenazim with polyglot Livournais merchants as well as with Arabic-speaking, indigenous peddlers. The Crémieux Decree made this presumption a legal reality in Algeria. The protectorate system and, to an even greater extent, French Jewish organizations like the AIU, made it into a cultural and ideological fact in Morocco and Tunisia.

In both the Metropole and the colonies, these various negotiations of nativeness often had unintended consequences. The Republican obligation to deny the corporate character of Jewishness from a position of collectivity constantly reinvoked the specter of unassimilable Jewish difference—a specter that at times led to violent and even murderous attempts to remove Jews from the national body. In the colonies, the necessity of emphasizing Jewish distinctiveness as a way of distinguishing Jews from Muslims and gaining access to legal or cultural Frenchness had the potential to reify particular forms of Jewishness as the most relevant collective, terminal identity. European anti-Semites and even Metropolitan Ashkenazim ceaselessly reminded North African Jews of the ways in which their particular forms of Jewishness left them inescapably close to "Arabs." Moroccan and Tunisian colonial administrators worked to assure that Jews remained distinct from European colonists. Native North African Jewishness thus both opened and closed the door to Frenchness. This paradox was most evident in Morocco and Tunisia, where the end of French colonialism and influence revealed both the profound rifts that had developed between

Jews and Muslims *and* those that occurred between Jews and France. As a result, most Moroccan and Tunisian Jews emigrated to Israel, where Jewishness defined religious and political identities.

But not all Moroccan or Tunisian Jews went to Israel; about 55,000 Tunisian and 50,000 Moroccan Jews, along with almost 125,000 Algerian Jews, chose France in the years following decolonization. They brought their particular forms of liminality and sense of belonging with them from the colonies to the Metropole. As we will see in the next chapter, this sense of self and other would help transform the institutional face of French Judaism.

Two   Arab, Jew, Arab Jew

> It is as if the [French] authorities were holding back, acting as
> spectators to the conflict opposing two "immigrant" communities
> fundamentally foreign to France; a conflict imagined as emerging
> from tensions external to the French scene. . . . It is very likely that
> this understanding has become part of [French] public opinion. This
> would imply a sudden denationalization of the Jewish community,
> leaving it assimilated to a community whose members were (and
> still are, to a large extent) foreign nationals and recent immigrants.
> . . . [But, in fact, t]he position of Judaism in the Republic is in no
> way comparable to that of Islam. . . . In relation to its roots in the
> nation, it must be remembered that the "Jewish community" as such
> is in no way an "immigrant community."[1]
>
> —Trigano 2000:22–25

The arrival of almost 250,000 North African Jews in the Metropole
transformed post-Holocaust French Jewry. It more than doubled the
metropolitan Jewish population, almost instantly turning the longer-
settled Ashkenazi population into a minority, and introduced colonially
inflected concepts of Jewishness and Frenchness into the Metropole.
This massive change in French Jewry coincided with wider, post-1970s
shifts in conceptions of Republicanism and the space for difference
in Metropolitan France, shifts spurred in part by the way "decolonization"[2] challenged France's long-standing domestic and colonial
mission civilisatrice (Silverstein 2004; Weber 1976). As a result, an
internally divided French Jewry began asking questions about what it
meant to be a French Jew at the same time that the general French
public started reevaluating Frenchness. Ultimately, this reevaluation
created significant social space for some forms of public difference
while simultaneously making others inimical to Frenchness.

This chapter explores the paradox that this structural conjuncture
created for a reconfigured French Jewish population. I suggest that
postcolonial political and social changes invited French Jews to express
their religious, cultural, and ethnic distinctiveness in new ways while
also raising questions about whether Frenchness could tolerate such
difference. Sephardim responded to this new mode of interpellation by

successfully challenging Ashkenazi claims to "represent" French Jewry and by establishing public forms of Jewishness that would have horrified many 19th and early 20th-century "state Jews." But, as the chapter's opening citation suggests, this process has been haunted by the resurgent specter of Jewish foreignness, a phantom that divided Jews internally and threatened to exclude them collectively from the nation. I will argue that by the early 2000s, many French Jews—whether Sephardi or Ashkenazi—had responded to this double menace by adopting a logic of Jewish autochthony to France. Thus instead of emphasizing the structural, if not cultural, commonalities between Jews and all other French minorities, many Jews insisted that they were (at the very least) more "native" to Europe and France than other "others," particularly Arab Muslims.[3] But, as I also hope to illustrate, some of the discourses and practices used to establish these kinds of claims were ambiguous, calling renewed attention to internal Jewish cleavages and Muslim Jewish proximities, with serious implications for how younger generations negotiated relationships between and among Jewishness, Arabness, and Frenchness.

Multicultural France?

France is not a multicultural society in Anglo-American terms (Taylor 1994). Ethno-religious differences are not politically recognized, and there is great opposition to doing so (de Montvalon and van Eeckhout 2006). Political and social representation is still imagined in universal rather than experiential terms, thus making the Anglo-American obsession with political and workplace "diversity" a marginal part of public debate.[4] This discomfort with recognizing and thus authorizing ethno-religious groups extends beyond those directly involved in politics. Although more and more French researchers are borrowing terms like "ethnicity" and even "race" from Anglo-Saxon academics, using them often creates public scandals. The only formal letter I received after my exclusion from Jewish schools (see Introduction) noted that it was impossible to use a term like "racialization" in a French context. In 2005, when an elite French university hosted a series of discussions about the possibilities and drawbacks of importing the category "race" into French sociological inquiry, most of the question-and-answer session was consumed by academics denouncing the decision to even discuss such a dangerous idea.[5]

But this deep discomfort with multiculturalism conceals the ways in which postcolonial France has created space for public difference. In part, this liberalization was tied to the "lessons" of colonialism, which created new possibilities for the expression and understanding of domestic pluralism. By the late 1970s, to some in the opinion-shaping French public, anticolonial revolts and the gradual revelation of colonial realities (Fanon 1967; Memmi 1991) highlighted the gap between state claims—a "civilizing" mission that would turn "natives" into "good Frenchmen"—and practices that presumed and helped realize incommensurable differences between ethno-racially defined groups (Cole 2010; Colonna 1997; Lorcin 1995; Silverstein 2004; Stoler 1997). As a result, assimilation appeared to be not only impossible but also undesirable, a violent deformation of valid alternative lifeways (Silverstein 2004). In a strange way, then, the moral of failed and failing Republican colonial experiments was part of what colonialism had assumed all along—that cultural traits were "given," immutable, and closely tied to particular (quasi-biologically defined) populations (Taguieff 2001).[6]

This foregrounding of Herderian conceptions of culture and identity coincided with the opening of public space to nonnormative expressive practices in France. As early as 1951, the *loi Deixonne* cracked the foundation of the Jacobin edifice by authorizing the teaching of provincial languages in universities and introducing decentralization measures that favored the expression of local difference (Silverstein 2004:73). By the 1970s, regional groups like Bretons and Corsicans began demanding more autonomy and public recognition for cultural forms imagined to be endangered by the Paris-centered practices that passed as national identity (MacDonald 1989; Safran 1985). In part as a response to these demands, by the late 1970s high school students could force public schools to teach a particular regional or foreign language by assembling ten age-mates interested in pursuing the same course of instruction (*L'Arche* 1979:9. In the early 1980s, the Socialist government headed by François Mitterrand opened the public sphere to such expressions of difference, calling for a "flowering of regional cultures and

languages that constitute one of the riches of the French cultural patrimony" (cited in Safran 1985:41). Under Mitterrand, Corsica became an
independent region, government grants were given to regional cultural
initiatives, the national Department of Education recognized and even
encouraged the systematic teaching of regional languages, and radio
and television airways were opened to foreign languages and nonstate
actors (Blatt 1997:42–43; Safran 1985). For a short period of time, these
legislative changes encouraged public pluralization—what 1980s Socialists called "le droit à la différence" [the right to difference]—to an un-
precedented degree. It suggested that diversity in expressive practices,
far from undermining the national project, might be one mode of its
realization (Comaroff and Comaroff 2000:16).

However, not all forms of social and cultural difference (or bearers
of that difference) were treated the same way in this pluralizing national
public (Warner 1992). In the decades following World War II, France
increased its recruitment of Algerian, Moroccan, and Tunisian laborers
for reconstruction and reindustrialization efforts (Weil 2005:16). These
laborers were predominantly single men, commonly referred to as
"guest workers," who were given company lodging in temporary dor-
mitories. For most French citizens, there was no question that these
men would return "home" when the Metropole no longer had any use
for them. By the 1970s, as France entered a 20-year economic down-
turn, it became clear that most of these men would not or could not
leave France. Some had brought their wives and/or children to France
between 1962 and 1974, a period during which circulation between
Algeria and France was relatively unregulated (ibid.:16). Even more
brought their families after the government froze all immigration except for family reunification in 1974. Although generally not possess-
ing French citizenship themselves, many had raised French children in
France.[7] From "guest workers," North African Muslims became "immigrants" or simply "Arabs"—a term that glossed over the myriad of
ethno-cultural differences among North Africans and indexed colonial
constructions of savagery and foreignness (Lorcin 1995; Stora 1992).
Facing a general panic about job competition in a declining economy,
right-wing and then left-wing governments made "zero immigration"
a central part of their political platforms (Silverman 1992; Weil 2005).
At the same time, political parties on both sides of the aisle began dis-

cussion of voluntary and (in extremis) forced "repatriation" of North Africans and their children (Weil 2005:19).

Starting in the late 1960s and more dramatically in the 1970s, a rash of new programs dedicated to promoting immigrant "culture" appeared. Motivated by the same logic about the internal connections among territory, biology, and culture that helped liberalize the French public sphere, these programs had a rather radically different intent (Escafré-Dublet 2008:3–4).[8] Rather than assume that immigrant difference could become part of a pluralized Frenchness, those whose places of birth or expressive practices were imagined as too different from the French norm were to be excluded from French nation (ibid.). In other words, while on one level absolute homogeneity of cultural practice had ceased to be the centerpiece of the national project by the 1980s— no one, excepting some Bretons themselves, thought that the inhabitants of Brittany were not "French"—on another, it continued to index fitness for national belonging for nonwhite, non-Christian populations.

As a result, through a range of business initiatives, government laws, and representational practices, North African difference was cultivated as an insurance policy against eventual assimilation.[9] In the 1960s and 1970s, housing complexes for immigrant workers and industries (like auto manufacturing) with high concentrations of North African Muslims constructed prayer rooms for employees, whether the workers themselves requested such accommodations or not (Davidson 2012). In the 1970s, Valéry Giscard d'Estaing's right-wing government, in consultation with North African states, began a television series that tied the cultural practices of immigrant groups living in France to their "home" countries (Escafré-Dublet 2008). In addition, d'Estaing's government signed foreign-language contracts with the countries that provided much of France's immigrant labor. These contracts placed foreign teachers paid by foreign governments in French public schools as a means of providing language education to (often French-born) children whose "native" language was assumed to be something other than French (Boyzon-Fradet and Boulot 1991:241). Children so designated might spend up to 27 hours a week in special classes with a teacher neither trained in nor familiar with the standard school curriculum (ibid.). This meant that "culturally" appropriate education was provided *instead of* access to a standardized national curriculum imagined as the key to the construction of French Republican subjects. In other words, speaking Arabic and being French, unlike speaking Breton and being French, were framed as contradictory propositions.

Many of these policies continued under the left-wing government of François Mitterrand (Escafré-Dublet 2008). Despite a stated commitment to immigrants' "right to difference" within the French political community, both the logistics of French immigration law and many of the cultural programs associated with that legal regime—notably the television and language programs just mentioned—remained in place (Escafré-Dublet 2008; Silverman 1992; Weil 2005). In addition, the far-right Front National under the leadership of Jean-Marie Le Pen almost immediately and very successfully seized the left's language of difference as a "nonracist" justification for their cultivation of mainstream xenophobia, support for forced repatriation, and agitation for restrictive reform of the nationality code. This tactical move, which illustrates how the logic of multiculturalism is closely tied to Herderian conceptions of community (Tagueiff 2001), led the Front to significant gains in the 1983 municipal elections (Vichniac 1991). Ultimately, then, the creation of space for minority difference within France left North African Muslims, regardless of their nationality, enclosed in a cultural world much of the French public imagined as radically other (Davidson 2012; Shepard 2006).

As numerous scholars have noted, since the middle of the 1980s the pendulum has swung away from multiculturalism and back toward more Jacobin understandings of Republicanism (Blatt 1997; Escafré-Dublet 2008; Mandel forthcoming; McKesson 1994; Vichniac 1991). Discussion of the need to "assimilate" or "integrate" Muslims into a Republican national model has since come to dominate French conversations about "immigrants." But Pandora's Box had been opened. The presence of cultural and ethnic difference—and particularly North African ethnic and cultural difference—has remained in the public sphere. In the 1980s young, well-educated second- and third-generation North African Muslims who called themselves *beurs*, street slang for *Arabe*,[10] began revalorizing the very cultural practices that had initially been used to marginalize North African immigrants. Although they did so in conjunction with politically affiliated antiracist organizations, thus in the name of Republican universality (they were not, for instance, demanding *beur* political representation), this further reified "Arabs" in the French national imaginary (Silverstein 2004). By 1990, members of the French government were working to construct a Muslim council modeled on Napoleon's Jewish Consistoire. Like the Consistoire, it was intended as an intermediary between and among the "Muslim community," the state, and the general French public. Then Interior Minister Nicolas Sarkozy brought the project to completion in 2003 with the creation of the Conseil Français du Culte Musulman (French Islamic Council, CFCM), an organization whose mission he described as literally and metaphorically "fighting the Islam of basements and garages" and bringing Muslim practice into the light of the French public sphere (Bowen 2011; Coroller and Licht 2003). At the time, Sarkozy had also defied his center-right party and its president (Union pour un Mouvement Populaire, or UMP) by advocating both ethnic census questions and affirmative action. Politicians, he argued, could not hope to "integrate" France's "visible minorities" if they continued to deny "their particularities and their identity" (de Montvalon and van Eeckhout 2006).

But while Sarkozy's (then) considerable popularity rested in part on his willingness to break French political taboos and, as his supporters said, "call a spade a spade," establishing the political and social space for a French Arab-Muslim "community" inspired considerable fear about denaturing French society and politics.[11] In June 2004, the French equivalent of the FBI released a report warning that at least 300 poor neighborhoods in France were showing dangerous signs of Muslim "ethnic withdrawal" (cited in Bensoussan 2004:3). The signs of this retreat from French society? They included "ethnic shops," halal butchers, women in headscarves, and mosques—all public manifestations of private particularity in part encouraged by the state and now read as evidence of its inability to control borders, bodies, or minds. The decade-long crisis over Islamic head-coverings in public schools has also been framed as a battle between a weakened Republic and illegitimate ethnic interests. In conference after conference and conversation after conversation, non-Muslims described veiled schoolgirls as embodying the antidemocratic, coercive, and misogynistic tendencies of an all-powerful Muslim community. (For an in-depth discussion of the debate about veiling in France, see Bowen 2007.) Stripping girls and schools of such symbols became synonymous with reclaiming physical and moral space for the Republic from the foreign religious concerns that had colonized it (Fernando 2009). The commission charged with offering legislative recommendations about the veil noted:

> [S]ome young girls and women wear the veil voluntarily, but others do so under duress or pressure. Such is the case for pre-adolescent girls, who are forced, sometimes violently, to wear the veil. Young veiled women can show themselves in public housing complexes and in the street without fear of being mocked or mistreated, the way they would be if they left their hair uncovered. Paradoxically, then, the veil offers them the protection that the Republic should provide. (Stasi Commission 2004:102–103)

Over and against this kind of analysis, I am suggesting that government practices helped create a two-tiered space for difference in the Metropole. On the one hand, the differences displayed by groups that could claim native rootedness, or autochthony, in France were framed as building blocks of a diverse national public. This was most obvious for regional groups whose identity claims were inextricably linked to French political geography. Breton children, for example, were never forced to choose between the national curriculum and "their" (long-forgotten) language; they could have both. This space for autochthonous difference also, although to a lesser extent, could be made to accommodate (some) Jews, whose forms of distinction could *not* be rooted in a purely territorial imaginary. Beginning in the 1970s and 1980s, Jewish groups began to insist on a distinctively Jewish experience of World War II. Written work about the "Shoah"—the Hebrew term used to refer to the massacre of Jews during World War II—started appearing, as did special Jewish commemorations and demands for recognition (Conan and Rousso 1994; Rousso 1991). These demands and the responses they elicited mirrored the pattern already discussed for regional groups—they were assertions of difference that were inextricably tied to the experience of Republican Frenchness. Insisting that the French government recognize the Shoah as a uniquely Jewish experience relied on the simultaneous evocation of group distinction *and* connection to the Metropolitan national community. It was the French Republic's betrayal of Jews, its transformation of law-abiding, integrated French citizens into racialized others, that led to the necessity of acknowledging Jewish difference. By the 1980s the Jewish Holocaust thus had literally become a part of French national history, taught in public schools as a lesson about difference *and* national community. In contrast, the public space created for "immigrant" practices beginning in the 1960s and 1970s reinforced the distance between French identity—no matter how diverse it appeared to be—and foreign dispositions and actions. Even if practices such as speaking Arabic, praying in a mosque, or wearing a headscarf actually were closely tied to Metropolitan life conditions, they invariably indexed an elsewhere and an otherwise.

Oriental Fundamentalists versus *Jambon-Beurre*: Public Pluralism and the Shifting Face of Jewishness

Beginning in the 1970s, then, Frenchness was becoming less about absolute homogeneity of public practice and the absence of subnational corporate affiliation and more about "elevating to a first principle the ineffable interests and connections, at once material and moral, that flow from 'native' rootedness, and special rights, in a place of birth" (Comaroff and Comaroff 2000:16).[12] What did this mean for North African Jews and, by extension, French Jews more generally? Most Jews who identified themselves as Sephardim, like North African Muslims, had not been born in Metropolitan France. They could not claim any literal historical or genealogical connection to emerging Holocaust-centered narratives of French and European Jewishness (see below). And, as we have seen, many arrived in France with a far more ambivalent conception of the potential relationship between Jewishness and Frenchness than their Ashkenazi counterparts. How were the potentially thorny relationships between and among place of birth, expressive cultural practice, and national identity to be negotiated?

By the 1970s and 1980s Metropolitan Jewry had, once again, become relatively invisible and comfortably middle-class. The same could not be said about many of the North African immigrants who settled in and around Paris. North African Jewish immigrants came from a wide range of class backgrounds—from families of very wealthy merchants to those of impoverished artisans. But almost all were negatively impacted by the move to a differently structured economy that demanded new kinds of diplomas and social networks. Jews who had held civil service positions in colonial North Africa were quickly reassigned to Metropolitan posts,[13] but tens of thousands of immigrant shopkeepers, restaurant owners, retail merchants, and artisans had more trouble finding similarly skilled work (Bensimon 1971:67; Poirier 1998:93–94). To make matters worse, many of the most economically fragile immigrants—in particular, non-French, low-skilled Tunisians—arrived after 1963, when the French economy had begun its downward slide, making economic integration considerably harder (Bensimon 971:71; Poirier 1998:93–94). Furthermore, many North African Jewish immigrants, in particular almost all Algerian Jews,[14] abandoned what worldly wealth they did posses in the rush to flee increasingly precarious political situations.

This economic divide between Sephardim and Ashkenazim was doubled by the spatial politics of North African resettlement. The French government attempted (but failed) to evenly distribute Algerian *rapatriés,* including Jews, throughout the country, thereby avoiding any concentrated strain on local economies or resources. But like generations of Jewish immigrants before them, many North African Jews—Algerians included—settled in Paris. Severe postwar housing shortages in the city made reasonably priced lodging hard to find. As French citizens and official rapatriés, Algerian Jews benefited from government resettlement programs that gave them priority for residence in newly constructed *cités,* semiurban housing communities for middle-income families concentrated in northern and eastern Parisian suburbs like Sarcelles, Aulnay-sous-Bois, Bondy, and Créteil (Bensimon 1971:56; Bensimon and DellaPergola 1984:72). Although typically excluded from government assistance, many Moroccan and Tunisian Jews later joined Algerians in these same housing complexes (Podselver 1996:78). Others clustered in relatively inexpensive peripheral neighborhoods around Paris, particularly the 12th, 18th, 19th, and 20th arrondissements (Bensimon and DellaPergola 1984:72; Poirier 1998:94). Neighborhoods that previously had housed impoverished Eastern European Jews, such as Belleville, gradually acquired a new population. Even the heart of the former Parisian shtetl, Rue des Rosiers in the Marais, gradually lost its Eastern European–style delis, bakeries, and markets to North African shopkeepers selling Oriental pastries and couscous.

Far from sharing physical spaces and daily practices with longer-established Ashkenazim, these residence patterns meant that North African Jews often lived in close social and cultural proximity to North African Muslims, who also settled in large numbers in the semi-urban housing projects that ring Paris to the north and east. In addition to living in the same relatively low-cost apartment buildings, North African Jews and Muslims shared culinary practices, some religious rituals (see chapter 1), and a mutually comprehensible language other than French. In the late 1960s and early 1970s, the overwhelming majority of Sephardi adults and a substantial plurality of Sephardi youth, including Algerians, spoke Arabic.[15] Some Sephardim even shared legal predicaments and concerns with North African Muslims. In the late 1960s and early 1970s, considerable numbers of Moroccan and Tunisian Jews still did not possess French citizenship; some had established permanent residence in France illegally, having arrived as tourists and stayed after their tourist visas were no longer valid.[16] As a result, moves to restrict immigration and access to French citizenship considerably impacted Moroccan and Tunisian Jews as well as North African Muslims (Allouche-Benayoun and Bensimon 1998:343).[17]

A number of my informants alluded to these commonalities by talking about what Arabs and Jews "should" share in France. A Moroccan-born mother of two told me that at age 14 or 15, in the early 1970s, one of her best friends was a "Muslim girl." Having moved to Paris as a young child, she explained, "I was in a public school. There were very few Jews in this school. The people who, the adolescents who were most likely to resemble me in my culture and my reactions, they were Muslim girls." There is even some indication that Jews and Arabs were at times mistaken for one another and that the two categories themselves interchangeably indicated foreignness. In the late 1980s and early 1990s *Actualité Juive* published two stories about violent assaults against Jews that included anti-Semitic and anti-Arab epithets. In December 1988 a group identified as tied to the far-right Front National screamed, "Dirty Yids [*youpins*], dirty Arabs," while attacking Jews wearing kippot in front of the Eiffel Tower. Two years later, the same newspaper reported on a Jewish teacher assaulted in her home by two masked individuals crying "dirty Jew," "dirty Arab" (C. M. 1990:5). In 1993, one of *Tribune Juive*'s writers called attention to the Department of Education's confusion of "Arab" and Sephardi children. For the purposes of the "native" language classes destined for immigrant children, teachers and department officials apparently mistook Jews with Arabic (or simply Arabic-sounding) names for Arab Muslims:

> [S]everal Jewish children have been the victims of "misunderstandings" . . . [c]reated in large part by ignorant teachers. For them, there is no distinction: Ben Gurion and Ben Bella are both Arabs. These quick confusions, this prejudice in the face of names could be dismissed as mere nothings. But when a Jewish mother receives, via her son, a libelous pamphlet in Arabic, it is disturbing. . . . If one wants to be French, it is better to be named Dupont. . . . It seems unimportant if the child is French, was born in France: "his national language . . . his country" are in North Africa. (Waintrop 1993:23)

Even racist police practices suggested the constant threat of confusion, this time because of the physiognomic similarities between "Arabs" and North African Jews. In 1981 Dan Lewer wrote: "There is a racist climate and the problem with immigrant workers proves it. We no longer find Jews at police stations in the wee hours of the morning, but immigrant workers. And if Jews happen to be there, it's because a policeman has made a mistake because of their dark skin" (Lewer 1981:13). In 1985, then president of the UEJF and supporter of the antiracist organization SOS-Racisme, Eric Ghebali, went further than Lewer. Where Lewer saw an accident born of physical resemblance, Ghebali imagined physiognomy indexing a shared structural position.[18] Explaining an initiative that would bring young Jews and Muslims together to discuss dealing with French racism, Ghebali noted that he thought it critical for "young Jews, who are often themselves second generation immigrants, to participate in this new fight that, this time, affects all *basanés* [slang for dark-skinned people]" (cited in Silbert 1985:15).

This proximity to France's quintessentially foreign population and distance from "native" Jews was reinforced by patterns of adaptation and community development. To a large extent geographically, economically, and socially isolated from Ashkenazim, newly arrived Sephardim recreated their own local worlds. A Jewish press directed at a North African audience appeared, including publications that had existed in North Africa, like *Information Juive* from Algiers, and entirely new creations, like the religious newspaper *Actualité Juive*. Groups dedicated to reconstituting networks for Jews from particular cities sprang up, as did national associations focused on the preservation and elaboration of "Moroccan," "Tunisian," or, more rarely, "Algerian" forms of Jewishness (Poirier 1998:173). Neighborhoods with large concentrations of Jewish immigrants began to develop the infrastructure that facilitated a marked ethnic and often religiously observant life. Beginning in the late 1970s and early 1980s, Jewish day schools, long a very marginal part of French Jewish life, opened by the score in peripheral neighborhoods and the suburbs. Many of these day schools were directly affiliated with networks that had previously educated Jews in North Africa, for example, the Alliance Israélite Universelle and Ozar Hatorah. Kosher restaurants, supermarkets, and butcher shops sprang up, as did Jewish bookstores and boutiques selling ritual paraphernalia like seder plates, Kiddush cups, and challah covers. In addition, between 1960 and 1977 the number of synagogues and community centers in Paris more than doubled, from 30 to over 71 (Tapia 1986:221). A large number of these institutions were not affiliated with or recognized by the Consistoire.[19]

Sarcelles, an urban conglomeration (*banlieue*) just north of Paris that is closely associated with immigrants more generally and with Sephardim in particular, provides a case in point. Over the course of the 1960s and 1970s an identifiable "Jewish quarter" emerged, attracting ever-greater concentrations of North African Jews. Even those who had been living in other, more upwardly mobile neighborhoods were drawn to the newly established (1964) synagogue—which ultimately offered services from all three North African national traditions—and the incredible concentration of Jewish businesses catering to an observant Sephardi public (Podselver 1996). By the early 1990s Jews made up about 15 percent of the Sarçellois population, a number that has led to considerable talk about Jewish political influence in local elections and even an attempt to establish an all-Jewish electoral list (Benveniste 2002; Podselver 1994:37).

This kind of alternative Jewish institutional and cultural world testifies, at least in part, to initial North African alienation and exclusion from Ashkenazi-controlled Jewish organizations (Poirier 1998:86). Not only did North Africans find the Franco-Jewish practices of mainstream institutions like the Consistoire un-Jewish, and even "Christian," few Ashkenazi elites were willing to countenance sharing their power as community "representatives" with newcomers. While institutions like the Fonds Social Juif Unifié (FSJU), Conseil Représentatif des Institutions Juives de France (CRIF), the Comité d'Action Sociale Israélite de Paris (CASIP), and the Consistoire did provide housing aid, job advice, clothing, and food to new arrivals,[20] these kinds of programs clearly styled Sephardim as charity cases rather than leaders. But as French cultural politics shifted toward greater tolerance for public difference, Sephardi challenges to the Ashkenazi monopoly over powerful institutional positions started working, creating a crisis of representation and representativity.

In the summer of 1980, the first North African Jew—Algerian-born René Sirat—was elected to a major community position as chief rabbi of the national Consistoire. Far from viewing this election as a nonevent, the establishment Jewish press waxed long about the significance of the shift in leadership. Adam Loss, the editor of FSJU's flagship magazine *L'Arche*, described Sirat's election as a "profound change" that "confirmed a new reality" in the nature of the Jewish community (Loss 1980a:17).[21] Less neutrally, Jean-François Kahn, the editor of the left-leaning national weekly *Marianne*, claimed that Sephardi Jews living in the suburbs were organizing against the entrenched Jewish leadership and that a newly vocal group of hardliners were working to oppose the rest of the largely progressive community (Kahn 1980). To his readers, this comment would have been easy to decode: relatively poor, reactionary immigrants were trying (unsuccessfully) to impose their atavistic religious practices on all of French Jewry.

This theme—poorer, flamboyantly religious immigrants trying to oust a progressive bourgeoisie with privatized religious practice—became a leitmotif in intra-Jewish conversations about the change sweeping through French Jewish practice and institutions. Not surprisingly, Sirat would be one of the first Sephardim publicly described as a "fundamentalist," a term most often associated with Arab Muslims. By 1985 he had provoked the public ire of much of the remaining Ashkenazi establishment and a good number of Sephardim, including the lay portion of the Consistoire, by refusing to convert or to recognize the out-of-state conversion of Guy de Rothschild's bride (Trigano 1994:187).[22] This religious opposition struck a nerve. Guy was not only a Rothschild and the head of the FSJU; his religious practices and political positions represented the last gasp of bourgeois Franco-Judaism. He was patently uncomfortable with growing public assertions of militant Jewishness, favoring clearer lines between public citizenship and private religiosity. And he had long advocated fighting Jewish battles in universalist terms, including rolling the fight against anti-Semitism into a more general battle against racism (de Rothschild 1980). In response to what seemed to be a frontal attack on Franco-Judaism itself, Jacquot Grunewald, the editor of *Tribune Juive* and no political friend of Rothschild, accused Sirat of trying to turn French Judaism into a "form of fundamentalism" (Grunewald 1985a:8).

These accusations are hardly unusual; they appear in various guises in almost any context in which there is an established Jewish community and a more observant, immigrant one. But the French context in the 1970s and 1980s contained at least one decisive particularism. Behind all of this talk about "fundamentalism" lay the veiled but powerful implication that Jewish newcomers were like Muslims, and therefore were engaged in practices tinged with inassimilable foreignness. French colonial stereotypes and the bloody Algerian struggle for independence had helped link fanaticism indelibly to Arab Muslims in particular and perhaps Islam more generally (Shepard 2006; Silverstein 2004). In addition, in the late 1970s and the 1980s, the Jewish press was quite preoccupied with the rise of radical Islam, with Iran as the model for developments in the rest of the Muslim world (see, e.g., Berg 1982:56–57; Dishon 1979:18; Ghariani 1986:8; Kriegel 1979:24–25). All of the intra-Jewish conversation about "fundamentalism" and fanaticism played out in this heavily charged context. Jewish writers accusing (primarily) Sephardim of being irrational and divisive fanatics were at the very least unconsciously tapping into this fund of associations, using it to frighten their readers into action or agreement. It could be argued that they were surreptitiously calling the Jews with whom they disagreed "Arabs."

Those seeking to displace the old guard of Jewish leaders also hardly minced words, even embracing the label "fanatic" as a happy alternative to a form of Frenchness that they thought completely dissolved Jewish collective identity. In 1982 Gerard Touaty, a regular columnist with *Actualité Juive*, denounced the Jewish establishment as peopled with weak men who "spoke timidly with government ministers after bombs were dropped on Jews, and then went home to eat ham and butter sandwiches [*jambon-beurre*]" (1982a). "Why ask for synagogue protection," he queried, "when you never go there?" (ibid.). The term jambon-beurre has two meanings in the sentence. It indexes a total disregard for Jewish dietary restrictions: both ham *and* the consumption of dairy and meat together are considered unclean. In addition, it references assimilation to the lifeways of the nominally Catholic, average Frenchman, colloquially known as a jambon-beurre. For Touaty, either disqualified Jewish leaders from their representative pretensions. A few months later, Touaty wrote a column titled "Apology for a Little Fanaticism," in which he encouraged Jews to reject Western assumptions about the relationship between religion and rationality:

> The little Tunisian or Polish Jew lost in the cold halls of a university who rediscovers his roots, who makes *techouva* [literally a return, usually applied to religious practices], who disturbs those around him with his *kashrut* and his *tefilin* [phylacteries], that Jew is the product of a free choice. After having fully lived as a little Frenchman, his change of course is a choice; he weighed the pros and the cons. . . . [T]he real fanatics are those who watch TV and go jogging on Saturday morning [the Jewish Sabbath], who are still attached to the old, colorless West that offers us only sadness and misery. (1982b)

This imagined opposition between Western society and French social norms, on the one hand, and Jewish authenticity, on the other, did not always lead to calls for stringent religious observance. Shmuel Trigano, the Algerian-born philosopher cited at the beginning of this chapter, argued that the very nature of French society had created both Jewish extremes: the "self-hating" assimilation implied by Franco-Judaism and the religious extremism implicit in Sephardi attraction to Eastern European forms of ultraorthodox religious practice (Trigano 1980; Podselver 1992, see below).[23] He begged Jews to reject both dangerous accommodations with Western societies, whether they lived in France or in Israel. "We must free the Jewish idea from its Western cage; we have to rethink Jewish destiny" (Trigano 1979b:37). Although he never outlined what such a non-Western Jewish future would look like, he insisted that the path itself would be found by those least corrupted by Western lifeways, namely the Jews of the "Sephardi world" (Trigano 1979a:39).

Some of the tensions that came to a head with initial Sephardi attempts to gain and reframe leadership roles have since disappeared from public view. By the time I did my fieldwork, most of the leadership and staff of old establishment Jewish institutions were first- and second-generation North African Jews.[24] But this did not mean that internal, ethnicized tensions within French Jewry had disappeared. In fact, they seemed to have become more rather than less significant as Sephardim gained power and prominence. In 1988, a demographic survey sponsored by the FSJU found that 50 percent of Jews interviewed identified themselves as "Sephardi," 34 percent as "Ashkenazi," and 16 percent as "neither" (Cohen 2002:12). In a 2002 follow-up study, the number of Sephardim jumped to 70 percent, the number of Ashkenazim dropped to 24 percent, and 6 percent claimed to be both Sephardi and Ashkenazi (ibid.). Notably, in the 14 years that separated the two studies, "neither" disappeared as an experiential category completely, suggesting that it was no longer possible to escape ethnic identification within Jewishness.

Given the continued salience of this internal ethnicized politics and a larger social and political context that (at least officially) was recommitted to Republican integration, it was not surprising that the debate over French Jewishness continued to rage during my fieldwork. When Roger Cukierman, former president of the CRIF and one of the few Holocaust survivors who still held a community leadership position in the mid-2000s,[25] described French politics in explicitly ethnicized terms, he provoked discomfort among his own largely bourgeois board members and staff who thought he should stick to defending Republican principles. Infamously, comments he made after the 2002 first-round presidential elections—in which the far-right candidate Jean-Marie Le Pen amassed more votes than the sitting Socialist prime minister Lionel Jospin—created considerable consternation within the CRIF. Cukierman told the Israeli newspaper *Ha'aretz* that

Le Pen's victory was a welcome political sign for Jews; it made it clear that "Muslims needed to calm down [*se tenir tranquille*]" (*Le Monde* 2002b; Laske 2002). A whole range of Jewish leaders immediately denounced Cukierman, notably CRIF board member and socialist legislator Michel Dreyfus-Schmidt, who publicly demanded that the CRIF president resign for being patently un-Republican (*Le Monde* 2002a).[26] In 2005, Cukierman was again in the hot seat. At the CRIF's annual gala dinner, an event attended by French politicians, he denounced then President Jacques Chirac and his government for cultivating anti-Semitism through misguided foreign policy in the Middle East (Ternsien 2005). In response, Théo Klein, a former president of the CRIF, told *Le Monde*: "In my understanding, the president of the CRIF should evoke general problems and seek to elucidate them with ideas from the Jewish community. But one must always put the general interest of the country first, before any particular interests" (cited in ibid.). There could be no more classic invocation of the delicate balancing act involved in Franco-Judaism.

But at the same time, a vocal portion of the Jewish public continued to dismiss Jewish leaders as far too willing to respect Franco-Jewish traditions. Jewish elites were often characterized as silent and assimilationist, unwilling or unable to stand up for Jews as Jews regardless of the social consequences. And, in moments of perceived crisis, a whole range of alternatives seemed to proliferate.[27] When I first arrived in Paris, neighborhoods associated with high concentrations of (usually North African) Jews were plastered with posters for the Jewish Defense League and the Betar. Both are far-right youth movements with roots in Israeli (not French) politics; both are deeply prone to racializing narratives of Jewishness and are shadowed by histories of violence against Arabs and Muslims in both France and Israel. Even for those who would never consider joining such movements, their confrontational style and disregard for Republican and democratic norms can be appealing. According to Eric, a second-generation business school student of mixed Algerian and Tunisian ancestry:

> I think that the Jews of France should not behave like victims. . . . I think that a child who is called "dirty Jew" at school should respond. He should go to school, and he should punch the guy in

> the face. . . . From my perspective, most of the Jews who live in the
> [upper-middle-class] neighborhood where we live, they are—how can
> I say it?—cowards. They are people who don't have enough indepen-
> dence, I think. And from my perspective, I think that the institutions,
> the Jewish organizations that are a bit more, how shall I say it?—
> radical—they are useful to show that Jews are not weak. When I see
> that Dieudonné [a black comedian sued and exonerated repeatedly for
> anti-Semitism] does shows in front of an audience of 3,000 people, it's
> an anti-Semitic show that's live for two hours, and the people applaud;
> I would like the Betar to put a bomb in the, I want them to threaten
> Dieudonné, yes, I really want that— . . . I want there to be a reaction.

From such a perspective, even Cukierman's discourse is Rothschild-
esque. As a middle-aged man with a heavy North African accent told
the CRIF president after a public debate:

> We are being given very prudent responses to subjects. You are re-
> sponding [to journalist and audience questions] with a very political
> discourse. And perhaps that's not the discourse we wanted to hear.
> . . . I would just like to say that you are someone whom I respect,
> that I respect the positions that you have taken. But nevertheless, I
> find that you are, on a political level we would like to have a little less
> euphemistic language because, as a Jew. . . . What we hear officially in
> the media and what we live in France, even if it is not yet a disaster, I
> think there is a big gap. . . . And I find that you are taken in with your
> meetings with such and such a European political person, but the vast
> majority of Jews have a daily life that is different.

And indeed, there is an enormous gap even in the language used by
the wealthy, articulate Cukierman and his Sephardi interlocuter.

In this last example, the classed differences in education and discourse are too striking to ignore. Although the issues and practices
that separate French Jews were heavily class-inflected (see chapter 5),
they were still likely to be understood in terms of intra-Jewish ethnic
distinctions. They became evidence of deep cultural and even biological differences between Ashkenazim and Sephardim. The growing visibility of Jews' presence in Paris is a case in point. Many Jews who
welcomed growing Jewish publicity attributed it to the "Sephardim"
who had breathed life back into a moribund French Judaism that had
all but disappeared after the Holocaust. More than one person claimed

that French Jewry would no longer exist if not for the arrival of the Sephardim. Some even went so far as to assume that there were no Ashkenazim left in France. A teacher in a Jewish school queried, "Where are they? Do you see them? They're certainly not here." Among some Jews, even internal differences among North African Jews mattered, with presumably Frenchified Algerian Jews offering little in the way of Jewish renewal. A Moroccan-born Jewish school director proudly attributed much of the public transformation of Jewish practice to Moroccans, who had brought their "double culture," including Jewish and general knowledge, to bear on everything from schooling practices to butcher shops. "The Algerians," he noted, "they know nothing of Jewish schooling because they always had public schools. They couldn't understand why people were opening Jewish schools when there were neighborhood schools just around the corner. . . . Ninety-eight percent of Jewish school directors in France are Moroccan."

Those who viewed this visibility as a disturbing transgression of French social norms also associated it with Sephardim. An upper-middle-class college student whose mother was born in Tunisia and father in Morocco talked about her embarrassment when faced with such public Jewish practices:

> Sometimes I'm ashamed of the way people behave. Over there in the street, there are all these kosher butcher shops, all those who double park in their big SUV Mercedes and who block the entire street without thinking about it, I find that shameful. . . . It's true sometimes I'm ashamed when there's a woman yelling in a restaurant, or who has a bizarre reaction, or who doesn't realize that the person across from her is not Jewish and starts to say: "the Arabs, I want to kill them" or "one should only marry Jews" or something like that. . . . I think it gives people a negative image. It's true that I'm Sephardi, but I think Sephardi Jews have created a very bad image. . . . Ashkenazim are more reserved, more discreet, much more integrated as well. They melt into the crowd. For an Ashkenazi, unless he has a very distinctive family name, you won't know he's a Jew.

For this student, Sephardiness was an inversion of the social norms associated with polite, bourgeois French society. It meant engaging in conspicuous consumption; loudly embracing racist, reactionary politics; and rejecting tolerant openness in favor of clannishness (see chapter 6).

Ashkenazim, on the other hand, were invisible precisely because they embodied mainstream French values.

Scores of people echoed this vision in softened terms, linking lingering tensions over ways of being Jewish to the "different mentalities" that accompanied being Ashkenazi or Sephardi. When I asked if one could talk meaningfully about tensions between Ashkenazim and Sephardim in France, an Ashkenazi English teacher in a religious school said yes, noting that history, culture, everything separated the two groups. She added with evident sadness that the influx of Sephardim had turned Ashkenazim into a "dying race, and I use the word 'race' very intentionally." Sephardim, in turn, told me that Ashkenazim were "cold," "distant," or "reserved," all terms that the same people used to describe the non-Jewish "French," with whom they claimed to have little in common. Eric explained:

> I find that Ashkenazi Jews have a different mentality than Sephardi Jews. . . . Because, I don't know, I would say that most Ashkenazim have a certain self-reserve, a certain distance that Sephardi Jews don't have. I know this is a generalization. But I think there is much more familiarity, many more things in common among Sephardi Jews than between a Sephardi Jew and an Ashkenazi Jew. I know that I would have less, I would have fewer ties, I could be best-friends with a guy who is Ashkenazi, I don't care. . . . But it's not as easy. I don't know how to say it. I feel that it's a bit two different universes.

Assimilated Jews of whatever origin were even characterized as "Ashkenazim." Ben, a college student whose mother was born in Algeria, described his family as "assimilated. . . . We are very French, very much in the Republican model; there are a number of them [family members] who have put aside anything related to the religion. . . . We are almost like the Ashkenazim from Eastern Europe, the Ashkenazim who come from France." After quizzing me on my (scant) knowledge of religious Judaism, a school director shook his head sadly and asked whether I was Ashkenazi.

Many of my Sephardi informants in turn characterized themselves as "warm," "outgoing," "loud," and "joyful," descriptions that eerily echo the classed and racialized language found in Orientalist literature (Said 1978). This kind of dichotomous characterization extended beyond popular culture into official Jewish representations of French Jews. In 2005, a permanent exhibit about French Jews in the Musée d'art et d'histoire du Judaïsme (Museum of Jewish Art and History) in Paris played on such assumptions. It represented Ashkenazim through literate and predominantly masculine aspects of religious life and ritual: books codifying rabbinical commentary, Torah scrolls, the silver ornaments used to decorate sacred texts, and marriage contracts. North African Jews, in stark contrast, were depicted through domestic objects: heavily embroidered and gilded women's clothing, amulets described as part of elaborate webs of superstition, and cooking implements. Once again, Ashkenazim were given a monopoly on the traits most closely associated with Western identity and the exercise of French citizenship: rationality, literacy, and intellectual debate. Sephardim, in contrast, were the ethnicized, feminized, exotic other.

A small number of my interlocutors even embraced the description of Sephardim as "Arabs," thus further underscoring both biological and cultural differences from "European" Jews. During my fieldwork, a teacher at Brith Abraham called herself an "Arab Jew" as part of an attempt to get her middle-school class to understand identity in more complex, cultural terms. She explained that the term accurately described her "dual culture," provoking peals of uncomfortable laughter and a chorus of "No! Madame! You can't say that!" from her students. A middle-aged woman at a conference on the Israeli-Palestinian conflict announced that she needed to correct the general public's usage of the word "Arab" in relation to "Muslim." "Arab" in the Bible means "nomad," she continued. "I, for example, am a Jewish Arab. When you start thinking about the words, nothing that has been said means anything anymore." A Moroccan-born high school student likewise told me that he was an Arab Jew, prompting instant ridicule from his French-born peers. And a senior in a public high school, whose parents hailed from Algeria, waxed long about "Western" attempts to divide Jews from their Arab heritage and brothers:

> I think that Westerners wanted to make a problem develop between
> Arabs and Jews. . . . But fundamentally, we were always brothers.
> For 2,000 years we've been persecuted. From the Egyptians, in all
> of our history we've always been persecuted. But I think we've never

had problems with the *rebeu* [street slang for Arab; see n. 10], with the Arabs. When we were chased out of Spain . . . we were brothers. We have always lived together as brothers in Algeria, in Morocco, in Tunisia. And all of a sudden, since there has been Israel . . . there is a hatred between Jews and Arabs. In 60 years, while for the 2,000 previous years we were like brothers. Mohammed says it in the Quran. He says that Jews and Muslims are cousins. We have the same chosen father. I have Muslim friends. They know it. We have the same culture. . . . We really have the same culture. . . . We are all Sephardim, the majority of Jews, because the majority of the Ashkenazim were killed in the camps. . . . Even in terms of the holidays, like Kippur, we cut lamb and they cut lamb. We are really like brothers, like cousins. And I don't know why we hate each other so much because we are so similar. When I talk to an Arab, for me, it's like I'm talking to a Jew.

But many of my informants, despite frequent self-presentation in orientalized terms, were very uncomfortable with the notion of being ascribed "Arabness." Shmuel Trigano, who, as we have seen, imagines Sephardi cultural worlds as diametrically opposed to those of European Jews, has long hated the term. In the context of growing French awareness of Ashkenazi discrimination against North African Jewry in Israel, Trigano wrote:

> Some people even go to the point of saying that the Sephardi dimension introduces Arabness in Israel, which is the same as saying that the Ashkenazi dimension is "aryanism" in Judaism. . . . The Sephardi Jew is therefore not an "Arab Jew," because that would be as absurd as talking about an "Aryan Jew." He is even less an Arab of the Jewish religion because that would be as absurd as talking about an Aryan or European of the Mosaic confession. (1980b:14)

Although hardly formulating their discomfort as critiques of racialized thought, few of my interlocutors agreed with the Brith Abraham teacher who imagined herself as "culturally" Arab. Arabophone adults told me that they were "ashamed" to speak Arabic in public, perhaps because Arabic has long been associated with a stigmatized, colonized population. Those who had been born in France sometimes stressed the importance of being native to France or Europe as a way of distinguishing themselves from those born in North Africa. At times, Sephardim uncomfortably joked that Ashkenazim assumed they were all

"Arabs." In the teachers' lounge of a day school, I overheard an economics instructor talking about her son's "intermarriage" to an Ashkenazi girl who refused to participate in the Sephardi family's ritual observances. The teacher's tone suggested that her daughter-in-law, described as coming from a family that lived in one of the wealthiest parts of Paris, rejected Sephardi practice out of prejudice and pride. In response, another teacher told the (largely North African–born) assembly the following joke: A group of Ashkenazi wise men got together to discuss Maimonides. One of them claimed he simply could not understand a particular passage. His colleagues tried repeatedly to explain it to him but could not do so to the perplexed man's satisfaction. So the group decided to call in the great sage himself. Maimonides entered wearing his turban and caftan, dressed as he would have been at the time he lived. Upon seeing him, the perplexed man cried: "Why should I listen to this Arab?" Everyone laughed bitterly.

Not surprisingly, these kinds of conversations about internal Jewish divisions made some people uncomfortable. The Algerian-born head of youth programs for the FSJU told me that any discussion of an Ashkenazi/Sephardi division was misplaced; he had never felt any tensions and therefore did not think they existed. Charles Szlakmann had made a similar point years earlier in an article criticizing press coverage of the "Jewish community." He accused newspapers of discussing "the Ashkenazim" and "the Sephardim," in ways that if replaced with the terms "the blacks" or "the Arabs" would cause serious and warranted consternation in antiracist circles (1990:11). These are ideological statements about the moral and ontological unity of the Jewish "community," in France and elsewhere. And, in a sense, both men are right. Neither Sephardim nor Ashkenazim are tightly bounded groups with clear religious, cultural, or even socioeconomic traits. We have seen the significant historical and cultural differences among North African Jews. In addition, there are plenty of Jews with North African ancestry who are "invisible" in French society, while there are also Jews from long-settled Ashkenazi families who do not embody the class and cultural practices associated with the bourgeois Parisian public. But just because no dichotomous mode of classification can actually encompass complicated social realities does not mean that the stereotypes themselves do not have real social effects (Herzfeld 1997:26). The imagined cultural, and at times even biological, divide between Ashkenazim and Sephardim structures how differences in class, religious observance, and expressive practices have been understood. In a very real sense, the constant mobilization of stereotypes about Ashkenaziness and Sephardiness helped produce the reified cultural worlds seemingly indexed by the terms.[28]

From Strangers to Autochthones?

In the pluralized public context of the 1970s and 1980s, Jewish politics shifted dramatically from a discreet embrace of Franco-Judaism to a much more public display of social, cultural, and religious difference. Much of the internal Jewish argument around this shift took place in ethnicized language, with relatively newly arrived Sephardim accused of fanaticism, foreignness, nonnative birth and customs, and even "Arabness." These kinds of characterizations illustrated how dangerously close public forms of post-1980s Jewish practice were to the line described at the beginning of this chapter—the line that divided acceptable internal forms of French difference from inassimilable culture-cum-racial alterity. How did Sephardim and French Jewry more generally deal with this threat? How, in other words, could French Jews who embraced public difference still do so within the contradictory bounds of Frenchness? As the kinds of Jewish-Muslim proximities evident within the post-1970s Jewish community registered on a wider national scale, French Jews had to rethink the relationship between and among Frenchness, Jewishness, and Arabness. This rethinking took on a number of different forms. But by the Second Intifada, many French Jews—whether Sephardi or Ashkenazi—had begun to think of Jews as autochthonous to Europe, an argument that allowed simultaneously for irreducible Jewish difference and unique Jewish elective affinity to Frenchness.

This was certainly not always the case. Immediately after World War II, Jewish *résistants*, many of immigrant origin, formed a series of associations dedicated to fighting all forms of racism and to transforming French immigration policy (Noiriel 2007:486–487). Although these groups quickly split along political lines, the alliance was renewed in the late 1970s and early 1980s, just as opposition to immigration from North Africa began uniting political agendas on the left and right. Despite the growing significance of the Arab-Israeli conflict for identity politics among Jews and Muslims, the French Jewish press and French Jewish institutions continued to depict Jews as defenders of or, more rarely, cosufferers with *Maghrebins*—a stance Maud Mandel has called "pluriculturalism" (forthcoming; also see Mandel's chapter 6). In 1985, just after the bombing of a movie theater showing a film about Adolf Eichmann, the editor of *Tribune Juive* noted: "The development in France of an often murderous racism, even if it does not directly target the Jewish community, is intolerable to the Jewish community. Racism cannot be divided. Jews who only yesterday were its privileged victims feel directly attacked" (Grunewald 1985b:17). The pro-immigrant, antiracist stance among writers in the Jewish press was even occasionally defended as both a humanitarian issue and a specifically *Jewish* cause. In a 1986 editorial tellingly titled "Because You Were Strangers," Henri Smolarski urged Jews to oppose legislation that would authorize the expulsion of (even legal) immigrants who had broken the law. He argued that biblical injunctions made such opposition a moral requirement for Jews, "because the stranger is part of the human race. Because he is the Other. Because every man is in exile. Because no boundaries between men are legitimate. Because no people is the proprietor of the land it inhabits" (Smolarski 1986:4). The CRIF executive board agreed.

This clearly is not an argument about Jewish autochthony. Quite the contrary. It is a deliberate and continuous referencing of "foreign" Jewish origins—or, at the very least, the perception of their "foreignness"—in the service of an anti-essentialist vision of the nation. This, however, did not necessarily mean that Jewish leaders believed Jews and Muslims shared a structural position in contemporary France. In a way, encouraging Jewish solidarity with "immigrants" who were victims of racism and discrimination helped nativize and nationalize French Jews, Ashkenazim, and Sephardim alike. Dan Lewer's comments about no longer finding Jews in police stations point to a sense of historical succession—once foreign, Jews now count as "French." Jacquot Grunewald echoed this assumption. Arguing that French Jews should reach out to Arab Muslims despite disagreements over Israel, he noted: "The Arab population . . . the Arab immigrants, the immigrant workers, . . . to a certain extent recall to our memory what we formerly have been in our history" (1983:14). When writers suggested that Jews had passed through the phase in which Arab foreigners were currently stuck, having themselves been immigrants who suffered from discrimination, they underscored their own integration into the French social fabric and Arab exclusion from it. Jewish organizations thus provided a ground for Jewish unity—all Jews had been immigrants, or treated as such—*and* for Jewish Frenchness by making common cause with Arab Muslim immigrants.

But the subtle distinction between Jews who had been nonnative and Muslims who continued to be so became harder and harder to sustain in the 1980s. To begin with, second- and third-generation North African Muslim immigrants gained French citizenship and became politically active in their own right, thus eliminating the literal national divide between groups. In addition, and perhaps more significantly, the kinds of public Jewish practices that had become increasingly commonplace by the late 1970s and 1980s were mirrored by practices adopted by Arab Muslims. In the words of Chantal Benayoun (1993), a sociologist who has compared North African Jews and Muslims: "A symbolic proximity organized references and preferences, claims and myths, . . . there is a symmetry in identitarian practices, political mobilizations, and public confrontations" (101). This is, in part, a reference to the increasing public religiosity of both Jews and Muslims. But it also points to the way Jews and "Arabs" were, from the late 1970s on, mobilizing around the Israeli-Palestinian conflict—often in parallel and dialectically opposed ways (see below).

As a result, by the late 1980s, when the "headscarf affair" became a potent national symbol of the Republic's "failure" to integrate immigrants, Jewish activists and writers were retreating from their earlier commitment to a common antiracist cause (see Mandel forthcoming). Even before the first Gulf War in the early 1990s, many of the antiracist coalitions that prominently included Jews and Muslims began disintegrating, torn apart by (respective) accusations of anti-Semitism and militant Zionism (e.g., Azeroual 1990:10–11; Derai and Azeroual 1990:4–5; also see Mandel forthcoming).[29] At the same time, attempts to draw parallels between Arab Muslim predicaments and Jewish history or contemporary reality began to be described as evidence of false consciousness, at best, if not dangerous delusion. In 1989, *Tribune Juive* published a letter to the editor that denounced attempts to associate Muslim and Jewish practices through legislation against the wearing of religious symbols in school.

> Let's be clear: Banning the kippa or the Jewish star from even secular schools would be an intolerable attack on human rights. Secularism can certainly accommodate religious expressions that do not have expansionist or hegemonic designs (the way Islam does!). In addition, Christians AND JEWS are at home here. . . . Islam is waging a systematic offensive against our tolerant, Judeo-Christian society. We cannot accept the wearing of the *chador* [sic] in class. (Charrier 1989:30; emphasis in the original)

The following month, another reader shared similar sentiments. He noted that until recently, no one had ever thought of questioning a Jewish child's right to miss school for Shabbat or to wear a kippa in class. "But the time has come for complete confusion, for calling into question established rights that did not bother anyone" (Strouf 1990:25). Joseph Sitruk earned the ire of those who typically supported him—relatively observant Jews—by arguing that *both* the veil and the kippa should be allowed in public schools. The team of reporters interviewing the chief rabbi for *Actualité Juive* asked him three times, evidently with increasing incomprehension, why he could not defend the kippa without the headscarf (Benattar et al. 1989:n.p.). Sitruk's position was more consistent than that of the *Actualité Juive* editorial board, which advocated creating the space for public Jewish practices while condemning visible forms of Muslim identity as foreign and dangerous.

What made this illogical and inherently contradictory position so self-evident, both to the editors of *Actualité Juive* and to the Jewish press's readers cited above? In part, it may have been the growing power of discourses about Jewish "particularism" that countered those of the Jewish stranger (see Mandel forthcoming, especially chapter 6). These discourses insisted on irreducible Jewish difference and on Jews' privileged relationship to Frenchness-cum-Europeanness. One form of this alternative understanding appeared in Jewish discourse about Israel. By the late 1970s, discussion of Jewish community politics vis-à-vis Israel had become commonplace in the French Jewish press. These articles implied that French Jews, whatever their often vast and seemingly growing differences, were unified in support of Israel. Grunewald noted in a 1979 editorial:

> The religious revival [among French Jews] is accompanied by hellish descent into superstition and fetishism; the extremes—both assimilation and [religious] radicalism—are so different from one another that they do not even think about fighting each other. . . . The only light that can guide this community remains Israel. . . . She [Israel] is vital to the Jewish community in France: Israel is the community's greatest common denominator. (Grunewald 1979:14–15)

Often, "supporting" Israel meant opposing mainstream French foreign policy. Raymond Lindon wrote: "[F]or Jews who seem to me to be authentic, who see Israel as either a second homeland or an eternal refuge, the choice made during elections hinges on each party's attitude toward Israel. And, unfortunately, it has become clear over the last several years that the political parties are all in favor of Arab countries because they are desperate for oil" (Lindon 1979:14–15). Just a few months later Henri Hajdenberg, then president of the short-lived *Renouveau Juif* (Jewish Renewal) and future president of the CRIF, published a letter denouncing the right-wing Valéry Giscard d'Estaing government for collaboration, this time with the Palestinians: "The 700,000 Jews in France should not be deceived. Our generation has to face being abandoned by yet another French government. It is another style of collaboration that will hurt our people: supporting an organization that wants to destroy the Jewish state. . . . [W]e have broken with this government" (Hajdenberg 1980b:2–3).[30] He later added that while Jews had the same "domestic" preoccupations as all other French people, particularly unemployment, "there are moments when there is no question about how to choose between problems with no life or death consequences and the survival of our people" (Hajdenberg 1980a:xiv).

These were not just assertions about the centrality of Jewish difference; Jews were increasingly engaged in forms of public mobilization that seemed to underscore the rupture between Jewishness and mainstream Frenchness. For the first time, Jewish writers and leaders began talking about the translation of Jewish cultural and political unity into an ethno-religious lobby whose electoral weight should and would be used to force changes in French politics (e.g., Hajdenberg 1985). In the early 1980s, Renouveau Juif created electoral maps indicating districts in which Jews were supposedly numerous enough to influence local elections. A number of Jewish writers and readers called for the Jewish press and organizations like the CRIF to publish (black)lists of candidates who "act against the security interests of the state of Israel" as a means of discouraging Jews from voting for them (Grossman 1980:5; Grunewald 1980b:8). Adam Loss railed against the "Jewish community" for not insisting on its political priorities in the public sphere "when the very existence of the state of Israel is in question, and despite the fact that public officials explicitly try to appeal to Jews on this issue, particularly just before large elections" (1980b:17). There were also articles that celebrated the successes tied to the "Jewish vote." When right-wing incumbent Valéry Giscard d'Estaing was defeated in presidential elections by socialist François Mitterrand, the Jewish press and its readers lauded the power of the Jewish *vote sanction* congratulating Jews who had voted against their material interests in order to elect a candidate who was ostensibly a "friend of Israel" (Eytan 1981:4–6; Eytan 1983:6; Grunewald 1986:19; Wahl 1982:n.p.).[31] Even Jewish writers and officials who downplayed the electoral impact of the "Jewish vote" insisted that Jewishness implied a homogenous set of political concerns. When interviewed by *Tribune Juive* in 1993, then chief rabbi Joseph Sitruk noted:

> The attempt to seduce the [Jewish] community has always surprised me because outside certain districts, where there is a large concentration of Jews and therefore electoral influence, the "Jewish vote" does not exist. . . . The Jewish community does not have numerical weight but influence. There are points on which the community is virtually unanimous: the fight against racism, anti-Semitism, and xenophobia, and support for Israel. A candidate who does not defend these things in his program cannot attract the sympathy of the community. Beyond these points, what tips the balance in favor of one candidate over another is the attention he pays to the community's specific problems: the development of private schools and more open legislation that provides greater religious liberty in explicit terms. We want to be good Frenchmen and good Jews. (cited in Derai and Cohen 1993:8–9)

In some ways, the French political establishment echoed this logic of Jewish political particularism (Birnbaum 2000:6). After Giscard d'Estaing's defeat, some of his supporters apparently accused Jews of acting as a "lobby" that grounded its politics in ethnic concerns about a foreign country (Liscia 1980:36–37). More often, politicians comforted Sitruk in his belief that the pursuit of an explicit Jewish agenda was not incompatible with being "good Frenchmen." Even while denying the existence of the "Jewish vote," politicians agreed to do interviews in the Jewish press that focused heavily on Middle Eastern politics and personal relationships to the state of Israel (e.g., Lellouche 1986b:5; Lellouche 1986a:7). They also joined CRIF- and FSJU-sponsored trips to Israel, ensuring significant publicity and glowing coverage in the Jewish press. Reine Silbert summarized this active courtship in the following terms: "In any case, one certainty remains: if Jewish voters want to vote Jewish they need to look at the bottom of the electoral lists. At the top, there's no problem. They are all, all, all for Israel, all, all, all for the defense of Jewish particularities. The rest is just a question of nuance" (Silbert 1986:16). By the 1990s, the general public discussion of the "Jewish vote" seems to have become so commonplace that a number of political scientists committed to Republican ideals published works attempting to disprove the existence of such a phenomenon (Benayoun 1984; Schnapper and Strudel 1983; Strudel 1996).

Focusing the construction of Jewish Frenchness around Jewish loyalty toward Israel seems to emphasize Jewish foreignness and irreducible difference. These stories about the "Jewish vote" privileged Zionist accounts that root Jewish cultural and biological origins in the land of the contemporary State of Israel. In addition, they suggested that Jews could not or would not engage in the kind of abstraction from personal interests that French Republican politics ideally requires (Scott 2005); instead, Jews remained focused almost exclusively on a narrow, foreign political agenda that inevitably raised questions about Jewish Frenchness. Jewish writers themselves claimed that spiritual and material attachment to a foreign power (Israel) prevented Jews from fully appreciating the domestic concerns that drove most electoral choices, a position that eerily echoed two hundred years of anti-Semitic assertions about Jews' double loyalty and the impossibility of Jewish Frenchness. Furthermore, imaging support for Israel as a universal Jewish trait dissolved the particularities of a *national* community into a global, diasporic one. By founding "authentic" Jewishness on a particular affective and political relationship with Israel, French Jews appeared to have more in common with, for example, American Jews than with non-Jewish French nationals.

But there is another side to the story. By the 1980s, Jewish elites imagined this narrative about Jewish difference as confirming the natural affinity between and among Jewish sensibilities, French national attachments, and European sociocultural norms. How so? If Jews opposed French politics, they did so on the grounds that they represented a betrayal of French and Western values. In the 1980s Jewish writers repeatedly accused politicians of selling out to morally questionable, culturally alien governments. At a time when politicians increasingly described French industry and national identity as besieged by foreign Arabs, accusing French officials of coddling Arab governments hinted at a form of disloyalty that touched more than just French Jews. Hajdenberg's use of the term "collaboration" (see above) indexes this vision of state treachery against the "native" nation, at least partially embodied by its Jewish citizens. The Vichy state's willing sacrifice of Jews symbolized its larger betrayal of Enlightenment-inspired French values and Republican culture. Thus, while Jewish political discourse may have created the conditions of possibility for alienating Jews from particular government practices, it did not necessarily imply a dichotomy between Israel-supporting Jews and native Frenchness. The cover of the May 15-21, 1981 edition of *Tribune Juive* was adorned with Marianne, the personification of the French Republic, wearing a T-shirt that read *"j'aime Israël"* (I love Israel). Just a few months earlier, Raymond Lindon had noted that while Jews may be "detached" from the French political establishment and "attached" to Israel, they were not alienated from French culture or from the "French population" (Lindon 1979:15). French Jews go to Israel, even if they think they are going forever, with "Victor Hugo under one arm" (ibid.).

The explanations the French Jewish press offered for the anti-Semitic acts that bloodied Paris in the early 1980s reflected this vision of native Jewish interests endangered by literal foreigners. Some Jewish writers quickly attributed the bombing of a liberal synagogue on Rue Copérnic, the attack on a Jewish student dining hall in Montmartre, and the drive-by shooting of a Jewish restaurant in the Marais to *external* sources, namely an Arab country or a Palestinian terrorist group, not to Arab Muslim immigrants or their descendants (Ya'ari 1983:5).[32] A number of Jewish writers even suggested that these "international terrorists" underscored how deeply Jews were rooted in Western society and democracy. Jews and Israel, they argued, were attacked because they embodied the Occidental values that so threatened religious radicals and dictators in the Arab world. As Grunewald noted just after the bombing of Copérnic: "Anti-Semitism has never been less of an end unto itself. It is rather part of the process that seeks to kill democracy everywhere it exists" (1980a:5). Never, in the words of another *Tribune Juive* writer, had the general French public so well-supported and closely identified with the "Jewish community" than when it was attacked in such a brutal manner (Eytan 1980:7).

But this dichotomy between a Jewish population defending its Western material and moral interests and a set of external aliens violating French sensibilities was, like so much else in this tale of Jewish self-representation, hard to maintain. The elaboration of a foreign nation as not only a reference point but a literal (if never seen) homeland (even if only a "second" homeland in Lindon's terms) mirrored the indelible foreign national origins—passed seemingly genealogically in families—attributed to North African Muslims. As Jewish demonstrations expressing unconditional support for Israel multiplied in the 1980s and 1990s, North African Muslims began leading countermarches declaring their solidarity with the Arab Muslims imagined as victims of American and Israeli violence. During the first Gulf War in 1991, as some began predicting Jewish-Muslim street violence, Sitruk and the head of the *mosquée de Paris* (the flagship Parisian mosque built during the colonial period) signed a petition calling for calm in "their" respective communities—a move that more than hinted at potential political and social parallels between Jews and Muslims (Derai 1991:1). The same kinds of mirror-image mobilization around ostensibly foreign conflicts have become ever more obvious since 2000. In one of a series of similar incidents, protestors demonstrating against the American war in Iraq and Israeli President Ariel Sharon's Palestinian policies attacked two Jews from the left-wing Zionist youth movement Hashomer Hatzair, one of whom was wearing a kippa while watching the protest. In another, members of the Ligue de défense juive (Jewish Defense League, LDJ) beat representatives of a far-left, pro-Palestinian student group who were testifying in front of a university tribunal.

At the same time, government officials began underscoring other, equally sensitive similarities. By the late 1980s, teachers and Department of Education administrators suggested that certain increasingly visible Jewish and Muslim practices challenged French Republican values in the same way. Partially as a way of averting charges that Islam and Islam alone had been targeted, official government statements and administrative rulings often spoke of kippot and Jewish stars in the same terms as veils, advocating that all such symbols be banned from public school classrooms. When the issue resurfaced in the first decades of the new millennium, the conflation of Jewish and Muslim practices was retained. The Stasi commission (the extraparliamentary group formed in 2003 to conduct hearings on and make recommendations about the presence of religious symbols in French public life) included headscarves, kippot, and (improbably) "large crosses" in the list of symbols that unacceptably challenged French secularism and Republican values in classrooms, hospitals, and government offices (Stasi commission 2004:150). While mostly dedicated to denouncing explicitly Muslim challenges to Republican religious neutrality, the commission's report also included some (very) subtle attacks on Jewish practice that would have been recognized by those concerned.[33] The 2004 legislation banning religious symbols from public schools contained the same language used by the commission.[34]

As a result, at least since the beginning of the second Palestinian Intifada and the concomitant rise in anti-Semitic discourse and acts in France, French Jewish discourse has shifted again. Rather than insist on Jewish Frenchness over and against an imagined external other, many Jewish elites have now recast Muslims as an inassimilable, interiorized threat. It has thus become commonplace to insist that Jews are native, whatever they might do, while Muslims are not, whatever their citizenship status. Georges Bensoussan, a Jewish historian and editor of *Les territoires perdus de la République* (The Lost Lands of the Republic),[35] a work cited in all contemporary discussions of Muslim "integration," denounced comparing Jewish and Muslim practices as a kind of false consciousness.

> In the face of t[he] disintegration of the social fabric, many figures of authority . . . tend to deny, ignore, and conceal recognized facts which are splitting French society in two. . . . Rare cases of Jewish children refusing to go to school on Saturdays are blown up out of all proportion; such cases are all the rarer . . . in the French public school system since the vast majority of children of practicing Jews go to Jewish schools. People talk of students refusing to eat meat which has not been slaughtered in accordance with religious law, while intimating that this refers to Muslim students as well as their Jewish fellows. The latter, however, are at least ten times more numerous than the former. (Bensoussan 2004:4)

Bensoussan has even gone so far as to suggest that the problem posed by Arab Muslims in France has less to do with the development of explicitly Muslim practices and more to do with Arabness itself. This ties Arab Muslim foreignness more explicitly to a racial identity than to religious practices, thus potentially sparing public Jewish religiosity from attack. He writes: "It is striking to note that aside from the Paris Mosque . . . only *non-Arab* Muslim organizations . . . have distanced themselves from this belligerent position [in favor of the veil]. This underlines still further the Arab rather than the Muslim aspect of this war of entrenched positions against a republican and secular France" (ibid.:5, emphasis in original).

Bensoussan is not alone. Trigano, as we have seen, has consistently viewed any comparison between French Jews and Muslims as a dangerous conflation that threatens Jews' position in France. Recently, he has even gone so far as to erase the national origins of a large plurality of French Jews. In denouncing what he considers the entirely inappropriate assimilation of the "Jewish community" to an "immigrant community," he wrote:

> The editorialists often insinuate, surreptitiously, that this "Jewish (immigrant) community" indexes North African Jews who have lived in France since the 1960s. . . . The 120,000 Jews from Algeria who made up the largest group of North African Jews in 1962 have been French since 1870. . . . To assimilate them to the newly arrived North African

immigrant community constitutes one of the worst regressions that could exist . . . they became French precisely so that they could leave Muslim society, in which their status was hardly admirable. (2001:25)

Trigano thus collapses Moroccan and Tunisian Jewish experience into Algerian history, turning all North African Jews into French nationals. He also denies any possible common cause between Muslims and Jews. In his 2003 book *La demission de la République* (The Failure of the Republic), Trigano accuses French society of "protecting" and "socializing" Arabs by "denationalizing the Jewish community" (16).

A number of my adult informants noted that the French public increasingly puts Arabs and Jews "back to back," erasing the lines that should separate a perfectly "integrated" population from one that cannot help but remain alien. Jewish leaders complained that the post-2000 rise of anti-Semitism in France was being depicted as an intercommunal war with little impact on "the French" rather than an assault on Western values launched by those who have remained outside the French Republic. In a press conference he gave in 2004, then CRIF president Roger Cukierman attributed contemporary anti-Semitism in France to Muslims who were "insufficiently integrat[ed] into French society," and deplored the fact that that same society "sees the current wave of anti-Semitic incidents as part of the Jewish-Arab conflict and therefore does not think it is implicated." "I dare to hope," he continued,

> that a sincere government will help them [Muslims] with their social integration. I think this is the issue sine qua non for civil peace and for the democratic evolution of this country. . . . What we [Jews] need is for anti-Semitic incidents to cease. That is all we need, because we are citizens who are perfectly well integrated into this country. We have no problem with integration. Jews have lived in France for hundreds of years; we are an integral part of French society. The only problem that we have today is a wave of anti-Semitic acts that is unacceptable for Jews and unacceptable for France.

At the time, the president of the Union des Etudiants Juifs de France, who frequently disagreed with Cukierman's politics, concurred. The erroneous construction of Jews as foreigners was, he told me, his "greatest fear." While he believed the French government had evolved on the issue, "in the general public, there is often this idea that we should put people in the same boat. In the general public, it's the Jews and the Arabs are nice, but they are not in their own country, and they should go fight each other elsewhere. . . . It's not said like that, but that's the meaning, the subtext. The Jews have the status of foreigners."

On a more popular level, this kind of discourse sometimes translated into European identity narratives and even Europeanized religious practice, both of which have become ways of making territorial claims denied to Arab Muslims. In some cases, this was as simple as emphasizing a literal geography of birth. The mother of a Brith Abraham senior, whose parents were born in Tunisia, told me that she was "proud" to have been born in France and that she thought her European birth "much better than having been born in North Africa." In more symbolic form, the very term "Sephardi" indexes a history that turns all North African Jews into once and future Europeans. As noted in chapter 1, the term—which has existed for centuries but has been recently popularized through Israeli practices[36]—is derived from the Hebrew word for "Spanish" or "Spain." It breaks with the notion of biological and/or cultural commonalities between North African and Middle Eastern Jews and Muslims by giving Jews a European genealogy. The Iberian peninsula becomes the implied point of origin for virtually all Sephardim, regardless of the complicated realities of their literal family histories. Their presence in the "Arab" world thus is linked inextricably to the *reconquista* and the 1492 expulsion, events that have become an integral part of a larger post-Holocaust narrative about the possibilities and impossibilities of European Jewishness.

This symbolic link to a European past was evident in the creative genealogies some Sephardim constructed.[37] At Brith Abraham, a well-read high-school philosophy teacher whose mother was born and raised in Algeria told me that North African Jews were descended from 15th-century Spanish immigrants. When I asked whether there were any "indigenous" Jews whose presence antedated the Iberian expulsion order, he acknowledged that some people living in backward mountainous regions of Tunisia or Morocco might not have had European origins, but virtually all Algerian Jews did. Note the not-insignificant racialized link between imagined cultural superiority (Algerians versus those in the backward mountainous regions of Morocco and Tunisia) and a European genealogy. A number of people I spoke with even turned this vague collective genealogy into the framework for understanding their own family histories. A college student working for the UEJF told me that his mother's Constantinian family had originally come from Spain, while his father's Moroccan family was actually English, descended from the 19th-century English notable Sir Moses Montefiore.[38] The story was rather confused and confusing:

> In doing our genealogical tree, we discovered where we came from, the name Sebag, which is my name, originally it was Montefiore-Sebag. . . . [Montefiore] was an English sire who was in Spain for a while, who was a British détaché in Spain, who had family over there, and in fact, during the Inquisition in Spain. Some left for Spain, some left for Morocco [he meant this as a correction], others left for England, and that was how the family was divided. There was a part that went to Spain, to Morocco [again a correction]. And that's us, and another part went back to England where they came from.

These kinds of claims became so self-evident over the course of the 1980s and 1990s that an exasperated reader of the Jewish press wrote a letter to the editor of *Actualité Juive* recalling the stakes of the distinction between Sephardim and Jews from North Africa. "It is not possible to accept the erroneous extension by which, for the last few decades, our North African co-religionists, who are *Arab Jews*, have become Sephardim" (Hasson 1992:2, emphasis mine).

Some Sephardim also adopted practices coded as European. Laurence Podselver (1986, 1992, 2002) has written about the attraction of struggling, second- and third-generation Sephardim to the Lubavitcher movement (see chapter 1). Trigano has also commented on the trend, which he noted with derision teaches young Sephardim to read Maimonides and Yehuda Halevi in Yiddish rather than in the Arabic original (1980a). "Who has not at some point run across these religious Sephardim who have adopted everything associated with Ashkenazi modes of religiosity (including the clothes, fur hats, and wigs for women . . . as if it were the only authentic form?," he queried (ibid.:20). A significant plurality of recently created Jewish schools drew heavily on European forms of orthodoxy while catering almost entirely to the children and grandchildren of North African immigrants. The head of the Education Department at the FSJU described an intellectual and experiential "gap" between Sephardi administrators and their predominantly Sephardi pupils. He noted that school administrations had adopted the yeshiva in its Eastern European incarnations as the baseline for school practices. That meant focusing heavily on the Gemara (commentary on the oral Torah or the Mishnah), the Talmud (the Gemara and commentary on the Gemara), and Halakhah (Jewish law and orthopraxis), to the exclusion of almost everything else. In North Africa, he insisted, the curriculum and pedagogy were different; they focused on horizontal diffusion, not on intellectual gymnastics, and included a wider range of texts, particularly the Zohar (a 13th-century mystic text). "It was a humanist education that has been rejected by the Eastern European orthodox and by [French Jewish school networks]. . . . The administration has been Ashkenazified; it has internalized the religious and cultural framework of an entirely different civilization."

Recasting the Holocaust as a universal Jewish experience has also become a means of regrounding Sephardim in European narratives of Jewish identity. When I asked a middle-aged man born and raised in Algeria whether he had ever felt tensions between Ashkenazim and Sephardim in France, he tellingly answered: "There is no difference . . . or at least no important difference. During World War II they did not ask whether a Jew was Ashkenazi or Sephardi before putting him in a concentration camp. They went after all the Jews, there was no difference."[39] As early as 1980, at least one Jewish leader expressed his surprise and pleasure that of the Jews in the French delegation at the commemoration of the Warsaw ghetto uprising, "three-quarters [of the attendees] were of North African origin," young people whose "families had not suffered either directly or indirectly from Nazi persecution" (Hajdenberg 1980a:viii). Throughout my fieldwork, the Holocaust was an ever-present reference and trope at Jewish conferences and debates with audiences comprised primarily of Sephardim, many of whom felt they were "reliving" events of the 1930s and 1940s through contemporary anti-Semitism. Typically, during an evening at the Centre Communautaire de Paris (Paris Community Center) dedicated to discussion of Israel in French politics, a woman who peppered her expressions with Arabic moaned: "I feel like we are going to be eaten by them! It's another Holocaust getting under way!" When the surprised speaker asked her to explain what the parallels were between France in the late 1930s and the early 2000s, she became defensive. Flustered, she shouted: "I don't know! I didn't live through it; I don't know what happened. All I know is they tried to kill Jews all over Europe just because they were Jews!"

This defensiveness is hardly surprising. If Holocaust narratives helped some Sephardim lay claim to European history, these attempts at establishing North African "nativeness" in Europe were often rejected. We have seen Trigano's ire for those Sephardim who embraced Hasidism. A day school student even talked about his Lubavitcher math teacher as a "convert" who had abandoned a more authentic, North African form of Jewish practice for alien ways. The rejection could also come from Ashkenazim who were reluctant to share *their* past, in whatever form, with Sephardim. While there were many Ashkenazim who saw Sephardi internalization of Holocaust narratives as produced by and productive of global Jewish unity, some viewed Sephardim as, at best, interlopers and, at worst, as holier-than-thou judges.[40] A Brith Abraham art and Jewish history teacher, who lost several family members in the Holocaust, explained that there was a fundamental gap between Ashkenazim and Sephardim on the issue. "It's like someone losing their mother," she told me. "If you haven't lost yours, you can empathize. You have a mother too, you can imagine what it would be like. But you can't really know what it feels like until you've experienced it. And this confusion sometimes leads them [Sephardim] to extremes." Richard Marienstras, the outspoken advocate for the reconstruction of shtetl culture and European Diasporic practices, apparently requested that Sephardim refrain from talking about the Holocaust. "It's very inconsiderate of people whose community was spared . . . to give lessons on being Jewish" (cited in Szlakmann 1990:11). In a letter to *Actualité Juive*'s editor, a reader wrote:

> As a practicing Ashkenazi Jew, I deny all my Sephardi brothers the
> right to comment, appreciate, weigh, and most importantly, judge
> this tragic part of our history. Because it is clear that only the Sephardi
> fringe, which has little or no direct familial experience (Jews from Sa-
> lonica excepted) with these black times, allows itself to take sides on
> the unspeakable. So about this issue, my Sephardi brothers, particularly
> if you consider yourselves religious, keep silent, silent! (Jarville 2000:4)

Some of my Sephardi informants carefully commented on this rejection, describing it as a betrayal of the Jewish universalism they believe did or should exist. According to Eric's friend Frédéric, also a business major:

There are some, I know that I have to take precautions and everything because you can't talk about the whole, but I have the impression that the Ashkenazi people feels . . . like it was weakened by the war . . . because some of their parents were deported and everything. At the same time, they make others feel like they are the only ones who suffered from that, do you see what I mean? And the fact that I wasn't, that my grandparents were not deported, and that those in other families weren't deported, we can't. . . . They make it seem like they suffered more from that, at least in their language. And I find that is a bit unjustified. Because in a people, you suffer for others, do you see what I mean? It's a union. From my perspective, if the grandparents of an Ashkenazi Jew were deported, I feel even more pain for them than they do for themselves.

Eric, who I was interviewing at the same time, added: "I'm pretty much in agreement with him. . . . But for me, there isn't a difference. For me, the Jews, Ashkenazi or Sephardi, they are Jews. . . . But it's true that, in terms of fact, the Sephardi are a people from North Africa, and the traditions are completely different. . . . It's complicated to talk about it, I have trouble."

French and Foreign?

If the explosion of public Jewishness in the late 1970s and 1980s challenged one of the central tenets of Franco-Judaism, the more recent assertion of Jewish autochthony did not. Although it moved away from the homogeneity of values and practices that underlay Franco-Jewish assertions of elective affinity, the insistence that Jews had a long-standing, powerful, and permanent claim to Frenchness echoed the assumptions of Metropolitan Jews throughout the late 19th and early 20th centuries. But this claim was made in a potentially new way, through the public evocation of a foiled population eternally denied the possibility of naturalization. For many Jews and non-Jews alike, Arab

Muslims remained foreign regardless of the number of generations actually spent in France. Religious and cultural differences were one of the foundations for this argument, with Arab Muslim expressive practices cited as evidence of indelibly alien dispositions and values. But religious and cultural differences may also have been one of the reasons Jews were making this negative and differential argument at all. Some Jewish expressive practices—both political and religious—divided French Jews along lines imagined in ethno-national terms *and* potentially threatened all Jews with what Trigano called "denationalization."

Despite the insistence that the distinct ontology of the "Jewish community," whatever its practices, made any parallels between Jews and Muslims fictitious or irrelevant, such comparisons were part of the language of everyday Jewish life. Almost all of my informants turned "Jewish" and "Arab" into parallel, mutually exclusive ethno-national categories distinct from Frenchness. Eric, the business major, described his neighborhood in the following terms: "It's a diverse neighborhood; there are French people, a few Jews, but not a lot of Arabs." Did that mean, I asked, that neither Jews nor Arabs counted as French? He and his friend Frédéric laughed uncomfortably, quipping that only a sociologist could ask such a question: "It's familiar language," Eric continued. "For Jews, we call them *feuj* [the syllabic inversion of the French word for Jew, *juif*], for Arabs we call them *rebeu*. And French, in fact that means Christian. . . . It's the same thing as white." Frédéric tried to come to the rescue: "Often we say 'Arab' in order to say 'Muslim.' . . . In Arab countries there are lots of Muslims. And we think of Muslims when we think of Arab countries." And what about the Jews, including your grandparents, who lived in those Arab countries, I queried. The question, I was told, was "too hot to handle."

In Eric and Frédéric's widely shared reading, being French was first and foremost an ethno-religious identity ("whiteness" and Christianity), and thus a priori excluded both Muslims *and* Jews on the same racialized grounds. But they were also uncomfortable with erasing distinctions between the excluded groups. Whereas all Muslims were imagined as coming from elsewhere and thus could be readily reduced to that imagined ("Arab") origin, they were not quite willing to apply the same logic to Jews. Jews might not be "really" French, but they were certainly not quite as "other" as Arabs. And their ethno-religious otherness did not disqualify them—at least at times—from imagining themselves not just as legal citizens but as French nationals with a shared commitment to a political and social community that runs parallel to the affective ties of Jewishness. As James Gibson (2004) has noted in the context of a similar kind of development in South Africa, this suggests a retooling of classic conceptions of national identity based on exclusive attachment, whether that attachment is formulated in political or ethno-racial terms. National identity stops being an either-or proposition, becoming a "both, and" one.[41] Jewish elites and many Sephardi adults were thus increasingly likely to articulate an understanding of Jewishness as a distinct ontological and therefore cultural and political position. *And* they would insist with Trigano, Cukierman, and Eric and Frédéric that Jews were meaningfully tied to the French nation in ways that were impossible for Arab Muslims.

This may be a radical rethinking of Franco-Judaism, but it is not entirely a rejection of it. The "elective affinity" between Jewishness as religious practice and Frenchness became grounded in a mythically imagined place-of-birth and could not be vitiated by expressive culture. In addition, the same suspension of disbelief or ability to simultaneously hold contradictory positions that long characterized Franco-Judaism remained. But none of those responsible for articulating a vision of simultaneous Jewish nativeness and radical alterity were educated in Jewish schools, which are the heart of the state-supported Jewish project of cultivated, public difference. And, as we will see over the next two chapters, this seemingly paradoxical embrace of *both* embodied Jewish distinction and French national identity was not so obvious for those who inhabit this new social location.

Three   Four Cubits of Jewish Schooling

May 6, 2004. I was supposed to be "testing" a 10th-grade class at Beit Sarah on their willingness to learn English with a native speaker, but the conversation had quickly degenerated into French. The 15 girls in the room found me an improbable proposition in France, and they wondered audibly what life could be like for an American Jew in Paris. "Do you like French people?" someone asked above the din. Surprised that they would be asking whether I liked *them*, I answered that I had met lots of nice people in France. A discontented murmur arose. "Why do you like them?" someone else queried. "Why don't *you*?" I answered back. The litany of stereotypes with which they responded— "they are aloof," "they are hypocrites," "they don't say hello to you," "they are nice to your face and say nasty things about Jews behind your back"—suggested that no one in the room considered herself "French." "Don't you all at least have 'French' friends?" I asked awkwardly, scare quotes and all. Headshakes with tongue clicks, air blown through pursed lips, rolled eyes, and a couple of yeses. "You have French friends!?" a group of girls shouted in surprise at one of the students who had said yes. "Impossible!" After class, a student clarified: "We have French passports, but that's it. Otherwise, we're Jewish!"

In the last chapter, we saw the ambivalence among Jewish institutional elites about the nature of and relationship between Frenchness and Jewishness. On the one hand, there was a growing embrace of Jewishness as a form of incommensurable difference, and thus a rejection of possible social or political commonalities with either post-Christians or other religious minorities. On the other hand, there was an unwillingness to imagine a complete rupture with a national community rooted in the sociocultural manifestations of shared French and European ancestry. French Jews might be Jews first and foremost, but they were also indelibly French, whatever post-Christian whites had to say about it. But this was less obviously the case with the 10th-grade class described above and with adolescent day school students more generally. Many could not imagine themselves as meaningfully tied to Frenchness or even intimately socializing with anyone who so identified.

There was nothing about the sociology of these 10th-grade girls or the Jewish day school population more generally that would have made this inevitable. Most day school students were born and raised in France. They were overwhelmingly the children and grandchildren of North African immigrants who, all things considered, had been remarkably upwardly mobile. Often solidly middle class, many day school students' parents were living a version of the immigrant dream: they had achieved sufficient prosperity to invest heavily in their children's education and future. And they made choices—in this case for parochial education—that reflected many of the same values and assumptions as their similarly classed, Christian or post-Christian neighbors. In addition, most day school students spoke French as their first and often only language; and with few exceptions, French was their household language, spoken between their parents if not between their parents and their grandparents. And while a minority came from highly observant families whose ritual observances separated them from non-Jews, this was the exception rather than the rule, even in *haredi* (ultra-orthodox) schools like Beit Sarah.

So why was it impossible for those who attended a government-funded French school and learned the French national curriculum to imagine even being friends with "French" people? Why was it so obvious, even to those with such friends, that they themselves were not "French"? How had it happened, for these students but not necessarily their parents or even teachers, that Jewishness came to stand in opposition to and not just in tension with identification as French nationals?

In Liisa Malkki's (1995) work on Burundian refugees living in two very different physical and social contexts, she seems to have asked similar questions. Why, in one case, did refugees identify in ethno-racial terms as the embodiment of a "true" and "pure" Hutu nation while "Hutu-ness" became relatively insignificant, fluid, and contextual in the other? What made a particular primordialized narrative about self, community, and other so much more significant among one group? Her answers revolved around the connection between spatial configurations and social relations in identity construction. The refugees who understood themselves through ethno-national "mythico-history" lived in an isolated camp peopled exclusively with Burundian Hutu refugees, who initially shared little with one another outside the experience of Tutsi violence and exile (1995:54–55). Almost all interactions with non-Burundian "others" were structured by the hierarchical social world of refugee camp administration, thereby establishing clear boundaries between those *of* the camp and those simply *in* it. People made sense of this pronounced separation, this in-gathering of otherwise unconnected men and women, and the heteronomy and precariousness that inevitably characterized camp life by figuring themselves as members of a nation-in-exile (1995:3). They told and retold stories about a collective national past and present that called on the Burundi past and camp present as foils. Malkki notes: "The camp had become a central means of asserting separateness from 'other' categories, of resisting any form of 'nationalization,' and was in this sense a locus of categorical purity. Never intended as such by its architects, the camp had become the most central place from which to imagine a 'pure' Hutu national identity" (ibid.:3). In stark contrast, the refugees who were scattered across an urban environment inhabited by a nationally and ethnically diverse population did not imagine themselves in national terms, or even as "Hutu" at all. Instead, they characterized themselves in cosmopolitan terms, resisting classification into ethnic or national categories, and moving situationally among various nested identities. "The opposition between the historical-national thought of camp refugees," Malkki argues, "and the cosmopolitan ways of town refugees made it possible to discern how the social, imaginative processes of constructing nationness and identity can come to be influenced by the local, everyday circumstances of life in exile, and how the spatial and social isolation of refugees can figure in these processes" (ibid.:3).

Although I am not writing about refugees or the totalizing conditions of a refugee camp, Malkki's insight may help explain—at least in part—how and why day school adolescents denationalized themselves, insisting that they never had been and never would be connected to a "French" moral and political community. I begin the discussion in this chapter by exploring why this is counterintuitive; to do so, I outline the potentially shared structural positions and concerns that link Jewish schooling and private schooling more generally in France. I then examine Jewish schools' legal exceptionalism vis-à-vis state authorities, teasing out the forms of physical and social isolation (inadvertently?) presupposed and entailed by that exceptionalism. I argue that the resulting alienation from wider social networks has encouraged day students to abstract themselves from the nested social contexts that enveloped them, creating a privileged space for narrating ethno-religious difference as the foundation for a primordialized moral community. At the same time, the material conditions that underwrote the construction of this community—the particular mix of social and economic circumstances that made day schooling possible and popular in France—were occluded, preventing students from recognizing the national, cultural, and class specificities that defined their practices (see chapter 5). In the process, government-funded Jewish schooling quietly contributed to a national nightmare: the replacement of an imagined French national community with an equally imagined Jewish one.

Public Anxieties and Private Education

In 1959 the French government transformed secular education, passing a law that allowed state financing of private religious schools under certain conditions. Called the "Debré law" after its sponsor, Gaullist Prime Minister Michel Debré, the measure was intended as a compromise, a way of ending the ideological battle between Catholic and secular schooling that had plagued the Third Republic (1871–1940). Faced with a demographic explosion in the school-aged population, politicians were struggling with ways to quickly expand school capacity (Bellengier 2004). The left argued for state-absorption of all existing private institutions, thus eliminating *libre,* or independent, education all together (Journal Officiel 1959: 3595–3614). On the right, politicians demanded that the state fund private education unconditionally in the name of "free "choice." Debré offered a middle ground—the rapprochement of public and private educational spheres while preserving the "special character" of religious schools. He argued that private schools, the overwhelming majority of which were Catholic, were already part of the public educational system and had earned their "letters of Republican nobility" by accepting the (primarily Jewish) children banned from public schools during the Vichy period (ibid.:3596). The proposed law, he noted, would simply expand and codify the terms of this collaborative relationship.

To accomplish this, the law abolished some of the structural and pedagogical boundaries between public and private institutions (Poucet 2005). Private secondary schools were given the option of remaining completely independent and receiving no funds or entering into a *contrat d'association* with the state.[1] Schools that chose the contractual relationship would henceforth be staffed with state-appointed, state-salaried instructors who, once approved by the principal, would teach the national curriculum. They would also be granted per-student funds for regular operating expenses, like heat, electricity, and building maintenance (Bellengier 2004:33). In return, contracted schools were expected to respect the basic principles of French national education and Republican *laïcité*: enrollment of students regardless of "origins, beliefs or opinions," respect for individual conscience and freedom from religious compulsion, faithful implementation of the Department of Education's standard national curriculum, submission to the same pedagogical inspection regime as public institutions, compliance with national standards of class size, and adherence to basic health codes (ibid.; Journal Officiel 1959:3595–3614).[2] Faithfully echoing the founder of modern education in France, Jules Ferry, the 1959 commission that studied the issue of public subsidies for private schools claimed that such an accommodation would allow the *laïc* state to fulfill one of its primary roles: the preservation of the child's conscience as it developed in the family (Journal Officiel 1959:3600). Families would have the option of "choosing" a school that reflected their values.

Religious institutions were thus largely allowed to preserve their religious missions from state interference. As Debré noted, the state was offering and asking for "tolerance." "The state is in no way asking private schools, at least those marked by their religious affiliations, to abandon their special character. The contract they sign will nonetheless impose obligations . . . that it would be unthinkable not to impose. I am speaking of acceptance of all children, regardless of their origins or their religion, and liberty of conscience" (Journal Officiel 1959:3597). Debré's government intended this as a guarantee that privately raised funds—student tuition, donations, and grants—could be used for optional religion courses that would supplement the national curriculum, either before or after standard school hours. But "special character" was never legally defined, making it a subject of continuous legal contention (Poucet 2005:5). For decades, Catholic schools insisted that their "special character" involved the infusion of all instruction with Christian principles and Catholic theology, thereby abolishing any attempt to distinguish between core Republican education and supplemental religious instruction (ibid.:6–10). Under the right-wing governments that held power throughout the 1970s, this interpretation received significant legislative and judicial support, reinforcing private education's autonomy without curtailing its financial entitlements.[3] When the left took control of the government in 1981 with the election of François Mitterrand, overturning these legislative changes took a backseat to more systematic attempts to retool the entire relationship between public and private schools. This preference for systemic change allowed the patently un-Republican legislation and precedents established in the 1970s to remain in force for an additional four years.[4] Even once the left abandoned a holistic approach in favor of more immediate attempts to curtail the power of private education, "special character" continued to be a potent argument for otherwise unthinkable legal concessions.[5]

But at the same time, Catholic schools began to change their song. Increasingly interested in attracting the growing non- or post-Catholic public looking for educational alternatives, Catholic schools could no longer proudly emphasize totalizing practices and opposition to French democratic politics. Instead, Catholic leaders restyled parochial education as more authentically inclusive and democratic than public schooling. If the Republic seemed to demand that children leave their ethno-religious affiliations at the school gates, Catholic schools claimed to accommodate all forms of religious difference without resorting to either secular or religious proselytism. When public schools contemplated excluding veiled Muslim girls and turbaned Sikh boys (first in 1989 and then definitively in 2005), Catholic schools offered themselves as refuges from state-sanctioned religious intolerance. As the secretary general of Catholic education noted in an interview with *Libération*: Catholic schooling "recognizes the place of each child" and refuses "to exclude those who are 'unlike the others'" (cited in Davidenkoff 2005:18). He added: "Catholic education, which represents 97.7% of contracted private education and 2 million students, is not public education or private education or even public supported private education. It is instruction associated with the public service of education . . . and clearly participates in Republican schooling" (cited in ibid.).[6]

Jewish schooling benefited from the same legal and social shifts as Catholic institutions. Over the 1980s and 1990s, 50 new Jewish schools were created, more than doubling the number of institutions extant at the end of the 1970s (Petit-Ohayon 2003).[7] The number of students enrolled increased proportionally, rising from about 3,200 at the end of the 1970s to 16,000 in the late 1980s, and then doubling over the course of the 1990s to reach 30,000 in 2002 (Haymann 1978; Petit-Ohayon 2003).

This spectacular increase cannot simply be attributed to parents' sudden interest in assuring a religious education for their children. It is true that a large number of day school students came from families that had "returned" to more intense religious practice over the last decade or two. Many of the students I interviewed described parents who did not keep kosher or observe holidays before marrying or having children. Some had since introduced Shabbat and stricter kashrut observance, at least within the home.[8] Jewish schooling, in turn, contributed to this process as children brought home the more rigorous practices learned in school and refused their parents' compromises. Few students, however, described themselves or their families as "really" religious. The category most often used was "traditionalist," a term that suggests deep ethnic attachment to Jewishness rather than stringent observance of Jewish law. For most, being "traditionalist" meant doing distinctively "Jewish" things on a weekly if not daily basis. Many, particularly the girls at Beit Sarah, attended synagogue regularly with their peers. Most day school students paid some attention to Jewish dietary restrictions, even if that meant eating the McFish at McDonald's instead of a Big Mac. Almost all described wanting to follow in their parents' footsteps by becoming more observant, or what they often called more "serious," as they got older, married, and began to have families. And for almost everyone, marrying a non-Jew was simply unthinkable, both because of the impact it would have on parents and because of their own convictions.

If they were not necessarily religious, what kinds of families put their children into Jewish schooling in Paris? And why? Although fear of anti-Semitism in public schools may be driving an increasingly diverse Jewish population toward day schools, in 2004-2005 most of the students in Jewish day schools were the children of lower-middle- to middle-class Moroccan and Tunisian Jews.[9] Although there certainly were some self-identified Algerian Jews in the day schools I attended, these students often had a parent who was born in either Morocco or Tunisia. This demography did not, for reasons stated below, reflect the ethnic diversity of the contemporary French Jewish population. According to the 2002 FSJU Jewish population study *Les Juifs de France: Valeurs et Identité* (The Jews of France: Values and Identity), 70 percent of the French Jewish population was Sephardi, 24 percent was Ashkenazi, and 6 percent was "both" (Cohen 2002:12). Of the more than 50 percent of the Jewish population born outside the Metropole, the largest plurality was Algerian (21%), followed by Moroccans (11.2%) and then Tunisians (10.6%) (ibid.:11). Jews with Algerian ancestry therefore most likely comprise the largest plurality in the French Sephardi population.

There was somewhat more socioeconomic than ethnic diversity in contracted schools. Tuition rates were kept down by heavy state subsidies, which covered 50 to 60 percent of contracted schools' budgets. In addition, the Jewish Agency, a quasi-governmental Israeli institution dedicated to promoting Jewish immigration to Israel, provided funds for programs that encouraged attachment to the state of Israel and "feeling of belonging to a French and world Jewish community" (Elkouby 1979:69). Parents were called on to pay for defined services, particularly cafeteria expenses, religious education, busing, upkeep, and hall monitors. But each family's contribution was calculated on a sliding scale based on income, and school directors insisted that they had never turned away a family for financial reasons. A number of parents with whom I spoke were at least temporarily unemployed, and some students described their own economic conditions as straitened, particularly in the context of the very expensive fashions considered "Jewish" among their wealthier school peers (see chapter 6). Poorer parents, however, still complained bitterly about school officials who were all too willing to mix educational and financial decisions.[10]

Despite this relative economic diversity, most students seemed to come from petit bourgeois homes with solidly middle-class incomes but little social capital in Paris's steeply hierarchical social order (Bourdieu 1984). Teachers consistently described their students in precisely these terms, noting (often with derision) that students' families were well off but not cultured, more interested in material well-being than education. The students I interviewed often had two working parents, both engaged in midlevel white-collar jobs. Many fathers were salesmen, small business owners, or employees in electronics or technology-related companies. Mothers tended to be teachers (sometimes in Jewish schools), secretaries, and nurses. Parents with the most schooling were often doctors or dentists, professions valued for their independence and flexibility rather than their economic or social prestige.[11] Very few parents seemed to work in the public sector, which still represents the majority of jobs in France and, throughout the 19th and early 20th centuries, served as the most important means of economic and social ascension for Jews (Birnbaum 1996). And none of the students I met had parents in highly paid, education-intensive positions like finance.

There are several related reasons for the overrepresentation of these particularly ethnicized and classed families in Jewish schools. The first is rooted in the different configuration of colonial identities in Algeria, on the one hand, and Morocco and Tunisia, on the other. In Algeria, where Jewishness was a route to both cultural and legal Frenchness, many Jewish families developed an early and deep commitment to Republican schooling, which both underwrote and presupposed Jewish difference from "native" Muslims. This carried over into the Metropole as a preference for public schooling and an embrace of bourgeois-style assimilation. As we saw in chapter 1, there were no similar options during the colonial period for Moroccan and Tunisian Jews, for whom even French-language schools were first and foremost Jewish. These divergent histories were evident not only in school demography but also in the way day school students talked about Jewishness. Some day school students did not identify Algerian Jews as "Jewish" in the same way as they referred to Moroccan and Tunisian Jews. Like upwardly mobile and assimilated Ashkenazim, they had become "invisible." As a result, students' lunchtime jokes about "Jewish" traits always featured the speech and gestures of Moroccan or Tunisian Jews. Some adolescents even took this logic one step further, insisting that "Algerians look less Jewish than Moroccans and Tunisians."

The particular colonial experiences of Moroccan and Tunisian Jews continued to impact school choices in another way as well. Like many non-Jewish families in the dominated fraction of the French middle class, religious schooling is a way to deal with anxieties about race and class. Because Tunisian and Moroccan immigrants faced greater legal, cultural, and economic obstacles to rapid upward mobility than did their (already French) Algerian counterparts and (longer-established) Ashkenazim, they were disproportionately represented within this socioeconomic group. As a result, unlike Ashkenazim and Algerians, many Moroccan and Tunisian families still lived in rough, lower-middle-class, semiurban neighborhoods: Aubervilliers, Bondy, Bobigny, Créteil, Sarcelles, Saint-Germain-des-Prés (Strudel 1996). Those who lived in Paris itself often had homes on the literal and figurative margins of the city, in the 18th, 19th, and 20th arrondissements. These neighborhoods typically have large concentrations of recent immigrants, relatively high unemployment, and public schools that have suffered considerably from proportionally declining investment in education (Battut et al. 1995). For many middle-class Jewish and non-Jewish parents in these areas, public schools have therefore become synonymous with danger and failure. They are associated with chaos: overwhelmed teachers, drugs, sex, and violence. And these problems are often viewed as indissociable from the ethno-racial composition of the schools, which is increasingly likely to be majority-minority (Battut et al. 1995; Brenner et al. 2002; Lefebvre and Bonnivard 2005).

For some middle-class parents in socioeconomically mixed neighborhoods, private schools provide a haven from these problems.[12] Until the mid-1980s, the budget for private religious schooling grew relative to that of public schools (Georgel and Thorel 1995:95).[13] While enrollment in public schools increased by almost 41 percent in the postwar period (from 7.6 to 10.7 million), the number of students in private schools remained relatively stable. In 1959, 1.7 million students were enrolled in private schools; by 2004, that number had increased by 18 percent to just over two million (Georgel and Thorel 1995:88).[14] This means that the percentage of French children in private schools declined while the allocation of resources between public and private institutions remained constant. As a result, private schools have remained wealthier and less diverse than their public counterparts. In the 1992-1993 school year, private schools educated 17 percent of France's school-aged children, but only 2.9 percent of France's foreign-born population (Georgel and Thorel 1995:95). France keeps no official statistics on second- and third-generation children who possess French citizenship, but anecdotal evidence from students and parents in a range of Catholic schools suggests that their numbers remain low as well.[15] This means that in general private schools face fewer challenges than public schools, which have high numbers of socially and economically disadvantaged children.

Middle-class parents of all backgrounds thus saw private schools as a place where their children would be safe, insulated from the academic and disciplinary problems associated with "immigrants" and overwhelmed, indifferent teachers. A history teacher at Brith Abraham described her (Jewish) sister's decision to put her young daughter in a Catholic school in precisely these terms, as purely a question of safety. The little girl was being beaten up daily on the playground of her public school for no apparent reason, and parents felt that the school was doing nothing to take care of the problem. Worse, when the child complained about the incidents to the principal, she was told to find the teacher, who then directed her to the principal, and on and on. The parents ultimately put her in a Catholic school simply to escape the violence and the inaction.

Furthermore, lower-middle- to middle-class parents who themselves have relatively limited education are not particularly adept at making the complicated, cumbersome public school bureaucracy work to their advantage. Parisian elites, regardless of where they live, almost invariably put their children in public schools. This partially reflects a geography of social standing, meaning that such families often live in neighborhoods with wealthier (and whiter) schools. But it also reflects, as Bourdieu (1984) noted long ago, a particular embodied knowledge that may or may not have anything to do with material riches. A limited number of Parisian public schools (Henri-IV, Louis-le-Grand, and Montaigne, to name a few) provide privileged paths to the preparatory schools (*classes préparatoires*) that have the best success rates at placing students into prestigious semipublic universities (*grandes écoles*). These universities, in turn, lead to the most socially coveted positions, generally public-sector careers. Those who have benefited from this system are both invested in it and know how to manipulate it. They sign their children up for German, Russian, or Chinese, languages taught only in well-regarded public schools that may be outside their usual school district. Or they use personal connections to get *derogation* from the Department of Education, special dispensations that exempt a child from geographical school-districting guidelines. Day school parents—like many middle-class families with ties to commerce or liberal occupations—neither have this knowledge nor these social aspirations for their children. None of the students I met had parents who had attended a grande école, and only two of the scores of seniors I got to know expressed interest in pursuing the two to three years of coursework required before sitting for the grandes écoles competitive exams. Instead, most students planned to attend the "*fac*" (the public university system that accepts all French students with a baccalauréat) and enter well-paying liberal professions. Many, particularly boys, said they wanted to become "international businessmen," a dream that was often shared by their parents.

For parents with this kind of social and economic standing, private schools often look more accessible or personalized than public schools (Battut et al. 1995). Private schools can provide a "second chance" for children who are in danger of being thrown out of their academic program of choice or of being *orienté*, literally "guided," to a technical track.[16] Private schools also have the reputation for being "user friendly," meaning they are considerably more open to parental input and criticism than their public counterparts. To some extent, this may be an illusion. Most private schools expel students who are at risk of failing the general baccalauréat exam, a strategy designed to artificially improve passing rates.[17] But there is also a reality to the perception that private education is more child-centered than bureaucratic. The economic realities of private schooling depend to some extent on a liberal model of attracting and keeping "clients." Although heavily subsidized by governmental and private sources, most schools could not continue to operate without revenue from tuition payments. At least in Jewish schools, this means that teachers and administrators worry about parental opinions and therefore about the messages students carry home.[18]

For many Parisians, including Moroccan and Tunisian Jews, private schooling may thus provide a way of shoring-up overlapping class and ethno-racial distinctions. For upwardly mobile but precariously positioned families, private schooling suggests a middle-class commitment to education and the resources to back up that commitment.[19] It also appears to assure a child's future class status through the purchase of services imagined as better adapted for academic and therefore financial success. The Tunisian-born mother of a Brith Abraham senior, who had never completed her own high school education, described the tuition payments she could barely afford as the structural equivalent of mortgage payments. She lived in subsidized public housing and would never be able to buy her own home, but private schooling would allow her son to earn enough money to purchase one (or more) for her. "With what I paid for school I could have bought ten houses! It's that expensive, the houses, I mean school. Everything that I put into education I didn't put into the apartment for me. At least I'll have given you a good education," she said turning to her son. "We put everything on you."[20]

In addition, private schooling reinforces the ethno-religious and racial distinctions that tend to naturalize differences in class. Jewish students and parents openly admitted that Jewish schooling provided a means of escaping contact with nonwhite populations. The Moroccan-born father of two boys enrolled in Beit Ya'acov told me that he had "to put them [his sons] in Jewish school and there are so few choices. . . . I could not have put them in public schools with Arabs or blacks. . . . They would have been hit and brutalized. . . . That's the way it is with Arabs and blacks; they don't like Jews." A Brith Abraham junior who attended public school until high school described her decision to enroll in a Jewish institution as a reaction to her "extreme discomfort" at being "the only Jew in a school with 500 Muslims." Marion, a ninth-grader at Brith Abraham, told a similar story: "I was in public school through sixth grade, but as soon as I was supposed to go to middle school my mother put me in [Brith

Abraham]. The public schools in Bondy [a low-income suburb of Paris] are filled with Arabs and blacks. And my mother did not want me in school with Arabs and blacks." Students at Beit Sarah so regularly claimed that they were enrolled in a Jewish school because public schools had "too many Arabs and blacks" that the school director told them to stop. On the day a television station was scheduled to film a special on private education in his school, he coached students on how to answer reporters' questions: "When they ask you why you attend school here, do NOT say that there are too many blacks and Arabs in public school. That is NOT why you are here. You are here for the religious education."

As a number of these comments suggest, parents and administrators *did* think there were specifically "Jewish" reasons for putting children into day schools. Most parents and school officials viewed contemporary anti-Semitism as a uniquely Jewish problem, not as part and parcel of an increase in teenage, school-based violence in difficult neighborhoods (Laronche 2006; Rollot 2007:10). In addition, for many reasons, Catholic schools remained unthinkable to some (although not all) parents.[21] And finally, for a growing number of Jewish families who were making a "return" to various forms of rigorous practice, Jewish schooling alone provided the conditions of possibility for a truly "Jewish" life. An observant history teacher at Brith Sarah, for example, put her young daughter in a private Jewish school because of Shabbat: "I wanted to respect Shabbat. If I had put her in public school, that wouldn't have been possible because I would have had to send her to school on Saturdays."

But, as we have seen, the concerns that lead Jewish parents to seek private schools were both narrower and broader than "Jewishness." Only particularly classed and ethnicized Jews sought recourse to Jewish schools, meaning that the Jewish school population was hardly "representative" of French Jewry or even of French Sephardim. At the same time, the explosion in all forms of private schooling has been fueled by classed and raced anxieties about educational achievement, upward mobility, and physical security. The fear of "Arabs" and "blacks" that led Sephardim to flee poor, peripheral Parisian public schools coincided with a more general white post-Catholic exodus from the same schools for similar reasons. As we saw in the last chapter, when first-, second-, and third-generation Sephardim described "immigrants" as culturally alien freeloaders who collect welfare checks and set cars on fire, they echoed a larger nationalist political discourse with increasing resonance among working class (post-)Catholics living in "mixed" neighborhoods (Wieviorka 1992). It is very important to note that there is nothing particularly "Jewish" about such stereotypes, but quite a bit that is typically "French" (and increasingly European) in such concerns and commentaries (see chapter 2).

The Vanishing State

For all these similarities among parents of parochial students, Jewish schools were not simply a different flavor of Catholic institution. If Catholic schools capitalized on the massive changes in the market for parochial schooling by emphasizing their inclusiveness and tolerance of religious difference, Jewish schools went in the opposite direction. Much of the explosive growth in Jewish schooling over the last 20 years has come from very observant institutions that embrace illiberal forms of Judaism. Schools the FSJU categorizes as "orthodox" combined with those of the ultraorthodox (haredi) Ozar Hatorah and Lubavitcher networks account for 30 of the 50 new institutions created in France over the course of the 1980s and 1990s (Petit-Ohayon 2003). In 2002, almost two-thirds of elementary-aged children in French Jewish schools were enrolled in orthodox or ultraorthodox institutions; the same was true for 50 percent of middle-school-aged students and 30 percent of high school students (ibid.). In Paris, five of the eight largest school networks were either orthodox or ultraorthodox, accounting for almost a third of the 21,300 young Parisians enrolled in Jewish institutions (ibid.). In addition, a number of schools that were not typically considered or labeled "orthodox"—the institutions in the Alliance Israélite Universelle network, for example—slowly had been moving toward more pronounced forms of religious practice. They had recently adopted more stringent dress codes, forbidden boys and girls from sitting together in secular classes, tried to stop students of different sexes from greeting each other with "bises"—the Parisian double-cheek kiss common among social intimates—and introduced more intensive religious instruction. Since almost half of the government contracts awarded to Jewish schools have been granted within the last 20 years, government funds probably disproportionately subsidize highly observant institutions (ibid.).

These schools did not embrace the form of multiculturalism that Catholic institutions have increasingly glossed as "Republican." While even the most religiously observant day schools employed non-Jews as secular teachers, custodial staff, and kitchen workers, even the least religious systematically refused non-Jewish students.[22] In violation of the terms of the contrat d'association with the state, the vast majority of subsidized Parisian Jewish schools conditioned enrollment on providing Halakhic proof of Jewishness. This requirement was typically satisfied by the presentation of a ketubah, a contract certifying that the applicant's parents were married by a consistorial or ultraorthodox rabbi and therefore were both considered Jewish either by birth or conversion.[23] In cases of intermarriage, children of Jewish mothers were eligible if the maternal grandmother's ketubah could be produced. Because Jewish law locates religious transmission in the maternal line, children with Jewish fathers and non-Jewish mothers were refused.[24]

Despite increasingly vocal concerns about Republican law and democratic norms losing ground to ascriptive forms of religious authority, very little public attention was paid to the way Jewish schools violated laïcité. This silence started with the Department of Education, the entity responsible for inspecting contracted government schools and thus ensuring compliance with current law. Among Education Nationale officials and inspectors, non-Jews' exclusion from day schools was a well-kept public secret, known but studiously ignored. When I asked the Department of Education official in charge of developing antiracist programs for schools whether Jewish schools discriminated against non-Jews, she told me that while she was not knowledgeable on the subject, she might be able to put me in touch with retired officials who were. "Why only retired officials?" I asked. "Because," she continued, "it's a politically sensitive topic that active employees might be uncomfortable discussing." A high-ranking school inspector was more straightforward on the issue: "We have a 'see no evil, hear no evil, speak no evil' policy with respect to Jewish institutions, including schools," he told me. In other words, they did not ask or tell.

In the last chapter, we saw that some Jewish elites worried about their ability to maintain this kind of categorical distinction between Jews and Jewish institutions, on the one hand, and the practitioners and practices of other embodied religious, notably Islam, on the other. Jewish school networks were not entirely immune from this kind of concern. A historian of European Jewry who happened to attend a board meeting for a well-established Jewish school network reported one distraught board member's sense of this shift: "We can no longer use the Shoah to get them [government officials] to do what we want!" My exclusion from day schools revealed similar anxieties about calling public, non-Jewish attention to practices that might be interpreted as evidence of Jewish divergence from Republican norms. School officials' discourse seemed haunted by fears of being accused of racial intolerance and/or "fundamentalism" and thus of being publicly denounced as un-Republican. Although some teachers and (to a lesser extent) administrators also worried about producing good Republican citizens (see chapters 4 and 5), school principals seemed most concerned about maintaining the appearance of Jewish schooling's willing participation in the construction of a multicultural *national* community.

Nevertheless, as my brief account of French colonialism suggests (see chapter 1), Jews are not Muslims in French political imaginaries. This was very clear in conversations with the head of the Department of Education at the FSJU, the man responsible for overseeing contract negotiations between Jewish schools and the state. When I asked him whether growing public concern about totalizing religious practices and self-segregation would have an impact on government policy vis-à-vis Jewish schools, he laughed. The state, he confided, does not look closely at Jewish schools; inspectors are happy if there are the right number of children in each class. Beyond that, he added, "We can give so many reasons for why there are no non-Jewish children, and non-Jews have so many reasons not to put their children in Jewish schools. It will have no impact at all."

In some ways, this insouciance seemed justified. Public secrets are by definition difficult to discuss in an audible fashion (Taussig 1999:5). Not only was the state relatively uninterested in details of Jewish schooling, but the news media also ignored most attempts to roll Jewish schools into a larger conversation about secularism and the Republic. In 1989, just before the exclusion of two veiled Muslim girls from public schools launched the first explosive national debate about education and laïcité, four teachers from a haredi school held a public press conference denouncing the gap between Republican principles and their school's programs. They claimed that the school administration had become so "fundamentalist" that it was impossible to fulfill national curriculum requirements (Azeroual 1989b). On the one hand, the press conference attracted the ink and ire of the Jewish press.[25] The following week, a press release from the Association des Directeurs d'Ecoles Juives de France (ADEJF), the association of Jewish school directors in France, appeared in both *Tribune Juive* and *Actualité Juive*:

> The Association was outraged that problems internal to Ozar Hatorah's middle/high school in Créteil were communicated by a handful of teachers to the national media via press conference. The Association also vehemently objects to the use of the term "fundamentalist'" to describe an institution whose educational mission is to promote traditional Jewish values. (ADEJF 1989b:32)

Jewish media coverage continued for a few more weeks as teachers and administrators traded recriminations, suggesting that this was indeed a serious controversy. But on the other hand, the mainstream printed press seems to have entirely ignored the issue. Even when a non-Jewish teacher became the only person involved to be fired, there seems to have been no public attempt to further examine the situation.[26]

This same inaudibility was evident during my fieldwork. The Stasi commission (see chapter 2) alluded to ethno-racial discrimination in private schools,[27] but it buried the allusion in generalities on page 91 of a 100-page report: "Certain contracted private schools accept only the students who can prove that they have the same religious affiliation as the establishment; these schools also do not teach the parts of the national curriculum that do not seem to conform to their vision of the world. All of these attitudes are illegal" (Stasi commission 2004:91–92). With none of the supporting anecdotes that accompanied the rest of the report, most of which focused on Muslim challenges to the "neutrality" of public institutions, the observation never attracted media or government attention. Similarly, at an academic conference on the French Republic and laïcité held at an elite Parisian university in October 2005, the conversation revolved exclusively around Islam until Didier Leschi, the head of the Bureau central des cultes (the Central Office of Religions in the Interior Ministry), exploded: "Why does everyone keep talking about Islam when we all know that fundamentalist Jewish education is the real problem!" The audience apparently met the outburst with dead silence and quickly returned to discussing Muslim practice.[28]

In some contexts, ignoring certain Jewish institutional practices allowed the French government to preserve the appearance of a commitment to Republican individualism and bureaucratic rationality. Paraphrasing the Education Nationale official who offered to refer me to her retired colleagues: we do not and cannot know for sure, so we cannot act. But occasionally Jewish schools demanded more than selective blindness. Just after the adoption of the 2005 law on religious symbols that introduced limited recognition of non-Christian religious holidays in schools, the Department of Education scheduled part of the baccalauréat exam on Shavouth, the annual commemoration of Moses' reception of the Torah on Mount Sinai. Shavouth is *yom tov*, a significant holiday to observant Jews during which "work" is not permitted.[29] Shavouth was not, however, among the state-recognized Jewish holidays, and adding it would have required the renegotiation of the number of sanctioned days for each religious group. The students at Beit Sarah were in a panic. For the first time, they, like veiled girls in public schools, might be forced to choose between religious obligations, on the one hand, and their social and material prospects, on the other. Sarah, a senior whose arrival at Beit Sarah in middle school coincided with an increasing commitment to religious practice, was near tears:

> I know the way the government approached the issue of the veil, and I know Christians. So I know they won't understand if I try to explain to them why I cannot take the test! There are lots of people in my family who are not religious. And I know they will tell me to take the test and make up the holiday afterwards. They don't understand. They have no idea what it's like to have made this commitment, to have changed their life, and to be incapable of going back to the way it was before.[30]

Zoé noted that her problems were even closer to home: "I'm worried about that in terms of my parents. My mother already told me not to get a zero on a section. I don't want to break the holiday, but the bac[calauréat] is a choice about my future. I'm going to try to resist my mother. I'll go, but I won't write anything. That way they can't disqualify me."

While his students worried and strategized, Beit Sarah's principal seemed relatively unconcerned. He had previously assured me that one of Beit Sarah's chief financial patrons, a wealthy Ashkenazi American, "had the ear" of both the United States Congress and Jacques Chirac, then president of France. This, he implied, would allow the school network to weather any political storm. For the present case, he had already contacted the chief rabbi, Joseph Sitruk, and the issue was being worked on "quietly" so that it would not get mixed up with "the veil" and public discussions about laïcité. Much to the relief of his students, the exam dates were changed with no public announcement or explanation. It was as if nothing had happened. In response to my questions about the Department of Education's unexplained about-face, Beit Sarah's disciplinary dean warned me not to talk about such things. "After the law on the veil, it would not be good if Muslims knew the date had been changed for Jews." In any case, she added, the rules *should* be different for Jews. "We cannot write, we cannot ride in a car, etcetera. For them, it's no big deal if a test falls on Ramadan or Christmas. The worst thing that can happen is that they miss a family meal together once every ten years. But for us, it's impossible."

Why, at least in this context, did it seem so obvious that things *should* be different for Jews generally and Jewish schools in particular? As the social fiction of Franco-Judaism cracked around public Jewish practice for both Jews and non-Jews, why did state institutions, major media outlets, and respected intellectuals collude in preserving the illusion of a seamless connection between Republican educational principles and Jewish practices?

I have only provisional historical and sociological answers to these questions. The first and most obvious relates to the impact of the Holocaust on French governmental practice. As a historian of European Jewry noted during my fieldwork, a commitment to strengthening the rule of law and, more particularly, the rule of *one* law for all might logically have been *the* lesson Jews took from the experience of World War II. In both France and Germany, the proliferation of legal exceptions and wholesale exclusions created a predicament that no strong Jewish communal structure could rectify. But in many ways, the political lesson taken from the Holocaust in France has been just the opposite. As we saw in the last chapter, Jewish institutional structures and leaders' legitimacy was often tied to the ability to wrest concessions for Jews—and sometimes Jews alone—from the government. *Actualité Juive*'s editorial board thus found it completely incomprehensible that Chief Rabbi Joseph Sitruk refused to urge the government to accept the kippa but not the veil in public schools. And, quietly, the government often seemed to echo this understanding. As one high-ranking education official noted, after the Holocaust the French government could not afford to deal with Jewish organizations as it would with other institutions. Given the history of the French state, no bureaucrat or department wanted to be thought of as taking action against Jews qua Jews. So, paradoxically, Jewishness became the most relevant facet of these institutions' identities, rendering them untouchable. This can be viewed as placing Jews outside any national project, turning them into a tiny number of internal aliens (roughly 0.8% of the population), whose dispositions and actions are irrelevant to concerns about national cohesion and community.

But an alternative sociological explanation is also possible. The widespread willingness to ignore or more rarely to facilitate Jewish schools' deviations from legal and public norms might, at least partially, reflect the success of arguments about Jewish autochthony (see chapter 2). It suggests that differences in Jewish expressive practices were generally (although not universally) viewed with more benevolence and considerably less anxiety than their Muslim equivalents, even in the highly sensitive domain of education and subject formation. Whatever Jews did or did not do, their actions did not and seemingly could not threaten national cultural projects. As a result, they did not need to be flagged as meaningfully different or even different at all.[31]

If there are still "fundamentalist" Catholic schools—and there certainly are at least a few—many Jewish institutions can be placed in the same category. They may not be Republican, but no one would question whether or not they were "French." Here the contrast with

Muslim institutions, only one of which is currently under government contract in Metropolitan France, is instructive. Even with the promise of government subsidies a distant dream, Muslim schools routinely include assurances that Jewish schools have never made: the proposed school will be "open to everyone"; will not mandate the wearing of "religious signs," like the veil; and will make religious instruction optional (*Le Temps* 2007; Portes 2003; Vidaline 2007). Nonetheless, local and national officials have used every legal pretext possible—such as insufficient attention to environmental and safety issues or the specter of "terrorist" financing—to prevent such schools from opening or operating (e.g., Agence France Presse 2006; Landrin 2006:12).

The results were clearer than the cause. State practices helped carve out an extralegal space for Jewish schools and Jewish religious practices, confirming the disciplinary dean's insistence on Jewish exceptionalism. School policies that directly undermined government claims about core Republican values were ignored; and tensions that were part and parcel of larger social struggles over religion and citizenship were resolved through backroom deals that benefited religious Jews alone. While perhaps imagined as quiet compensation to a small population for the horrors of the Holocaust, I will suggest that the result was (ironically) further alienation from the daily practices of French citizenship. This exemption from public debates about the relationship among religious authority, social identity, and Republican citizenship became the foundation for constructing a lived reality structured by the opposition between "Jewishness" and any other form of identification.[32]

The Vanishing Nation

In theory, this development should not have been possible. The Debré law created the foundation for shared dispositions and horizons that were national in scope. Students in contracted and public schools did similar kinds of things, in similar ways, at similar times, thus giving students all over the country a common set of intellectual and experiential references. Despite occasional claims to the contrary, Jewish schooling, including religious instruction, was conducted almost exclusively in French.[33] Day school students were required to take and pass national exams in order to receive their diplomas. The content of secular courses, which were taught by state-trained and -salaried teachers, therefore closely followed nationally established guidelines. And those guidelines still tended to be vaguely "nationalist," in the sense that Anglo-American politics and policies systematically appeared as foils for their French counterparts and "Europe" remained an administrative abstraction.

There were also a myriad of more subtle ways in which public and day school students resembled one another. Institutional micropractices, the kinds of minute bodily regulations that Foucault (1977) described as the essence of subject formation, were similar across school contexts. Modes of authority, the value placed on particular disciplines (math and science were for "smart" students, social sciences and literature for those who struggle), the desks students learned to sit in, and systems for evaluating student performance were more or less uniform across France. A middle- or high-school student history notebook—a material manifestation of what students learned and how they were expected to have learned it—was a good illustration of these practices. The textual content, outlining techniques, handwriting, and even ink colors used by a day school student were comparable to those of a child in public school. Both would have learned to take notes only when the teacher dictated; both would have used their desk partners for help with spelling; and both would have changed from blue to red when shifting outline levels. In addition, like struggling French students everywhere, day schoolers fixated on the failings highlighted by France's precocious ability tracking. They regularly called themselves "zeros"; sweated about passing to the next grade level; and insisted that they would fail, even before knowing what they would be required to do (see Hamon 2004). They also could not imagine a social world outside the confines of French educational structures. Even when discussing their burning desire to go to university in the United States or Israel, day school students projected distinctly French structures onto their imagined foreign ideal: the baccalauréat, free public universities that function through attrition, elite (often inaccessible) classes préparatoires that lead to the privileged world of the grandes écoles, career choices made at 18 in a context of high unemployment, and the irreversibility of educational paths from high school on.

Even outside school, day school students were in many ways indistinguishable from their public-school age-mates. Like all French adolescents, they watched lots of television, particularly the reruns of old American television shows that aired nightly on the three major national channels. Although of American origin, these shows bound French adolescents into a particular kind of viewing community that would be unrecognizable to an audience anywhere outside France (Abu-Lughod 2005). They knew nothing about the voices of the original characters because the shows were dubbed rather than subtitled, and they were stuck in a very particular kind of time warp in which *"Friends," "Charmed"* (pronounced "sharm-ed"), and *"Jerry Springer"* remained hot shows long after they had come off the air in the United States. Among high school students, the plot twists of the most recently aired episodes were hashed over again and again at lunch. Also like most adolescents, day students claimed that they did not read the newspaper. Instead, they got their information from the eight o'clock network news or (to a much lesser extent) from the Internet.[34] And finally, like all of their age-mates, they were glued to their cell phones, sending text messages to one another in an abbreviated, coded language common to their generation but scorned by educators and adults.

Nonetheless, there was little recognition that these everyday banalities constituted a shared adolescent French universe that transcended the particularities of Jewish schooling, a fact that had even begun to alarm some journalists with the French Jewish press. In June 2000 a reporter for *Actualité Juive* conducted a series of interviews with Jewish school students. Surprised by the results, he wondered in print whether Jewish schools were capable of producing French citizens. He insisted that all students responded to his questions similarly, describing "French" people and Jews as virtually two different species. "We have nothing in common; we do not have the same mentality; we have nothing to say to one another—everyone said the same thing. You can feel the discomfort, the fear of the other. When you listen to them, you get the feeling that French society is composed exclusively of depraved people who will lead you straight to hell" (Derczansky 2000:n.p.).

As the vignette with which this chapter began suggests, the students I interacted with routinely insisted on incommensurable differences between Jews and "the French," without any of the ambivalence evident in their parents' generation. High school boys from Beit Ya'acov were shocked and surprised when I asked if their mothers were French. "Of course not," one snapped back, "they are Jewish!" Similarly, students at both Beit Sarah and Brith Abraham told me time and time again that they were not "French," that "France was not [their] country," and that "the French" and the "the Jews" had nothing in common. Joshua, a Brith Abraham senior, explained: "In fact, when we say 'French,' we think of non-Jews and non-Muslims. We know that we are French. But that means, there is always this gap." Teachers at Brith Abraham even complained that confusion about national identity had seeped into uncertainty about citizenship. Apparently, many students did not know how to answer questions about nationality on government forms, writing in "Tunisian" or "Moroccan" depending on where their parents had been born.

How did Jewishness and Frenchness come to stand for unambiguously, mutually exclusive identities in the context of day schools, to the point where "Moroccan" or "Tunisian" nationality seemed more appropriate? In different ways, much of what students did, saw, and heard every day occluded the material foundations for forms of identification that transcended and crosscut Jewishness. While Jewish kids did lots of things that were not specifically Jewish and might be characterized as typically "French," attending a Jewish school often meant leaving any non-Jewish social network. The very structure of schooling isolated students from their own neighbors and the wider French social world. Typically, Jewish schools started somewhat later than their public counterparts, a concession to some students' considerable commutes. They also ended later, in part because of their start times. But the late days were also the result of augmenting the already heavily charged state program with considerable hours of religious instruction. At Beit Sarah, all middle- and high-school students, except twelfth-graders, attended ten hours of religious instruction (kodesh) every week. At Brith Abraham, the load was more variable by grade level, ranging anywhere from three to six hours of Jewish history and/or kodesh per week.[35] But even with this relatively light load of kodesh, the school day began at 8:30 A.M. and did not end until 5 P.M., with only a thirty-minute lunch break in the middle.[36]

As a result of this kind of schedule, day school students did not have much opportunity to meet or play with children from other kinds of schools. Particularly during the Parisian winter, many students who commuted long distances left for school before it was light and returned home well after dark. As a result, very few students participated in after-school activities, Jewish or otherwise.[37] In fact, by high school, most students had given up any programs in which they were previously involved. A high school student at Beit Sarah complained about her daily grind: she did not get home until after 6 P.M. and therefore no longer had time to take dance classes at the local athletic center. Although she still tried to play sports with neighborhood friends, homework made even that rather difficult.

The rhythm of the annual Jewish calendar itself also added to day schoolers' isolation. Day school vacations were clustered around Jewish holidays (Rosh Hashanah, Yom Kippur, Succoth, Purim, Passover, and Shavuoth) rather than the Catholic observances that structured public-school breaks. Since the state mandated the number of school days required in government-financed institutions, Jewish schools made up for vacation-time associated with religious observances when public schools were not in session.[38] Although longer summer and winter vacations overlapped to a large extent, Jewish and non-Jewish families were much more likely to travel during those periods.[39] As a result, when day school students were home looking for neighborhood play-mates, their options were limited to other day school students.

The absence of non-Jewish playmates seemed inextricably tied to day schooling. Kevin, a tenth-grader enrolled in a public school whose younger sister was in a Jewish school, claimed to have lots of non-Jewish friends. His sister, on the other hand, no longer hung out with anyone who was not Jewish. This does not imply that Jewishness was never a central, structuring identity for public (or Catholic) school students. As all forms of identification in France are increasingly ethnicized, Jewishness may be playing a larger and larger role in self-understanding in all contexts. When Eli, a turbulent middle-school student kicked out of Brith Abraham for disciplinary infractions, found himself enrolled in a public school for the first time, it took him all of three days to identify the ten other students he claimed were Jewish. When I wondered at his ability to have located these students so quickly among the hundreds if not thousands of other unknown middle-schoolers, he laughed at my surprise. Between the telltale sartorial signs (particularly red-string wrist bands, see chapter 6), egregious last names, and the shared interest in identifying a Jewish peer group, he said it had been extraordinarily easy. But far from having found "all" the Jews in his school, it is likely that Eli found only the Jewish students who, like him, *wanted* to be found and therefore foregrounded their Jewishness, which typically meant stereotyped Sephardiness.[40] As Kevin explained: "The clothes, the skin color, when there's a Jew, we know he's a Jew. . . . The Ashkenazim . . . there are some who make themselves visible and others who make themselves less visible. But for the Sephardi Tunisian Jews, they call so much attention to themselves."

While ethno-religious identification was increasingly important for some Jewish students outside Jewish day schools, it had an open, fluid quality that might not (and perhaps could not) have excluded intimate relationships with non-Jews or Jews who did not meet Halakhic criteria. The mother of a teenager enrolled in a Catholic high school described her daughter, Jennifer, as interested exclusively in Jewish issues and Jewish friends. But she also explained Jennifer's tendency to "convert" classmates to Judaism. At the time, her latest conquest was a girl the mother described as "Asian," who had taken to dressing like Jennifer, right down to the Jewish star they both wore around their necks. Although her mother insisted that Jennifer preferred "real" Jews, she would take what she could get.

This kind of flexibility also seemed to hold for day school students who had previously been enrolled in public institutions. Many had stories about the "French" and even "Arabs" with whom they had regularly played both inside and outside school as younger children. But since enrolling in a Jewish institution, all equally acknowledged gradually and inevitably losing contact with those friends. Some noted that while they were still on amicable terms with these old friends, they no longer had time to maintain such relationships. Kevin's sister, Alicia, who left public school for a Jewish institution in middle school, noted:

> Everyone still lives in the same neighborhood. When I was in sixth grade, I would see them [her elementary school friends] almost every Friday night, because I got home early. But then I stopped seeing

them completely. But just recently, I saw them again because we all had to take the *brevet* [a standardized national test taken at the end of eighth grade], and we all took it together in the same school. So all of my friends from both worlds were together, it was kind of funny.

Zoé, a senior at Beit Sarah who attended public school until middle school, described her shifting friendships as a conscious choice:

> I had no bad experiences in public schools. And in a way I'm glad that I had a chance to meet people from different backgrounds, different religions etc. But if I had to do it over again, I'd rather be in a Jewish school the entire time. . . . I used to have [non-Jewish] friends, but things changed when I came to [Beit Sarah]. I no longer felt close to them or like I had anything to share with them, so we grew apart.

Those who had spent their entire childhood in a Jewish school often noted that they did not know any non-Jews at all. Jason, a senior at Brith Abraham, told me it was partially for that reason that his parents were "proud" that he was in a Jewish school: "They are happy that . . . I stay with Jewish friends in a Jewish context. I don't have any *goy* friends. I've never had any *goy* friends. I don't even know what that would be like. I was never in a *laïque* [public] school, so for me that's totally normal [to have only Jewish friends]."

As Zoé and Jason's comments suggest, even if day school students had time to play with neighborhood children, they might not do so. Day school students were multiply discouraged from initiating and maintaining social relationships with non-Jews. Architecturally, Jewish day schools are like fortresses. Both Beit Sarah and Brith Abraham are separated from the street by high walls, with single entry points that are open only for a few minutes at the beginning and end of school. Many French public schools share this kind of structure, marking an ideological separation between the sordid adult world of work and politics, on the one hand, and the almost sacred space of "neutral" schooling, on the other.

In Jewish day schools, this separation extended one step further: the "outside" was figured as both a physical and ideological threat to the "inside." This was, in part, motivated by concerns about rising anti-Semitism. As previously noted, there has been an increase in reported anti-Semitic incidents in France post-2000. Jewish organizations have recorded several nocturnal attempts to burn down Parisian day schools (CRIF 2002a; CRIF 2005; *Observatoire du Monde Juif* 2001:3), as well as incidents of schools being vandalized (windows broken, money and materials stolen, occasional anti-Semitic graffiti) (see CRIF 2006; *Observatoire du Monde Juif* 2001.[41] In addition, the same organizations have documented cases of day school students being insulted and/or physically assaulted, sometimes while leaving school. All such attacks on Jews are classed as anti-Semitic, whether or not the motivations are clear. Sometimes such aggressions appeared class-based: cell phones were stolen, money was demanded. But other times insults were also proffered—"dirty Jew," "Jew, we'll have your skin!"—suggesting a proximity between socioeconomic and ethno-religious identities that made distinctions between the two hard to sustain (see below and chapter 6). At other times, class seemed to have little to do with the violence, as when rock-throwing youth (perhaps consciously imitating Palestinians from the first Intifada?) greeted Jewish adolescents as they left the Tenouji school in the northern Parisian suburbs (see, e.g., *Observatoire du Monde Juif* 2001:2).[42]

Assessing the prevalence of and motivations for such attacks on Jewish adolescents is complicated (see chapter 6) and well beyond the scope of this book;[43] but day schools' responses were very clear. Day school officials reinforced visible security measures, thus figuring the French street as an existential threat to Jews as Jews. Both Beit Sarah and Brith Abraham had video cameras mounted on their gates and intercom systems that allowed school personnel to question anyone seeking entrance. Brith Abraham and a number of other Jewish schools had *vigils*, or private security guards, who watched the gates all day. At the beginning and end of each school day, uniformed French *gendarmes* surrounded building perimeters. Students were instructed not to congregate in front of or in the vicinity of the school, not to travel in conspicuous groups, and to go directly home. At Brith Abraham, parents paid for private buses to pick up and drop off students who lived at a considerable distance, allowing them to avoid the public transportation most Parisian students take to school.[44] These measures did not necessarily increase school security. The buses—conspicuous blue-and-white tourist charters—became targets of attack (*Observatoire du Monde Juif* 2001:3, 4). Similarly, the police presence called attention to schools and to the children leaving them. One student who had attended two different Jewish high schools in Paris claimed that the security cameras and police presence simply displaced those who were looking to bother Jewish students, making them harder to monitor and catch.

But all these attempts at securing buildings and students did reinforce students' sense of insecurity. Although only a handful of the students I interviewed had direct experience with urban violence, anti-Semitic or otherwise, many—particularly girls—had deeply internalized this message. On a crowded public bus one afternoon after school, a female junior at Brith Abraham told me: "I'm afraid to ride the Metro. I'm afraid to ride the RER [regional express railroad connecting Paris to its suburbs]. After about 7 o'clock at night I won't leave my house alone. And when I see a group of *Maghrebins* [North African] boys or men, I panic." A 13-year-old girl from the same school could not believe that I used public transportation to get to school from the center of Paris: "Isn't it terrifying?" she asked in genuine wonder. A 14-year-old girl at Brith Abraham accused of stealing became inconsolable when her parents and the administration threatened to put her in a "non-Jewish school," a verdict that seemed to her to be the equivalent of a death sentence. A 17-year-old boy at Beit Ya'acov summed up Jewish physical insecurity in France very simply: "it's the religious intermixture. Jews will never be safe as long as they live with Christians."

This terror of the world outside school walls was also evident in the telling and retelling of a handful of anti-Semitic incidents that students had standardized and narrativized. Scores of students in lots of different contexts told me about the "friend" or "friend of a friend" who had been forced by "Arabs" to swallow the Jewish star around her neck. The scene was said to have taken place on public transportation, and the white post-Christian public riding the bus/train/metro failed or refused to intervene to help the victim. Regardless of its veracity,[45] this particular story crystallized a number of themes that had become central to day schoolers' imaginaries. First, it highlighted the ubiquity of violent, senseless anti-Semitism, an anti-Semitism with no pecuniary motive that crouched just outside school grounds, menacing everyone. It also spoke to the fear of the uncontrolled, socially mixed spaces of public transport, places where Jews might find themselves face-to-face with "Arabs" and surrounded by a completely apathetic "French" public. The slowness with which Prime Minister Lionel Jospin reacted to initial reports of anti-Semitism in 2000 and 2001 was often held up as inconvertible proof of "French" indifference to Jewish well-being. The apotheosis of this trope occurred in 2004, when a deranged woman manufactured a fictitious but culturally plausible accusation of violent anti-Semitism on the commuter railroad.[46] The swallowed star also emphasized an imagined homology between appearance and essence embraced by many Jewish adolescents. The aggressors were tautologically described as "Arab" both because Jewish children thought they "looked" Arab and because their violent behavior confirmed this categorization—even if and when they happened to have black skin (see below). Insisting that a Jew had been forced to eat an external identifying mark projected precisely the same kind of logic onto the aggressors themselves; the internalization of the Jewish star made it both indelible and unnecessary. You always already are what you eat.

To some extent, adults shared student concerns about rampant "Arab" anti-Semitism and "French" indifference. But the level of anxiety created by the constant narration of such events surprised even some day school teachers and administrators. When I told a religion teacher at Brith Abraham that some of the students seemed terrorized, he interrupted me: "Terrorized but nothing has ever happened to them. . . . There are facts [about anti-Semitism] and then there are fantasies about those facts. I don't know where those fantasies come from, but it's clear that the students have them."[47] The principal at Beit Sarah, perhaps ignorant of the ways in which anti-Semitic (and all intraethnic) violence had become generation-specific (see chapter 6), told me that he could not relate to student fears.[48] "I walk around all the time in a kippa and have never had a problem. I really don't know what they are talking about." He also insisted—echoing most other Jewish institutional heads—that the right-wing government under then President Jacques Chirac had gone to extraordinary lengths to address anti-Semitism and protect Jews. Neither the Republic nor its government could be characterized as anti-Semitic or indifferent to Jews.

In other words, regardless of what might have been intended by particular security measures or day school officials, the social geography of Jewish schooling both presupposed and authorized particular kinds of narratives about self and other. For many day schoolers, Jewish schools appeared to be heavily fortified havens in a hostile "French" world. This sense of being in a besieged "bubble," as many Jewish educators and students called the Jewish school environment, was then reinforced by relations with surrounding institutions and individuals. Both Brith Abraham and Beit Sarah were located just meters away from public institutions with which students had no organized interaction. Brith Abraham shared a playing field with a public middle school and high school. But the students never played games together and saw one another only as the field changed hands. Beit Sarah's ten-foot-high perimeter fence looked catty-corner onto a public middle school. During lunch, Jewish girls eating behind the fence and public school boys and girls walking and talking in the street stared at one another through the bars in tense, distrustful silence. At least one teacher warned Beit Sarah's principal that this combination of proximity and unbridgeable distance would inevitably lead to potentially dangerous misunderstandings. And indeed, the only interactions with public school students that I heard about were tense ones.[49] While I was meeting with a disciplinary dean at Brith Abraham, a tenth-grade boy came in to announce that there had been problems with "guys of Maghrebi origin" on the shared playing field. One afternoon outside Beit Sarah, two middle school girls claimed that "blacks [masculine]" from the middle school across the street had yelled "it smells like Jew here" [*ça pue le feuj ici*] while passing them on the street. When I asked the girls how they had responded, one claimed she screamed "dirty blacks" [*sales noirs*] as the boys ran away. But despite a history of such simmering tensions, neither the Beit Sarah nor the Brith Abraham principals seemed interested in joint programs that might help defuse some of the ill-will. Notably, when the UEJF proposed integrating Brith Abraham and local public school students into a new program about racism and anti-Semitism, the principal pointedly declined the offer.[50]

From inside Jewish school walls, then, the French nation, at best, appeared reduced to an insignificant abstraction and, at worst, to a hostile camp filled with unknown but feared adversaries. And Jewish school administrators were either unaware of or uninterested in mitigating the sense of siege prevalent among students.

Conclusion

"Jews are not safe in France because they will never be safe as long as they live with Christians." There are few sentences that better summarize Jewish day school students' sense of the social and spiritual danger associated with living in non-Jewish society in general and France in particular. In Liisa Malkki's account of Hutu refugees, it is in large part physical isolation that allows for the elaboration of similarly narrow bonds of trust and belonging. In contrast, refugees settled in mixed ethnic and national urban areas did not and perhaps could not construct such stories about themselves. But as we have seen, it was not just the literal isolation of day school students that mattered. In many ways they were not isolated; unlike Hutus living in refugee camps, day school students shared apartment buildings, buses, playing fields and street corners with non-Jewish neighbors. It was, however, not enough to live next door to non-Jews.

The structure and experience of day schools discouraged young Jews from recognizing the social ties that bound them to those neighbors. In the process, Jewish schools became privileged locations for the narrating of Jewish incommensurability in relation to a variety of racially and religiously defined "others": non-Jews generally, "Arabs," "blacks," or "the French." French non-Jews came to be perceived as harboring either deadly hostility or murderous indifference to Jews, whose physical well-being and even survival was thus constantly in jeopardy. The heavily fortified, highly charged physical and symbolic boundaries of Jewish schools—their gates, buses, and temporarily inhabited playing fields—were some of the only regular sites for Jewish/non-Jewish social interactions, with predictable results. This, in turn, discouraged recognition of commonality across religious lines and inhibited the creation of any context in which day schoolers' assumptions about being and belonging might, however temporarily, look less certain.

But these certainties could be disrupted. Kevin, who had always been in a public high school, told me:

When we [Jews] are in a *laïc* [secular] environment, this is funny, that is what I say to my Arab friends. I have lots of Arab friends. I'm very liberal; I have friends from all religions and of all colors. . . . When we are with them, we don't care. We don't care if we are *rebeu* [slang for Arab], Catholic, Arab, Catholic, Muslim and all that. But when we are in a family [Jewish] environment, there is a hatred that develops; let's say that we become racists. We have extreme ideas. And it's completely the opposite of what we are normally. . . . For my [Jewish] friends, when they are with Muslims, everything is fine. . . . We admire them. They are our friends. We sit next to them in class and all. And when you hear them [his Jewish friends] talk about people behind their backs: "Ah, all these Arabs, we have to kill them all." And even them [the "Arabs"], I've heard them because they've told me: "Oh, the Jews, we don't like them."

He later described his contextual transformation into a "racist" as against his will and his reason, as a kind of communal effervescence that emerged inevitably from all-Jewish adolescent gatherings. "I really believe what I say; we [Muslims and Jews] should not fight. But tomorrow, when I find myself with my Jewish friends who are going to say the Arabs this, the Arabs that, they are going to fan the flames of hatred, so I will end up thinking things I don't really think." Joshua, a Brith Abraham senior who spent elementary and middle school in public institutions, suggested that *any* kind of regular social contact across ethno-religious lines helped interrupt this kind of circuit, turning group boundaries and categories into objects of play rather than charged sites of hatred:

When I was in middle school, when I was in elementary school in a public school . . . I got along well with everyone, with Arabs as well as with French people. Sometimes I yelled at an Arab, or I got into an argument with a friend. Sometimes they [friend/Arab] would say, "Yeah, it's a little Jew." But it wasn't, I don't know if they were thinking about what they were saying. It was really only when we were in an argument. I fought with people every night at public school, but it wasn't because of my religion. It was just like that. We just fought all the time. Every night we organized a fight. "Yeah," we said, "tonight we beat each other up!" But we did it laughing.

This is hardly a recipe for acceptable bourgeois tolerance. But even a standing engagement to fight can be a method of community-building that (temporarily) transcends recognized religious differences. Joshua certainly knew "what" all of his friends were—Muslim "Arabs" or post-Christian "French" people—but that neither kept them apart nor defined their social interactions. Jason, a Brith Abraham senior who was always in a Jewish school, explained that isolation from non-Jews made it almost impossible to engage in this kind of play:

> [W]e always stay with other Jews [*on reste entre nous*], and we've learned to stick together, to proudly keep links with the Jewish community and everything. So we are always together. We don't marry, we cannot go out with *goyot* [Hebrew feminine plural for non-Jews]. We can't hang out with the Arabs, the girls, either. . . . And because we make this distinction, they ask what we have, why we are always so happy together. And unconsciously, they decide to do the same thing. [They say:] We can laugh together. On Saturday, you are not going to bug me by saying it's Shabbat. . . . What bothers them [the non-Jews], is that we . . . I think if we laughed with them and went out with them, it would be different.

Jason's point is well taken. Most day school students were hardly laughing. The day school experience provided the context in which Kevin's segmentary narratives about racial difference and hatred were almost never disrupted. Jewish day school students had very few occasions to leave "the family," an appropriately biological metaphor for day school students' sense of Jewish incommensurability (see chapter 4). This helped turn an otherwise unseen and unknown national public into a series of enemy camps. In such a context, Anderson's vision of the nation as an internally boundary-less, horizontal fraternity appears impossible, a potentially dangerous deception that ignores the ethno-religious foundation for true moral and political community. But it was not only the isolation of Jewish day schoolers from non-Jews that made heterogeneous community seem so chimerical. As we will see over the course of the next two chapters, the experience of day schooling reified and homogenized Jewishness itself, laying the groundwork for alternative ethno-national imaginaries.

Four   Religion to Race

June 10, 2004. Margot came bounding up to me in Brith Abraham's courtyard and breathlessly inquired if I had watched TF3, one of the major public television stations, the night before. To her great disappointment, I had not. I had apparently missed seeing one of her cousins, a musician, who was on the news because he had performed at the wedding of an "Arab" man and a Jewish woman. The news report, I gathered from Margot's rather excited and therefore garbled explanation, had focused on the wedding—supposedly an anomaly in the context of significant tensions between Muslims and Jews—not on her cousin.

So I asked what she thought of the marriage. "It's not a good thing," she sighed. She went on to explain that people were born with a religion and therefore were obliged to live their whole lives within it. What about the possibility of conversion, a central tenet of even the most stringent forms of Judaism, I asked. She was not sure; there was a hall monitor she really liked who had converted. "In terms of practices, she's more Jewish than I am," Margot explained. But in general she thought a religion should not and maybe even could not be changed. I backtracked; no one had converted for this wedding. The bride was still a Jew, I noted, which meant that her kids would be Jewish. "That's even worse," Margot exploded. The kids will be both, she insisted impatiently, Jewish through the mother and Muslim through the father.

In Margot's description, Jewishness and Muslimness are inescapable, heritable essences automatically passed to the child from both mother and father. Many of her classmates shared this presumption, even if they disagreed with the mode of transmission Margot articulated. Two middle-school girls from Beit Sarah—both of whom claimed to be worried about Muslim proselytism if a planned mosque was built near their synagogue—also insisted that conversion was impossible. One explained that it was not "normal" for either a Muslim or a Jew to change religions. In any case, the other added, a Muslim who tried to convert to Judaism would always be a Muslim (and vice versa) because he or she "had been born that way and blessed by their god at birth." Similarly, during a discussion about the 2004 American elections, a class of middle-school boys from Beit Ya'acov told me that John Kerry was Jewish. No, I insisted, he was a practicing Christian. Impossible, a student explained. If one of his grandparents or parents was a Jew, he too was Jewish. Despite the protests from one of their classmates, most of the boys agreed that neither conversion nor lineage (from the paternal or maternal line) were relevant because, "according to the Halakhah," even a converted Jew was still a Jew.

In all of these examples, day school students refused the possibility of conversion and therefore understood Jewishness in what Shmuel Eisenstadt and Bernhard Giesen (1995) call "primordial" terms—as a form of identity that is given in nature, innate, unalterable, and frequently styled as radically incommensurable with other kinds of identities. Eisenstadt and Giesen write: "[Primordial attributes] seem to be fundamentally exempted from communication between, or reflexivity by the members of primordial community, they are simply unalterably different, and this difference conveys inferiority and danger at the same time. Strangers are frequently considered as demonic, or as endowed with a strong and hostile identity which threatens the existence of primordial communities" (1995:78–79). At the same time, many of these same students appealed to an entirely different mode of identity construction—not to nature, but to the sacred or transcendent realm (divine blessing, the Halakhah)—as a way of explaining their invocation of an unchangeable Jewish essence. Where primordial identities are understood as always already constituted, identities rooted in the sacred or transcendent often foreground the constant spiritual and ritual work required for belonging (ibid.). Why, then, did students see these two very different modes of grounding community as linked? The previous chapter explored how government policies and day school practices (sometimes inadvertently) underwrote an experience of disjuncture between "French" and "Jewish" worlds. This chapter asks whether and how the content of Jewish schooling played into this sense of alienation. What, given students' simultaneous invocation of the natural and the transcendent, was the relationship between the religious education students received in day schools and their understandings of Jewishness as a primordial form of incommensurable difference? To what extent did figuring Jewishness as primordial contribute to day school students' sense that "Frenchness" and "Muslimness" were both irreducibly different *and* dangerous for Jews? In other words, what role, if any, did religious education play in making it more difficult for adolescents to generalize trust beyond Jewishness and live with difference?

I will suggest that day school students' understanding of Jewishness as a fragile and threatened primordial identity was not necessarily the result of an orthodox Jewish education. Contrary to many of the contemporary French presumptions about the inextricable link between traditional religion and atavism (including primordialism and racism, see below), I will argue that secular assumptions about personhood and identity indelibly shaped what day school students heard and, more importantly, how they understood religious lessons about the content and meaning of Jewish identity. In the process, adolescents transformed a religious mode of identity construction rooted in the everyday work of following God's law (what I will call *becoming*) into a set of fixed, primordially given identity traits (what I will call *being*). In other words, the explosive combination of secular presumptions about personhood and religious conceptions of Jewish community created the grounds for primordialized and racialized understandings of Jewishness.

Race, Religion, and the Republic

As we saw with popular discussions of Islam and Muslim schooling in France (see chapters 2 and 3), there are strong presumptions about the relationships between and among embodied religious traditions, primordial identities like race or ethnicity, and racism.[1] In the first place, embodied religious identities are regularly conflated with ethno-racial categories, leading to the contemporary confusion over the terms "Muslim, "Arab," and even "immigrant" (Fernando 2009).[2] In addition, current incarnations of French Enlightenment tradition associate both orthopraxis and orthodoxy not only with the stifling of individual autonomy (see Brown 2006; Fernando 2010; Mahmood 2005) but also with reactionary intolerance for pluralism or diversity (Roy 2004). In one widely circulating form, this Enlightenment narrative suggests that pious Islam, which is rooted in the close management of bodies and the ritualization of everyday life, inevitably leads to an understanding of identities in rooted, racialized, and exclusive terms (Brenner et al. 2002; Hirsi Ali 2007; Taguieff 2005). This association is evident in a range of public discourses and policies that link various forms of intolerance—racism, sexism, homophobia—with embodied religiosity. One of the arguments used repeatedly to support the 2004 ban on "ostentatious" religious symbols in French public schools linked Muslim veiling practices to anti-Semitism (Bowen 2007:1, 107, 163, 209). In *Les territoires perdus de la République*,[3] the editors noted the "invariable correlation" between the increase in observant Islamic practice, "the degradation of women's social status," and an "increase in anti-Semitism" (Brenner et al. 2002:46).[4] Only by ending particular kinds of embodied religious practices, so the argument goes, will young Europeans of immigrant origin learn to think of identity in civic and individualized terms, as a reflection of a personal rather than collective essence, and as amenable to rational reflection and choice rather than heteronomous submission to divine will. Fighting essentialism is thus viewed as synonymous with eliminating certain conceptions of religion and forms of religiosity (Roy 2004).

Although this discourse focuses on Islam rather than Judaism, it nonetheless suggests that there is nothing surprising about racism among children and young adults educated within an embodied religious tradition. Observant Judaism, like Islam, closely manages bodies and ritualizes many aspects of everyday practice, making it impossible to contain it within the binaries—public/private, action/belief, state/religion—that animate secular states. In addition, again as in observant Islam, gendered and religiously marked bodies are crucial to the forms of distinction that crosscut and mark the boundaries of Jewishness. Within this framework, then, Sephardi youth's primoridalizing tendencies should be tied directly to their religious education. This seems to have been what Didier Leschi, the head of the Bureau central des cultes, was saying when he accused Jewish schools of being *intégristes*, a term in France that is closely associated with self-ghettoization and ethnicized separatism.

This kind of argument makes two rather problematic presumptions. In the first place, it supposes that embodied religions are *necessarily* primordializing while simultaneously ignoring how and why Republican understandings of the secular self are prone to producing identities perceived as fixed and given in nature. Although Judaism is difficult to characterize in the terms of traditional social science—it is and has been either simultaneously or in different contexts an ethnicity, a nation, and a religion (Boyarin 2004)—traditional rabbinic Judaism has seldom been satisfied with the assumption that Judaism is a fixed, transmissible identity that is a given in the natural order of things.[5] It is indeed the case that lineage, and particularly maternal lineage, is central to current Halakhic definitions of Jewishness. And at least since the institutionalization of Christianity in Europe, Judaism has not sought converts or styled itself as a universal salvation religion. But observant Judaism, like many illiberal religious traditions, is better described as embracing what Eisenstadt and Giesen (1995) refer to as a "sacred" or "cultural" rather than "primordial" mode of identity construction. They write: "[Cultural] constructions of collective identities overcome the problem of the fragility and fluidity of social boundaries by relating the collectivity to an unchanging and eternal realm of the sacred and the sublime . . . [and they are] often presented as a human construction in accordance with some divine commandment" (82–83). This implies several things. First and foremost, the daily work of becoming a proper member of such a community is not concealed through naturalization; instead it is highlighted. As a result, the performance of appropriate morality and required rituals are central to being recognized as a full member of the group. In other words, "cultural" identities are those that focus on the continuous process of *becoming* a fully cultured part of the community; they do not assume that either an inner mental state (belief) or physical make-up (race) produce identity and belonging.

In addition, boundaries between groups are differently configured. Eisenstadt and Geisen note: "The boundaries between inside and outside can be crossed by communication, education, and conversion, and—at least in principle—everyone is invited to do so," opening "cultural" communities up to universalistic orientations (ibid.:83). As previously noted, this is more complicated for Judaism than for Islam, Christianity, Buddhism, or Hinduism because of the historical conditions that made Jewish proselytism impossible. However, traditional Judaism has always embraced the possibility of conversion—a possibility that "primordialist" forms of identification systematically refuse. This does not mean that there is agreement over how and why conversions can be performed. Over the last 100 years alone, Halakhically rooted Orthodox rabbinical rulings have run the gamut from very liberal approaches (reluctantly) sanctioning conversion for marriage to unusually draconian attempts to excommunicate converts who fail to continue stringent observance of Jewish law after successfully completing the process of orthodox conversion (Ellenson 1985). But despite these restrictions, conversion is not only possible but also often imagined as transformative, turning non-Jewish bodies into thoroughly Jewish ones (Kahn 2005). And even when conversion is not a possibility—as in the case of rabbis who excommunicate nonobservant converts—the logic of traditional Judaism remains focused on a process of becoming in relation to divine command. Being a Jew means observing the divine commandments regulating every aspect of Jewish life.

The logic of becoming is reflected even in the aspects of traditional Jewish thought that might otherwise seem primordializing.[6] Take, for example, the emphasis on filiation that makes Jewish maternity a key vector of Jewish transmission. In her examination of Halakhic rulings related to the Jewishness of gametes used in assisted reproduction in Israel, Susan Kahn (2005) found that it was not genetic material that determined the Jewishness of the baby.[7] Rather, it was the religious status of the womb in which the fetus was carried and by extension the presumed environment in which the child would be raised that determined the religious identity of the child. For similar reasons, after symbolic circumcision and ritual immersion, Falasha—Ethiopian Jews airlifted out of refugee camps and resettled in Israel—were accepted as fully Jewish by the Israeli religious hierarchy. In contrast, in the context of a racially driven HIV/AIDS scare common to scores of Western democracies, secular Israeli state officials continued to see Falasha blood as carrying irreducible racial difference that left Ethiopian Jews tainted and unlike unmarked (white) Israeli Jews (Seeman 1999).

Contrast this understanding of Jewishness with the way in which secular Frenchness is discursively framed. French Republicanism has long had a performative strain, or what Eisenstadt and Giesen (1995) ideally typify as a "civic" mode of identity construction. The mission civilisatrice described in chapter 2 only made sense if identity could be acquired through familiarity with and enactment of "implicit rules of conduct, traditions and social routines" (ibid.:80). But Republican Frenchness has always been Janus-faced, allowing for full assimilation through individual choice (the "civic" side) while simultaneously styling some individuals as nonassimilable members of primordial collectivities. Recall the limits of the mission civilisatrice, which allowed certain kinds of bodies—particularly those that were white and Christian—to fully embody "Frenchness" while other kinds of bodies seemed indelibly marked by difference and distance from proper norms. In other words, "conversion" to Frenchness was often impossible because of characteristics imagined as innate to particular individuals and groups. Further complicating the notions of becoming implicit in some aspects of French Republicanism, post-Enlightenment French secularism radically decollectivized social groups, replacing logics that were by their very nature heteronomous (subordination to God, women subordinate to men, etc.) with an emphasis on individualism and autonomy. As a result, French Republican philosophy (like most Protestant-inspired, post-Enlightenment Western political ideologies) conjured up an image of society peopled with individuals whose behaviors were largely determined by a post- or presocial, reasoned, and interiorized self (Seligman 2000). This interiorized self became a privileged source of "authentic" behavior, thus linking identity to a more-or-less static internal state (being) rather than to any work-in-the-world (becoming), including external behavioral manifestations.

In addition, this split between the "real" source of self (being) and actions (becoming), which were supposed to be secondary and derivative, made appeals to a shared inner essence (being again) a privileged ground for the reconstitution of meaningful community (Brown 2006; Seligman 2000; Seligman et al. 2008).[8] Thus, throughout much of the 20th century, it was possible for the French state to formally deny categories of people—women, Muslims, Jews—full access to public Frenchness, regardless of how closely members of those groups adhered to France's implicit civic codes (Fanon 1967). At the same time, both the French state and the French public assumed that these groups were, by nature, internally homogenous, despite abundant evidence of their heterogeneity (see Brown 2006 on Jews; Davidson 2012 on Muslims; Scott 1996 on women). French secularism, in other words, helped produce very modern and deeply anchored notions of race as an inescapable, interior essence that *should* (whether or not it did) have exterior manifestations.

This brings me to the second problem with French accounts of the relationship between religious education and primordialization or racialization. Contemporary French anxieties about certain forms of religious education greatly overstate the power of educational content to determine student identities and destinies. This overstatement has long been common in French nationalist narratives,[9] Jewish justifications for parochial education,[10] and even some sociological analyses of schooling (see, e.g., Bourdieu and Passeron 1990; Foley 1990; Luykx 1999). Most anthropological accounts of schooling have moved beyond presuming that "explicit" or "implicit" classroom agendas are unproblematically transmitted to students (Ferguson 2001; Hall 2002; Willis 1977). And there has been increased attention to the ways in which schooling is only one site of socialization, and an increasingly marginalized one at that (Dolby 2001; Hall 2002). If classroom lessons ever did have the power to decisively shape youth practices, those days are most likely long gone, chased out by the multiplication of sites of peer-based socialization—everything from social networking to texting, on-line chatting, and cell phones.

Given religious Judaism's focus on becoming and the difficulty of equating schooling with socialization, why focus an account of adolescent racializing practices on Jewish schooling at all? Because the unique combination of secular presumptions and religious logics in most Jewish schools made particularly nefarious forms of systemic incomprehension and reinterpretation possible.

Individualizing Collectivity

The post-Enlightenment tendency to primordialize identity as internal and given in nature was not just part of the ideological scaffolding of contemporary French social and political culture. Students and teachers constantly evoked this kind of understanding of self. Not surprisingly, given my account of the logic of liberal Republicanism, the most explicit naturalization of Jewish identity came from secular teachers. Mme. Amsallem, a state-paid art instructor as well a Jewish history teacher, used a biological analogy to explain the prophet Ezra Ha-Sofer's injunction against intermarriage: "You know that in Judaism," she told her sixth-grade students,

> the child is the fruit—and not just in Judaism—is the fruit of its mother. So if the mother is Jewish, the child is Jewish. It's normal. If the tree is Jewish, the fruit is Jewish. We don't see apples that grow on a pear tree. If the tree is a pear tree, the fruit will be . . . [Students respond: "pears"] pears. If the tree is an apple tree, the fruit will be . . . [Students: "apples"]. And if it's an orange tree, it will be . . . [Students: "oranges"]. Have we ever seen apples growing on an orange tree? [Students: "No."]. No. So if the mother is Jewish, her fruit, her child, is Jewish. If she isn't Jewish, even if the gardener was Jewish, the fruit. . . . You are going to say that now we are going to look for DNA, that's true. But at that time, you know that there wasn't any DNA and all that.

In this account, even more obviously than in student stories about the impossibility of conversion, Jewishness was depicted as a germ line, a heritable trait that presumably could be traced through DNA. Furthermore, Mme. Amsallem implied that "Jewish" DNA determined morphology and physiology, making it "unnatural" to bring together those who did not share the same genes.[11] Thus, differences in fruit kind, like differences in human populations, were genetically determined.

In some ways, this interpretation of Ezra may not be unusual. The Ezra story certainly lends itself to naturalization. In the postbiblical narrative, Ezra encouraged the Israelites to cast off their non-Jewish wives and children in the interest of purifying what he called the "holy seed" of Judaism. Indeed, some scholars have seen in Ezra's ban on all forms of intermarriage a racial conception of Jewishness, in which all Gentiles were presumed to be innately polluting (Alon 1977). But Ezra certainly does not have to be understood this way from either a secular or a religious position. Solomon Zeitlin (1960), for example, has argued that Ezra's injunction can be best understood in reference to his sociopolitical context. In this reading, the delegitimation of mixed marriages and their offspring was a successful attempt to undermine one (intermarried) Jewish faction's biblically supported claims to the priesthood and the Temple. From a more religious perspective, Ezra's edict can be understood as a rearticulation (and perhaps extension) of biblical injunctions against Israelites marrying into one of the seven idolatrous Canaanite nations (Cohen 1983). This biblical prohibition had less to do with racial or even ritual purity than preventing apostasy and acculturation through socialization among nonmonotheistic peoples (Hayes 1999).

In many ways, it is irrelevant which of these interpretations best reflects Ezra's intent (as if such a thing could possibly be known). It is also not particularly important to know which, if any, of these possible views is most common in recent rabbinical thought. What is significant is that all of these various interpretations have Jewish scholarly and sometimes even religious support (Hayes 1999). In a class devoted to what Mme. Amsallem called "secular" Jewish history, any—or, even better, all—of these interpretations could have been used to "explain" what looks like a particularly intolerant moment in canonical Jewish history. In fact, presenting a plethora of explanations would have given Mme. Amsallem's class a form that more closely mirrored traditional religious pedagogy (see below). Furthermore, Mme. Amsallem had personal reasons to avoid a naturalized explanation. The child of Holocaust survivors, she resented and denounced student "racism," and even lectured one of her classes about the moral horror of racializing Jewishness after the Holocaust.

After her comments about DNA, Mme. Amsallem seemed to think better of her approach. She backtracked, noting the centrality of women to child-rearing and the construction of a kosher home—all arguments about the ways in which Jewishness is about becoming rather than naturalized being. But her first pedagogical instinct, her first attempt to reach her students, had been with a single categorical explanation that rested on an interiorized and naturalized conception of identity in general, and Jewishness in particular. Given that on some level (whether conscious or not), she shared this notion of identity with her students, it was predictable that the DNA illustration—and not her subsequent attempts to explain intermarriage injunctions through socialization—resonated most deeply. It spawned a series of student questions in subsequent lessons about conversion and its impossibilities, to which Mme. Amsallem responded with annoyance. She insisted repeatedly that Ezra's injunction had not applied to women who had converted, but to those whose idolatry threatened the religious practices of their families. So while she did not see her own explanation as barring conversion, her students logically thought it did—she had been talking about nature, not culture. As a result, she should not have been surprised by her students' questions and confusions—they mirrored her own inability to avoid reducing Jewishness to an essence.

Mme. Amsallem's example was unusually biological. But many other secular teachers offered naturalized understandings of identity, sometimes despite their stated interest in combating students' primordializing tendencies. Mme. Haddad, a secular history teacher at Brith Abraham, devoted several hours of her middle-school civic education class to deconstructing and critiquing students' assumptions about "blacks," "Arabs," "Jews," and "the French." As noted in chapter 3, she even tried to undermine the false, racialized dichotomy her students posited between "Arab" and "Jew" by describing herself as an "Arab Jew." But at the same time, she offered reductionist accounts of the relationship between national and ethno-religious identities, implying that nations were first and foremost natural artifacts of culturally homogenous, ethnically bounded communities. Her account of Woodrow Wilson's 14 points and the end of World War I, which slid into a discussion of the Balfour Declaration, provides a case point. "What are the states that . . . are going to create problems [in the interwar period]," Mme. Haddad asked rhetorically. Remember the principles of the 14 points, she exhorted her students:

> One people, one state. What is the example here of, Czechoslovakia. Chezko-slova, chezk. We see already that there are two ethnic groups in this state, and this will be a problem. . . . Hungary was a defeated state, you agree with me? And what happened? We amputated from her a number of regions, including Transylvania [which] had 2.5 million Hungarians. That means that in Romania right now, there is a very large ethnic minority. So did we apply the principle of self-determination? No, because the Hungarians should be in Hungary and they were nevertheless put in Romania. So we already have a problem. Wilson's points were definitely applied, but to the winners.

The losers were stripped of their lands. . . . Second example, Germany. Germany was divided in two by the Danzig corridor that went to Poland . . . Germany was divided in two; is this manageable? No!

She applied the same logic to the "problem" of the Jewish state: "In 1917 the Balfour Declaration promises a homeland to Jews in Palestine and at the same time promises to the Arabs that they will have a Palestinian state. It's started badly already." Her students agreed.

Here again, we see the contradiction between a conscious antiracist project and the underlying conceptions of identity that haunt mainstream conceptions of self and community. Mme. Haddad might argue against understanding Jewishness or Arabness in naturalized terms, and yet her presentation of post–World War I conflict depends on just such an understanding. Maintaining the possibility of being *both* Jewish and Arab would seem difficult given Mme. Haddad's argument that, already in 1917, Jews and Arabs were mutually exclusive and hostile populations. Not surprisingly, Mme. Haddad's students were far more willing to assent to this underlying assumption—communal incompatibility and the impossibility of national pluralism—than to the hybridity and perhaps even indeterminacy implied by Jewish Arabness. And they were more than willing to push this mutual exclusivity further back than 1917. Mme. Haddad had a world history timeline in her classroom that used the word "Palestine" to describe part of the Middle East in the period several thousand years before the birth of Jesus; students had scratched it out and replaced it with "Israel." If Mme. Haddad, despite her antiracism, could not articulate a non-naturalized community, her students clearly embraced that notion as a seemingly eternal truth about all collective identities.

Collectivizing Individuality

Students thus sometimes loudly articulated their secular teachers' presumptions about community and identity, in large part because both groups shared those presumptions. The same cannot be said about the religious conceptions offered in kodesh classes. There was a difference between the seemingly self-evident naturalization, if not racialization, of nation-states—a key trope in French national imaginaries and media—and the notions of community underlying religious instruction. In contrast to secular teachers' ethno-nationalism, which presumed an individually embodied cultural if not biological essence, religious teachers often (but certainly not always) described identity in collective terms, rendering the individual a by-product of communal ties that demanded submission vis-à-vis a higher power. When this kind of collective religious community was evoked in class, students found it incomprehensible and frustrating, provoking conversations that painfully illustrated the incommensurability between some religious worldviews and students' "common sense."

A conversation between tenth-graders at a haredi day school and Mme. Benayoun—a very pious religious instructor—about the conditions under which Temple sacrifices (*korbanot*) were *pigul* (meaning invalid and therefore inedible) exemplified both this conceptual gap and the frustrated silence around it. In her summary of a complex and potentially highly symbolic Talmudic discussion of the relationship between intention and action, Mme. Benayoun gave her students rules that had to be followed. One seemed particularly problematic to them: a cohen, or high priest, who had "impure thoughts" during the slaughter of a sacrificial animal, not only invalidated the sacrifice but also put the entire community at risk. All those who ate the corrupted offering, Mme. Benayoun insisted, were in danger of being killed because God would be angered by such an "abomination." A number of students protested that this rule was unjust because it held innocent people responsible for actions other than their own. Faced with these protests—which were hardly unusual among her tenth-graders—Mme. Benayoun seemed at a loss about how to directly address students' concerns. In the guise of an answer, she bizarrely responded that it was very important for the Jewish community to wisely choose its *cohanim* (plural for "cohen") so that such things would not occur.

Neither the students' incomprehension nor Mme. Benayoun's confusion were surprising. This "rule" about sacrificial purity violated mainstream secular understandings of personhood in a number of ways. It challenged a conception of community rooted in discrete and differentiated individuals by presuming that the thoughts of a leader could have (potentially lethal) divine consequences for followers. In addition, it undermined the central distinction between thought and action, outside and inside—distinctions that are part of Enlight-enment-inspired conceptions of the moral self. Here what the priest thinks—does he plan to eat the sacrifice after it is no longer valid?—can completely undermine an otherwise impeccably executed set of ritual actions. In other words, thought seems to dramatically transform reality.[12] Although students certainly did not articulate their discomfort in those terms, their somewhat hostile questions highlighted the disconnect between their assumptions about community and self, on the one hand, and this alternative sense of community and personhood. Similarly, Mme. Benayoun's response[13] spoke to her inability to address (or perhaps even understand) the differences between traditional Jewish and modern post-Enlightenment concepts of interiority and exteriority, intent and action, individual and community.

Although she may not have known it, Mme. Benayoun missed an exegetical moment that illustrates how deeply traditional Judaism is focused on becoming rather than being. In the Torah, the discussion of ritual sacrifice does not focus on intent; rather it minutely enumerates the actions required for expiation, thereby firmly locating communal atonement in the realm of action-in-the-world. In contrast, the Talmudic and Halakhic elaborations of the Torah deal almost exclusively with the problem of intent, downplaying a whole host of ritual mistakes (Linzer 2011). This reversal of typical Halakhic concern may show the limits of traditional Judaism's view of action—whatever the intent—as entailing the transformation of internal states (ibid.). In cases where action—like sacrifice—*could* be viewed as similar to idolatry, medieval religious thinkers made intention do work in the world and provided a theoretical justification for the viability of Judaism outside a context (Jewish sovereignty and an extant Temple) in which sacrifice was possible or desirable. In contrast, other actions—like Torah study or general observance of Jewish law—carried merit even if good intentions were lacking. Mme. Benayoun had neither the training nor the mandate for this kind of exegetical work. But my point is that a different type of deeply religious Jewish education *could* work against assumptions that privilege static states of being over an emphasis on individual and collective becoming. In other words, the context of government-funded Jewish schooling may have overdetermined the misinterpretation I describe, but this was not tied to the nature of religious Judaism itself.

Religious departures from some of the fundamental presumptions of secular personhood were hardly unusual. In a myriad of different ways and in different contexts, kodesh teachers contradicted student assumptions about autonomy, personal agency, and individuality. These violations of unstated secular assumptions occasionally provoked student dissent and even ire. For example, "choice," defined in liberal thought as the exercise of autonomous personal agency, appeared in far more complex terms in religion classes. For many religion instructors, Jews made only one significant "choice": whether or not to submit to the "yoke" of the mitzvoth and thereby fully realize the crucial transcendent aspect of Jewish identity. To paraphrase a famous Talmudic saying, God controls everything except whether man fears him. In teachers' lectures, individual Jews were therefore responsible for their ritual observance before God and were encouraged to work unfailingly toward the performance of the 613 mitzvoth. But not only did God always already know the outcome of that "choice," no other outcomes seemed to be in human hands. An argument between a Beit Sarah tenth-grader, Rebecca, and M. Attias, a haredi religious instructor, exemplified these clashing conceptions of choice and human agency. During a lecture about balancing desires for material objects (houses, cars, etc.) with piety and ritual observance, Rebecca interrupted and insisted: "It's not bad to break Shabbat if you have to do work for your family." M. Attias objected: "If you work five out of seven or six out of seven days, you are still going to earn money." Rebecca continued to protest: "My father has no choice; he doesn't want to, but he has to." M. Attias responded with a story about a rabbi who had been asked a similar question. In the guise of an answer, the rabbi queried: If you put a storage container on the roof of your house to collect water, would you get more water out of it if you put in seven spigots instead of one?" Bewildered, Rebecca, yelled out, "Yes." "No," M. Attias, continued, "the water in the container is the money God has decided to give you for the week; if you work five days or six, it will come out exactly the same." Frustrated now, Rebecca continued to protest: "If you work more, you earn more."

> M. Attias: "It comes from God, and you will make up the clients during the week."
>
> Rebecca: "You can't tell your boss that God will make up for your clients"

M. Attias: "It's a question of faith; you have to believe."
Rebecca [trying deliberately to provoke what she hoped was a more "reasonable" response from the teacher]: "It's the same at school. God decides whether we have to repeat the grade or not, so it's useless to work at school. He decides on Yom Kippur."
M. Attias [clearly backed into a corner]: "No, God lets us do some things independently."

Here, Rebecca confrontationally pointed to what she saw as the hypocrisy and inadequacy of religious conceptions of free will. M. Attias paradoxically seemed to presuppose absolute autonomy in the world of work: Rebecca's father was presumed to be free to "choose" not to work in order to observe the mitzvoth, meaning he was subject to no real (or meaningful) structural constraints on his activities (i.e., no boss to whom his absence must be explained). At the same time, however, M. Attias denied that people ultimately have an impact on the results of their own actions: God had already determined whether Rebecca's father would be rich or poor, whether he worked or not seemed to have little to do with the outcome. In contrast to M. Attias, Rebecca, and probably many of her quieter classmates, were far more comfortable with an equally paradoxical alternative. She knew that her father was socially heteronomous, a wage laborer beholden to a particular boss and to an economic system that ensured that he would always have one. But she also presumed a certain degree of individual autonomy; despite this social heteronomy, she assumed her father's necessary independence from divine law and the optional aspect of Jewish performance. For Rebecca, her father's Jewishness existed independently of his attempts to realize God's will; God would understand if he broke the rules because being trumped becoming.[14] For M. Attias, the opposite was true.

A similar failed attempt to bridge these two divergent positions occurred in another class, around what one student saw as the coercive aspects of biblical Judaism. After a lecture in Mme. Chitrit's tenth-grade class about the requirement that non-Jewish slaves in Jewish households partially convert to Judaism,[15] Giborah asked in outrage how the Torah could oblige a non-Jew to become a Jew, particularly one with less than full Jewish rights. "The Torah *obliges* her to be Jewish?" Giborah asked in shock. "Why is this not a choice!?" Giborah's distress, like Rebecca's, was driven by her commitment to individual autonomy. As in Protestant and Enlightenment conceptions, Giborah insisted that religion should be a free "choice," driven by individualized belief and commitment. In contrast, the biblical injunction points not only to multiple forms of heteronomy—slavery, divine obligation—but also to the privileging of collective interests, particularly the problem of Jewish social and religious separation (see below). As a result, Mme. Chitrit tried to revise Giborah's frame of reference, suggesting that "choice" was not an appropriate way of understanding the issue. In an attempt to explain the framework in which such compulsion operated, she noted: "You cannot even imagine what it's like to be a slave. You do not have any will; you do what others tell you to do. But if you work in a Jewish household, the Torah obliges you to convert to a certain point." When it became clear that she was not making any headway with Giborah, who continued to be outraged and incredulous, she abandoned that approach, instead attempting to minimize the significance of the gap Giborah had stumbled into. Mme. Chitrit continued: "There are certain cases like this. But don't worry, it doesn't happen very often."

Context not Content

Secular teachers' lessons were animated by assumptions, if not explicit political engagements, that frequently mirrored those of their students. Many religion teachers, on the other hand, offered explanations and examples that rested on quite different ideological foundations. As a result, they often shocked and bewildered their students. But this is not the whole story. Just as significantly, their mode of teaching religion made it virtually impossible for students to understand sometimes very complicated religious practices in terms other than those of primordial community or race. Teachers, for a variety of reasons described below, did not allow their students to engage with rabbinical thought in a traditional way. Instead of foregrounding debate and dissent, which have always been a central part of both Talmudic study and Halakhic law, kodesh teachers offered rules that students were left to integrate and understand through already-existing ideological frameworks. Although it is very hard to speculate whether changes in pedagogy would have impacted outcome, debate *might* have forced students to (at least) intellectually engage the differences between their common sense and religious understandings. Focusing exclusively on *dinnim*, or general consensus positions, discouraged such engagement. And this actually pleased many students. While some, like Rebecca and Giborah, butted heads with instructors, most found it far easier to memorize lists of rules than to confront the epistemological and ontological gaps that made what they learned in religion class a foreign world.

Why this failure to fully engage the form and content of Jewish tradition? In the first place, kodesh teachers were overwhelmingly pious men and women looking for part-time work that would not compromise their religious convictions or practices. The men were often yeshiva scholars who had renounced secular pursuits and education for a life of Torah-learning. The women, many of whom had spent a year or two in a Jewish seminary, were predominantly haredi housewives with large families and considerable domestic responsibilities. In contrast to secular teachers, who were trained by the state, few had any pedagogical training. Although the FSJU runs a diploma-issuing Jewish pedagogical program through the Centre André Neher, it was optional; and a number of haredi teachers and administrators contested the right of an ostensibly secular cultural organization to certify religious instructors. In fact, pedagogical ignorance was sometimes seen as a benefit rather than a drawback. The director of Beit Sarah, for example, noted that he always chose kodesh teachers for their visible piety rather than their knowledge or pedagogical skill.[16]

But the incommensurability of student logics and religious messages was not just a product of poor pedagogy. There are at least two structural trends in religious education that may be implicated (Friedman 1987; Hefner and Zaman 2007; Soloveitchik 1994). First, as Haym Soloveitchik (1994) and Menachem Friedman (1987) have documented in both American and Israeli Jewish education, there has been a turn away from mimesis, a mode of transmission that privileged lived practice over abstract legal rulings, toward maximalist interpretations of the oral (Mishnah) and written Torah. This has increased the centrality of text and textual sources in the governance of everyday life, not just in yeshiva study. It has also sidelined the quest to find leniency that animated rabbinical Judaism and Halakhic debate for most of the medieval and early modern period. Despite the range of opinions on any one issue—from the size of the amount of matzah to be eaten during the first Passover seder to the style of women's head coverings—the most stringent interpretations are taken as the most "authentic" and therefore "true."

Second, and simultaneously, Jewish religious education has been democratized. Historically, Jewish religious instruction was gendered; only boys studied Torah and Talmud, while girls instead learned to pray and perform the daily duties of a Jewish homemaker through mimesis. In fact, there are Talmudic sayings that liken the teaching of Torah to women with similar instruction for animals. With the post-Enlightenment transition to more egalitarian schooling, Jewish schools followed suit. Different Jewish traditions have taken various approaches to teaching girls, from allowing them to learn the same things as boys (more or less the case at Brith Abraham) to creating a separate girl's curriculum (definitely the case at Beit Sarah). This too has led to simplification in *both* girls' and boys' instruction (perhaps in part because girls and boys are taught by the same teachers, albeit at different times of day). Again in contrast to a yeshiva education, this has led Jewish day schooling to focus on dinnim instead of the complicated dialectics that—at least since the Middle Ages—observant Jews believed permitted human interpretation of divine will.

As we saw in relation to Mme. Benayoun's class on korbanot, or animal sacrifices, this meant that there was very little sustained debate in religion classrooms. Some teachers articulated this as part of a conscious agenda. Mme. Grunspan, a very thoughtful Brith Abraham religion instructor, explained that she was trying to teach children to defer to and respect (religious) authority. She claimed that day school children grew up thinking that nothing was sacred because ambient French popular culture taught them to challenge authority of all kinds loudly and impertinently:

> They all watch these television programs with the journalists who
> want to show off and look like know-it-alls. They interrupt the invited
> guests constantly. . . . A student, copying what he's seen on TV, will

tell a teacher that he's "totally wrong" or that he's in "total disagreement" with what the teacher just said. They have to learn that this is not an appropriate way to speak to someone like a teacher. . . . Ten years ago, the journalist really just asked the questions and stayed in the background, but today kids have learned a really different model and need to be resocialized at school.

So rather than teach them to argue, she encouraged "respect" and therefore silence. But this was an unusually articulate and reasoned position. Many teachers were simply uncomfortable with student questions, sometimes so uncomfortable they chastised students for their curiosity. In (yet another) attempt to argue over the concept of choice (see above), Shoshanna, a Beit Sarah tenth-grader, asked Mme. Benayoun why someone ignorant of the dinnim associated with Shabbat should be punished for turning on the lights and whether turning them on accidentally (out of habit, for example) was a serious offense. For Shoshanna, these questions were motivated by concerns about individual intention and the distinction between exterior action and internal belief. But Mme. Benayoun saw them as frustrating and irrelevant. In the first place, she might have seen these distinctions as misplaced; in a practice-oriented worldview, what you *meant* to do when turning on the lights is far less significant than the action itself. In addition, she saw Shoshanna's questions as a distraction from the central point of her lesson on Shabbat dinnim. "Why are you asking these questions?" she demanded. "Do you typically transgress Shabbat? It's death if you do!" When Shoshanna tried to ask another series of questions about a (confusing) interpretation of a biblical passage, Mme. Benayoun humiliated her for her trouble: she was accused of being "insubordinate" and acting inappropriately for a "Jewish girl."

I have thus far highlighted student reactions that, however inarticulately, plunge headlong into the gap between a liberal focus on internal states and a religious preoccupation with becoming through practice. But this tended to be the exception rather than the rule. Kodesh teachers were not the only people in school who struggled with the difficulty and complexity of debate and dissent. Students had, to a large, extent, internalized rules-based forms of religious instruction and rejected attempts to break that mold.[17] One of the only Ashkenazi instructors at Beit Sarah, a sixtysomething man who everyone called "rabbi," was particularly appreciated because his classes were essentially lists of rules. In one class that seemed to fascinate tenth-grade girls, he asked and answered questions about Shabbat observance: Can one open a bottle of wine on Shabbat? [Yes, doing so does not create a new object.] A soda bottle? [No, unless you puncture the cap so that it can no longer be used. Otherwise one has created a new object, a bottle cap.] A packet of sugar? [Yes, but you cannot tear it in any place with words; tearing words violates the injunction against erasing on Shabbat.] Can you tear off a paper towel on Shabbat? [No.] What if there is a cake with writing on it, can it be cut and eaten? [It can only be cut and eaten if the words are made of the same ingredients as the cake, otherwise cutting into the letters also violates rules about erasing.] After class, a self-described "unreligious" student sighed contently: "Finally, a kodesh teacher who knows how to speak to me!"

Although they had far fewer hours of religious instruction, students at Brith Abraham reacted similarly. A "modern" orthodox kodesh instructor—M. Ayoun—regularly ran up against student discomfort with open-ended discussion. In a class with senior girls who were unaccustomed to his teaching style, a student asked whether Judaism allowed girls to wear pants. In response, he asked the class to think about the problem of pants in Jewish discussions of modesty: Why were pants discouraged? Did it have something to do with pants themselves? Could one be immodestly dressed yet wear a skirt? In other words, he was asking them to think about what kind of gendered subject religious Judaism cultivated and what this subject had to do with the performance or display of sexual difference. This in turn might have forced them to confront the differences between that ideal subject and their everyday assumptions and practices—which were hardly modest, whether or not they were wearing skirts. Student confusion and frustration was palpable, culminating in an exasperated attempt to end the conversation entirely: So does that mean we can wear them or not? After class, M. Ayoun talked about how hard it was to poke holes in the litany of certainties day school children had been learning since *gan*, or kindergarten. He continued to hope that his classes would unsettle them just enough to provoke questions or thought, but he was frequently disappointed. Many students expressed equal ambivalence about him and his methods, noting that their favorite kodesh classes were those that were directly "relevant" to their lives. Jennifer and Naomi, two very different eleventh-graders, explained the role of religious instruction on the bus one afternoon:

> Jennifer: School tries to give people a good foundation; it tries to give us direction for our future lives. They want to make that foundation so firmly engrained that, when we move on in our lives [to non-Jewish contexts], we will have already chosen a path that we will go further along and not leave.
>
> Naomi: In *kodesh* classes in particular, we get a list of things that we can and cannot do in a whole bunch of precise circumstances. The difference with [M. Ayoun] is incredible. He says we are free individuals, and we can choose to live our lives however we want. It's like he opens the door to thought. He then presents us with different ways of thinking about these choices, but he never insists on anything.
>
> Jennifer: That's okay coming from [M. Ayoun] because he is neutral, but it could be very dangerous if it came from someone who presented ideas in a biased way.

I asked if the threat of "biased" presentation was not a very good reason for M. Ayoun's insistence on providing a range of possible interpretations. Naomi agreed, but only for older students. Jennifer disagreed, noting that it would be confusing for anyone. In any case, as she later explained, there was really only one "right" way to be Jewish; sure lots of people did lots of different things, but real Jewishness was spelled out in black and white in the Torah.[18]

This turn away from debate and contextualization was particularly problematic given the ease with which students turned to primordialist conceptions of Jewishness to understand religious practices and ideas. For many kodesh teachers, as for observant Jews in general, Jewishness presupposed and entailed following the biblical command to be *kaddosh*, often glossed as "holy" or "separate," in every aspect of daily life (e.g., Deuteronomy 7:6). Under the influence of postexilic rabbinic Judaism, this has come to mean conscious and conspicuous separation from what are often biblically termed "the nations," or non-Jews and surrounding non-Jewish society (Heilman 1994; Katz 1961a; Neusner 1996; Soloveitchik 1994). Those who strive to embody this distinctive and totalizing form of Jewishness[19] imagine themselves as not only guaranteeing a place in God's favor but also contributing to a larger Jewish eschatological project—the "return" to a theocratic Israel and the concomitant arrival of the Messiah. In a certain kind of context, this project is not about racial separation but about ritual purity; in Mary Douglas's terms, it is about managing structural dangers, not the physical or biological threat created by non-Jews. In fact, Jewish historians have argued that the threat of social and cultural proximity between Jews and non-Jews fueled ever more rigorous attempts to establish boundaries in certain places (intimacy and marriage) while necessarily leaving others (commerce, daily interactions) rather open (Berger 2002; Katz 1961a; Soloveitchik 1978). This is very different than either presuming stable ontological difference (race) or attempting to create the presumption of that difference through absolute hierarchical segregation (Jim Crow).

But when the rules governing Jewish separation are presented without their accompanying religious logic, they can appear to be about a primordialist notion of Jewish being rather than part of a ritual program of becoming appropriately subject to God's divine plan. A lesson at Beit Sarah about *bishul akum*, or forbidden forms of cooking, illustrates the slippage between these two different understandings. Mlle. Chicheportiche, an imposing and (unusually) unmarried religion teacher, told seniors at Beit Sarah that wine touched or even looked at by a non-Jew was no longer kosher and therefore unfit for consumption. "If a *goy* so much looks at my glass, I can't drink it; I throw it out. Others might [drink it], but I would rather be safe than sorry." The same teacher instructed students never to share a meal with non-Jews or even to eat kosher foods cooked by a non-Jew because "the beginning of intermarriage is a meal together." A student, who was perhaps shocked by how this sounded, noted that this could not really apply to "a [female] Jew and a *goya* [female non-Jew]," who "logically would not marry one another." Mlle. Chicheportiche shouted in response:

> God forbid, God forbid. . . . The Torah that created us says that the table is a sacred space. We can be friends, [as in saying] good morning, good evening, but not at the table. I would never invite my neighbor, a *goya*, even if I've known her for 20 years. I would never even go to her apartment, because the day that she tells me to come in, I'll have to tell her to come in. And after that it's finished, it's

hopeless. My children and her children will start playing together in the courtyard. And they can't do that; it's forbidden!

She also warned students about ever feeling spiritually safe with non-Jews:

> I recently saw a guy I know. How's it going? [I ask.] He tells me he has a problem. What? My son is 26, and he has gotten involved with a non-Jewish girl. I'm sick [he says], and I don't know what to do. And I say: How did he meet her? At the university. It starts with classes together and then it goes further. You think it's not true? Remember when we talked about hurting God. It's [hopeless] if we don't put ramparts and walls and everything up. . . . Don't tell yourself that you're the son of a rabbi, [so you're safe]. Don't believe it. . . . We have to take care of ourselves. We decide to keep them [non-Jews] at arm's-length. I say that for our ears only. How many times have the teachers, my colleagues, said to me, "Come on, let's get a pizza amongst ourselves, a kosher one!" Never!

Mlle. Chicheportiche's discussion was an idiosyncratic mixture of a particularly stringent, medieval Ashkenazi interpretation of Jewish law and modern intolerance. During the period of Halakhic elaboration now glossed as *tosafist* in medieval Northern Europe (commonly called *Ashkenaz*), it was indeed the case that wine touched by a Gentile after a certain point in its production was no longer considered kosher.[20] This (very onerous) legal stricture grew out of Talmudic concerns about *avodah zarah*, literally foreign work, which referred to idolatry and idolaters.[21] Rabbinic writers in the first centuries of the common era assumed that wine in non-Jewish hands was first and foremost used as a libation for idols, making it and anything with which it came in contact a source of apostasy and an affront to the one true God (Porton 1988:252). The ban on libation wine was extended to any food that might contain wine or be used in heathen religious rituals. The restrictions on consuming kosher food cooked by non-Jews were also influenced by fears of aiding and abetting idolatry. The Talmudic term generally used for forbidden instances of such cooking, "bishul akum," directly references idolaters (akum). But early rabbis were also deeply concerned about the social implications of eating and, more particularly, drinking with the pagan nations. Such intimate social intercourse, it was argued, might lead to sexual intercourse and intermarriage. As the Talmud notes: "Their wine was forbidden on account of their daughters" (cited in Katz 1961a:47). Indeed, well into the medieval period, when concerns about libation wine had virtually disappeared, some rabbinical scholars—but certainly not all[22]—continued to conflate Christians with idolaters, leaving the blanket Talmudic injunctions intact (Katz 1961a; Soloveitchik 1978). And even when rabbinical scholars reinterpreted those injunctions so as to disassociate Christians from idolaters, thus allowing for more Gentile contact with wine (particularly in its production phases) and Jewish contact with Gentile wine (for purposes of trade and debt repayment), the Ashkenazi prohibition against social (rather than simply economic) intercourse around wine and food remained (Soloveitchik 1978). Established social practice and medieval Ashkenazi revulsion at the perceived idolatry of Christians prevented this reclassification from vitiating the Halakhic prohibitions on commensality (Berger 2002; Katz 1961a; Soloveitchik 1978). But this shift allowed for the loosening of a range of other social restrictions separating Jews and Gentiles, including, for example, the relatively intimate exchange of gifts. In non-Ashkenazi contexts it had more direct consequences. There were several attempts by Sephardi Halakhists to abolish the restrictions entirely (Soloveitchik 1978:178). And in places like Italy and Eastern Europe, widespread pragmatic dispensations made consumption of "Gentile" wine common (Katz 1961b).[23]

Most crucially for the point I am trying to make, Mlle. Chicheportiche presented a particularly stringent medieval Halakhic interpretation without explaining its history or complexity. She then added her own very modern disgust, disgust that in many ways defies other Halakhic injunctions. The idea that wine merely *looked* at by a non-Jew would be dangerous and undrinkable is not part of any Halakhic interpretation because it has nothing to do with the forms of interaction Jewish law strives to regulate. Her insistence that she refused to drink wine seen by a Gentile because she would rather be "safe than sorry" sounds suspiciously like modern racism with its theories of innate contagion. One has only to think of the widespread accusations in the Southern United States against African Americans who were accused of violating white women with their eyes. The same extra-Halakhic disgust applies to Mlle. Chicheportiche's horror at the idea of socializing with business colleagues, allowing Jewish and non-Jewish children to play together or attend the same university classes, or inviting a non-Jewish neighbor into her house. Even in medieval Ashkenaz, maintaining cordial and even friendly relations with business partners was necessary and permitted; Jewish children were commonly apprenticed with other non-Jews to Gentile master tradesmen; and visiting non-Jewish households was regulated (in terms of ritual and food) but common (Katz 1961b). In fact, the importance of maintaining Christian good will for the sake of Jewish communal safety—what was called "preventing resentment" or "promoting peaceful relations"—*and* the glorification of God through exemplary Jewish conduct was a common Halakhic justification for behaviors that allowed for the (temporary) crossing of Jewish-Gentile boundaries (ibid.). Instead, Mlle. Chicheportiche describes a world in which even the most basic social contact between Jews and non-Jews is unthinkable, turning non-Jewish neighbors into dangerous physical as well as spiritual enemies.

Student (mis)interpretations of these kinds of comments highlighted the disjuncture between what religious teachers may have intended and the secularized message about identity they were in fact communicating. After Mlle. Chicheportiche read a biblical passage in which the cries of young Ishmael—Abraham's son with his non-Jewish servant Hagar—were heard and heeded by God, a shocked student asked: "God listens to the prayers of non-Jews?" It would be hard to characterize Mlle. Chicheportiche as an anti-primordialist, but she was evidently disturbed by the question. Like the student who suggested that those born into different religions were blessed by "their" gods at birth, this question presumed that monotheism was impossible because religion stood for indelible differences in being, not for the work of realizing the will of a universal transcendent force. In the process, the single God of Jewish monotheism was transformed into a tribal deity who jealously protected Jews and ignored everyone else. Trying to reinforce the central message of monotheism, Mlle. Chicheportiche shot back:

> Of course, and so what! There's a little bird that cries; he doesn't have anything to eat. What does *HaShem* [literally the name, one of the most common ways religious Jews refer to God] do? He makes sure

> that the rain falls so that the worms come out of the earth so that the little bird can find something to eat. You need to know that. He does that for everyone. He's good, *HaShem*; he feeds everyone. And when I say everyone, that means everyone, even the little ant that you don't see but who sees you. *HaShem* feeds it.

But this reply may very well have reinforced the presumption that fueled the question in the first place. HaShem may feed everyone, but the only examples given were zoological ones.

Other students expressed similar confusion about how to differentiate between Jewish being and Jewish becoming. Four tenth-graders at Beit Sarah struggled particularly with God's creation of non-Jews and their role in what kodesh teachers portrayed as a deeply Judeo-centric universe. Shoshanna in particular noted that she had long been disturbed by the seeming pointlessness of non-Jews. "If the world exists for Jews, why create non-Jews at all?" she claimed to have long asked herself. In other words, she could not understand why the divine rules linking appropriate Jewishness to world health and renewal did not simultaneously imply both the cosmic and physical irrelevance of non-Jews.

Conclusion

Shoshanna's confusion brings us back to where we started—religious justifications for clearly primordialist understandings of Jewishness. Her nagging discomfort with non-Jewish *existence*, what we have called "being"—rather than just religious mission, what we have called "becoming"—highlights the gap between what students were probably taught and the terms in which they were capable of understanding those lessons. It also shows that at least some students suspected that this gap existed and that their modes of interpretation and comprehension did not do justice to what they were supposed to be learning. (When girls at Beit Sarah were particularly frustrated with a question, some of them shouted: Go talk to the kodesh teachers! They know better than we do!) This disjuncture and the (very vague) discomfort about it, far more than the content of religious instruction, is what makes the context of Jewish schools important for understanding at least some of the forms of primordialization going on among teen-agers. As I have shown, there were two interesting things happening in Jewish day schools. On the one hand, the presentation of Judaism and irreducibly collective religious logics as a set of decontextualized rules collapsed the rich traditions of rabbinic Judaism into textual literalism. In the process, a multivocal tradition in which both the content and boundaries of Jewishness have long been the subject of heated debate was flattened into a single, static conception of Jewish-ness. On the other hand, students were free to understand these rules through the secular logics that shaped the contours of their everyday lives. Teachers' refusal to seriously engage questions and the tendency to downplay the radical disjunctures between religious and secular thought meant that students were often left to translate epistemologi-cal and ontological differences into a language with which they were familiar. Often that language did not maintain the principal idea teach-ers may have intended to communicate. And in many cases, students did not even fully realize what they were doing. It may certainly have seemed like discussions about the practical modes of creating Jewish purity and fulfilling obligations were (also? actually?) conversations about Jewish superiority and primordial difference.

In light of this, how can we understand Margot's concern about the children of a mixed marriage being both Muslim through the father and Jewish through the mother? Traditional Judaism traces Judaism through matriline while traditional Islam ascribes religious community through patriline. But in both cases, these logics of transmission reflect communal identities rooted in becoming. As previously mentioned, Judaism views maternal influence as decisive for creating the appropri-ate moral and physical environment for Jewishness; traditional Islam sees male moral and religious authority as stronger and therefore as deterministic (Bringa 1995). As a result, it is improbable that Margot's religious teachers were primarily concerned that the child of a mixed Muslim-Jewish marriage would be "both" Jewish and Muslim; instead, it is far more likely that they were worried that the child would be "nothing" because of the impossibility of fulfilling two competing, embodied traditions. What about the assertion that it is "written" in the Halakhah that John Kerry is Jewish? While the Halakhah almost always allows conversion *into* Judaism (albeit sometimes reluctantly), there is a strain of Halakhic thinking that makes conversion *out* of Judaism difficult if not impossible (Boyarin 2004). But this Halakhic conversation grew, to a large extent, out of the problem of *forced* conversion in medieval Christendom and, to a lesser extent, in Muslim lands. The strain of Halakhic thinking that refused to recognize conversion out of Judaism was an attempt to ensure that Jews forced to leave Judaism still counted as Jews. Furthermore, at least some of this discussion privileged practice and continued observance of Jewish law over a vision of conversion as a decisive shift in an internal state. Maimonides, for example, wrote an extensive and scathing rebuttal to a European rabbi who insisted that observing Jewish law after (even forced) conversion compounded the apostasy and God's displeasure. Maimonides claimed just the opposite: the importance of becoming, that is, continuing to attempt to respect God's law, over and against some imagined shift in being—in this case, conversion to Islam (Halkin and Hartman 1985). It is thus not in any simple, literalist way that John Kerry's "Jewishness" is "written" in the Halakhah or that, in a terrifying return of Nazi logic, one Jewish grandparent makes anyone indelibly Jewish. But day school students often transformed these (and other) complicated, contextual stories about Jewish law and epistemology into stories about Jewish racial difference. And this transformation was underwritten by Jewish religion teachers' failure to pedagogically address students' secular presumptions about personhood and collective identity.

In other words, even though race was not central to the conceptions of Judaism taught in day schools, the experience of day schooling often confirmed student assumptions about the primordial nature of Jewishness. Day schools were thus uniquely configured stages that facilitated certain conceptions of Jewishness while making others more difficult. But what were the conceptions of Jewishness that students enacted inside and outside day schools? And given many students' discomfort with the idea of life in France, where were they located?

Five   Domesticating Diaspora

November 8, 2004. In an eleventh-grade English class at Beit Sarah, we were reading an extract from Richard Goldstein's "The New Anti-Semitism" (1994). In the text, Goldstein announces his short-lived adolescent confidence that American Jews "did not need the promised land," because they had found their own haven in the United States (1994: 204). After the meaning of this sentence became clear, students began objecting. "That line," someone began explaining to the class, "it does not mean to say that we do not need Israel. All Jews need Israel, even if they don't think so. And we need to return to Israel because it is our land and our country." Another student, Jessica, asked me what I felt when I was in Israel, when I was standing at the Kotel, or Western Wall. "Because when I'm in Israel, I feel like I'm home, I'm moved," she added defensively. A third student noted: "It is written in the Bible that Israel belongs to the Jews and that the Jews have to go back. All Jews believe in the Bible, so all Jews know they have to go back to Israel." Given how frightened they were about anti-Semitic violence in France, I asked whether they worried about terrorist attacks in Israel. They did not. Besides, Jessica added: "Everyone will eventually have to go back to Israel, so isn't it better to go now rather than later? . . . Wouldn't you rather die in your own country rather than live ten more years someplace else?" Jessica's comment made me think of Levina, another eleventh-grader, who recently had told me: "I don't feel French; I feel Israeli [*israélienne*]. When there are reports of events on the news, none of us particularly care about what happens in France or in Europe. But we all feel directly concerned about what happens in Israel." Levina apparently had no relatives in Israel, "just friends. . . . But it is our land. God gave it to the Jews so it belongs to the Jews." Jessica was trying to get my attention again: "You may think we are brainwashed and everything," Jessica added, "but it has nothing to do with that."

Among day school students, this conversation about national identity and belonging was both typical and somewhat surprising. It was typical because I had similar conversations with scores of students in all three day schools. Almost all agreed that their days in France were numbered and that they should seriously contemplate leaving. Many insisted that a "return" to Israel was the only way to guarantee long-term Jewish safety. And even when they acknowledged that Israel did not necessarily guarantee immediate security, death "at home" seemed to hold fewer horrors than continued life in France. But despite Jessica's "brainwashing" comment, Beit Sarah was not officially a Zionist institution. In fact, the Jewish press and a number of parents had accused it of ignoring the Jewish national question and remaining too narrowly focused on politically indifferent orthopraxis. But Jessica, Levina, and scores of other Beit Sarah students articulated a militantly Zionist understanding of Jewishness, turning Israel into the "central building block of any future-oriented life project" (Bunzl 2003:156). To a somewhat lesser extent, the opposite was also true. At Brith Abraham, an openly and deeply Zionist institution, some students spoke of the United States as a paradise on earth where Jews could literally wear their Jewishness on their sleeves without constraint or fear.

How and why was this the case? Why were students committed Zionists at an institution historically dedicated to educating future generations of Diasporic Jews? On the other hand, why did a number of the students in a committed Zionist school dream about a specifically Jewish future in the United States? I will suggest that day school students' construction of an imagined Jewish future in Israel or the United States had little to do with explicit school ideology, let alone "brainwashing." Rather, it grew out of the way Jewishness itself was imagined and lived within day schools of all orientations. In the last chapter, we saw the ways in which students' secular understandings of personhood contributed to the (mis)interpretation of religious teachings about Jewish community and identity. In this chapter, I will argue that day school students' conceptions of Jewishness were rooted in the projection of their particular forms of being and seeing onto an imagined global Jewish community instantiated through Israel. In the process, children developed their own Herderian conception of community—one in which membership in the "Jewish community" came to rest on essential sameness, not on the daily work of "subjunctive" social imagination (Seligman et al. 2008) or argumentative engagement with a common discursive paradigm (Asad 1993). Jewishness thus became not only a shared genealogy but also a common set of ideological orientations and expressive practices.

Homogenizing Jewishness

Stanley Tambiah (1990) and Arjun Appadurai (1996) have looked at the complementary roles of abstraction, generalization, and particularization in their work on ethnic conflicts. Both authors emphasize the importance of thinking about the ways in which specific experiences and events come to be figured and refigured as tokens of a type. Tambiah pays particular attention to what he calls "focalization and transvaluation" (1990:750). "By focalization," he writes,

> I mean the process of progressive denudation of local incidents and disputes of their particulars of context and aggregating them, thereby narrowing their concrete richness. Transvaluation refers to the parallel process of assimilating particulars to a larger, collective, more enduring, and therefore less context-bound, cause or interest. The processes of focalization and transvaluation thereby contribute to a progressive polarization and dichotomization of issues and partisans. (1990:750)

Appadurai (1996) sees this two-way telescoping—up to generalities from stripped-down particulars and down to specifics from unmoored generalities—getting pulled into highly localized "structures of feeling" that, in turn, influence the way in which a whole range of experiences and events can be interpreted and understood (1996:156).

In many ways, this is precisely what happened to "Jewishness" within the context of day schools. As we saw in chapter 3, only a particularly classed and ethnicized segment of France's Jewish population enrolled their children in day schools. The physical, social, and ideological isolation of day schooling helped efface the ties that bound day-school students to their similarly classed and socially positioned peers, creating the perception of absolute difference between French Jews and non-Jews. At the same time, the particularities of Moroccan and Tunisian families settled in peripheral Parisian neighborhoods came to stand for universal Jewishness. As a result, what was "normal" in this relatively tight-knit world became the model of Jewishness writ large.

In addition to sharing national origins, migration histories, and class status, the students, Jewish teachers, and administrators in day schools across Paris often knew one another and were related, creating links across generation and geography. The principals at Beit Sarah and Brith Abraham grew up together in Morocco, working at the same summer camp as when they were children and then choosing the same career path after decolonization. One parent described the staff at Brith Abraham as the "Moroccan mafia," a reference to the fact that many of the teachers and administrators were of Moroccan origin and were related to the school principal. The principal's sister and spouse, for example, occupied significant administrative and pedagogical positions in the school, and their children attended the school. A Beit Sarah kodesh teacher spent almost an hour taking roll the first day of class because every name called had to be placed into a web of relationships with former students, teachers, friends, and relatives. Nearly every adolescent I met asked whether I knew a cousin, sister, brother, or friend who attended or taught in a Jewish school in another part of Paris. Jacob, a college student educated exclusively in contracted haredi institutions, summed this up as what he called the inevitable "proximity" among Jewish teachers, students, and parents. "The teacher is your niece's friend, or your aunt's friend, or your cousin's friend. . . . It was always like that—relationships in which you know someone who knows someone who knows your son's teacher."

This is not to say that the myriad of ethnic, historical, and class differences among French Jews had no resonance within day-school walls. In some ways, day schools were haunted by the forms of Jewishness that they inadvertently and intentionally excluded, potentially exploding any myth of homogenous Jewish universalism. Teachers were all too aware of the ethnic, class, and religious specificities of the children they taught. They chatted casually about the imagined differences between Ashkenazim and Sephardim and about the virtually total absence of the former from Jewish schools. As I noted in chapter 3, teachers also complained about students' behavioral problems and their lack of "culture," predicaments that they linked to class in general and parents' petit bourgeois materialism in particular.

Even the students recognized some diversity within their limited universe. Everyone knew where their parents and their grandparents were born, and they made jokes about the behavioral and even physical distinctions between and among Algerians, Moroccans, and Tunisians. There was thus at least some awareness of the historical and perhaps even cultural specificities that crosscut general beliefs about "Jewishness." In addition, day-school students knew that there was a wide spectrum of religious practice within and across schools. Debra, an eleventh-grader at Beit Sarah, asked me rhetorically how many of the girls in her class I thought were "religious." "Only two!" she cried. "There are sixteen girls in my class, and most of them wear pants and have boyfriends. At least three or four don't even do Shabbat. And I have my belly button pierced.[1] In the eighth and tenth grades there are even more with belly button piercings!" These hierarchies of religious observance sometimes led to the exiling of particular people or institutions from "Jewishness" entirely. As Jennifer noted, those who violate Jewish law may still be Jewish, but they are not appropriately Jewish. A Beit Sarah tenth-grader was less charitable. She explained that she could not attend Brith Abraham, which was much closer to her parents' house, because a coeducational school that made daily prayer optional could not really be "Jewish."

Particularly in a place like Brith Abraham, class distinctions were just as frequently a subject of conversation as religious discrepancies. Everyone knew who could afford to buy expensive clothes and who could not, and social groups tended to follow socioeconomic lines. Children from lower-middle-class families complained that wealthier students betrayed the "Jewish community" by refusing to speak to or go out with those who either could not or would not dress like them. They also frequently claimed different "values" than their wealthier counterparts. Mélanie, a tenth-grader, explained that, while "the school is full of spoiled kids who live off their parents' money," she, however, had learned "independence" from an older sister and worked to pay for her own clothes and Saturday night outings.

But these kinds of conversations about the national, religious, and class diversity within Jewishness rarely filtered into the messages about Jewishness conveyed through the social environment or classroom. In some ways, this was a conscious policy. During our first interview, the principal of Beit Sarah noted that while he "would be very happy to have an American Jew discuss Jewish life in America," he did not want his students exposed to the different kinds of Judaism that exist in the United States. "We try to give students a particular kind of education and a particular kind of relationship with Judaism. I don't want them to discover that there are other ways [of being Jewish] that might be better or might be worse, but would tempt them to stray from the path they are on and what they are learning."

Accordingly, school rules at least partially shielded students from the array of religious practices and ideological allegiances represented among Jewish faculty and staff. At Beit Sarah, all female teachers were required to wear skirts and modest tops, and all Jewish men were told to cover their heads. Similarly, at Brith Abraham male Jewish teachers were strongly encouraged to wear kippot like their students.[2] In both institutions, teachers who chose not to purchase kosher meals in the cafeteria ate in the teachers' lounge, out of student sight. Students were forbidden to bring nonkosher food to school. The few who did bring their own lunches were exiled to the hallways or courtyards—again out of sight of the majority eating in the cafeteria. In addition, some teachers had the impression that their classroom speech was policed by the administration. The English teacher regularly responsible for the class in which I taught Goldstein's text asked me never to present it again. She was worried the school director would be displeased by its portrayal of orthodox Jews—described as being an all-too-visible source of mainstream Jewish shame—and accuse her of undermining the school's mission (Goldstein 1994:205–207). This institutional insistence on homogeneity also extended into politics. A Beit Sarah history teacher was reprimanded for identifying Tel Aviv as the capital of Israel—a faux pas the principal insisted relied on concealing part of the "truth" and therefore equaled "telling a lie." Similarly, a history teacher at Brith Abraham told me that the principal had disciplined her for being too "Francophile" and insufficiently "Israelophile" in her classes. "Thinking is becoming a crime here," she whispered.

The occlusion of Jewish heterogeneity was also a by-product of the way religious practice was taught. Kodesh teachers came from a variety of ideologically distinct forms of orthodoxy: some were Hasidim, others Misnagdim (literally "opponents" of Hasidism), and still others "modern" orthodox. But they did not position themselves in relation to those distinct traditions. Instead, as we saw in chapter 4, they spoke in the name of a homogenized and rule-bound "Jewishness" that, occasionally, was not consistent across teachers and grades. Kodesh teachers not only effaced the existence of other (especially non-Halakhic) forms of Judaism, they also erased the historical and cultural particularities of their own practices. The "we" of Jewish schooling took little account of its primarily Sephardi audience and the influence of Ashkenazi forms of orthodoxy on day school religious instruction. On the rare occasions that kodesh teachers acknowledged that they were addressing Sephardim and not "Jews" generally, they reduced the differences between the two populations to minor variations in practice. In stark contrast to intra-adult discussions of the Ashkenazi-Sephardi divide, here the distinctions appeared meaningless, tiny flaws in an otherwise completely uniform set of global Jewish practices. A Beit Sarah kodesh teacher, for example, told students that while Ashkenazi women say a *brucha*, or blessing, over the *lulav* and the *etrog*, the palm fronds and Middle Eastern fruit that are at the center of the harvest festival of Succoth, Sephardi women do not. She also noted that Ashkenazi women say far more *bruchoth*, plural for brucha, than their Sephardi counterparts. But she neither offered nor was asked for an explanation of these diverging practices, thus implying that they were phenomenological and not linked to different conceptions of women's roles. Similarly, a kodesh teacher at Brith Abraham reduced divergent observances of *niddah*, or family purity laws, to virtually meaningless custom. She explained that the "only" difference between Ashkenazi and Sephardi practices had to do with the number of days between the end of a woman's period and authorized sexual relations. She offered no textual or ideological motivation for the divergent counting practices, nor did the students ask for any. She also encouraged students to observe the Ashkenazi ritual on the grounds that it was "simpler," when in fact it was more stringent.[3]

If the differences in practice tied to historical and ethnic specificities were occluded or dismissed as phenomenological, students' relatively homogenous socioeconomic status was assumed as a necessary condition of observant Jewishness.[4] For many kodesh teachers, God was the direct source of worldly wealth or poverty. And while relative wealth was not necessarily described in Protestant terms as a divine reward for good behavior—it could also be a test of faith—many of the religious practices kodesh teachers described as essential to "Jewish" observance required considerable disposable income. Teachers claimed that eating processed food not certified kosher by the Beit Din was just as bad as eating nonkosher meat. But instructors never discussed the vast differences in cost that made purchasing "listed" cans of string beans and sacks of flour—in addition to meat and milk products—a stretch for lower-income families.[5] Failing to exclusively eat listed items was instead associated with moral and even physical weakness that students should address through teshouva, or repentance, and "return" to full observance. Thus the lines between facility (you were hungry and the nonkosher candy was there) and necessity (buying unlisted canned vegetables as a way of making the purchase of kosher meat possible) became impossibly blurred. In the process, a social question about wealth and religious observance was reduced to an individualized issue of self-control. Similarly, in religious imaginaries, a kosher kitchen seemed to require two of everything—two refrigerators, two sinks, two ovens, two dishwashers—a prohibitively expensive proposition that only the wealthiest day school families might be able to afford (Jacobson 2006). But the pressure to do so was nonetheless significant. A Brith Abraham mother who was at the end of a home construction project described investing extremely heavily in the kitchen—which indeed had two of everything—a decision that meant furniture and finished bathrooms would have to wait. And as we saw in chapter 4, some kodesh teachers even described "Jewish" lifestyles in terms that indexed not only middle- to upper-middle-class incomes but also self-employment. Thus M. Attias argued that all Jews should negotiate their own work hours so as not to break the Sabbath (see chapter 4).

For many students, although certainly not all, these kinds of presentations and practices helped naturalize their own realities as comprising "Jewishness" in general. In the first place, students had trouble recognizing the Jewishness of those who did not share their ethnic particularities. For most students, the term "Ashkenazi" had no clear referent. The idea that I, like the vast majority of American Jews, did not have roots in North Africa made no sense to many of them. When I described myself as "Ashkenazi," students occasionally even asked whether that meant my family was from Morocco or from Tunisia. Jacob, a college student educated in a subsidized haredi Jewish school from kindergarten through twelfth grade, condensed the ways in which being a particular kind of Sephardi Jew with a particular familial history blurred into Jewishness writ large:

> There were only Jews in school. . . . I say that, and I remember that there was this one kid. In one of my classes I had a François Grunwald I can't imagine how that one was Jewish. But he drew really well, and he wanted to go to a school that required at least one year in private school before entry. And so he ended up *chez nous* [lit., in our house]. I never knew whether he was Jewish or not.
> Kimberly: Why didn't you think he was Jewish? . . . Why are you even asking yourself the question?
> Jacob: Because . . . because, I have to tell you—yes, it's really an important element—in my school 80 to 90 percent were Sephardi.
> Kimberly: From where?
> Jacob: Yes, it was very varied.
> Kimberly: Algeria, Tunisia, Morocco?
> Jacob: No, I don't know. They were Sephardi, 90 percent.
> Kimberly: So national origins weren't important?
> Jacob: No, not really. But there were always little things about the Moroccans, the Tunisians, because. . . .
> Kimberly: But not the Algerians?
> Jacob: No, not the Algerians.
> Kimberly: Was that because there weren't any?
> Jacob: Maybe there weren't any. Yes, certainly there were not. I don't know everything, but I know that those in my class were almost all Moroccans and Tunisians. Maybe there was an Algerian, I don't know. It didn't strike me at the time. But it was, you have to know it was a Jewish school in the 19th arrondissement, therefore . . . boys' private, religious school. . . . That means very focused on family, the rabbi, everyone knew one another.
> Kimberly: And he wasn't like everyone else?

> Jacob: Yes. . . . I think he did one year [at school]. There were little things. He was friends with everyone, but not more than that. Like I said, I got there in first grade and stayed until the bac[calauréat],[6] and I remained the guy who showed up in first grade and not in preschool. That means that a guy who only spends a year and stuff. . . . It's maybe that plus the fact that he had a different name.
> Kimberly: There weren't a lot of French names like his?
> Jacob: No. . . . There were a lot of Yonathans, Michaels, Davids, and Moshes. Even the last names were all similar. There were lots of Ben somethings and Cohens.

Since it seems highly unlikely that a non-Jew would have been allowed to enroll in a haredi institution, François Grunwald may very well have been from an Ashkenazi family. But that never occurred to Jacob. He simply assumed that his difference—he was not from a known family, did not reflect the established pattern of enrollment, had first and last names that differed from those of his classmates—meant non-Jewishness. As a result, Jacob never thought to question why, in his version of Jewishness, there were so few students named "François"—he just wondered why there might be any at all.

I heard virtually the same story from Jason and Joshua, both Brith Abraham seniors, about two black students—Salomé and Eric—who briefly attended sixth grade with them. Jason explained that when he first met them, "I asked myself questions. They are here, but they are black, and this is a Jewish school. But Salomé, I think she was a real black, I don't know." What does it mean to be a "real black"? I asked. "That means she is not Jewish," he explained. Joshua, who had previously insisted that Salomé was at least a "half-Jew" because her mother was Jewish and evidently white, clarified: "There were no signs of Jewishness." Again, I had to ask what that meant.

> Jason: In France, there are no black Jews.
> Joshua: Yes there are.
> Jason: I've never seen any!
> Joshua: We just do not notice them. . . . It's rare. I know that in the synagogue I sometimes go to, I have an uncle who officiates at this synagogue. And when we go to his synagogue, sometimes there are blacks who come. And it's true, it seems really strange.
> Jason: Saying "Shabbat Shalom" to a black, it's . . . .

Joshua: Yeah, when we see blacks we think non-Jews. We just do not
   have the experience.
       . . .
Jason: For us, blacks are like Arabs.
Joshua: They go together.
Jason: For us, it's the same thing. . . . There's a black, there's an Arab.
   . . . To explain, there's a word: *caillera* [*racaille*, or scum, inverted].
   For us, when you say "a group of scum," that means Arabs and
   blacks.

Joshua, who spent elementary school and part of middle school in
a public institution, knew there were black Jews in France. But some-
how their existence did not register—they were immediately visible
but as he said, "we just do not notice them," leaving him with insufficient experience to naturalize such a possibility. And while he insisted
that Salomé was Jewish over Jason's objections, she remained nonetheless a "half-Jew," a term that directly indexed quasi-biological notions
of "half-blood" and illicit intermixture. Jason, on the other hand, who
had always been in a Jewish school, could not even acknowledge the
possibility of black Jewishness. Even after Brith Abraham sanctioned
Salomé and Eric's Halakhic status by accepting them as students,
Jason still maintained that he had never seen a black Jew in France.[7] If
François Grunwald's name and whiteness exiled him to the category
"French," Jason suggested that dark skin left Salomé and Eric equally
non-Jewish, even "Arab." Jewishness thereby remained the exclusive
province of those most like Jason and Joshua.

Danger and Redemption: Israel at Brith Abraham

If Jewishness was "focalized" in day school contexts, stripped of the
complexities of history, geography, and class and reduced only to its
local incarnations, it was equally the object of "transvaluation." At
Brith Abraham, day schoolers were openly encouraged to project their
understandings of their own Jewishness onto Israel. The principal and
administrators at Brith Abraham were up-front about their commitment to promoting Israel as an alternative site of national identification for students. In my first meeting with one of the academic deans,

I asked about the school's educational goals. The dean replied: "We share the goals of *éducation nationale*: success on the bac[calauréat], integration into French society through employment. . . . We [also] try to bring students to practice and live their Judaism, hopefully through *aliyah* [emigration to Israel]. We recognize that there are contradictions between these two goals, but we try to avoid creating schizophrenic children." On another occasion, the principal went even further, suggesting that life in France was useful insofar as it pushed children closer to Israel. "Life in America," she added, "is too easy; who would leave a land of milk and honey to go to war? At least in France they [students] are uncomfortable; France is somewhere between the United States and Israel in terms of difficulty of life." She may have even encouraged students in their uncomfortable alienation from any sense of national community. When teachers asked her how they should respond to student fears and their stereotypes about "Arabs," the principal refused to even acknowledge the legitimacy of the question. Rather, she instructed teachers to "understand" adolescent anxieties and scolded those who wanted to offer a more intellectual approach to the problem. In other words, the students' alienation described in chapter 3 served a desired end, encouraging them to look for "home" elsewhere.

Where that elsewhere *should* lie was clearly indicated in every aspect of daily life at the schools. Political Zionism—associated with all Israeli governments since 1948—is premised on the idea that Jews everywhere form a single nation and that Israel, in either its theocratic biblical or quasi-secular modern form, is the sovereign state of that nation. The corollary of this premise is that all Jews will eventually "return" to Israel. They may do so of their own free will or they may be forced to flee untenable positions in the Diaspora. In either case, the promise implied in the hyphen between the Jewish nation and the Israeli state is inevitably slated to become a sociological reality. The "law of return," which allows any person defined as "Jewish" by the Israeli state to acquire citizenship, turns all Diasporic Jews into potential Israelis. As a result, the Israeli government often claims to speak for and represent the interests of Jews globally, regardless of whether they happen to already be Israeli citizens or not. Israeli Prime Minister Ariel Sharon's July 2004 call for all French Jews to make aliyah, although hardly appreciated by

French Jewish institutional elites, perfectly reflected this logic. As one of my adult informants noted, why should Sharon take less interest in the physical well-being of French Jews than the French foreign minister would take of French citizens vacationing in Israel?

This is precisely the message that Brith Abraham offered its students. In school decorations and celebrations, representations of Israel occupied the place that might have been reserved for French national imagery. A display of miniature plastic flags from around the world hung from the lunchroom rafters, but the tiny European, North American, and South American flags were dwarfed by the large Israeli flag, made of cloth, hanging in their midst. Similarly, while no classrooms had maps of either France or the European Union when I arrived,[8] most were equipped with borderless satellite maps of Israel that included portions of Lebanon, Syria, Jordan, and Egypt—a visual representation of the Israeli hard right's commitment to "Greater Israel," which includes the West Bank and Gaza Strip. Some classrooms also had panoramic photos of Jerusalem taken from the Mount of Olives, as if windows in the Parisian suburbs opened onto the Western Wall and the Dome of the Rock. Hebrew-language posters made by the KKL (*Keren Kayemeth Leisrael*), a charitable, quasi-governmental institution organized in 1901 to facilitate both the creation of a Jewish state and the "return" of Jews to Palestine, also covered many of the walls. One particularly prevalent series commemorated the 50th anniversary of Israeli independence with photos of all the country's prime ministers from 1948 to 1998. Even the student work on display focused on Israeli issues rather than their French equivalents. A student project that memorialized and honored Israeli soldiers captured by militant Palestinian groups had been left hanging for at least a year in a history classroom. The ongoing national conversation about two French journalists taken hostage in Iraq in August 2004 did not, however, echo in school classrooms.

If these kinds of images made Israel the only represented site for national identification, other practices encouraged students to think of their Jewishness as sufficient for rendering them Israeli. In the cafeteria, students waiting in line for food service faced a map of the Middle East labeled "David and Goliath." The map schematically represented the number of Israelis relative to the surrounding Muslim population. All

Israelis were depicted as Jewish soldiers—armed blue men marked with a Star of David—while by contrast the inhabitants of the surrounding states were shown as an indistinguishable group of armed green men wearing the Islamic crescent. In the case of Israel, such a depiction conflated religion with national identity. This map served to entirely efface Israel's considerable non-Jewish population, creating a mythical, militarized Jewish unity for an extremely diverse and politically cantankerous country. At the same time, it suggested that any Jew, anywhere in the world, could and perhaps should join this besieged army of blue men. Day school students were thus interpellated as potential Israelis. For the rest of the Middle East, this imagery similarly suggested that religion was the true basis for politics and collective action. Regardless of nationality, all Muslims were shown united in an overarching military goal—the elimination of Israel. In the process, the map elided the vast cultural, political, and social differences among putatively "Muslim" countries, suggesting that Turkey (which has a long-standing peace treaty with Israel) was indistinguishable from Syria.

School activities functioned similarly, turning school grounds into an extension of Tel Aviv. France admittedly has few national holidays that are collectively celebrated and even fewer that occur during the school year. Bastille Day on July 14, for example, falls just after the end of the term. But those that do fall within the school calendar, such as the *fête du huit mai* (the May 8 national holiday celebrating victory at the end of World War II), or the November 11 Armistice Day (commemorating the end of World War I), were not observed at the day schools. There were no associated lessons, no assemblies, and no special lunchtime observances for these holidays. In contrast, Israeli Independence Day, *Yom Ha'atzmaout*, completely transformed the normal school day. For Yom Ha'atzmaout, children and teachers were asked to come dressed in blue and white and to bring Israeli flags. Some students even dressed themselves in the Israeli flag, tying it around their waists as a skirt or shoulders as a cape. Common spaces were decorated with Israeli flags. The school served a special lunch of falafel, French fries (a student favorite), and pita; hired a DJ to play Israeli and American music while students ate; and suspended afternoon classes for a party in the courtyard. The party began with the whole school gathered around the principal for the singing of "Hatikvah," the Israeli national anthem. Throughout the afternoon students took turns waving a gigantic Israeli flag in the middle of the school courtyard.[9]

Brith Abraham students were also told that Jewish destiny lies in Israel. The school's approach to Jewish history was deeply Zionist, linking France in particular and Europe more generally with a narrative of Jewish martyrdom and suffering—what the school principal described in an assembly as "two thousand years of being persecuted and killed without cease." Jewish history was a required subject for all sixth- through ninth-graders at Brith Abraham. It met for three hours a week and was designed to be cumulative. The curriculum, which was probably at least partially paid for by the Jewish Agency, began and ended in Israel.[10] In the sixth grade, Jewish history started with a literal reading of the Bible's "historical" events, from the destruction of the First Temple to the definitive exile from Palestine that occurred around 70 C.E. In the seventh grade, students learned about Jewish life in France and medieval Europe more generally, a tale heavily sprinkled with discriminatory decrees, expulsion orders, and state-sanctioned pogroms. In the eighth grade, they moved to the rise of the nation-state and the emergence of modern anti-Semitism, particularly focusing on Jewish persecution in 19th-century Republican France. And in the ninth grade, they learned about the Holocaust, Zionism, and the creation of modern Israel.

This progression mobilizes a secularized version of a particular form of biblical exegesis that associates *galut*, or exile, with sin and suffering, and equates redemption with a "return" to Israel. It is a circular history that begins and ends in the same time/place. And it writes Jews who have remained in the Diaspora out of what is properly considered "Jewish" history entirely. During the school's observance of *Yom Ha'Shoah*, the Israeli day of remembrance for Holocaust victims, the principal summed up this understanding of history:

> It is wonderful to hear these young voices. [The fourth and fifth graders had just sung "Aveinu Malkeinu," Our Father, Our King, a prayer for divine forgiveness typically recited on Rosh Hashanah and Yom Kippur.] It is wonderful that we have returned to our land of Israel. But at what price? It is wonderful to hear the voices of these young people, but it comes after the terrible suffering and death of the Shoah. The terrible suffering of 2,000 years of exile and 2,000 years of

being persecuted and killed without cease. It comes as anti-Semitism raises its head again in France. We have noticed and appreciated the festivities held this year for the landing in Normandy in July 1944, for the liberation of Paris in August 1944. But I must note that for six months after the liberation of Paris, six long, devastating, and deadly months, the concentration camps continued to function, until 1945. And even worse, after the concentration camps closed came the death marches and the thousands lost in the death marches.

In this telling, there is little difference between occupied and liberated France—both were deadly for Jews. And the invocation of renewed anti-Semitism suggests that living in France continues to be a singularly risky proposition. Thus the "price" that Jews have paid for Israel is borne entirely by the past and present Diaspora. The principal made no mention of the ways in which Israelis themselves suffer for the continued existence of the Jewish state. There was no mention of Palestinian terrorism, not a word about the physical and psychological toll of a militarized society. Instead, it is those who remain in Europe who run all the risks.

There is undeniably considerable suffering in the history of Europe's Jews, and much of it was dwelled upon in Brith Abraham's Jewish history classes. One typical text, which was circulated as part of Mme. Amsallem's Jewish history class, described "the French" as the only population that responded "zealously" to a 13th-century papal order to destroy the Talmud, resulting in the public "execution" of the text by fire (Garson n.d.). The article ended with a note about the rapid deterioration of both Jewish learning and Jewish living conditions in Paris, resulting in the emigration of France's leading Torah scholars to "Eretz Yisrael," the Hebrew term for the biblical land of Israel. Mme. Amsallem who doubled as a state-paid history and art instructor, described such lessons as necessary correctives to French nationalist histories. In such histories, she noted, figures like Louis IX, the king responsible for the "zealous" execution of the papal order, were all too likely to be called "Saint" when they were, in fact, merciless killers of Jews. Even small victories were sometimes depicted as crushing defeats. Thus Mme. Amsallem claimed that a 9th-century decree granting freedom of religion and commerce to a rabbi and his grandson proved that Jews were "not men."[11] "Do you understand?" she asked her sixth-grade students. "You have to know that this only applies to two Jews. They are given privileges, but that is not a good thing. If they had been freemen, like most men, they would not have needed these privileges." The fact that neither she nor her students knew anything about life in 9th-century France, including what it might have meant to be a "freeman" or to have "rights," seemed totally irrelevant. Similarly, the lesson of the Dreyfus Affair was not that democratic rule and values triumphed over racialized military interests, but that Jews were "subhuman." M. Rosenblum, a twentysomething Jewish history teacher, told his ninth-grade class: "We've been talking about Jews becoming French and becoming citizens, and we've seen that it does not give them equal rights. . . . Anti-Semitism at the end of the 19th century makes life impossible outside a Jewish state. . . . Jews had believed that they became entirely men in the eyes of non-Jews. . . . They believed that, but they continued to be 'subhuman.' . . . They learned with bitterness that being citizens does not necessarily mean equality in a human sense."

Even when non-Jews were not slaughtering Jews, they were putting them under enormous pressure to convert or "assimilate," thus creating the conditions for what students and even some teachers considered a kind of treasonous self-hatred. Mme. Amsallem regularly described Jewish apostates as "wanting to kill their previous identity" and therefore as "extremely dangerous for Jews." In a summary of their discussions of 19th-century French Jews, M. Bensaïd—a state-paid French teacher as well as a Jewish history instructor—noted:

> We have above all seen examples of Jews who assimilated. The problem is that those who assimilate, they lose their religious identity because for them assimilating means putting aside their religious practices and identity. Sometimes they assimilate completely—they lose their identity; they change their name; they convert. . . . Integration in France, what is the cost? . . . It is paid at the expense of their identity and through the rejection of their religion.

The class responded with noisy disdain for those who made such compromises.

Teachers, particularly history teachers of all stripes, were often keenly aware that such flattened depictions of European Jewish life fueled rather than stymied student tendencies to *faire l'amalgame*, or conflate unlike things. After telling her ninth-grade class a transfigured version of Eleazar's martyrdom, a story in which a Jewish courtier commits suicide rather than fulfill his Christian king's order to convert, an Ashkenazi kodesh teacher explained that she did not typically indulge in such bleak tales. "I want to help students to get away from thinking of Jewish history as a series of massacres and oppressions. I do not want them to think of Judaism as a permanent condition of martyrdom, to think that they are always persecuted by others." Similarly, a state-paid history teacher told me that it was very difficult to teach the Holocaust to his day school students because of their curious mix of absolute ignorance and profound certainty. He tried to go beyond the state-mandated curriculum in order to talk to students about the emergence of murderous anti-Semitism and to contextualize the Jewish Holocaust within the larger bloodbath of World War II. In other words, he struggled to provide a historicized reading of an event that students thought needed no explanation. For them, Jews were simply fated to suffer at all times and in all places at non-Jewish hands. Mme. Haddad, a history and civic education teacher, became so frustrated with her seventh-graders' systematic conflations of the contemporary French context with the Holocaust that she began mocking them:

> Of course, of course, everyone knows that French society is particularly anti-Semitic. They [the French] are all rotten to the core. And we are all going to end up in crematoriums like in 1940. [Screaming now] Can you compare Kristallnacht with what you are experiencing? I'm not saying that anti-Semitism doesn't exist. But now, that a small problem like that [gestures] ends up in the mouths of our beloved students like that [gestures], I'm not convinced.[12]

These moments of specificity, however, swam in a vast sea of undifferentiated "Jewish" experience in which the Diasporic past and present slid inevitably backward and forward into the horror of the Holocaust. The arc of the Jewish history program lent itself to this, turning the Holocaust into both the end of European Jewish history and the logical climax of Brith Abraham's curriculum. Even state-paid history teachers sometimes played fast and loose with chronology and historical context. Mme. Amsallem thus seamlessly conflated the situation and sensibilities of contemporary French Jews with those expelled from 15th-century

Spain. She told her eighth-grade students that even though Spanish Jews were allowed to immigrate to Holland after 1492, they should not be "naïve" about what that meant:

> We [the Jews] are a rejected people, so we always have this thirst to be loved. As soon as something is not negative, we think that they [non-Jews] "love" us. France was the first country to give support to Israel. So Jews and Israelis said that France and de Gaulle *loved* us. But France just had economic interests and wanted to counter the USSR. But when this was no longer profitable, Jews decided that there was a great break in the "love story." . . . I don't mean to say that the Dutch are not nice, but don't fall into the trap. Jews were economically useful. And as long as the state thinks we are useful, we are respected. As soon as the Republic thinks it can pass them up, it's a different story.

The use of the term "Republic" in the last sentence seemed intentionally ambiguous, simultaneously referencing both the early modern Dutch government and the French Fifth Republic, which might also no longer have a "use" for its Jews.[13] If the past lived in the present, the modern horrors of the Holocaust could also be traced backward in time. By suggesting that 19th-century Jews were viewed as "subhuman," M. Rosenblum invoked one of those traces, projecting the outcome of Nazi propaganda and brutality back into the past. He immediately regretted this telescoping of history, adding: "Maybe I'm exaggerating a little," but a student had already taken up the chorus: "Yeah, they were treated like animals!"

In a school that primarily educates the children and grandchildren of North African immigrants, the absence of information about non-European Sephardim is striking. The editor of *L'Arche* magazine, Meïr Waintrater, explained early on in my fieldwork that while the history of North African Jews was necessarily part of the history of the Jews, it certainly could not be counted as "Jewish history." Mme. Amsallem echoed this, noting that she simply "did not have time" to talk about North African Jewry. "But," she added, "I try to make it very clear that those good Jews who were emancipated by the Crémieux Decree were terribly treated in the period before colonization. If the Jews from Morocco and Tunisia wanted French citizenship even when they couldn't have it, there had to be a reason." In other words, if Sephardim wanted

French protection despite France's considerable anti-Semitic record, things had to have been pretty awful for them. Their stories could thus be safely folded into the larger Zionist narrative about the inevitable pain and suffering associated with Diasporic life. Any differences from the European experience became mere phenomenology, not worth the time their study would have required in a Jewish history class.

But if, according to this view, the only historical Diaspora was European, Europe was stuck in a particular time: the period between 1933 and 1945. This turned all Jewish interactions with non-Jews into a prologue to genocide. It mattered little whether the non-Jew was Louis IX or Adolf Hitler; the means may have changed, but the goals remained the same. Thus, even after lessons in which time and place were crucial for the message being communicated, students could not see the significance or specificity of the historical context. For example, after a lecture given by Mme. Amsallem on why Roman persecution of Jews prior to the fall of the second temple was neither "anti-Semitic" nor "genocidal," one of her sixth-grade students confidently asserted: "Yeah, they [the Romans] wanted all the Jews to die!"

Europe, including France, was thus continuously invoked as a place where Jews suffered and died at the hands of non-Jews. But what was Israel? Despite the deeply Zionist arc to history at Brith Abraham, students were given very little information about the contemporary state of Israel's history, geography, politics, or demographics. Mme. Amsallem told me that after lecturing on Jews' continuous presence in Israel, the Balfour Declaration, and the 1948 Arab-Israeli war she barely had time to squeeze in basic information about the geography and government of Israel. "It's appalling how little these kids who go to Eilat [a coastal town on Israel's southernmost border known for attracting French tourists] every summer know; they have absolutely no sense of Israeli geography." A haredi kodesh teacher echoed this assessment of student ignorance. She noted that most students have some family members in Israel and many vacation there. But when they do so, they stay with family members in French-speaking enclaves like Eilat and Netanya,

> so they have no real idea of what happens in Israeli society more generally. They have no understanding of Israeli politics and seemingly no interest in it; they barely even know who the Israeli prime minister

is. Whatever vague notions they might have are quickly forced into a Manichaean opposition—"we" [Israelis/French Jews] are the good side; "they" [Palestinians/Muslims everywhere] are the bad side. As soon as you have a more nuanced position on Israel, they look at you and start to wonder whether you can really be a Jew.

Even when teachers attempted to address Israel-related issues that one might imagine as crucial to adolescent identity construction, students were not interested. M. Rosenblum's lectures on Zionism were almost entirely drowned out by his seventh-graders' noisy indifference.

This ironic disinterest seems crucial to the work of transvaluation, of projecting deracinated local dispositions and sensibilities onto distant peoples and spaces. In a sense, Israel has become a pure negative differential, defined less by what it was than what it was not. It was not an ethno-religiously mixed space, like France, but a homogenously Jewish one. It was not a site of Jewish persecution or suffering but a space of safety and security. If life in France appeared to demand assimilation, the adulteration of practice, and the dissolution of group boundaries, Israel came to look like an ideal "Jewish community": clearly bounded, biologically and socially self-perpetuating, and unified through relatively uncompromised religious activity. All of the visual props associated with Israel, from the David and Goliath poster with its neat rows of blue soldiers to the graffitied Israeli flags carved into student desks, became the ground onto which adolescents projected day-school social relations. They could imagine the day school's microcosm of (relatively) shared ethnicity, class, religious practice, and familial connections as the macrostructure of Israeli society. Israel, precisely because it remained largely unknown, was a blank canvas onto which this artificially Herderian community was projected as an eternal and essential Jewish truth.

Often inadvertently, teachers, some of whom did not necessarily share the administration's commitment to aliyah, confirmed this message. In a civic education class, Mme. Haddad told her students that France demanded compromises from people of all faiths; these compromises included respect for a strict separation of private belief from public action. For Jews, this made wearing a kippa in public places potentially offensive if not outright illegal. "What would an employer think?" Mme. Haddad asked her horrified students, many of whom were noisily insisting that the kippa was a religious "obligation."

> Mme. Haddad: He [the boss] is going to feel a little attacked. He's going to say, *oh la la*, this one wears a kippa every day. What's he going to do to me with his holidays. . . . Oh no, what if he's a fundamentalist? . . . Do you understand now when I see lots of young people in the 19th [arrondissement] going to synagogue, I see lots of young people wearing the kippa, and I don't think that's good!
>
> Female student [significantly misinterpreting the reason for Mme. Haddad's displeasure]: But Madame, we are surrounded by Jews. Nothing can happen to us!
>
> Mme. Haddad: So if nothing can happen to me, I can impose myself on others?! The religion is still. . . . No mademoiselle, either you decide to fit into the mold or you go to Israel.

Mme. Haddad also tried to convince her students that they did not *have* to leave France in order to remain authentic Jews. Wearing a kippa was not a religious obligation except when eating, she explained, making it possible to be a good Jew and a good French person. But no one found her assertions credible. "I'm trying to understand why we have to wear it all the time [in school]," one highly skeptical student noted. In other words, Mme. Haddad inadvertently reinforced the message that the "authentic" forms of Jewish practice cultivated in school could only be completely realized in Israel.

For many students, particularly those with little experience in Israel, these kinds of representations proved powerful. Aurélie, a middle school student who had recently transferred from a public institution to a school in the same network as Brith Abraham, explained that she could not wait to go to Israel with her class. It would be her first trip, and she was particularly excited about the possibility of seeing the "Wailing Wall," which she suggested symbolized the way in which Israel represents the "entire religion," and thus all Jews. This interest, she noted, was of relatively recent date:

> It's true that before I wasn't concerned [about Israel]. I didn't think about it. It didn't happen that everyone went to Israel, and I didn't think about whether I wanted to go. There were three or four people who were Jewish [in public school], so I didn't talk about it. . . .

I hadn't been to Israel even once, and their destination wasn't Israel. And we didn't talk about the land or religion. We didn't talk about Israel. And now, I talk about it much more often. All of my classes and everything about the religion makes Israel appear all the time.

Jennifer, an eleventh-grader who had attended a public middle school before enrolling in a more orthodox Parisian school and then finally in Brith Abraham, made a similar remark. She tied her growing interest in a potential future life in Israel to the nation-state's ubiquity in daily discourse at school: "The school is extremely Zionist, there is no question about that. . . . Three years ago it would never have occurred to me to be interested in making aliyah. But the teachers repeat that Israel is 'our land'; they organize trips to Israel. Everyone talks about it all the time. And so now I'm thinking about something that would never have occurred to me before."

The constant evocation of Israel as a foil for the Diasporic dangers of interethnic coexistence and assimilation encouraged Brith Abraham students to transpose their experience of day school "community" onto the Holy Land's empty sociological terrain. At Brith Abraham, the Diaspora became synonymous with Europe and social pathology: promiscuous intermixture, forced assimilation, and genocide. Israel, in turn, appeared as the antithesis of this dangerous universe and therefore as an extension of the school itself. From within school walls, the particularities of day school students could be imagined as the shared patrimony of an entire ethno-nation. This had as much to do with what students did *not* learn as with what they actually did.

Once and Future Israelis?: Beit Sarah

At Brith Abraham, the modern state of Israel was the end point of a secular narrative of Jewish suffering and redemption that served as a foil for the dangers of Diasporic life. Beit Sarah offered students no such story. But as the vignette with which this chapter opens suggests, Beit Sarah's students were no less committed to Israel as an "actual homeland" than their Brith Abraham counterparts. How and why?

Within the organized Parisian Jewish community, Beit Sarah had a reputation for being "anti-Zionist" or, at the very least, "a-Zionist."

While this designation hardly reflects a mainstream meaning of the term,[14] it does index haredi Judaism's discomfort with the secular messianism implicit in a Zionist vision of Jewish history. Traditional rabbinic Judaism links the end of galut to the coming of the Messiah, not to the 1948 Israeli declaration of independence. As Michael Rosenak notes in his study of "fundamentalist" education in Israel, "Haredim [may] differ in dress, read different . . . newspapers, and entertain diverse accommodations with the Zionists and their Hebrew-speaking culture. . . . But all haredim consider the State of Israel and its epoch to be a continuation of Galut, albeit in the Holy Land" (1993:381). Many haredi institutions therefore carefully distinguish between the "State of Israel" in its modern incarnation and Eretz Yisrael the divinely given land of Israel (Association des Directeurs d'Ecoles Juives de France 1978). To paraphrase M. Petit-Ohayon, the head of education at Fonds Social Juif Unifié (FSJU): for many "Torah-true" Jews, one makes aliyah to Eretz Yisrael, *not* to the State of Israel. This means settling in places like the ultrareligious Jerusalem enclave Mea Shearim; it does not mean moving to Tel Aviv or to any other "secular" city iconic of the modern nation-state.

It would, however, be hard to characterize the principal of Beit Sarah as indifferent to the modern State of Israel. His wife, children, and grandchildren all lived in Israel, and he fully intended to follow them upon retirement. He imagined his role as head of a religious school in France as a sacrifice, viewing his decision to move from Morocco to France in 1974 as a concession to divine will and the good of the Jewish people, not as a personal choice about national allegiance or lifestyle.[15] He even embraced many of the political positions typically associated with Zionism. I have already recounted his reprimand of the non-Jewish history teacher who identified Tel Aviv as the capital of Israel. He also chastised me for trying "to tell our students that French colonization was the same as Jewish colonization in Israel."[16] "We try," he continued,

> to teach our children that the "Occupied Territories" are not occupied, that it is not really colonization because there are Jews who still have land titles to houses that are 1,800 years old. We have always had

a connection to Israel. And that has nothing to do with the French who landed in North Africa like extraterrestrials.

Despite this, he did not imagine Israel as the only "natural" pole of national identification for his students. In conversations with me, he denounced the use of aliyah as a solution for anti-Semitism or Jewish political insecurity. He did not appreciate Ariel Sharon's infamous call for French Jews to emigrate en masse, noting that such talk undermined "community" attempts to rehabilitate the conservative French government. "I'm very worried about young people in Jewish schools of all persuasions," he told me. "They all want to go to Israel with their eyes closed; they are fleeing France. . . . They should be much more worried about the Arabs in Israel than the Arabs in France."[17] Instead, he suggested, aliyah should be motivated by religious conviction, by the desire to more fully live Judaism's 613 mitzvoth. Only such a motivation would ensure that those who go actually stay. This is a far cry from hope expressed by the principal of Brith Abraham that adolescent "discomfort" in France would result in a mass exodus for Israel.

This difference in perspective filtered into the kinds of representations of Israel present within school walls. Beit Sarah did not mark holidays like Yom Ha'atzmaout or Yom Ha'Shoah—quintessentially Israeli state constructs—with the pomp and circumstance prevalent at Brith Abraham.[18] Although Beit Sarah's principal objected to community reports that his institution "ignored" these festivities, I neither witnessed special activities nor heard about plans for them.[19] In addition, there were no political decorations at Beit Sarah: no posters of Israeli state officials, no advertisements for Israeli military service, no homage to captured Israeli soldiers, and no schematic (David-and-Goliath) depictions of the Palestinian-Israeli conflict. The events advertised within Beit Sarah's walls were largely limited to rabbinical conferences and Lubavitcher-organized religious observances, not the announcements for colloquia about Israeli politics and predicaments often posted at Brith Abraham. Some school administrators even tried to limit expressions of student Zionism. A Lubavitcher disciplinary dean upbraided a group of tenth-grade girls who had written "Israël, je t'aime" ("Israel, I love you") and "Israël vaincra" ("Israel will be victorious") in large colorful letters on their class blackboard. In response to the students' protestations "What's the problem, we are all Jews here!" the dean claimed that the message was a "provocation" and that it had to be erased immediately.

This does not mean that there were no representations of Israel at Beit Sarah. The school was filled with images that mapped biblical narratives onto the landscape of the modern Israeli state. The principal's office was lined with full-color photographs of Jerusalem. Just behind his desk was an enormous poster of the Kotel with the Dome of the Rock and the Mount of Olives in the background. Drawings of biblical sites, composed out of Hebrew text describing them, hung in the hallways. Classrooms contained the same borderless satellite maps of Israel found at Brith Abraham, but here they had been labeled with the Hebrew names of biblically significant cities. A number of blackboards had been adorned with full-color artists' renditions of the *Beit Hamigdash*, or Jerusalem Temple. While I was doing my research, a tenth-grade kodesh class worked for days creating a wall-sized paper replica of the Kotel. For the rest of the year it covered the entire wall in the back of their classroom.

Contrary to the representations of Israel at Brith Abraham, these images did not invite students to imagine themselves as potential Israelis—as the soldiers, students, and voters who make up a contemporary nation-state.[20] Instead, these visual props collapsed the distance between an imagined biblical past and the lived present in Israel. Biblical stories were literally mapped onto the topography of the Israeli nation-state, implying historical continuity through geography. These forms of mapping seemed to be a small-scale version of what Nadia Abu El-Haj (1998) found in Israeli museumology and archaeology. She notes that the display and naming practices used with Iron Age and Roman artifacts creates an aura of identity between the ancient Israelite world and contemporary Israeli Judaism. She writes:

> The whole practice of labeling objects "Arab," "Jewish," "Christian," or "Muslim," of naming a period "Israelite" instead of "Iron Age" or "Herodian" instead of "early Roman"—all names or "cultures" presumed to have a correspondence in particular contemporary groups of citizens, residents, and tourists . . . [conveys] the notion that the archaeological record contains the distinct heritages of what are iden-

tified as culturally, religiously, or nationally distinguishable modern population groups. (Abu El-Haj 1998:174)

She further argues that by integrating historical monuments into the newly rebuilt "Jewish quarter" in Jerusalem, archaeologists and urban planners ensured that "the present inhabits the past," creating a city "that has risen out of the ashes of a past whose tradition it perpetuates. These archaeological objects imbue the quarter's built environment with signs of a specific *historicity*, not just of a particular history" (Abu El-Haj 1998:178; emphasis in original).

The same might be said of Beit Sarah's various depictions of Israel. Within school walls, contemporary Jerusalem was collapsed into the city ruled by David and Solomon; the constant juxtaposition of models of the beit hamigdash and the Western Wall created a visible, tangible connection between the two. On classroom satellite maps, Tel Aviv's central bus station and "Abraham's grave" existed on the same plane, making it reasonable to talk about the number of kilometers between the two rather than the historical and ontological wedge that separates such distinct objects. In addition, the presence of the "past and the present in the present" flattened differences between historical and contemporary inhabitants (Bloch 1977). Biblical Jews became indistinguishable from contemporary Israelis, who were thought to have inherited both a sacred geography and an unchanging set of practices from their ancestors.

This aura of unbroken continuity, if not identity, between the biblical past and the Israeli present was reinforced by the particular way in which Hebrew was used at Beit Sarah. At Brith Abraham, Hebrew writing was relatively rare, a fairly conspicuous absence in a Zionist school.[21] At Beit Sarah, in contrast, virtually all of the visible text was in Hebrew. On the first floor, the doorpost leading into the restroom located just to the right of the school entrance bore a sign entirely in Hebrew, reminding students of the appropriate prayers associated with going to the bathroom and washing up. In the main staircase leading from the first to the second floors, five separate images of books depicted the five books of the Torah—*beresheit, shemos, vayikra, bamidbar, devarim.* On the third floor, most of one wall was covered by a student-made poster illustrating some of the forbidden forms of work on Shabbat, with the Hebrew legend "Forbidden: Respect Shabbat!" Another student poster, a huge drawing of lips with a shushing finger, warned students about *lashona hara*, or unkind speech. The principal's office was surrounded by prints with advice about proper behavior. Student artwork recounting dinnim (religious obligations), biblical events, and key legal texts, all in Hebrew, hung in classrooms. In fact, there was so much Hebrew text that I assumed, upon first visiting the school, that the language of daily interaction if not instruction would be Hebrew. I was stunned when a number of students explained that they had very rudimentary Hebrew skills.

This admission points to an important fact: Beit Sarah's engagement with Hebrew remained primarily script-based. As at Brith Abraham, only students with immediate family members who were born or raised in Israel spoke anything approaching fluent Hebrew.[22] And although students spoke of Hebrew as "their" language, they were seldom called on to understand it orally or speak it. When an ultra-orthodox Israeli rabbi came to address the students, it would have been unthinkable not to simultaneously translate his remarks into French. Modern Hebrew classes, like those at Brith Abraham, were optional. Even in the advanced Hebrew classes taught primarily by Israelis, the instruction was often given in French; grammatical rules, difficult passages, and homework assignments were all explained in the students' mother tongue. And although students were obviously encouraged to respond to Hebrew questions in Hebrew, many resorted to French.

Students were thus invited to take modern Hebrew, with fairly paltry results. But they were *required* to sit through extensive instruction in biblical Hebrew. They started learning the Hebrew alphabet and the recitation of daily prayers at the beginning of elementary school. By high school, they were expected to be able to read and translate the daily liturgy, the Torah, and some commentaries (particularly Rashi) with relative ease. Kodesh tests included untranslated passages from the Bible or Mishnah that students were expected to explain. Although students responded to these questions in French, they could not do so if they had not understood the original text.[23]

What emerged from this focus on textual literacy? As noted in the last chapter, recent literature on Jewish and Muslim religious education emphasizes the ways in which texts and textual literacy are being elevated over and against lived practice (El-Or 1994; Friedman 1987; Hefner 2007; Jacobson 2006; Soloveitchik 1994). Menachem Friedman (1987) and Hayim Soloveitchik (1994), for example, discuss the ways in which yeshiva-style learning is being mobilized against the sedimented traditions of even highly observant families, in part because all contemporary practices are viewed as tainted by assimilation and compromise. At the same time, the bar for minimally acceptable practice has risen considerably and rapidly, transforming the meaning and content of religious orthodoxy from one generation to the next (Hefner 2007; Soloveitchik 1994). This makes very particular notions of religious authenticity crucial and widespread. It turns traditional family practices into textually unfounded "superstitions," or even worse, syncretisms, and encourages the grounding of all action in the seemingly ancient and static written word. So, in a sense, recapturing universal Jewish "authenticity" requires a rupture with what may very well be acknowledged as immediate ancestral tradition. And very often this means abandoning Sephardi practices—everything from lentils to liturgy—for seemingly more rigorous text-based Ashkenazi alternatives. This is precisely what Shari Jacobson (2006) found among newly ultra-orthodox Sephardi women in Argentina. She notes:

> A refrain that Argentine Jewish women of Syrian descent assimilated and repeated is that Middle Eastern Judaism is like a family recipe: It has been passed from generation to generation and modified at each step along the way. As a result, it is no longer in keeping with the "authentic" form of Judaism that was handed by God to Moses on Mount Sinai. Paradoxically, by virtue of the allegedly modern nature of Europe and the assumed rationality of its peoples, haredi Judaism is reliably authentic. (2006:340)

All of these observations apply to education at Beit Sarah and, to a lesser extent, to Brith Abraham. Students were encouraged to cure themselves and their parents of heterodox practices. As a result, students routinely characterized themselves as "not really religious," despite relatively high levels of Sabbath and kashrut observance. When I asked why they did not consider the significant practical commitments they already engaged in as evidence of religiosity, they cited injunctions that they or family members continued to violate: wearing pants outside school, eating on minor Jewish fast days, dating boys, having mothers who did not cover their heads.[24] In addition, where even ultra-orthodox yeshiva learning is dialectical, dwelling on disagreement among rabbinic commentators, religious instruction at Beit Sarah offered students a single, authoritative interpretation as unchanging "divine law." This privileging of a particular, maximally restrictive legal interpretation significantly narrowed the bounds of acceptable Jewishness, potentially alienating students from alternative (even religious) conceptions of Jewish community. This was, at least in part, why students at Beit Sarah had trouble imagining anything less than ultra-orthodoxy as "real" Jewishness. And most importantly for my argument here, locating religious authenticity and authority in a static vision of text-based "law" laid the ground for projections of Jewish homogeneity across space and time. It meant that Jews at great social, temporal, or geographical distances—those whose lived practices were crucially *not* known—could be comfortably imagined as similar. Local particularisms thus incarnated authentic Jewish unity and community, but those particularisms were imagined as transcending regional or national boundaries.

In some ways, this is also what the focus on Hebrew as a written language accomplished. Whether or not students actually ended up literate in biblical Hebrew—and from my observations it appears that many did not—they were projected into what Benedict Anderson has called a "sacred silent language" community (1991:14). This kind of community closes the distance between geographically disparate groups—all of which are presumed to read and write the same language—and between the past and the present. In such a community, all Jews can theoretically communicate with one another across space and time, creating commensurability across uneven cultural and historical terrain. In addition, local use of a medium imagined as universally Jewish helps turn any evocation into a token of the larger type, and vice versa. In other words, by reading and writing biblical Hebrew, French Sephardim became archetypal "Jews" while simultaneously "Jewishness" became what French Sephardim did. This is itself a moment of both focalization and transvaluation. As Anderson has noted with respect to the use of Latin during the medieval period: "However vast Christendom might be . . . it manifested itself *variously* to particular Swabian or Andalusian communities as replications of themselves.

Figuring the Virgin Mary with 'Semitic' features or 'first-century' costumes . . . was unimaginable" (1991:23).

At the same time, the privileging of an exclusively written language avoided a central problem created by the intimate association of Hebrew with Jewishness. Since school-aged French children must also be taught to read (although not speak) French, the foregrounding of Hebrew literacy hid the contingent rather than essential relationship between language and being. This helps explain why children who could not and might never speak Hebrew nonetheless insisted that it was "their" language. It also ensured that there were no embarrassing disjunctures in pronunciation, vocabulary, or syntax that orality would have highlighted; this leveled distinctions between "native" speakers and those attempting to acquire language skills that they "should" have (always, already) possessed. Furthermore, the very fixity of the language used in sacred texts created an aura of absolute continuity with Jewish "forefathers," the biblical figures who were imagined to have written, worked, and prayed with the words recorded in the Torah. Beit Sarah's students reproduced that world in part through their own prayers and continuous engagement with sacred texts. This scriptural engagement with biblical Hebrew blasted Jewishness out of any kind of local or historical context, creating the illusion of undifferentiated experience and practice across time and place.

Beit Sarah's approach to Jewish history reinforced the ahistorical vision of Jewishness inscribed in the school's representational practices. During my fieldwork, Beit Sarah offered no Jewish history classes.[25] Given everything just described, this was not a surprise. Yosef Yerushalmi (1996) has suggested that while the Bible itself is a profoundly historical text, carefully distinguishing between times and places and foregrounding man's actions as the medium through which God becomes known in the world, later rabbinic texts are not. The *aggadah* or homiletic stories, laws, and commentaries found in the Talmud

> seem to play with Time as with an accordion, expanding and collapsing it at will. . . . In the world of aggadah Adam can instruct his son Seth in the Torah, Shem and Eber establish a house of study, the patriarchs institute the three daily prayer-services of normative Jewish liturgy, Og, King of Bashan, is present at Isaac's circumcision, and Noah prophesies the translation of the Bible into Greek. (ibid.:17)

In other words, the rabbinic compilers and writers of oral law were more interested in biblical hermeneutics than history. They also may have viewed the events and changes of their own period, almost none of which were recorded or commented upon, as so much "shifting sand," legible only with respect to the larger lessons of biblical history. In this reading, Jewish history is cyclic, a dialectic of Jewish sin and redemption, so concrete historical events are simply a replay, with slightly different details, of what came before (ibid.:24). Yerushalmi suggests:

> In its ensemble the Biblical record seemed capable of illuminating every further historical contingency. No fundamentally new conception of history had to be forged to accommodate Rome, or, for that matter, any of the other world empires that would arise subsequently. The catastrophe of the year 70 C.E. [the destruction of the Second Temple] was due, like that of 586 B.C.E. [the destruction of the First Temple], to sin, although the rabbis were well aware that the nature of the sin had changed and was no longer one of idolatry. (ibid.:22)

From such a perspective, teaching "Jewish history" as if it were something distinct from the biblical narratives that are part and parcel of instruction in Torah observance might seem pointless if not sacrilegious. In addition, as we have seen, the kind of Jewish history classes the Jewish Agency was willing to fund emphasized a secular teleology that explained Jewish suffering not through sin but due to national dispersion. Although the specificities of Jewish experience in a variety of Diasporic contexts are largely irrelevant to this story, a narrative of post-Exilic Jewish history is critical. For a community unified through biblical Hebrew, this is not the case. The important underlying structure of Jewish identity and history remains unchanged inside and outside Israel. Individuals may come and go, but categories, roles, and motivations remain the same, established by God's enduring relationship with Israel and played out through contemporary events.

These were precisely the terms in which kodesh teachers talked about the relationship between the biblical past and the present. M. Attias, one of a small handful of male religion instructors at Beit Sarah, told his seventh-grade class that giving a child a biblical name had a direct impact on his or her behavior. "If you have the name of someone who behaved badly in the Torah, it can make the child behave badly. Giving the name of someone who was good does the opposite. But I'm sure your parents only gave you good names!" Here, there was no historical logic at all, no cause-and-effect relationship between the behavior of King David and the comportment of little David from Sarcelles. The two, as Anderson has noted in another context, are related only vertically, through a divine plan that underwrites all observable action (1991:23–24). Similarly, Mme. Benayoun (see chapter 4) taught students about the sacrificial cult using the present tense, prompting a surreal exchange about what kinds of Temple offerings students could and could not eat. Not one of Mme. Benayoun's usually skeptical students seemed to think it was worth mentioning that the Temple no longer existed and therefore sacrifices were no longer made. In other words, kodesh classes taught children in a myriad of small ways that the events recorded in the Bible were not safely exiled to the past; they remained the prototype for what occurred and reoccurred cyclically in the present.[26]

Within this conception of history, not only did the play remain the same but the players did as well. When Yasser Arafat, the former president of the Palestinian Authority, lay dying in a French military hospital in the fall of 2004, Mme. Benayoun encouraged students to see a Haftorah portion from the Book of Samuel as a blueprint for how the Israelis should react to the situation. In the story, the Philistines launch a surprise attack on the Israelis as the Israelite High Priest Eli lies dying, a move that allows them to capture the Ark of the Covenant. For Mme. Benayoun, this story was a mirror image of the contemporary Israeli predicament, suggesting that the Israelis would be victorious if they launched a surprise attack on Palestinians.[27] This kind of parallel clearly emphasized the identity of, on the one hand, biblical Israelites and Jewish Israelis and, on the other, biblical "Philistines" and Palestinians.[28] The two groups were mortally opposed to one another in the past, fighting over the right to occupy and rule the biblical land of Israel, a situation that simply continued in the present.[29] In addition, the moral standing of both groups' claims had not changed. Although the Israelites lost the battle against the Philistines, largely as punishment for the sins of Eli's sons, they ultimately won the war: God made continued possession of the Ark deadly for the Philistines. God always has and therefore—in the long run—always will honor his promises to Jews.

Mme. Benayoun's lesson about the Book of Samuel was not an unusual one. Mlle. Chicheportiche—the teacher who refused to eat or drink with non-Jews (see Chapter 4)—also projected contemporary ethno-cultural categories into the past. Where Mme. Benayoun linked Palestinians to Philistines, Mlle. Chicheportiche conflated all "Arabs" with the descendents of Ishmael. In the biblical story of Ishmael's exile, God intervened to prevent the death of the young boy in the desert. God also promised to turn him into a "great nation"; the biblical passage ends with an image of Ishmael as a mounted, skilled hunter. After reading that description, Mlle. Chicheportiche exclaimed: "Ahh, it's characteristic of the Arab nation, the cavalier on his horse, the jihad, to conquer the world. It's really him." For Mlle. Chicheportiche, by the end of this short story Ishmael is already "the" Muslim Arab whose essential character traits will remain unchanged throughout history. She went on to note that Ishmael's name, which is the future tense of the Hebrew word *shema*, or to hear,

> means that the Arab nation will make *teshouva* [will repent]. . . . At the end of time it will go back to *HaShem*. It would be nice if it happened already. . . . I'm going to tell you now, it's personal, but it would have been better if he [Abraham] had sent him [Ishmael] elsewhere or kept him at his house; we would not have the problems that we have today![30]

If Ishmael stood for all Muslim "Arabs" across time and space, the "we" shifted between the group of French Jewish adolescents gathered in the room, the Jews of the biblical text, and "Jews" globally. Similarly, Mlle. Chicheportiche never specified the "problems" created by Ishmael's descendants, allowing students to slip between their experiences with and fears about "Arab" anti-Semitism and the Israeli-Palestinian conflict, with its defining "Jewish"/"Arab" opposition. By suggesting that these historically, geographically, and sociologically distinct "problems" were rooted in the same biblical narrative, Mlle. Chicheportiche made them appear interchangeable—so that they seemed to be emanations of a single underlying cause. The slippery "we" reinforced this conflation, likening French Jewish and Israeli experiences ontologically and epistemologically.

The text-centered projections offered by Mme. Benayoun and Mlle. Chicheportiche collapsed space and time, linking students to an ancient, ethnic story played out and replayed until the divinely ordained end of the world. In this story, students were not modern Israelis, but Israelites expected to faithfully reproduce a body of Jewish practice that had remained unchanged (despite massive changes) since biblical times. In some ways, this vision of unchanging Jewish community rendered place irrelevant in a way that would have been entirely alien to Brith Abraham's Zionist account of Jewish history. But at the same time, it reinscribed biblical land and therefore the contemporary State of Israel as the source of authentic Jewish practice. Whether or not they imagined contemporary Israelis in general as good Jews, Beit Sarah's kodesh teachers linked Jewishness to the social and religious geography of the contemporary Israeli nation-state, vitiating the traditional haredi distinction between "Eretz" and the modern State of Israel. As the principal of Beit Ya'acov (somewhat shockingly) noted: "At least if the students go to college in Israel, and they start to mess around with girls, they will be *Jewish* girls."

Once again, then, we have arrived at a vision of a homogenous ethno-religious community that is engaged in eminently familiar practices and incarnated in a particular place. This in-and-of-itself is a definition of ethno-nationalism, one that takes the model of the immediate school "family" and projects it onto Jewishness writ large. The collapse of general and particular Jewishness becomes most evident when this kind of community model gets challenged—particularly in Israel. This became clear in discussions I had with Beit Sarah tenth-graders who were crazy about Ne'hama Kramer's novel *Un cri sans réponse* (A Cry in the Dark). The book is a hysterical warning about the ways in which the Jewish nation-state is being biologically and spiritually compromised by the acceptance of non-Halakhic Jews. The culprits are "American rabbis" who will convert anyone for money; and the danger is that some of these "false" Jews may even act like real ones, thus making their detection almost impossible and the damage inflicted on "pure" Jewish lineages incalculable. The book therefore makes it clear that these are Jews "in name only," and they are no more welcome in the Jewish state than are Arab Muslims, who are more obvious and therefore less dangerous. The resonance with Nazi versions of the idealized Herderian community is striking, as was students' complete comfort with what seemed to be transparent racism. When Mme. Benayoun overheard us talking about the book, she added her own ringing endorsement: it was really a beautiful story with such an important message.

In a different way, other students expressed similar sentiments about the perils of imagined intermixture in Israel, *the* site of Jewish purity and particularity. Laure, a twelfth-grader, told me that she thought it was awful when people violated Jewish law in Israel, for example, by eating nonkosher food, because it rendered the "pure" land of Israel "impure." She added that she thought Israel should "limit the number of people who could move there. . . . There are more and more non-Jewish immigrants, particularly the Russians; and they shouldn't be allowed to be there." When I said that I thought most of the recent Russian immigrants identified as Jews, she retorted: "I've been to Israel a few times and seen them. They eat nonkosher food and try to impose their way of life on Israel. That should not be allowed because Israel is special and different. . . . They are corrupting Israel's culture!" For Laure, Russian Jews, whose culinary habits, (lack of) religious observance, and genealogies are deeply inflected by their communist past, do not register with Laure as "real" Jews. They therefore should not be allowed to "corrupt" Israel's imagined homogeneity. In other words, students expressed discomfort about differences in Jewish being (Kramer's argument about practicing Jews who are not really Jewish) and Jewish becoming (divergent versions of Jewish practice that would "corrupt" the imagined purity and homogeneity of authentic Judaism), instead invoking a fantasy of absolute identity in both essence and practice.

The American Dream?

If these narratives about Jewish being and belonging were, at least in part, driven by a discomfort with anything other than a primordialist conception of community, where did the United States fit in? At

Brith Abraham in particular students swamped me with requests for information about American universities and advice about admissions. Eager to earn my keep, I even proposed hosting an informational meeting for parents about the structure of the American university system, the application process, and tuition costs. In retrospect, it is not surprising that the principal rejected the proposal immediately, noting that she had no interest in "promoting aliyah to America." But even students who thought the entire Diaspora would ultimately "have to" move to Israel fantasized about life in America.

Given the constructions of authentic Jewishness as an ideal Herderian community, this seems counterintuitive. The United States is known in France as the birthplace of multiculturalism, affirmative action, and *communautarisme*, a word that implies the rancorous juxtaposition of mutually exclusive ethnic groups. This is the antithesis of many students' visions of and desires for Israel, which were rooted in the very real homogeneity of day schoolers' histories and dispositions. So what made "America" appealing?

In part, student fantasies about America were inseparable from popular-culture representations that have long led people to risk everything for a "better life" in the United States. In the television shows students watched, the movies they saw, and the songs they listened to, America appeared to be peopled with the beautiful, the happy, and the successful. Girls in particular always wanted to know which "stars" I had met or knew, and seemed not to believe the negative answer I always gave. Whenever I told students that I was American, they invariably sighed "*chomet!*" a slang word that literally means "mean" or "bad" but expresses admiration. It gradually became clear that for them, the "United States" equaled New York or Hollywood, cities whose streets were thought to teem with the rich, friendly, and famous.

But there also were specifically Jewish reasons that students dreamt of a future in the United States. To some extent, many students ethnicized America itself. For them, America *was* Jewish. A group of tenth-grade girls at Beit Sarah told me that they were sure their knowledge of Hebrew, which was better than their command of English, would allow them to work and live in the United States. Seventh-graders at Brith Abraham explained to me that what was beautiful about America was the way Jews literally could wear their identities on their sleeves. When I asked them to explain what that meant, many students painted America in the colors of their own imaginary: it was awash in identically dressed Jews; it had no anti-Semitism, or at least no worrisome anti-Semitism; and there were no "Arabs." This Judaizing of America was certainly tied to the United States' very public support of Israeli political objectives. But it was also tied to the way students had come to understand the relationship between class and Jewishness. Many students associated America with liberal capitalism and therefore, given the primarily liberal professions of their parents, with Jewishness. They denounced the French welfare state for cultivating dependence and sanctioning poverty and noted that America's laissez-faire system rewarded hard work and celebrated economic success—traits they also associated with Jewishness. Thus, while they knew that "making it" was a riskier business in America than in France, they nonetheless thought they would succeed. One high school student explained:

> We [Jews] are not viewed as noxious over there because it's a capitalist economy. . . . Jews are relatively rich in the U.S., and [President George W.] Bush's politics protect the rich. So it's good for Jews because over there Jews make lots of money. . . . [L]et's say that earning lots of money in France, let's say we [Jews] are critiqued. . . . Everything is related to money. That's where anti-Semitism develops. . . . The hatred for Jews is jealousy.

In other words, American "capitalism" is inherently more accepting of Jews in general because it favors the rich, and Jews are rich or potentially rich—even when those who were not particularly wealthy told the story.[31]

Even when American political economy was not conflated with Jewishness, American *communautarisme* seemed to promise autonomous and protected spaces for ethnic Jewish life. The concept conjures up images of strife-torn, deeply segregated, politically dysfunctional societies for most mainstream French people. But for some Jewish adolescents, it became the condition of possibility for authentic Jewish life. Inadvertently, France's nationalist secular curriculum may have emphasized this. In a range of contexts, textbooks and lessons highlighted the American tendency toward "ghettoization." Tenth-grade English textbooks used at Beit Sarah included a number of stories about the ghettoization of blacks in American (and, to a lesser extent, British) inner cities. Similarly, Brith Abraham's sixth-grade English class read a French novel about Jews in the American South that dwelled on the social barriers to intercourse across religion and race. Throughout high school, history, economics, and civic education classes repeated the same theme, dwelling on French national solidarity versus the fractal, ethnicized, and economically stratified ties that bind Americans. Although these references were intended to laud France's "race-blind" Republican history, the effect seemed to be somewhat the opposite. American ethnic enclaves may have appealed to many day school students, allowing them to think of American Jews as inhabiting a socially legitimated, quasi-self-sufficient world that did not necessarily include non-Jews.

Disrupting Transvaluation and Focalization

Regardless of the specific mechanisms involved, the foundation for the kind of focalization and transvaluation that occurred in day schools was the appearance of Jewish homogeneity. It was this homogeneity that facilitated the transformation of "me" into "we" and then the projection of that "we" onto spaces—primarily Israel and, to a lesser extent, the United States—that could be imagined as sustaining Herderian conceptions of community (Comaroff and Comaroff 2000). When this façade of homogenous Jewishness cracked, even slightly, social and moral community built on heterogeneity seemed to become possible for the first time. This, in turn, made "Frenchness" thinkable. Jacob, a college student who had spent 13 years in a contracted Parisian day school, told me that he first discovered that he was "French" when he joined the staunchly Republican UEJF (Union des Etudiants Juifs de France) at his public university. For the first time in his life, he noted, he met foreign Jews who helped him understand how much the way he viewed the world was "French." Just as significantly in his telling, he also met French Jews who did not share his (Tunisian) background, his degree of religiosity, or his social and political views. He repeatedly emphasized that for him, his "phase of integration . . . into French identity" happened (and, he believed, only could happen) from within a "Jewish milieu," but not in a Jewish school:

> I came from an environment where I was surrounded by . . . Jews who were like me. Not just because they were Jewish, but because they were exactly like me—from the 19th arrondissement, Moroccan or Tunisian, *chal* [a term that refers to a particular Jewish sartorial code, see chapter 6], not serious. . . . I never even got to meet a Jew who was a bit different from me. . . . At the UEJF, I met people from *Provence*, Jews from Provence. I met Jews who felt a whole lot more French than I did . . . I didn't feel French. . . . No, that's not quite right. I felt French, but I feel a lot more French now.

In a far less conscious way, Marion, a Brith Abraham ninth-grader, was also forced to recognize internal Jewish difference and therefore her Frenchness. While on the bus riding home from school, she showed me pictures of her most recent Israeli vacation, stopping at the photo of an adolescent boy. This was before he was beaten so badly that he had to spend the rest of the summer in the hospital, she told me. "By whom?" I asked. "By Israelis," she answered. "What?" I asked, convinced I had not understood. In response, she calmly noted: "Everyone knows about it. They look for French people to beat up because they think the French are messing up the country, but it's not true. . . . I know they don't want to beat me up because it's me, it's just because of the French thing." While offering an inelegant explanation for obvious, and unfortunately violent, intra-Jewish difference, Marion was suddenly "French." At the very site where Jewishness most clearly determines national identity, she was confronted with evidently salient national distinctions within Jewishness. Suddenly, shared Jewishness did not constitute sufficient ground for being "Israeli" or welcomed in Israel. In fact, it was quite the opposite. This certainly did not render Jewishness meaningless for Marion; she went on to explain that she wasn't afraid of the Israelis because she "knew" them, in contrast to the incomprehensibly violent "Arabs" in France. But the classification of French Jews as first and foremost "French" nonetheless produced some awareness of "the French thing" and therefore of the difficulty of sustaining the myth of absolute Jewish identity.

Marion's experience in Israel was unique only for its violence. Other Brith Abraham and Beit Sarah students who had spent considerable time in Israel sometimes confessed their discomfort with its ways and people. Some, like Laure, articulated this through the language of an ideal Herderian community. But others paid more attention to its implications for their own conceptions of community. Quietly, often when no one else was around, a handful noted that they never quite felt "at home" in Israel. Others (sometimes quite reluctantly) admitted that Israeli Jewishness was very different from their own assumptions and practices. Diana, a very observant twelfth-grader at Beit Sarah, told me: "I love Israel; I have a fabulous time when I'm there; and I would really like to move there. What is so nice is that I know everyone in Israel is just like me!" When I asked whether there was anything about Israeli customs or religious practices that she found surprising or alienating, she asked for clarification of the question: "I don't really speak enough Hebrew yet, but that's never bothered me. But I don't understand the question about culture; if we are all Jewish, we all have the same culture." I asked if she would be comfortable marrying an Israeli rather than a French Jew, who would be more likely to share her upbringing and experiences. "No," she backtracked, "I would rather marry a French Jew and go live with him in Israel." Even Mlle. Chicheportiche indirectly warned students not to assume that all Israelis were just like them. In a conversation about proper kashrut observance, she made fun of girls who thought all restaurants in Israel were by definition kosher.

Conclusion

Despite Brith Abraham's and Beit Sarah's different ideological orientations toward Zionism, students in both schools understood Jewishness as Israeliness; Israel, in turn, was imagined as an ethnically, culturally, and religiously homogenous community tied to the territory associated with the modern Middle Eastern state. At Brith Abraham, the work of narrowing the content of Judaism while projecting Jewish community outside of France relied on two aspects of everyday school life: the centrality of post-1948 Israel and the emptiness of the national category itself. At Beit Sarah, a similar form of focalization and transvaluation happened through the collapse of contemporary, homogenized, text-based religious practice into the unknown rituals and routines of biblical Israelites. In both cases, these projections relied as much on what students did not learn—about internal Jewish difference, about the modern Israeli nation-state, about the impossibility of a static Jewishness that transcends time and space—as on what they did. The heady combination of Israel's (variously incarnated) ubiquity and students' profound ignorance made it possible for adolescents to project their very local ways of being onto Jewishness-cum-Israeliness writ large. And it was only through confrontation with Jewish difference that day-school visions of Jewishness as a territorially grounded, culturally homogenous Herderian community were disrupted. How, then, did day school students cope with these kinds of disruptions in the world outside school walls?

October 27, 2004. I spent the morning in a sixth-grade Jewish history class at Brith Abraham. Mme. Amsallem, who had been running late, asked me to talk to the students about American Jews. The students envied my luck at coming from a place where they imagined there was no anti-Semitism and Jews could literally wear their identity on their sleeves. I thought they were confusing the United States with Crown Heights, in New York City, so I insisted that most U.S. Jews were not ultra-orthodox and, therefore, were indistinguishable from non-Jews. "That isn't true," one of the girls shot back, "you can always tell if someone's Jewish because of the *tête juive*" (which literally means "Jewish head"). Her classmates overwhelmingly agreed.

The teacher, half-listening while preparing her lesson, suddenly entered the conversation. A self-identified Ashkenazi Jew and the child of Holocaust survivors, she angrily denounced any attempt to link Jewishness to physical appearance as racist, even when clothing provided the identifying marker. She banged on the table for silence and told the following story: Her son went with three or four Jewish friends to the Champs-Elysées, a formerly posh shopping district now filled with large clothing chains and an abundance of McDonald's restaurants. One of those friends was wearing a Lacoste baseball cap. While walking down the street, her son and his friends passed a group of unknown Jewish boys, and one of those "idiot Jews" beat up the kid in the baseball cap. "A Jew hit another Jew," she shouted, "because of his hat!"

On a number of levels, this story was confusing. First, why did a Jewish kid beat up another unknown Jewish kid on the Champs-Elysées "because of his hat"? And second, why did Mme. Amsallem think this story about sartorially driven aggression exemplified students' racism? In analytical terms, fashion and race point to diametrically opposed conceptions of identity. If fashion is consciously constructed and always ephemeral, race is presumed to be given and unchanging. But the two seemed inextricably tied in Mme. Amsallem's telling of the baseball-cap tale. How and why? How can one understand the relationship between student discussions of legible Jewish physiognomy and a story about fashion-driven, intra-Jewish violence? What was the connection between clothing and Jewishness for these Parisian adolescents? And finally, what happened to the sense of Jewishness described in the last three chapters when day school students were in the ethnically and religiously mixed spaces of French public life?

As Mme. Amsallem's students already knew, and I slowly learned, the boy in the Lacoste baseball cap was not supposed to be Jewish; in fact, he was presumed to be "Arab." In this chapter, I will argue that his beating therefore both instantiated and challenged day school students' primordializing practices. In the mid-2000s the public face of Jewishness in Paris was defined sartorially, through the slippage between clothing and physiognomy. Day school students played a central, although far from exclusive, role in the construction of this highly visible Jewishness. Objectifying, primordializing, and individualizing Jewishness through conspicuous consumption made Frenchness possible for young "Arab Jews" in ways foreclosed to Arab Muslims. However, the work of inscribing Jewishness on the visible surfaces of the body led to ambivalent results. The very practices that helped construct distinctions between Jews and Muslims backfired, inadvertently foregrounding Arab-Jewish proximities and intra-Jewish divisions that many would rather have concealed. This, in turn, fueled ever more frantic and sometimes violent efforts to shore up uncertain boundaries.

Youth, Liminality, and (anti)Racism

Much social scientific work around youth culture and identity production would agree with Mme. Amsallem: the kind of violent incident described above is not supposed to happen. In the first place, Muslim youth, *not* Jewish youth, were publicly associated with violence in

France. In addition, English-language theoretical and ethnographic literature emphasizes the anti-essentialist and antiracist potential contained within youth identity and culture (Bhabha 1994; Hall 1990; Hebdige 1979). Although these theorists acknowledge that this potential is not always realized, it seems to reside almost inevitably in the multiply determined liminalities of many contemporary youth. They are depicted as "in-between" social roles (childhood/adulthood; consumption/production), cultures (country of origin/country of residence), even epistemological conditions (sincerity/authenticity) (Bhabha 1994:1; Hall 2002; Jackson 2008:175). For many of these authors, the link between social liminality and anti-essentialism has been reinforced in the contemporary moment by massive migration and rapid social change—phenomena that make totalizing identity narratives almost impossible to maintain. As a result, even when youth claims about community and identity may *appear* primordial, some writers insist that the practices on which those claims are based undermine assumptions about bounded, continuous traditions (Dolby 2001; Gopinath 1995; Jackson 2008). Youth are thus often described as "resisting" or denaturing hegemonic discourse, often through consumption practices (clothing, music, drugs) that create "sutured" or hybrid identities, thereby calling attention to otherwise unspoken social categories and assumptions.[1]

None of this fits the story discussed here. Some middle-class Sephardi teenagers engaged in the violent, racist actions typically attributed to disadvantaged, Arab Muslim youth, calling into question interpretations that reduce youth identity practices to class or Arab Muslim difference. At the same time, Jewish teenagers used widely circulating commodities to construct their Jewishness, therefore presumably accepting identity as a malleable, situational "choice." But adolescents understood their self-fashionings as reflections, rather than constructions, of Jewish authenticity. This strange doubling of choice and essence is part of the contradictions inherent in the postmodern moment. It powerfully illustrates the ways in which social forces associated with postmodernism may actually reinvigorate "modern" conceptions of self—particularly race as a mode of reading interior essence from exterior form.

Ambiguous Identities

As noted above, what appears first as a story of intentional Jewish-on-Jewish violence turns out to be considerably more complicated. The teacher's recitation provoked a shocked murmur among the students. One boy denounced the story as a lie. Another, Jonathan, noted that the teenager dressed in the Lacoste cap had "provoked" the unknown boys by disguising himself as a rebeu, a slang word for Arab. Since "everyone" knew that rebeu dressed like that, Jonathan insisted that such a disguise was a betrayal of one's Jewishness; it was therefore "normal" to be beaten up by another Jew for it. A third boy seemed rather unsettled by the turn of the conversation. He kept repeating, somewhat in shock, that he always wore Lacoste eyeglasses. Jonathan assured him that eyeglasses were "Jewish." Furious, Mme. Amsallem called for silence. She lectured the students on the unbearable hypocrisy of combining justified complaints about others' "racist" conduct toward them with their own "racist" behavior vis-à-vis those same "others," particularly given Jews' higher class status and greater educational opportunities. A number of students hardly appreciated these remarks, characterizing them as an attempt to excuse "Arab" anti-Semitism and therefore as "racist."

This conversation, like so much in contemporary French and French Jewish discourse, struggled to reimpose a neat divide between Jews and Arabs. As we have seen, the mainstream media depict Jews and Arabs violently disagreeing over a range of issues—peace in the Middle East, the way to fight racism and discrimination in France, the rightful place of religious expression in the French public sphere. If Muslims were associated with the marginalized, multiculturalist far left, article after article proclaimed French Jews' slide to the right (Benveniste 2002; Chombeau 2006; Gabizon 2006). These distinctions are perhaps even more dramatic when applied to young people. Adolescent and young adult Jews do not often count as "youth" (*les jeunes* in either French (or European) academic and political conversations. Since the first "headscarf affair" in 1989, the term has become increasingly associated with social danger in general and with "Arabs" in particular. These youth, often qualified as being from the *banlieues*, or semiurban housing projects that ring Paris to the north and east, are said to reject universalist social norms in favor of primordialized identities, often manifested through violent anti-Semitism (Brenner et al. 2002; Gaspard and Khosrokhavar 1995; Kepel 1987; Lorcerie 2003; Taguieff 2002; Trigano 2001; Wieviorka 2005). This primordialization is imagined as a retreat from "modernity," a verdict supported by reference to young people's supposedly premodern assumptions about religion, gender, and race, assumptions that are supposedly evident in the proliferation of "ethnic" shops, veiled women, mosques, and anti-Semitism in immigrant neighborhoods (Bensoussan 2004:3).

As noted in chapter 2, many of the same things could have been said about Parisian *Jewish* neighborhoods in the 9th, 11th, 18th, and 19th arrondissements, where kosher supermarkets and restaurants abut religious bookstores, and bewigged women circulate with large families. But such things were not usually said about Jews. If Arab "youth" were portrayed as potentially violent and socially disruptive, Jewish young people were most often invoked as the privileged victims of Muslim rage. In many public representations, Jewish adolescents and young adults featured as *the* minority success story and ultimately stood for the besieged Republic itself (Bensoussan 2004; Brenner et al. 2002; Rufin 2004).

Identity narratives forged in day schools reinforced this presumption of Jewish-Muslim difference. As we have seen over the last few chapters, whether intentionally or not, the experience of day schooling clarified and reified Jewish boundaries, eliminating any ambiguity that might have come from imagining Jewishness as fluid or internally heterogeneous. In addition, Arabs and Jews were portrayed as diametrically opposed populations engaged in a cosmic battle that Jews would ultimately win. Recall the David and Goliath poster, the description of Ishmael the "Arab" warrior, and the plan to defeat the Philistines-cum-Palestinians outlined in the Book of Samuel. Mme. Amsallem and her students echoed many of these assumptions. For students, "Arabs" dressed one way, Jews another way. In addition, "Arabs" were violent perpetrators, and Jews were victims. For Mme. Amsallem, "Arabs" were poor, uneducated, and therefore racist. Day school students were well educated and well off and therefore should be tolerant. But given the baseball cap incident, the conversation could not quite reestablish these dichotomies. Most obviously, and I will return to this, there was the unprovoked *Jewish* violence that lay at the heart of the story. If students argued that the boy in the cap was dangerously trying to "pass" as an Arab, the same could have been said about the members of the group that attacked him; they chose a lone, unprotected passerby because of his apparent ethnoreligious affiliation. This kind of story was told over and over again about anti-Semitic attacks. The so-called "Rudy H. incident" illustrates both this trope and the far more complex reality behind it. Rudy H., an adolescent Jew, was beaten in June 2008 by a group of youth identified by the media as "Maghrebi" and/or of "African" origin. Initially, the incident was reported as a savage attack on a lone, young Jew who was innocently headed to synagogue for Shabbat services (Agence France Presse 2008a; CRIF 2008; Midi Libre 2008; Serafini 2008). However, the incident was actually part of a series of interethnic turf wars between groups of adolescents.

Thus the story can be described as an example of the return of the repressed; it highlighted what was not supposed to exist. It pointed to the potential ways in which Jewish adolescent expressive practices—particularly those cultivated in day schools—ironically challenged attempts to solidify boundaries. Inadvertently, day school students seemed to cultivate dispositions that highlighted their social proximity to "Arabs."

How so? In the first place, they emphasized their connection to North African worlds that many of them had never seen. Day school students could not imagine being "French," but they identified themselves as "Moroccan" or "Tunisian" on official school forms (see chapter 3). Although adolescents neither spoke Arabic fluently nor intended to learn to speak it—insisting instead that they should focus on "their language," that is, Hebrew—their speech was nonetheless peppered with Arabic expressions picked up from parents and/or grandparents. This was particularly true when it came to describing Jewish family rituals: Shabbat delicacies, for example, were named in Arabic and linked to their country of origin. Students even adopted practices stereotypically associated with North Africans—elongated vowels, elaborate hand gestures, and loud, boisterous behavior. Kevin, the public school student mentioned in chapter 3, associated all visible Jewishness—which he identified as skin color, clothing, and attention-seeking behavior—with Tunisianness. An elementary school principal marveled at the way children whose parents spoke with no discernible accent had internalized the intonations and mannerisms of their more ethnically marked grandparents, a habit day school children called talking "Jewish."[2] Some adolescents also waxed nostalgic about their parents' experiences in North Africa, describing Algeria, Morocco, and Tunisia as vanished terrestrial paradises where Arabs and Jews shared social spaces and "got along," at least in part because Jews were economically and socially dominant. A few students even suggested that Jews and Arabs should still have far more in common than Jews and "French people."

In addition, students associated particular "Jewish" traits with certain national origins. Algerians—who were underrepresented in day schools and were widely presumed to be more "assimilated" because of their colonial history—were described as "looking" the least Jewish because of their "lighter skin." As Kevin noted, Tunisians were associated with the most ethnically marked characteristics. Typically, a Brith Abraham high school student said of one of her girlfriends: "She has to be from Tunisia because she talks so much and uses her hands so much!" The friend objected to the characterization, noting that she was not "Tunisian" but had Tunisian origins. When I asked if "origins" made a real difference, both responded immediately: "No. We are all Jews!" I asked Deborah, a middle-school student at a Parisian day school very much like Brith Abraham, what kinds of traits were associated with being "Tunisian." She explained:

> I don't know. A way of mimicking, the kinds of gestures, when you talk really loudly, things like that. After someone speaks really loudly, we realize: Ah, you're Tunisian! . . . But you can't rely on that. Me, in my school, I'll say: She's Moroccan, she's not good. But it's just for laughs. Because we're all Jews. We're all the . . . we're not all the same, but because we are all Jews we are all part of the same community, so everyone is the same.

This persistent certainty that everyone really is "the same," however, did not stop students from enthusiastically labeling one another by their parents' country of origin. And it seemed very important for them to be able to so classify those with whom they interacted; that is why I was asked whether Ashkenazim were from Morocco, Tunisia, or Algeria.

With some notable exceptions, parents and adults handled their North African origins very differently. They did not deny that their recent histories took place in North Africa, and they readily talked about their countries of origin. Most did not, however, refer to themselves as "Tunisians," "Moroccans," or "Algerians." And, as we saw in chapter 2, they often emphasized European genealogies, either because they were born in France or claimed descent from Jews who fled Europe during the Middle Ages. Remember the Brith Abraham parent—also from chapter 2—who described herself as "proud" of having been born in France, particularly vis-à-vis those who had the misfortune of a North African birth? Adolescents did not take this care. They saw their Jewishness as concomitant with particular geographical origins and saw those imagined geographical places as Jewish. In the process, "Tunisia," "Morocco," and, to a lesser extent, "Algeria" were transformed into Jewish spaces that hardly bore any resemblance to their French colonial or contemporary incarnations.

This kind of vision transformed all forms of Jewishness into a particular North African heritage and all North African family practices and experiences into "Jewish" ones. Students often seemed surprised when outside perception did not confirm this conflation. In response to a question about whether their parents and/or grandparents spoke "*Arabe,*" the French word for Arabic, a tenth-grader at Brith Abraham insisted that her parents and grandparents did not speak Arabic, but "Tunisian." This somewhat strange distinction may have been a way of writing Arab Muslimness out of the Tunisianness she associated with her parents and herself. When Mme. Haddad, a history teacher at Brith Abraham, tried to get her students to understand that by labeling themselves "Moroccan" or "Tunisian" they were inadvertently drawing parallels between themselves and "Arab" immigrants, many seemed angry and confused. After listening to a litany of student stereotypes about those immigrants, Mme. Haddad replied:

> I am a second-generation immigrant of Arab origin. I have an Oriental culture. Sometimes, I listen to Oriental music. I'm not ashamed. . . . I shocked you when I said [that I was] Arab, the daughter of [Tunisian] immigrants. [But you say,] "Me, I'm Moroccan! Me, I'm Tunisian." Why don't you define yourselves as French? . . . When you define yourselves, when you say, "Oh I'm Tunisian," when you define

yourselves in terms of your grandparents' origins, aren't you defining yourselves as immigrants? . . . You should say, "I'm French."

Her students started yelling so loudly it was virtually impossible for her to regain control of the class. One student retorted: "You can't be Arab because it's a religion. We are Tunisian." Another noted that she was "Israeli." Similarly, a student whose parents had taken her to North Africa to see their ancestral homes and villages, told me very quietly: "It's not at all like it used to be. There are now lots of Arabs!"

Although students seemed to imagine their North African origins in entirely Jewish terms, this emphasis on a shared geographical and cultural heritage undermined any attempt to maintain absolute Jewish distinctiveness vis-à-vis Arab Muslims. This was exacerbated by day school students' imaginaries of Jewishness, which had relatively little Jewish content. In fact, much of their understanding of Jewishness could be tied to the regional, cultural, and class particularities shared with Arab Muslims. Many of the last names adolescents associated with Jewishness are identical to or come from the same roots as Arabic names (Chouraqui 1998a:203). As we saw in the last chapter, Jacob inadvertently pointed to this commonality by identifying Jewish last names as "Cohen" or "Ben-something," a construction that means "son of" in both Hebrew and Arabic and is extraordinarily common in both populations. Thus, despite the violent derision of the editor of *l'Arche* magazine, the Department of Education's "confusion" about the difference between Jewish and Muslim last names is quite understandable (see chapter 2; Waintrop 1993). In addition, much of the texture of domestic Jewish ritual had a local North African flavor that recalled commonalities with Muslims from the same areas. The kinds of dishes prepared, their aromas, and Arabic names all invoked a universe that is at least partially shared across religious lines (Bahloul 1983. The music and singers many Jewish adults loved were common to both religious groups. Even Parisian wedding celebrations recalled nothing so much as an idealized and stereotyped North African heritage: a henna ceremony for the bride, "Oriental" music, elaborate costume changes, and even an occasional camel.

In addition, the physiognomic criteria young Jews cited as being hallmarks of Jewish identity were profoundly ambiguous. People they described as *typé*, or stereotypically Jewish, were often said to have dark skin, dark curly hair, and aquiline noses, traits that were more likely to be shared with North African Muslims than with most Parisian Ashkenazim. Underscoring this proximity, cases of "mistaken" identity occurred relatively frequently. A 13-year-old girl nervously giggling in a deserted school hallway told me that she had often been "taken" for an Arab. A 16-year-old boy claimed that an adult "Tunisian," who broke up a fistfight he was having with an "Arab" boy, took him for an "Arab Tunisian." An English teacher in a religious school told her class that, while eating a sandwich in the subway, a Muslim asked her what right she had to eat during Ramadan, provoking peals of anxious laughter from her students.

Looking the Part

There were (and are) serious material risks involved in being "mistaken" for an Arab in France. And whether Jewish adolescents consciously recognized this or not, their parents and teachers talked about it in a variety of ways. I overheard a conversation in which an older woman of Tunisian origin instructed a younger one in the art of being "recognized" as Jewish rather than "Arab" on the Parisian housing market, particularly when a last name was likely to be read as "Arab." An unemployed Moroccan-born man with two sons in a Jewish school told me that being "mistaken" for an Arab during a job interview guaranteed continued unemployment, but things went slightly better if the interviewer thought he was talking to a Jew. During a conversation on discrimination, a teenager whose father runs his own business confided: "Why would anyone hire Arabs if they could get someone else? My dad won't take them; they cause too many problems." Thus, while Jewish children often conflated "racism" exclusively with "anti-Semitism," they acknowledged that there was "discrimination" against "Arabs" in France. The baseball cap incident suggests yet another risk, with the added caveat that anti-Arab violence is probably less likely to come to police attention and/or be widely reported.[3]

But being perceived as Jewish could also be dangerous. This was particularly true for teenagers who lived in rougher Parisian neighborhoods. Reported incidents of anti-Semitism increased dramatically after 2000, and teenagers—particularly those who were readily identifiable—seemed to be privileged targets. We have seen that day school students viewed anti-Semitism as omnipresent and exceedingly dangerous. But despite deep concerns about anti-Semitism, the majority of the youth I met were more than willing to run the risk of being "seen" as Jewish.[4] In fact, most thought it frankly inevitable regardless of what they did or did not do (see below). But this did not stop them from flirting with danger by cultivating consumption and sartorial practices that, in Hebdige's terms, turned Jewishness into a "spectacular subculture," one that selectively and consciously engaged global fashion trends in an effort to communicate Jewish class and cultural distinctions while shoring-up group identity (1979:102; Bourdieu 1984). This sartorial complex emerged in the late 1980s and early 1990s, apparently as the brainchild of second-generation Tunisian immigrants whose parents were involved in the Parisian retail clothing industry. Then, as now, the practice was called *chalalah* (pronounced "sha-la-la"). No one I talked to seemed to know what the term meant or anything about its etymology. But as we shall see, there was something very fitting about describing this particular constellation of youth practices with a term that was all surface and no substance.

Chalalah was sumptuous in every sense of the word. Although favored brands and clothing items obviously varied with time, dressing chalalah usually meant wearing ostensibly expensive, tightly fitted, brightly colored, highly coordinated, and virtually unisex garments. When I began my fieldwork, many day school girls and boys were wearing what some described as "uniforms that cost 500 euros": closely fitted acid-washed jeans made by the Italian company Diesel; skin-tight T-shirts in day-glo colors manufactured by the originally American and now Luxembourg-based company von Dutch; and matching Converse high-top sneakers. Boys tended to favor racing jackets covered in advertisements, while girls wore zip-up sweatshirts. Both boys and girls wore their hair long (longer, however, for girls) and gelled into large, asymmetric styles. Many students also carried the latest brand of cell phone, placed visibly in the front pocket of their jeans.

Adolescents very often accessorized their clothing choices with Jewish or Israeli symbols. Boys and girls carried camouflage-colored pencil cases marked with the name of the Israeli army in Hebrew and English (*Tsahal* or Israeli Defense Forces, IDF). Many boys wore kippot, which were similarly marked. Students of both sexes tied red-string bracelets to their wrists, indexing the purchase of a wish or blessing from religious figures at the Western Wall in Jerusalem. They also wore necklaces or bracelets adorned with a giant sky-blue bead bought in Israel, IDF army dog-tags engraved with their names, stylized Israeli paratroopers, and/or Jewish stars (often several at a time) in every possible size and color. Girls favored Jewish stars covered in brightly colored rhinestones that matched their T-shirts, sneakers, and earrings. Boys seemed to prefer large silver stars, hung on leather ties or thick chains, or small, stylized scrolls marked with a star. Other symbols often worn as Jewish identity markers, such as the *chai*, the Hebrew symbol for "life," were relatively rare, a fact explained by one high-school student as a result of the sign's general illegibility in France—if only Jews could recognize it, its communication value was considered too limited. The *hamza*, the five-fingered hand worn by Christians, Jews, and Muslims in the Mediterranean basin as a means of warding off the evil eye, was even less common. I only saw one, worn by Giborah, a tenth-grader at Beit Sarah whose mother is Israeli. She explained her choice of symbol as a less "provocative" way of marking her faith than the Jewish star precisely because of the sign's ambiguity.

As Giborah's comment suggests, not everyone in day schools dressed "chal" (the nickname for "chalalah"), and very few of those who did were willing to think of themselves as chal, which is associated with superficiality and store-bought appearances. Instead, they characterized themselves as dressing like "Jews." But there was nonetheless a striking uniformity and opulence to student dress. Annabelle, a Brith Abraham student who had previously attended a public school, described her mother's horror when she first saw the student population. She apparently thought all the girls were dressed in identical clothes and earrings and wondered whether anyone in school did anything other than participate in a "daily fashion show." My fieldnotes were filled with attempts at counting those wearing what seemed to be "in" items—efforts that were quickly abandoned because of the sheer number of students involved. One of the more detailed descriptions from my notes gives a flavor for what many high-school girls looked like:

> pink, knee-high Ugg boots, skin-tight V-neck pink sweater, large Christian Dior glasses, wavy hair gelled to look wet, heart-shaped rhinestone watch, large charm bracelet adorned only with a three-dimensional Jewish star, a red string, and a Jewish star ring on just about every finger.

This kind of in-your-face visibility and legibility was an integral part of the claims to Jewishness that adolescents wanted to make. For many Jewish youth, *chalalisme* created a ground of Jewish practice that brought to life their understanding of Jewishness as a homogenous ethnic, class, and national identity. It potentially dissolved all of the internal Jewish differences day schools worked so hard to suppress, even outside school walls. It offered a way of circumventing arduous discussions about the distinctions between and among Ashkenazim and Sephardim, the observant and the nonobservant, the very wealthy and the middle class by aestheticizing thorny questions like who and what is a Jew. Jewishness became tantamount to a Sunday shopping trip, accessible to anyone with sufficient disposable income. As such, it opened up a pathway for the relatively painless reethnicization of Jews (often, although not exclusively, Ashkenazim) who had little, if any, contact with the histories or religious practices of day schoolers. At least in theory, this meant that an Ashkenazi Jew from the ritzy 16th arrondissement who dressed "chal" could be read as a "Tunisian," or simply as a "Jew," just like any average day-school student. And at times, chalalah seemed to work in precisely this way. A well-known French sociologist with Ashkenazi ancestry told me that her son, who was enrolled in an elite Parisian public high school, dressed "Jewish" despite his nominally Catholic upbringing and his complete disinterest in religious Judaism. He was not alone. A Moroccan-born woman married to a Parisian post-Christian described her teenage daughter, who has blue eyes and dirty-blond hair, as compensating for her "un-Jewish looks and name" with expensive jeans and Jewish stars. According to one of my college-aged informants, for some pale-skinned, fair-haired (often Ashkenazi) girls, dressing "chal" was the *only* way to ensure that self-identified Jewish (often Sephardi) boys would "read" them as "Jews" and thus as potential dates and/or wives.

By reducing Jewishness to style, chalalisme disassociated it from traditional sources of Jewish identity, particularly matrilineal descent and religious practice. This regrounding of Jewish identity was most evident in the discomfort contemporary youth practices inspired in some religious Jews. Beit Sarah's students were far more likely than those from Brith Abraham to disavow being "chal," noting that they knew better than to think of such practices as Jewishness. Diana, a serious, observant Beit Sarah twelfth-grader explained: "I don't need to be chalalah. I'm Jewish because I keep kosher, because I keep Shabbat, because I observe all Jewish holidays."

If Jewishness as style significantly lowered the barriers to entry, it also visibly reified the "Jewish community." At its most abstract level, this was accomplished through the clothing itself. Jewish adolescents who were enrolled in diverse schools—orthodox schools in lower-middle-class neighborhoods, traditionalist schools in leafy Parisian suburbs, and Catholic schools in the center of Paris—could be dressed virtually identically, regardless of their level of personal religious observance, family background, or even intellectual affinity for the idea of chalalisme. Jewish adolescents thus displayed their connection to other Jews who, echoing Anderson (1991), they might never meet but would recognize instantly. Furthermore, the practices associated with conspicuous teenage consumption helped ensure that Jews unconnected by family, schools, synagogues, or neighborhoods *would* meet. On public transportation, I watched them spread out and call to one another, attracting significant attention, including that of any unknown Jews who might be present. A number of students even described getting to know new Jews this way. In addition to traveling in groups, day school students bought clothing together, gathered in defined locations, patronized particular Parisian stores, and stopped to snack at certain restaurants. The Opéra Métro stop, with its regional rail-line connection, has long been a gathering place for suburban Jews spending the afternoon or evening in the city. Some adolescents shopped on Rue de Rivoli and/or Rue Etienne Marcel in the heart of the garment district on Wednesday and Friday afternoons. Le Paradis du Fruit, a restaurant chain specializing in fruit smoothies that contained no milk or meat products, was a preferred watering hole. Certain nightclubs had acquired a reputation for being *feuj*, the slang word for Jews. On Saturday night, the Champs-Elysées, which featured so prominently in the baseball cap story, was a (fading) haunt for contemporary Jewish *flâneurs*. And on Sundays, when almost all stores in Paris except those located in the Marais were closed, the neighborhood teemed with Jewish adolescents eating in kosher restaurants, shopping in local boutiques, and strolling in packs down the middle of the street. As one teenager told me, everyone knows where to go if they want to meet and hang out with other feuj.

I do not mean to suggest that Jewish youth opted out of religious practices. They did not. Religious observance was more marked among Beit Sarah students than among those at Brith Abraham. But in both cases students engaged in Jewish religious activities on a weekly, if not daily, basis. But many of these religious practices were also ethnicized in the sense that they were less about divine obligation than they were about social distinction. In particular, going to synagogue on Shabbat or for any Jewish holiday, whether or not one actually attended services, was a way of marking oneself publicly as Jewish. A Brith Abraham senior described hanging out with his school friends on the street outside his synagogue every Friday night. Mme. Haddad, the Brith Abraham history teacher, accused her students of turning Jewishness into a public spectacle by parading to synagogue on Shabbat in kippot (see chapter 5). Similarly, Beit Sarah students who regularly attended synagogue spent a lot of time outside of services, hanging out with friends in packs, seeing and being seen by those passing by. They knew very well that this led to their identification as Jews and sometimes to ethnic tensions. Girls complained that while they strolled around the lake near their Créteil synagogue on Saturday afternoons, "Arabs" would try to talk to them or harass them. The park in which Rudy H. was beaten, which is very close to a large Lubavitcher synagogue and school, was also known as a hangout for adolescent Jews on Shabbat. According to the rabbi of the synagogue, those who are most likely to be in the park are "trendy, not necessarily religious, but very strongly ethnically identified" (cited in Bordenave and Le Bars 2008).

With their particularly clad bodies, then, adolescents constructed a physical and geographical map of Jewishness that was resolutely local, even more specifically Parisian than French. But these practices also deterritorialized and reterritorialized Jewish youth, linking the particularities of Parisian adolescent Judaism to an imagined global Jewish community instantiated in Israel. Adolescents constructed elaborate stories about the invariably non-French brands they tended to favor, including improbably attributing design and production to Jews. American companies like Converse may also have been viewed as "Jewish," a product of the conflation of ultra-orthodox Crown Heights with "America" in teenage imaginaries. In a very literal sense, Israel was a privileged source for these globalized markers of Jewish identity. Awash in knockoffs and counterfeit merchandise, Israeli markets provided vacationing French youth with cheap "Diesel" jeans and "Converse" sneakers. Adolescents even established exchange networks that allowed those who had never spent time in Israel to benefit from these bargains. When I first began my fieldwork, girls in a religious school were working out the details for the Israeli purchase and French redistribution of a particular style of Birkenstock sandal.

If Israel was a privileged site for buying Jewishness, it was also an *object* of consumption, becoming an important means through which Jewish adolescents deterritorialized their local particularities. As we have seen (see chapter 5), even Sephardi teenagers who regularly summered in Israel did not speak modern Hebrew and had limited experience with larger Israeli society. When vacationing in Israel, they lived and played in a handful of Francophone "colonies" located in coastal cities (Eilat, Netanya, Ashdod), meeting and cementing ties with French Jews who may not have attended their schools or lived in their neighborhoods. Adolescents came to mistake these relatively wealthy, temporary communities of extended French families for "Israel," citing their instant comfort in these enclaves as proof that their Jewish roots were in Israel and that Israel felt like "home." The merchandising of Israel functioned similarly, allowing adolescents to dissolve Parisian Jewishness into an aestheticized Israeli identity. By purchasing and wearing flags, IDF T-shirts, and camouflage-colored school accessories, adolescents transcended the serious material difficulties that accompany Israeli citizenship, painlessly wrapping themselves in the fetishized surfaces of the militarized Israeli state.

As we have seen, these fetishized surfaces deeply penetrated adolescent consciousness. Many day school students spent a good portion of their class time idly doodling "I ♥ Israel" (as well as Israeli flags and Jewish stars) everywhere. School desks, chairs, and blackboards, as well as students' bookbags, pencil cases, and notebooks, were covered with the phrase. Almost always written in pop-culture English, which itself denied the French monolingualism of its authors, "Israel" became the equivalent of a beloved movie star—one whose real character would always remain inaccessible but whose public surfaces conferred intimate knowledge and close association.

In addition to connecting French Jews to Israel, this affective economy also provided the grounds of primordialized Jewish distinction. If Jews "loved" Israel, Arabs "hated" it. As adolescents told me repeatedly, this meant that being "for" Israel was the equivalent of being "for" Jews and therefore "against" Arabs. One high school student noted: "There is a conflict between Jews and Arabs in France. . . . So as soon as someone is pro-Arab, he is necessarily against Jews. It's like a soccer game, you can only root for one team." He was not alone in using a sports analogy to express his vision of Jewish-Arab relations. In 2004 an advertising campaign masterminded by the Betar, a youth movement affiliated with the right-wing Israeli Likud Party, echoed this logic. Attacking then French President Jacques Chirac for his "pro-Arab" Middle Eastern politics, a widely distributed poster demanded: "*Dis-moi qui tu supportes et je te dirai qui tu hais.*" This phrase is a double entendre that literally means, "Tell me who you support [in the sense of root for], and I'll tell you who you hate," but it is phonetically identical to saying, "Tell me who you support, and I'll tell you who you are." Political differences were thus largely stripped of their moral or ethical content and reduced to team loyalty rooted in ethnicized affect. In such a context, the public display of Israel-identified symbols clearly communicated which "teams" Jewish adolescents did and did not support, thus suggesting a neat boundary with "Arabs."

To reinforce the solidity of this frontier, young Jews policed their "territories" for any signs of the opposing team. Jewish protection services staffed largely by adolescents and young adults controlled the entrance to "community" events by examining bags and asking potential patrons: "Do you love Israel?" People wearing signs of pro-Palestinian politics in certain areas of the Marais were sometimes asked to leave by bands of Jewish teenagers in motorcycle helmets (Garcia 2004). Evidently, teenagers in Lacoste baseball caps were violently removed from the Champs-Elysées. And rival gangs organized along ethno-religious lines sometimes confronted one another in peripheral Parisian neighborhoods. The beating of Rudy H. turned out to be just that, a particularly vicious reprisal for a series of escalating skirmishes between a Jewish band and one alternatively described as "Maghrebi" and "African" (Bordenave and Le Bars 2008). In December 2007, Rudy H. himself had even been arrested with a group of friends for possession of dangerous objects (brass knuckles, projectiles) and presumed involvement in these territorial battles (Agence France Presse 2008b).

This double movement of internal homogenization and external distinction similarly characterized the class claims made by Jewish teenagers. By asserting affluence through sartorial splendor, Jewish adolescents shored up the connections between wealth and Jewishness. Whether adolescents bought full-price Diesel jeans at the Parisian boutique Replay or counterfeit versions in Israel, the very terms of chalalisme conflated Jewishness and socioeconomic success. In a sense, all teenagers who dressed "Jewish" also looked "rich," projecting an aura of upward mobility and seamless integration into the French economic system. An article on chalalisme published in the Paris *Observateur* in late April 2004 underscored precisely this point. It showed a picture of a girl wearing a large, fluorescent, pink-rhinestone Jewish star with matching T-shirt, earrings, and belt. The article also quoted one practitioner of chalalisme saying, "I'm rich, and I want to show it" (Cabourg and Gourdon 2004:22). To some extent, this assertion of purchasing power attempted to conceal the socioeconomic differences between Ashkenazim and Sephardim. But perhaps more importantly, day students saw their relative wealth as reinforcing the distinctions between "Arabs" and Jews. Jewish adolescents of both sexes routinely contrasted their ways of dressing, which they described as "classy" or simply "dressing well," with what they imagined as "Arab" sartorial practices. I was told repeatedly that while Jews cared deeply about what they wore and could afford to dress nicely, "Arabs don't care" and could not afford to buy good clothes. When I asked how "Arabs" dressed, I was almost invariably given a description of a male dressed in nondescript running pants, hooded sweatshirt, and uncoordinated sneakers. When I asked what kind of brands "Arabs" favored, students recited a short list of French clothing manufacturers, like Lacoste or Adidas, which were counterfactually described as "cheap."

This conflation of Jewishness with wealth and Arabs with poverty was often reinforced by delinquency and its interpretations. In 2004, the most common crime in France was cell-phone theft. For adolescents who rode public transportation to and from rough, peripheral neighborhoods, confrontations with young thieves could be a weekly occurrence. Jewish adolescents often filtered these encounters through the lens of anti-Semitism. As one 15-year-old boy bitterly explained: "Arab kids think that Jews are rich and therefore have good cell phones to steal." The decision to steal a Jew's cell phone was thus viewed as premeditated—the perpetrator targeted the victim because he was "known" to be Jewish—and therefore racist. The thieves themselves often played into this logic, calling victims of property crimes "dirty Jews." A 16-year-old girl who claimed to have been hit by "Arabs" while waiting for a bus in broad daylight recounted the incident in terms that had become almost formulaic: the "Arabs" asked for money; she gave them everything she had; they asked for more money and credit cards, neither of which she had; they called her a "dirty Jew" and hit her. In such encounters, Jewishness itself became a sign of economic inequality and differential access to the privileges of French citizenship, one that may have been all the more frustrating given the social and historical proximity between many North African Jews and Muslims.[5]

Ambiguous Identities, Again

If conscious practice has helped construct an imaginary of inevitable Jewish visibility, the baseball cap story underscored the fragility of this order. In the words of Arjun Appadurai:

> Real bodies in history betray the very cosmologies they are meant to encode. So the ethnic body . . . is itself potentially deceptive. Far from providing the map for a secure cosmology, a compass from which mixture, indeterminacy, and danger may be discovered, the ethnic body turns out to be itself unstable and deceptive. (1998:232)

In fact, I would argue that the very practices used to create Jewish "cosmological maps" were the means of their own undoing. In part, the reinscription of identity ambiguity was tied to Jewish adolescents' incessant slippage between style and physiognomy, or as Matthew Frye Jacobson describes it, between "social value" and racializing "perception" (2005:283–284). This is hardly new in the Western Jewish Diaspora. Sander Gilman analyzes the ways in which late 19th-century German Jews internalized racist notions of Jewish physical difference, worrying about the inevitable revelation of that difference even as objective signs of Jewish distinction (forms of dress, physical separation, etc.) disappeared. In Gilman's words:

> The Jew remains visible, even when the Jew gives up all cultural signs of his or her Jewishness and marries out of the "race." It is the inability to "pass" which is central here . . . Jews look different, they have a different appearance, and this appearance has pathognomonic significance. (1991:176)

While fully acknowledging that chalalah was a practice, not an essence, adolescents very often mistook sartorial codes for "Jewish" physiognomy. They insisted that ethno-religious identity was somatically fixed and universally legible, a fact that clothing reflected rather than constructed. How? The responses given to this question mobilized and inverted some of the classic canards of Western European anti-Semitic literature (Gilman 1991). Some students argued that Jewishness was visible through the gaze; the distinctiveness and benevolence of the "Jewish soul" shone in the eyes, particularly when those eyes happened to alight upon another Jew. The opposite was true when a Jew recognized and was recognized by an Arab, who would then radiate hostility. As one teenage girl phrased it: "A Jew looks at us with kindness, and an Arab looks at us with hatred and distrust." In both cases the logic was entirely circular, depending on unexplained prior recognition to unleash the silent bond or simmering hatred that supposedly sparked recognition. While discussions of the "Jewish soul" were often confined to religious students,[6] almost everyone talked about the "tête juive," a combination of vaguely defined physical characteristics that made Jewishness immediately legible to "Arabs," "the French," and other Jews, regardless of whether the person was wearing visible identity markers. But as noted above, the very criteria day-school students used to describe the tête juive were profoundly ambiguous. "Dark skin and dark curly hair" was a description as likely to exclude Jews (particularly, although not exclusively, Ashkenazim) as it was to include non-Jews (particularly, although not exclusively, Muslims of North African origin).[7] Others gave markers that were more clearly class-based, associating Jews with good teeth and Arabs with poor oral hygiene. But this, of course, also drew boundaries in unexpected places. To some extent Jewish children, particularly those who had been "mistaken" for Arabs, recognized the unpredictability of these supposed somatic signs. After commenting on the legibility of the "Jewish nose," a 17-year-old boy told me that he was viewed as "Arab" because of that same feature.

But if physiognomy was unreliable, sartorial markers were even more so because they were so widely accessible. While chalalah may have begun as an exclusively Jewish style, many adolescents acknowledged that others have since embraced it, including Arabs. The story about the Jewish girl who "converted" her "Asian" classmate to Judaism via chalalisme (see chapter 4) is a case in point. And this is precisely what somatic descriptions of Jewishness were meant to correct, explaining why so many teenagers insisted that they could distinguish between an Arab and a Jew even if both were naked. This seamless tracking between these two modes of "reading" Jewishness and the ever-retreating certainty associated with each one underwrote the social anxiety revealed by the baseball cap story. On the one hand, the decision to punch the teenager in the Lacoste hat suggests that his "Arabness" had been conclusively determined in advance. The hat and the face beneath it were collectively (mis)read as somatic indications of "Arabness." On the other hand, the punch was designed to reinforce the legibility of the difference between Arabs and Jews, literally marking the rebeu by wounding his flesh and signaling his exile from territory that had been claimed as Jewish. But both attempts to clearly somaticize difference failed. The student who denied the veracity of his teacher's story acknowledged this implicitly. He was willing to risk the displeasure of a volatile authority figure to save his categories from confusion—the boy who was hit could not have been a Jew. The boy who insisted that the beaten teenager got exactly what he deserved acknowledged it more explicitly. For him, the boy in the baseball cap was a race traitor trying to pass himself off as "Arab" with a clever disguise. Preventing such tricks demanded physically punishing those who attempted to hide their "true" identities, thus reestablishing the absolute parallel between surface and essence, exterior and interior.

If the practices associated with reading Jewish identity off bodily surfaces could not eliminate the identitarian ambiguity between Jews and Arabs, they also failed to transcend internal Jewish differences, both economic and ethnic. While many Jewish teenagers bought knockoffs and imitations, dressing chalalah was still an expensive endeavor. A number of middle- and high-school students I met worked as babysitters during the school year and held full-time jobs for at least one month during the summer to help finance their wardrobes. This was true for wealthier students whose parents refused to subsidize clothing purchases and for middle-class and lower-middle-class children whose families could not otherwise afford popular name brands. Nonetheless, the expense associated with dressing Jewish alienated poorer Jewish youth. Like any other educational institution, the Jewish schools in which I worked were segmented largely along class lines. Rich, popular students wore expensive "in" brands, and less well-to-do students bought similar-looking knockoffs and pouted over their socioeconomic exclusion. In many cases, very religious students rejected both possibilities; instead, they embraced more "traditional" Jewish dress associated with older generations (see below). Those unwilling or unable to afford the "real thing" complained that more privileged students refused to even speak with them, let alone become their friends. One disgruntled 15-year-old told me how ironic she found the contradiction between school discourses about Jewish unity and the student body's fragmentation into classed cliques.

Although adolescents often associated flashy dress and loud, attention-seeking behaviors with both universal "Jewishness" and "class," meaning wealth and good taste, many in the wider French Jewish world disagreed. Like so much about Jewish youth practices, there was little about chalalisme that could be characterized as explicitly Jewish. In fact, it largely flouted religious Judaism's notions of appropriate "Jewish" dress, which emphasized Jewish separation from mainstream consumer culture *and* intra-Jewish gender divisions. Conspicuous consumption and gender-neutral styles were therefore frowned upon as assimilationist in both material and spiritual senses. This could not be lost on students who frequented orthodox schools like Beit Sarah and even "traditionalist" institutions like Brith Abraham. Both had highly gendered, reasonably strict dress codes called tzniout, the Hebrew word for modesty. The spirit if not the letter of these codes forbid many aspects of adolescent sartorial practice. In orthodox schools, girls were not allowed to wear jeans or pants; short-sleeved, cut-off or low-cut shirts were grounds for being sent home; and large earrings or particularly noticeable jewelry had to be removed. The restrictions on boys were less stringent, but still significant. They were not allowed to have pierced ears, to use excessive hair gel, or to wear sleeveless shirts. In traditionalist schools girls were allowed, although not encouraged, to wear jeans and pants, and short-sleeved shirts were acceptable. All other orthodox rules held. In both contexts, religion teachers, disciplinary deans, and principals modeled the aesthetic they wanted children to emulate: dark trousers and light-colored oxford shirts with blue or black kippot for men; long, loose-fitting skirts and ample blouses covering elbows and collar bones for women.

"Jewish dress" was thus a daily field of contestation within Jewish institutions, with administrators and religion teachers disciplining girls for wearing wide-necked shirts, short skirts, and dangling earrings, and boys for the advertisements on their jackets and the amount of gel in their hair. In some cases, these battles even extended beyond school grounds. At Beit Sarah, religion teachers had been known to issue in-school punishments to girls caught wearing jeans outside school. In school, girls went to particularly great lengths to reconcile their notions of "classy" dress with restrictive tzniout requirements. Teachers at Brith Abraham often joked that girls dressed in "sexy tzniout," very form-fitting clothes that just barely covered the required parts and otherwise left little to the imagination. This was even more noticeable among Beit Sarah students, who had far more rules with which to contend. A number of girls would simply add a skin-tight, long-sleeved layer under the often plunging necklines of their favorite tops. Some used safety pins to temporarily close up skirt and blouse slits that otherwise would not have been acceptable. In addition, a number of girls changed as soon as they got into the Metro at the end of the school day, somewhat provocatively slipping jeans or shorts underneath a skirt that was then shoved into a backpack.

Teachers and administrators were not the only people who disapproved of student dress. Some parents happily funded and even occasionally shared the sartorial proclivities of their children. More often, however, the visually and politically aggressive aspects of chalalisme fractured Jews along generational lines, highlighting differences in conceptions of "appropriate" Jewishness and French-Jewishness. Parents, particularly mothers, of all degrees of religiosity fought with their children over "Jewish" clothing. An ultraorthodox mother described shopping for her teenage daughters with a ruler so she could make sure the T-shirts they were interested in buying were sufficiently long and wide for modest coverage. Less religious parents had somewhat different concerns. One observant, middle-class mother told me of her "embarrassment" about the flashy, attention-getting outfits and behaviors of her sons, blaming peer pressure at Jewish schools for instilling values alien to her own sense of "Jewishness." A 14-year-old, lower-middle-class girl described her relatively nonobservant mother as "horrified" by the way children in Jewish schools dressed. Another nonobservant mother described screaming fights with her daughter to get her to remove some identifying markers, particularly Jewish stars and Tsahal paraphernalia, which she considered dangerous in the current climate.

I would suggest that this notion of inappropriate, if not outright "dangerous" clothing extended beyond immediate fears about misspent time, wasted money, and unwanted, possibly anti-Semitic attention. It also spoke to clashing (highly gendered) notions of acceptable minority behavior in France. Where Jewish boys (and to a much lesser extent girls) were committed to aggressive self-defense if not outright provocation, many Jewish adults praised teenagers for their "restraint" and relative passivity vis-à-vis anti-Semitic bullies. We have already seen this with Mme. Amsallem's refusal to countenance Jewish racism as a response to "Arab" racism. Similarly, the head of youth programming at the Fonds Social Juif Unifié (FSJU) praised Jewish adolescents for their "self-restraint":

> During the violent period [of anti-Semitism], curiously, we didn't
> hear anything about the Betar. That means we didn't see the Betar

attack mosques or young Muslims. In that respect, young Jews dem-
onstrated a lot of self-restraint and responsibility. I heard about things
that in certain neighborhoods sounded like pogroms. . . . We haven't
seen any punitive expeditions, young Jews had an enormous amount
of self-restraint in relation to what happened, including the Betar.

This privileging of public discretion—what some referred to as "exemplary Jewish citizenship"—led to attempts to silence stories about certain Jewish youth practices, particularly those with a violent cast. The
story about the beating of the boy in the baseball cap, for example, was
never reported to the police because, in the words of the Jewish history teacher, "We [Jewish adults] wouldn't want such things to circulate outside the community." Other incidents of Jewish youth violence
also seemed never to have entered major media circuits (see n. 3). The
case of Rudy H., where the mainstream media revised their original
story within days of the incident, highlighting the ethnic gang–like
territorial disputes of which the incident was apparently a part, was an
exception to the rule.

But adolescents were not always amenable to such attempts to construct and preserve an image of public passivity. At a demonstration
against anti-Semitism, I watched as an intergenerational conflict over
the display of Israeli symbols degenerated into a potentially violent
confrontation between adolescent boys and a group of middle-aged
marchers. Against the wishes of the adults, who wanted to distinguish
between support for French Republican values and defense of Israel,
the adolescents insisted on their "right" to carry an Israeli flag. They
even threatened to "kill" anyone who tried to take their flag away.
The mother of one of the adolescents ultimately confiscated the flag,
but the boys got their revenge by telling an evidently drunk member
of the Betar about their plight. For several minutes he yelled at the
top of his lungs: "Where is that whore?" But mostly this aggression
was directed toward those imagined as racially "other." Boys at Brith
Abraham plainly relished my ill-disguised shock when they described
violent encounters with other ethnic groups. Four 14-year-olds once
spent an hour describing the havoc they wreaked on their lower-
middle-class, ethnically mixed neighborhood by smashing "Arab" and
"Portuguese" neighbors' cars and setting fire to balconies. The sto-

ries were most likely false, but they spoke volumes about the distance between teenage boys' idealized self-presentations and adult Jewish ideals of rationality and restraint.[8] In addition, like the newspapers, the FSJU either did not know or did not want to say that they knew about adolescent Jewish involvement in ethnicized conflict. A number of students at both Brith Abraham and Beit Sarah claimed that some Jewish boys actively sought to "provoke" interethnic conflict by wearing visible Jewish symbols only when encountering "Arabs." One Brith Abraham tenth-grader, who seemed to have been widely considered a race traitor for her "pro-Arab" understanding of the Palestinian conflict, told me that she had seen boys take kippot out of their pockets just as they crossed paths with teenagers identified as "Arab." I witnessed one such incident: three Jewish youth strolled back and forth through a minority-filled Parisian university library in brightly colored kippot decorated with Israeli flags. Their slow, seemingly aimless saunter may have been intended and was certainly received as a silent challenge.

If chalalisme's visual aggressiveness undermined intergenerational consensus on Jewishness, it also flew in the face of gendered, middle-class standards of respectable French self-presentation. Boys who dressed chalalah engaged in a kind of ghetto dandyism. They laid claim to economic status and upward mobility by embracing the brilliant, time-consuming sartorial forms that the Western bourgeoisie has long considered feminine. They spent as much time doing (and redoing) their hair as girls; some even used pocket mirrors for touch-up jobs in class. They often wore as much and the same jewelry as girls and favored similar form-fitting clothing styles. By refusing the more sober styles that have marked respectable middle-class European male consumers since the 18th century, Jewish boys inadvertently reinforced their own gendered and classed differences (Auslander 1996; Kuchta 1996). Loud, aggressive discourse and action of the kind described above may have helped boys recuperate the masculinity undermined by both effeminate dress and institutional discourses about Jewish docility.

But these very same practices vitiated chalalah girls' claims to femininity. Although it was far more acceptable for Jewish girls than boys to dress brilliantly, their vocal and physical gestures were expected to be more discreet than those of their male counterparts. As a number of anthropologists have noted with respect to African American girls, female "loudness" codes inability or unwillingness to conform to dominant assumptions about what it means to be a "good girl" or an appropriate female subject (Evans 1988; Fordham 1993). At Beit Sarah, teachers and administrators spent considerable time and energy trying to control the vocal volume and gestures associated with female conversation. During a state inspection required for the receipt of government funds, the disciplinary dean primarily seemed concerned that the inspector would find the school (and therefore its female students) "loud." She routed girls with a free period away from the classrooms in which the inspector was working and shushed all those walking in the hallways or talking in animated voices behind closed doors. While the inspection high-lighted anxieties about girls' vocal volume, bodily gestures were more regularly policed for their physical volume. Girls were not to take up a lot of space. A number of (particularly religious) instructors expected girls to keep their backs straight, their knees together, and their feet on the floor. Even a loose-limbed (and -hipped) walk could get a girl in trouble. I watched a teacher publicly humiliate a 16-year-old for what she considered a "revealing" walk that "showed [the student's] upper thighs" despite the length and cut of her skirt.

For some middle-class and upper-middle-class Jews, these various forms of ambiguously gendered, attention-seeking behaviors epito-mized the lack of "discretion" and "taste" characteristic of new money. A wealthy Ashkenazi law student described his university as riven by intra-Jewish conflict between those who dressed "chal" and those who were more discreet. He even accused the "chal" Jews of inspir-ing anti-Semitism among upper-middle-class Jews and non-Jews alike. His Ashkenazi girlfriend noted that she had attended a wealthy public high school where only Jews (but not all Jews) engaged in conspicu-ous consumption. In her view, those who were not *nouveaux riches* systematically underconsumed as a means of marking their class posi-tion, making those who were "chal" all the more visible and unset-tling. Mme. Amsallem revealed her own "racism" by emphasizing the relationship between class and chalalisme. When angrily commenting after class on student reactions to the baseball cap story, she derided them as "fake bourgeois" and *arrivistes*, or social climbers with money but no culture. "You won't find kids like them among the Orthodox," she noted, "because they have other values. You also won't find kids like them among the Liberals [Reformed Jews]; they are just like Mr. and Mrs. Anyone who have their own practices and go about their lives without needing to show everyone what they are. But in this socioeconomic group, this kind of attitude [excessive attention to dress and anti-Arab racism] is common." An orthodox kodesh teacher at Brith Abraham echoed this assessment:

> Their parents are reasonably financially successful. They are in commercial trades and can give their children a decent level of economic support. But the social level is nonexistent. Parents worry about children being well-dressed and clean, but they do not worry about their being well-behaved. They do not even learn to say "thank you" and "excuse me" because the parents never teach them to say such things.

She also thought religious observance made a difference, noting that it was obvious whose parents were *shomer Shabbat*, strictly observant of the Sabbath, and whose were not: "Those [shomer Shabbat] kids actually have the experience of 'getting' their parents at least once a week, so they are less starved for attention. But those who are not never get that time because their parents are always busy doing other things."

I have labeled most of these interlocutors as "Ashkenazim" because they self-identified in those terms. This is significant. Sephardi adults also often criticized student behavior; but they attributed their negative characteristics to class and lack of cultural capital, not to essentialized differences between Ashkenazim and Sephardim. A Sephardi history teacher at Brith Abraham thus noted:

> They [day school students] have a level of general culture that is extremely low. They don't know basic vocabulary words; they have no sense of geography or geopolitics. . . . Most of the students in the school come from families that are relatively well-off financially. But that doesn't open the door to a higher cultural level. Having money doesn't take you to the theater or to the library. It may remove the obstacles to doing those things, but it doesn't make them happen. Most of these kids have parents who are in commerce. If they don't happen to have a family member who is an educator or who is interested in education, all is lost.

In contrast, it is not hard to read Ashekanzi condemnations of Sephardi teenagers' taste and values as attempts to map the class differences spelled out above onto ethnic distinction. Indeed in some cases, people slipped freely between class and ethnic categories, translating youth behaviors, attitudes, and aptitudes into signs of inherent Sephardi difference. The Ashkenazi law student and his girlfriend did so explicitly. He characterized the nouveaux riches interested in dressing "chal" as Sephardim; she claimed that the flashiest Jews in her school were Tunisians. Ashkenazi teachers working in largely Sephardi Jewish schools also often associated students' visual and behavioral "loudness" with ethnicity. Bemoaning student actions inside and outside class, an Ashkenazi Spanish teacher noted: "The few Ashkenazi kids that I've ever taught are totally different. They are always cute, and quiet, and they get perfect scores on their tests. The others are . . ." and here she finished the sentence by grimacing, throwing out her arms and exhaling loudly, a series of gestures that suggested that Sephardi children are noisy and take up a lot of physical and visual space. "I have one Ashkenazi student this year," she continued, "and he always gets 20 out of 20 on his tests without any problem." An English teacher in a different Jewish school described the chaotic student behavior I witnessed in her class as "typical of that particular population with those origins." She then encouraged me to explore the "Ashkenazi-Sephardi division" in my research because it was crucial. "The Ashkenazi 'race,' and I use the word race intentionally," she noted, "is endangered."[9]

Thus chalalisme, through its very conspicuousness, splintered the French Jewish population, facilitating the recoding of internal Jewish class divisions as essential ethnic differences. This, in turn, reintroduced the specter of visible Sephardi foreignness and even "Arabness" over and against Ashkenazi invisibility in French society. As a young Ashkenazi teacher whose maternal grandparents immigrated from Poland before World War II noted:

When the Sephardim first started coming in the 1960s and 1970s, my grandmother was horrified; she saw them as Arabs. She still insists that the only thing uniting the two groups is religion; otherwise, we have nothing in common. With my fiancé [whose family is Algerian] I even find myself saying "you" to refer to Sephardim. He always stops me and asks who "you" is.

Not surprisingly, Sephardi adults were often quite conscious of this persistent disdain. The Beit Sarah teacher's bitter joke about Ashkenazim considering Maimonides an "Arab" (see chapter 3) illustrates this quite clearly. But even day school students who were relatively isolated from Jews who lived or practiced differently used ascriptions of "Arabness" as a weapon. A distraught 12-year-old at Beit Ya'acov reported a classmate's insult to a disciplinary dean: "He said I look like Bin Laden and then everyone started calling me 'Arab.'" What was true in the first years of middle school was also true among older teenagers. Seemingly for my benefit, a high school senior described his Moroccan-born classmate as an "Arab," prompting the shocked classmate to return the favor on the grounds that they both had North African ancestry. "No," the boy who initiated the exchange retorted, "at least I was born in France." Given the pejorative meanings of "Arabness" in both the wider French and French Jewish communities, French birth suddenly took on meaning.

Conclusion

If day schools worked to make Jewishness into a neatly bounded, nearly homogenous moral community that could be projected outward, even students' limited engagement with the French street made such a fiction difficult to maintain. As the Lacoste baseball cap story suggests, profound uncertainty haunted teenage efforts to actualize their primordialized understandings of Jewishness in the wider world. Many of the dispositions, traits, and practices they associated with Jewishness could instead be read as "Arab," and vice versa. In addition, the sartorial code that helped compensate for some of this ambiguity came with its own tensions, dividing Jews along lines of generation, class, religious observance, and ethnicity and thus hopelessly fragmenting Jewishness at the moment of its production. When adolescent signifying practices failed to sufficiently objectify social identities, as was inevitable, some youths resorted to force to ensure the symmetry between essence and choice.

In a sense, then, violent encounters were not only a result of increasingly clear ethnic boundaries—what people in France call "communautarization"—but a way of actually producing them, of shoring-up otherwise fuzzy distinctions (Appadurai 1998). In saying this, I do not intend to minimize anti-Semitism among Arab Muslim populations in France. But in a real sense, moments of sometimes brutal violence produced "Jews" and "Arabs" out of an otherwise very complicated mix of identities and affiliations. The anti-Semitic vitriol and anti-Arab racism that often accompanied these attacks canalized a whole range of potential socioeconomic tensions into race. This explains why day school students were so willing to characterize anyone they thought engaged in anti-Semitic behavior as "Arab," even when they described the person as "black." It also may explain why the accounts of anti-Semitic encounters published by the Service de Protection de la Communauté Juive (SPCJ) so often included the victim's perception that his or her attacker was an "Arab" or a "Maghrebin," without ever explaining how the person reached such a conclusion. But this was also not a one-way street. Young thieves or bullies who peppered their adolescent victims with anti-Semitic epithets also produced "Jews," whether or not those they targeted identified themselves as such. And they seemed to primarily construct this category out of one particular kind of (young) person: those who advertised wealth and ethnic identification, that is, those who were "chal."

In other words, the very fragility of adolescent identities ensured incessant investment in them. This investment coupled with the response it elicited—being called a "dirty Jew" on the bus or street—led Jewish adolescents to experience their lives even outside of school walls as defined and determined by ethno-religious origins. This, in turn, reinforced day students' Herderian assumptions about moral and political community. Their daily practices helped prove that "Arabs" and "Jews" could not live together. As a result, complex cultural, political, and economic motivations were routinely reduced to primordial difference, facilitating the reading of Frenchness itself as white and Catholic (or at least post-Catholic). This meant that, in the long run, French national interests and destinies could not coincide with those of either "Jews" or "Arabs." Coexistence may therefore have been theoretically possible, at least over short horizons, but national moral and political community appeared unthinkable. As a teenaged girl explained: "The French are allied with the Arabs to chase out the Jews. But once the

Jews are gone, the French will get rid of the Arabs." Interethnic national community was not only undesirable, it was a kind of suicide pact, first and foremost for Jews, but even for the "Arabs" and the "French."

Over the last few chapters, I examined how and why many young Parisian Sephardim did not and could not seem to imagine themselves as French. The context of day schooling played a significant role in making Frenchness seemingly more foreign and unknown than Israel, Morocco, Tunisia, and even the United States. But the practices that day school students carried out of school increasingly defined the public face of Jewishness in Paris and were therefore also partially responsible. The means adolescent Jews used to publicly distinguish themselves from "Arabs" ultimately made Jewish Frenchness impossible. In a way, Sephardi youth were faced with a terrible and almost colonial double-bind; they were threatened with exile twice, first as "Arabs" and then as "Jews." Arab Muslim exclusion from the national public encouraged young Sephardim to distinguish themselves through primordialized Jewishness. Forced to enact the essentializing logics of the French public sphere in order to (at least partially) escape them, young Jews constructed identities around a series of ethno-religious exclusions. They were *not* not French because they were not Arab; they were not Arab because they were Jewish. At the same time, foregrounding public Jewishness ran up against French political norms, threatening to put Jews back into the "foreign" if not "Arab" category. We are thus back to the paradox with which we started—the need to both preserve and deny difference from a position of difference (Scott 1996). In a sense, then, despite their claims to the contrary, Sephardi youth had thoroughly internalized mainstream French assumptions about national identity and difference, and that itself fueled the practices that led to their alienation. They were damned if they did and damned if they did not. By attempting to provisionally write themselves back into French national imaginaries, they were forced to assume subject positions that made such rewritings impossible.

Conclusion

I started my narrative by relating Margot's decision not to attend a demonstration against anti-Semitism because she considered herself "racist." There is more to this story than was initially stated. Although Margot refused to demonstrate because she could not attend an antiracist rally, the protest was not supposed to be against racism. Jewish institutions—the Conseil Représentatif des Institutions Juives de France (CRIF) and the Union des Etudiants Juifs de France (UEJF)—organized the demonstration. In doing so, they ignored requests from a range of antiracist groups to expand the theme so that it included opposition to anti-Arab and antiblack racism. This request was, and was understood as, an argument about the structural equivalence of Jews, blacks, and Arab Muslims vis-à-vis the white post-Christian majority. As we have seen, in the 1970s and even 1980s, some Jewish elites made this kind of argument about the nature of French racism and national exclusion. But by 2004, such a position was no longer acceptable or even thinkable for Jewish organizations. Rather, Jewish institutions maintained that such an understanding obscured rather than clarified the problem of hatred and exclusion in France. They insisted that anti-Semitism was qualitatively and quantitatively different from anti-immigrant racism and that immigrants, their children, and their grandchildren were very likely to be anti-Semites.

Many of the excluded antiracist groups marched nonetheless, loudly chanting that they were "against racism and anti-Semitism." But they did not march in the main cortege, and their ideological disagreement with the organizers was apparent in their physical distance. Most of those who marched with the main cortege seemed to be Jews. The event thus portrayed a very particular conception of minority being and belonging.

With slogans like *"synagogue brulée, République en danger"* (a burned synagogue means the Republic is in danger) and a plethora of French flags, the organizers established an intimate, exclusive connection between Jewishness and the trappings and values of the French nation. During the protest, the synagogue (but not the mosque, though a number of them had also been burned and vandalized) represented French Republican tolerance and democracy. In addition, the very public exclusion of antiracist groups largely associated with the defense of "Arabs" highlighted the rejection of any imagined commonalities between Muslims and Jews. Instead, Jews (perhaps unintentionally) styled themselves as part of a white post-Christian majority opposed to "immigrants," who threatened to destroy the Republic with their religious practices and intolerance. It hardly came as a surprise when, just a few months later, the secular Zionist youth organization, Hashomer Ha'atzair, (in)famously issued a petition signed by a number of prominent Jewish (and non-Jewish) intellectuals accusing blacks and Arabs of anti-Semitism *and* "anti-white" or "anti-French" racism. Alain Finkielkraut, one of the signatories and defenders of the petition, noted: "Today, a certain number of immigrants reconstitute their identities through hatred of Jews and France, a hatred that is both judeo-phobic and Franco-phobic" (cited in Van Eeckhout 2005). The message could not have been clearer: Jews and "the French" had a common foreign enemy.

This reshuffling of structural alliances and affinities is an ethnographic instance of one of the larger shifts outlined in this book. I have argued that Jewish elites and many Jewish adults produced a new synthesis between Franco-Jewish models and the more racialized concepts of Jewishness that emerged in the North African colonial context. They evoked "autochthony" as a ground for claiming both Jews' privileged relationship to Frenchness and Jewish ontological difference. In the process, they obscured most French Jews' immigrant origins and denied any structural commonalities or ethical obligations between Jews and other minority groups. This helped create certain kinds of lived social fictions about the relationship between "Jews" and "the French"; the two groups were often imagined as both incommensurable and the same. Day school principals' terror that I might reveal the public secret of adolescent intolerance spoke to this tension. It was not the difference from the French mainstream suggested by Jewish intolerance that posed a problem. In fact, crucial to my argument is the fact that Jewish intolerance of "Arabs" brought Jews and a wider (post-)Catholic French mainstream together. Rather, it was public attention to Jewish intolerance that seemed threatening. The day school mother (discussed in chapter 2) who was "proud" to have been born in France and not in North Africa, illustrated this in a slightly different way. She was "French" despite her conviction that "the French" were morally and culturally inferior to "the Jews."

But Margot's reaction, like those of many of her Sephardi day-school classmates, disrupted this kind of narrative. Her (in)actions and comments inadvertently collapsed the distance between Arabs and Jews posited by elite Jewish discourse. In the first place, she and the overwhelming majority of her classmates did not attend the demonstration. Some had been told by rabbis in their synagogues that it would be "dangerous." Others insisted that it was not "really about Jews." This seemed tied to the participation of one non-Jewish, antiracist organization—SOS-Racisme—that actually had very close ties to the organized Jewish community. But many others claimed simply that it was pointless. And that was not just an assessment about the depth and permanence of anti-Semitism in France. Day school students also did not participate in the wave of demonstrations against proposed high-school reforms that drew tens of thousands of young people into the Paris streets in 2005, disrupted many public schools, and made the headlines for months. According to a Brith Abraham senior who I interviewed after his graduation in 2005, the subject never even came up in conversations with his classmates and friends. This speaks to a profound disengagement from French politics, even when the issues addressed seem to have a direct relevance to students' lives. A Beit Sarah student summed up this disconnect: "We are not interested in what happens in France." As Jewish elites and institutions worked to tie Jews to France and French values, day school students dismissed such efforts as irrelevant to their present and future. Instead, they imagined themselves as displaced foreigners, biding their time until they could "return" to where they really belonged.

If being out of place in France turned "Jews" into temporary immigrants, Margot also suggested other parallels between Arabs and Jews. In some ways, her refusal to attend a demonstration against anti-

Semitism on the ground that she was "racist" reestablished the old structural parallels between Arabs and Jews. It suggested that both groups could equally be victims of "racism." Most day school students actually used the term "racism" almost exclusively to refer to anti-Semitism, thus vitiating a distinction that was central to Jewish institutions. At the same time, however, the evocation of Margot's "hatred" for Arabs reopened the ontological and cultural divide between the two groups. It created lines of primordialized distinction on the shared structural margins of French society. This, however, had unintended consequences. By engaging in precisely the same kinds of "intolerable intolerance" that many French Jews and non-Jews attributed to immigrants, particularly Arab Muslims, Margot underscored the ways in which young Jews and Arabs actually shared dispositions and practices. She thus further exiled herself from the values Jewish institutions insisted were the foundation of both French Republicanism and Jewish Frenchness.

This too encapsulates a central piece of my story. Rather than echo Jewish institutions and elites who claimed that Jews were "both, and"—simultaneously defined by their Jewishness *and* meaningfully and permanently connected to France—young Sephardim imagined Jewishness, Arabness, and Frenchness as mutually exclusive, primordialized identities. This left day school students with little interest in even attempting to create spaces in which deeply embodied differences could coexist. Thus even a demonstration staged for Jews, by Jews, and about Jews was viewed as a waste of time, a kind of naïve identity politics that could never eliminate the inherent danger of living with non-Jews. That danger could only be eliminated by living in the Jewish nation-state or, to a lesser extent, the imagined autonomous ethnic enclaves of the United States.

But imagining and enacting these pure spaces of Jewishness was not so easy. Adolescent Sephardim did not grow up in the Jewish enclaves French colonialism encouraged and sustained in Morocco and Tunisia. They lived in mixed neighborhoods, cheek-by-jowl with the children and grandchildren of other immigrants, where they were sometimes mistaken for Arab Muslims. As a result, adolescents attempted to project racialized Jewishness through market-based practices. What they wore, where they bought it, who they bought it with, and where and how they displayed it all contributed to the naturalization of Jewishness as essence, physiognomy, and shared practice. For many young Jews, then, identity was *both* a conscious choice of literal self-fashioning and an ineluctable essence (Comaroff and Comaroff 2007). While these might seem to be diametrically opposed ontologies of being and belonging, in practice they were dialectically linked, each reconfiguring the other and serving as proof of its authenticity. "Jewish" fashion rendered ambiguous physiognomy "Jewish," in the process confirming the "true" nature of the wearer—and vice versa. But when the incommensurability between these two understandings of the self became apparent—when appearance (the Lacoste cap) suddenly did not index the appropriate (Arab) essence—racialized violence stepped into the breach. This made Margot's racism a necessary part of youth identity practices. For many young Sephardi Jews, this "hatred" of Arabs helped make them unambiguously Jews.

A number of more general theoretical points grow out of this story about shifting patterns of Jewish identification in postcolonial France. In the first place, my tale suggests that the determination of self and other is not just negative and differential (Barth 1969), but also deeply dialectical. It is not simply, as Esther Benbassa (2003) has suggested, that Arab Muslims replaced Jews as the internalized "other" defining the limits of French national inclusion. Instead, since the colonial period in North Africa and the era of decolonization in the Metropole, the constitution of Jewish *Frenchness* has depended on continuously reinforcing the distinction between Jewishness and Arabness, particularly in relation to Sephardim. At the same time, Arab foreignness rests at least in part on claims that Islam is more corporeal, more problematically embodied than Judaism, and therefore more difficult to reconcile with Republican citizenship. This dialectic was evident in Jewish institutional and Sephardi adolescent discourse. On the one hand, growing Jewish attention to Islamic "fundamentalism" and Arab anti-Semitism highlighted Islam's supposedly inappropriate corporality. Muslims, so the story went, not only failed to separate private and public, belief and practice, foreign and French, they even turned religion into pure corporality—race—and attacked French Jews for being "Israelis." On the other hand, the growing publicity of Jewish practice, the increasing influence of orthodoxy and ultraorthodoxy on institutional Jewishness, the move toward Jewish self-ghettoization, and the forms of racialization common among many Sephardi youth underscored the importance of *Jewish* corporality. In other words, even practices that highlighted Jewish distinctiveness constantly threatened to produce Jewish/Muslim proximity, thus potentially fueling renewed attempts at distinction.

My story about emergent forms of Sephardi adolescent Jewishness also challenges the identity literature on liminality and hybridity. Where much postmodern and structuralist identity theory sees the liminality of migrants, young people, and even ethno-racial minorities (particularly Jews) as the key to deconstructing what Liisa Malkki (1995) has called "categorical identities," I point to the opposite possibility. In fact, in many ways, the more liminal French Jews were, the more likely they were to attempt to reroot their identities in an unchanging essence. So while some parents and teachers described themselves as "Arab Jews" and as "French Jews," adolescents were more prone to characterizing themselves in exclusive categorical terms. And they used race and racism to ensure that exclusivity. Far from heralding the advent of a postracial or even postidentitarian world, the double liminality of Sephardi youth led to a frantic attempt to create and police primordial distinctions and to ensure that outward practices and appearances "matched" internal essences.

To some extent, this was done through consumption itself. And this highlights a third narrative about contemporary identity that my story challenges. Beginning with Hebdige's (1979) seminal work on youth subcultures, the work of constructing meaningful identities through the tools and products of the global market has come to imply denaturalization. Because young people often rely heavily on consumption—clothes, music, movies, and drugs—to define a sense of self, youth identities are often described as obviously constructed and therefore categorically subversive. Sephardi youth *do* rely heavily on consumer choice to construct their sense of self—they consciously choose their clothes, friends, schools, and restaurants as a way of both reflecting and building Jewish identities. But in a sense, these choices have helped to overdetermine the renaturalization of Jewishness. The rage for rootedness in a period of deracination and rapid change made choice an insufficient ground on which to build the self (Comaroff and Comaroff 2007; Seligman 2000). There was always a gap between adolescents' conscious choices, which were obviously contingent and ultimately ambiguous, and what they thought *should be* a legible and inescapable primordial identity. So, once again, race and racism stepped into the breach, filling the void between ethno-religious transmission and consumption. Naturalization in the form of racialization, therefore, does not necessarily decline as identities become conscious constructs built through consumption; it may actually get called forth by the power of the market in an age of authenticity.

Furthermore, the racialization and Herderian rejections of multicultural community explored in this account ironically may be rooted in postcolonial state practices designed to open up public space for certain kinds of difference. The adolescents with whom I worked were the first to come of age within a newly configured, "multicultural" French public sphere. They were also the first generation to be educated within one of its hallmark institutions—barely regulated, government-funded Jewish day schools. Regardless of ideology or teacher practices, the physical and social isolation produced by these schools eliminated the possibility of sustained, meaningful interactions with non-Jews. At the same time, day school students were exposed to only a limited slice of French Jewishness. Students overwhelmingly shared family histories, socioeconomic positions, political ideologies, and religious practices. They projected this homogeneity onto Jewishness writ large, turning it into a universally homogenous way of being and seeing, not a subjunctive community (Seligman et al. 2008) or a context-specific engagement with a set of discursive practices (Asad 1993). This made difference of any sort appear incompatible with "real" community and produced an intolerant form of "integralism" (Holmes 2000). Rather than provide a framework for difference within the nation-state, France's particular form of limited multicultural practice may actually produce the conditions for its own impossibility.

This, in turn, leads me to one final general reflection about racism and intolerance in France and perhaps in other Western democracies. It would be too easy to associate Jewish (or Muslim) racism and intolerance with the very nature of illiberal religious practices. In fact, as we have seen, in many ways day schoolers' conception of Jewishness was not religious but primoridal. This was fueled in part by commonalities between Muslim and Jewish religious practices that might be socially dangerous for Jews. But it was also underwritten by Jewish day school students' very modern conceptions of self and identity. For most students, "authentic" identity was rooted in an individualized and yet collective internal essence (being) that simply expressed itself in external practice. This foundational presumption made religious conceptions of community as becoming incomprehensible, assimilable only through a transformation of practice into race. As a result, day schoolers' racism and intolerance had little to do with the content of their religious education, however illiberal it might have been. Instead, it was rooted in the un-narrated confrontation between two very different understandings of community in a context that greatly reduced the complexity of lived Jewish experience. Jewishness was reduced to an essence, and adolescent experience with Jewishness was limited to Jews who shared similar class, historical, and ethnic backgrounds. In other words, the phenomenon of simplifying and reifying Jewishness was not (just) about resurgent orthodoxy limiting the range and scope of behaviors that counted as Jewish. It was also about the reinterpretation of transcendent, performance-based communities through the lens of reductionist, secular understandings of the self in contexts of increasing ghettoization.

If this is what led to the racialization of religion or to the theocratization of race, it has serious political and theoretical implications. It suggests that neither Islam nor Judaism as embodied practices can be held solely responsible for the growth of sometimes violent intolerance of religious, ethnic, and gendered differences in France (or in Europe more generally). Instead, the focus must be shifted to the transformations of religious understandings taking place in contexts where individual autonomy and authenticity are highly valued. In this light, French attempts to establish and reinforce a version of laïcité, rooted in the necessity of deracinating individuals from certain kinds of ascriptive communities, may be fueling, not containing, the growing problem of minority self-primordialization. As violent intolerance between and among minority groups becomes a daily fact of life in some Parisian neighborhoods and on some school playgrounds, it is imperative that France rethink its 21st-century "Jewish question."

Notes

Introduction

1. All personal names are pseudonyms.

2. The police estimated turnout at 9,000, the demonstration organizers at 30,000.

3. For a discussion of Jewish reactions to racism and anti-Semitism in the immediate post-war period, see Noriel 2007: 486–487.

4. It is notoriously difficult to give accurate Jewish population demographics. Not only does one face the thorny question of who is a Jew, but it is also illegal to collect official census information on race, religion, or ethnicity in France. There are numerous problems with all of the population studies that attempt to count and classify French Jews. For example, the Fonds Social Juif Unifié (FSJU) has published studies (Cohen 2002) based on "Jewish" last names, a technique that is almost guaranteed to underestimate the European Jewish (Ashkenazi) population, which has far more intermarriage than the more recently installed North African (Sephardi) population.

5. In the 1980s, Israel invaded Lebanon and the first Palestinian Intifada began.

6. Immediately after the bombing, Raymond Barre noted that the attack had targeted "*Israélites* going to synagogue" but had killed "innocent Frenchmen." The statement, as many in the Jewish community and beyond angrily noted at the time, posited a distinction between Jews and the French (for a discussion of this historical moment, see Hyman 1998).

7. This demonstration may have marked a turning point; for the first time, some Jewish groups carried Israeli rather than French flags (Azeroual 1990:11).

8. All proper names have been changed to protect institutional identities. For the same reason, I have also chosen to dramatically limit the historical and contextual detail given about each institution. As the story of my expulsion suggests, the world in which I worked is a very small, interconnected one. And almost any significant details about institutional histories would probably allow for the identification of the schools in question.

9. I spent the least time in (and will talk the least about) Beit Ya'acov because my access to students and classes was severely restricted by the principal, who disliked the idea of a young, (then) unmarried woman wandering his hallways.

10. A 2002 study financed by the FSJU found that 48% of adult Parisian Jews had four years of schooling beyond the *baccalauréat* while only 28% of the general Parisian population had similar qualifications. The difference was even more marked on a national level: 31% of Jews as compared with 9% of the total population (Cohen 2002:17).

11. Benbassa's biography alone highlights the complexity of Jewishness for many in France; born in Turkey, she emigrated to Israel at the age of 15. A few years later, she made a kind of reverse *aliyah*, leaving Israel for France.

12. She has not, however, been sued for racial defamation, which is a crime in France. Other intellectuals have been. Edgar Morin, a sociologist who is often identified as a Jew in the media, was sued for an article on the Israeli-Palestinian conflict published in *Le Monde*.

13. I knew she was North African because she had, at another point during the discussion, made a joke in Arabic.

14. For many French Jews, the United Nations World Conference against Racism held in Durban, South Africa, in 2001 was a case in point. The conference committee passed a resolution declaring Israel a "racist" state. Pierre-André Taguieff, a philosopher who is regularly published in the Jewish press, has argued that Durban is a symptom of all that is wrong with Muslims in general and Muslims in France in particular (Taguieff 2002:130–145). For the reaction of some French Jewish elites to the accusations of Israeli racism at Durban, see Cukierman 2001; Tarnero 2001.

15. Historian Naomi Davidson (2012) suggests that French understandings of embodied Islam as a kind of inescapable, racial identity dates back to at least late 19th-century colonial practice and is evident even in Metropolitan attempts to "domesticate" Islam through institutions like the *grande mosquée de Paris*.

Chapter 1

1. In her book *Only Paradoxes to Offer* (1996), Joan Scott has made precisely this argument for gender difference in the French Republic. Anthropologist Mayanthi Fernando (2009) has made a slightly different, but related, argument for "secular" Muslims in contemporary France, whose assimilation to normative Republican values is always (and must always) be marked by their collective ethno-religious Muslim identity.

2. This story, which is hardly new, exemplifies what Gary Wilder (2005) has described as the simultaneously universalizing and particularizing aspects of both French colonialism and Republicanism (6).

3. Anti-Jewish measures began in the 7th century and intensified considerably in the 13th century. In 633, Jews were expelled from what would become France for the first time (Bourdrel 2004:21). Louis IX, also known as Saint Louis, introduced distinctive dress for Jews, restricted Jewish occupations, and even put the Talmud on trial for blasphemy (Benbassa 1997; Bourdrel 2004). In the 14th century, Jews were expelled twice. They were again ordered to leave France by

Catherine de Medici in 1615, just before she repealed the Edict of Nantes, which granted formal tolerance to Protestants.

4. Jews, however, were occasionally described as "foreign" to the Christian kingdom that gradually emerged in what would become France. But this had more to do with Jews' rejection of Christ than with a literal statement of origins. For example, in the 7th century, the archbishop of the area that is now Clermont-Ferrand implored Jews to "[s]tay with us in order to live like us or leave quickly. Return this land, in which you are foreigners [*étrangers*], to us; free us from contact with you or, if you stay here, share our faith" (cited in Bourdrel 2004:21–22). When Arab Muslim armies invaded the northern Mediterranean coast, the deicide accusation was transposed into the political register, becoming evidence of treason against the Christian state. In the 9th century, the archbishop of Toulouse claimed the right to slap Jews in front of the Cathedral on Easter, a practice he described as revenge for the Jewish-Muslim alliance that led to the (entirely imaginary) Arab conquest of that city (Benbassa 1997:28).

5. Hertzberg notes that 18th century Sephardim—who did *not* have their own civil courts, were relatively well-off economically, and tended to be lax in the application of many aspects of religious law—policed inside/outside boundaries with considerable zeal. The 1736 community charter for the Bordeaux *Sedaca*, or Jewish syndic, notes: "In order to safeguard our existence it is against our interests that any matter that concerns us should come to the knowledge of the gentiles. To ensure that no information should pass to them, we hereby decree that any individual who will inform the gentiles of any matter of consequence which can harm the Sedaca will be excommunicated and fined in accordance with the full rigor of the law" (cited in Hertzberg 1990:222).

Among Ashkenazi communities in places like Metz, the story seems to be reversed. By the 18th century, rabbinic courts found ways to cooperate with the increasingly powerful and centralized state's court system, particularly around economic issues like contract enforcement (Seligman and Weller 2012:187–188; also see Berkowitz 2010).

6. Their assimilation rested on the privatization of Judaism. Bordeaux's Jews largely rejected the Talmud as the basis for organized religious life, preferring direct interpretation of the *Pentatuach* (Benbassa 1997). This meant that the myriad of "hedges" the *Halakhah*, or Jewish law, builds around specific Biblical injunctions—hedges designed to highlight divinely ordained distinctions—were not considered obligations. This allowed, in some instances, for more open cultural and social exchange with non-Jewish populations.

7. And indeed, "Portuguese and Spanish" Jews were emancipated a full year and a half before the general emancipation of Jews living in French national territory (Hertzberg 1990; Hyman 1998; Scharzfuchs 1989).

8. Ironically, it seems to have been the reluctance of law enforcement officials to involve themselves in intra-religious conflicts that prevented the success of this strategy (Albert 1977).

9. For a detailed account of how "Franco-Judaism" impacted religious Jewish schooling and the 19th-century Jewish press, see further Haus (2002); Marrus (1971); and Albert (1977).

10. Just after the 1848 Revolution, at the beginning of the Second Republic, the chief rabbi of Strasbourg highlighted the transformation of Jews into proto-French nationals: "The flag flying today—don't you recognize it? It is the flag handed down by Moses to the people on Mount Sinai, the symbol of the rights of man proclaimed by our prophets at a time when the people were in slavery and subject to oppression. It is the Messiah's flag that will be raised one day over all the nations of the world. Today it is entrusted to the French people who, more than any other, deserve to gather the human family around it" (cited in Graetz 1996:231). Also see Marrus (1971) for an account of mid-19th-century Jewish religious discourse linking Judaism and the French nation-state.

11. Well into the 19th century, some local Alsatian governments insisted on taxing Jews at higher rates than other citizens, justifying the inequality with reference to continued Jewish involvement in usury. Eastern cities like Nancy established separate militia for Jews and non-Jews (Hyman 1998:33–34). Despite periodic suits, French courts did not find the *more judaico*—a special Jewish oath premised on Jewish perfidy—unconstitutional until 1846, when the Jewish lawyer and future Minister of Justice Adolphe Crémieux argued the case (Benbassa 1997:151).

12. Eugen Weber offers an important corrective to historians who view the Jewish question as *the* question facing modernizing France. During the 19th century, many departments did not have a single Jew and the majority had tiny scattered populations (1985:12–13). In addition, many of the charges leveled against Jews mirrored those against other groups that did not conform to the expectations of a rural, superstitious population. He notes, for example, that a Christian schoolteacher was stoned out of a village in the 1830s for reading a book in public (ibid.). As a result, the mere fact of Jewish literacy in a largely illiterate world rendered Jews "not only strange, but odd and threatening" (ibid.).

13. For a full account of the Dreyfus Affair and Jewish reactions to it, see Marrus (1971).

14. For an account of Jewish immigration to France at the end of the 19th century, see Green (1986).

15. Just after Dreyfus's public humiliation, Edouard Drumont, the anti-Semitic author of *La France Juive*, wrote: "The pathetic creature was not French. We understood everything from his actions, from his look, and from his face" (cited in Birnbaum 1998:82).

16. For a complete account of Vichy's anti-Semitic laws and their impact on Jews living in France, see Marrus and Paxton (1981); and Birnbaum (1996). For an account of the continuity between Republican logics and those of Vichy, see Noiriel (1999).

17. The criteria included French citizenship for five generations, lineage within a "notable" family, distinguished military service, or close relatives so distinguished (Marrus and Paxton 1981:99).

18. This is obviously a stark contrast to Nazi anti-Semitism, which was focused on rendering Jewishness visible among those who were most highly assimilated (Appadurai 1998; Bauman 1991).

19. As historians like Kim Munholland and John Sweets have noted, over the last thirty years there have been some dramatic changes in the historiography of wartime France. The Gaullist myth of a nation of *résistants* fell apart with the publication of Robert Paxton's (1972) iconoclastic work, *Vichy France: Old Guard and New Order*, and his subsequent book with Michael Marrus (1981), *Vichy France and the Jews.* This myth was replaced with a story about a nation of collaborators, including those who had served in the most hallowed institutions of the Third Republic, particularly the judiciary (see Ryan 1996; Weisberg 1996). There is no doubt that much of French civil society was deeply anti-Semitic, but neither extreme probably does justice to the complexity of the situation.

20. For some general, canonical accounts of French Jewry at various points in postrevolutionary French history, see Benbassa (1997); Birnbaum (1988, 1996, 2000); Graetz (1996); Hyman (1979, 1991, 1998); Schwarzfuchs (1975, 1979, 1989); and Winock (2004).

21. The first written evidence of Jewish presence in North Africa dates from 9th century B.C.E. Carthage, a city Palestinian Jews and Phoenicians coruled for almost 700 years prior to its fall to the Romans (Laskier 1983:8). The Roman destruction of Jerusalem and the Second Temple in the first century C.E. encouraged another wave of Jewish immigrants to settle in North Africa. Driven from urban areas by anti-Jewish measures introduced under the Holy Roman Empire, Jews resettled in inaccessible mountainous regions, entering into sustained contact with Berber-speaking populations. By the time of the Arab conquest in the 7th century, a significant number of Berber tribes had converted to Judaism.

22. Non-Muslims were forbidden to criticize or falsify the Quran, denigrate or insult the Prophet, make fun of or critique Islam, marry or engage in sexual relations with Muslim women (although both were permitted between a Muslim man and a Christian or Jewish woman), proselytize or in any way encourage someone to stray from the Muslim faith, or aid the enemies of the Islamic state (Chouraqui 1998a:94). Failure to observe any of these strictures annulled the contract, and thus any state commitment to the dhimmi's basic rights. The offending person was often subject to execution. In addition, in some times and places, dhimmi were also required to wear distinctive clothing, to restrain their public religious displays, and to pay an additional annual tax, called the *djyzia* (Chouraqui 1998a:91; Allouche-Benayoun and Bensimon 1998:16).

23. This does not mean the Jewish-Muslim distinction never had serious social and material consequences. When the economic climate worsened or the stability of a particular regime was threatened, Jews might be persecuted by state officials demanding ever-higher payments in exchange for protection. They also might have their shops, synagogues, and homes attacked by Muslim subjects all too willing to hold Jews responsible for their poverty. In much rarer cases, Jews

were even murdered in scenes that resembled Eastern European pogroms (Stillman 1980).

24. It is somewhat less clear whether Jews ate in Muslim homes given the greater stringency of Jewish dietary restrictions. Kosher cooking excludes foods forbidden to Muslims, but it includes other restrictions that are not observed in Islam. Muslims, for example, often cook meat with milk or butter—a combination forbidden to observant Jews. But Claude Tapia (1986) notes that Tunisian Jews often bought their food stuffs (particularly baked goods) from Muslim producers, whether or not the producer could guarantee that his products were "kosher" (50). In addition, Haim Zafrani insists that North African interpretations of Jewish law tended to be much more lax about dietary restrictions than those of the European tradition (2005:221).

25. By the 15th century, there was a *mellah*, or clearly demarked Jewish quarter, in Fès (Chouraqui 1998a:96).

26. A whole range of Jewish and Muslim rituals drew on a similarly shared repertoire of practices and projections about a common social and spiritual world. Drawing on tradition that perhaps predated Muslim conquest, Jews and Muslims often shared pilgrimage routes to *ghriba* [sanctuaries] or to the tombs of venerated saints (Allouche-Benayoun and Bensimon 1998:22). Jewish marriage customs closely resembled those of Muslims, particularly the tradition of putting henna on the hands and feet of the bride-to-be (Tapia 1986:34). "Superstitions" were also shared. Jews and Muslims frequented the same fortune-tellers and medicine men, feared the same demons and spirits, and shared the same amulets and remedies (most famously the symbol of the fish and the *hamza*, or five-fingered hand) (Chouraqui 1998a:203; Tapia 1986:31–32). Some forms of religious syncretism may have continued right up to the end of the colonial period. Joëlle Allouche-Benayoun's (1998) Algerian informants in France claimed that Muslims waited at the synagogue doors to hear the reading of the Ten Commandments on Shavuoth, the Jewish holiday commemorating the transmission of Jewish law from God to Moses (103–104). Some of her informants also reported that sterile Muslim women believed catching a glimpse of a *sefer Torah*, Torah scroll, would bring fertility (ibid.).

27. By the 19th century, when European powers began vying with the Ottomans for control in the region, dhimmitude seems to have been enforced in particularly degrading ways. Jews were taxed excessively, forced to remove their shoes in Muslim neighborhoods, required to dismount in a Muslim's presence, and constrained to wear specific colors and forms of clothing. On the eve of the French conquest of Algeria, for example, many Algerian Jews were subject to daily humiliations (Allouche-Benayoun and Bensimon 1998:26–27; Friedman 1988:3; Tapia 1986:34; Stillman 1980:17). During the same time period, Jews living outside the direct control of the Sherifian Sultan in Morocco were also subject to violent reprisals at the hands of local officials and nomadic tribes. Many European Jews who traveled to the area in the 19th century described Moroccan Jews as a poor, despised, pariah class (Stillman 1991:5).

28. Jews in Algiers might have had particular reasons for supporting the French invasion. Two Jewish bankers and commercial agents, Bacri and Busnach, were actually at the heart of the argument between the bey and the French consul that became the excuse for the French invasion. The bey retaliated by expelling all Jews from the city just before the French landing (Chouraqui 1998b:15–16).

29. In 1848, the Second Republic formally annexed Algerian territory that was then under French control, creating the departments of Algiers, Oran, and Constantine. These departments were, in theory, to be treated like any other departments in the Hexagon (Shepard 2006:21).

30. For a full account of the myriad of often contradictory changes in legal categories and their relationships in colonial Algeria, see Shepherd (2006).

31. The pressure paid off in 1845, when the Ministry of War authorized the creation of a consistorial system in Algeria. Within a short time, all three of the areas then firmly under French control—Algiers, Constantine, and Oran—had local consistories. And by 1867, all three of these had been formally annexed and subordinated to the Paris-based Consistoire Central (Chouraqui 1952:211; Sussman 2002:61).

32. Between 1865 and 1870, only 144 Algerian Jews had sought to become French citizens (Shepard 2006:29). Between 1865 and 1899, only 1,309 men classified as Muslim completed applications for French citizenship (ibid.:27).

33. In fact, an amendment to the decree, promulgated a year later, made access to Frenchness via Jewishness into a quasi-test of racial identity. In order to prevent Jews from other parts of the Maghreb from benefiting, the decree required proof of birth to or descent from Jews present in Algeria prior to 1830 (Shepard 2006:28–29 n. 27).

34. The Crémieux Decree made naturalized Jews and other French citizens legally indistinguishable, but local officials continued to count Jews and non-Jews separately in all censuses from 1871 to 1931 (Shepard 2006:35).

35. Even at the very end of the colonial period, only 13% of Muslim children attended French schools (Abitbol 1998:289).

36. It also certainly did not mean that all Algerian Jews accepted their own "Frenchness." Adolphe Crémieux famously insisted that Jewish emancipation should be obligatory rather than voluntary because Algerian Jews would never have chosen Frenchness over God's law (Friedman 1998:10). Not surprisingly, local religious leaders often strenuously opposed all of the changes entailed by the decree. By the turn of the century, some Algerian Jews had begun lobbying French Jewish institutions like the Alliance Israélite Universelle (Universal Israelite Alliance, AIU)—an organization dedicated to "civilizing" foreign Jews through French-language instruction—to help re-Judaize local Jews. Although religious conservatives in other North African contexts viewed AIU schools as shameless promoters of Jewish Frenchification (Laskier 1983), in the Algerian context *any* religious education at all would have been viewed by the observant as an improvement over the status quo. In 1902, a group of religious Algerian Jews specifically

asked the AIU board in France to create a network of Jewish schools in Algeria equivalent to what already existed in Morocco and Tunisia. The request was categorically refused.

37. In 1895, the French newspaper *l'Echo d'Oran* noted: "The famous decree, the cause of so much ill in Algeria, had thrown into play [*eût jeté dans la balance*] the enormous weight of unthinking votes that, depending on whether they go to the right or to the left, . . . create the majority" (cited in Trigano 2003:181).

38. This was one of the deadliest anti-Jewish riots in French history outside of World War II. Historians agree that this riot involved far more Muslim initiation and participation than previous instances of anti-Semitic violence. While Allouche-Benayoun (1998) maintains, as did contemporary Jewish observers, that Europeans were the instigators and Muslims simply their pawns, Abitbol links the Constantine pogrom to growing Arab nationalism and deteriorating relations between Zionists and Palestinians in Palestine (2005:193). For accounts that foreground French colonialism and anti-Semitism as a necessary framework for this riot, see Joshua Cole (2010) and Ethan Katz (2010).

39. Some Muslim religious and community leaders denounced the abrogation of the Crémieux Decree and the discrimination against Jews. Cheik-el-Okbi wrote in November 1942: "By putting down the Jew, one only brings him closer together with the Moslem. It was thought that at the abrogation of the Crémieux decree, the Moslems would rejoice; but the latter can easily see the dubious worth of a citizenship that the granting authority can take away after seventy years enjoyment" (cited in Marrus and Paxton 1981:195). The Algerian Jews interviewed by Friedman in the mid-1970s had memories of Muslim neighbors offering material and emotional support to Jews, while French "Catholics" adopted the ambient anti-Semitism of the time period (Friedman 1988:89).

40. The relationship between Jewishness and Frenchness was reinforced just before and after the Evian Accords. In July 1961, the Mozabite Jews living in southern Algeria, a region that had not been under French control in 1870 when the Crémieux Decree was passed, were accorded French citizenship en masse (Shepard 2006:244). These Jews had remained under "Mosaic law" throughout the colonial period, practiced polygamy, and had even escaped having to register under surnames with the colonial state. Their only claim to commonalities with French Algerian Jews was some essentialized notion of Jewishness.

41. On the one hand, the Front de Liberation Nationale (FLN), a major Algerian nationalist organization, pleaded with Algerian Jews to reclaim their rightful "native" heritage and to turn their backs on the always partial and contested citizenship rights that had been conferred on them "by the oppressors" (cited in Abitbol 1998a:294). On the other hand, the Organisation de l'armée secrete (OAS), a paramilitary group dedicated to keeping Algeria French, argued that Jews should support a French Algeria because of Muslim anti-Semitism and hostility toward Israel (Sussman 2002:135). For a full account of the complexity of these pleas and Algerian Jewish positions during the war, see Bensimon (1971) and Sussman (2002).

42. The historian Todd Shepard (2006) suggests that after 1961, this assimilation did indeed become possible as pro-French Algerian forces abandoned anti-Semitism and Metropolitan efforts to eliminate any distinction between "European" *pieds-noirs* and Algerian Jews (180-182). But even Shepard acknowledges that the complete collapse of distinction, if it ever occurred, was short-lived (ibid.:182).

43. Naturalization of any native Moroccan living in the country remained illegal until the end of the colonial period.

44. For accounts of the complexity of the relationships between native Jews, more recently settled and generally wealthier European Jews, and European colonial officials in Tunisia, see Allali et al. (1989); Chouraqui (1952); Sebag (1991); and Stillman (1980). For similar accounts about Morocco, see Abitbol (1998b) and Zafrani (2005).

45. This incident is recounted as follows: in 1857, Batto Sfez, the driver for the Jewish caïd responsible for collecting taxes for the bey, apparently insulted Islam during an argument with a Muslim. The bey chose to have the driver tried in recently established Malekite courts, which issued far stiffer penalties for dhimmi blasphemy than more traditional Tunisian *makhzan* courts. The driver was sentenced to death (Sebag 1991:117). Apparently, the entire European diplomatic corps pressed the Tunisian bey to void the death sentence.

46. The condemnation of Sfez in Tunisia was at least partially an attempt to shore up the bey's faltering power by proving his commitment to Islam and order. In Morocco, local caïds far from the center of Sherifian power used anti-Jewish violence as a response to growing political and economic distress (Chouraqui 1998, vol 2:37; Laskier 1983a:16).

47. Some Jews may have started viewing the European powers as omnipotent protectors whose mere presence allowed them to provoke Muslims in ways that would have been unthinkable in the precolonial period. As in Algeria, some Jews in Tunisia and Morocco supported French troops publicly, celebrating their victories and offering their services. In addition, it is possible that some Jews stopped using the customary forms of deference that regulated social relations between Muslims and non-Muslims under Islamic rule. When revoking the 1864 equality edict prompted by Sir Montefiore's visit, the Moroccan sultan invoked "Jewish arrogance" and "separatism" as the rationale behind his change of heart (Chouraqui 1998b:37). In 1874, the AIU secretary general, Isidore Loeb, and Adolphe Crémieux surprisingly echoed this sentiment. They wrote a joint letter to the leaders of the Moroccan Jewish community that emphasized the European powers' role in "rescu[ing] the righteous from the wicked," but also implored local Jews to "refrain from boasting about the help [you are getting] from foreign governments and of deliverance from afar. May the lips of those who boast [of such help] be silenced" (cited in Laskier 1983a:47).

48. After 1867, the AIU began training "native" Jews to be secular teachers, but they first had to be "Europeanized." They were trained at the *École* Normale

Israélite Orientale (Oriental Israelite Normal School) in Paris, where they were immersed in the principles of Franco-Judaism before being returned to posts in North Africa or the Middle East (Rodrigue 1990:188).

49. Wealthy native traders often sent their children to French public schools (Allali et al. 1989:44). Until the rise of Italian fascism in the interwar period, the Livournais tended to use the Italian schools operating in Tunisia. But at the time, most Jewish children probably did not go to modern schools at all. Limited enrollment and opposition to the transformation of local educational practices left many children entirely in the traditional system; girls were not educated outside the home and boys acquired the rudiments of written Hebrew and rote knowledge of religious observance in *khateb* run by elderly rabbis.

50. Yomtov Sémach, the Moroccan publisher of the AIU's early- 20th century mouthpiece *Paix et Droit* (Peace and Law), attacked the few (usually poor) Jews who decided to make aliyah in the 1920s and 1930s. He also condemned Jewish National Fund and Jewish Foundation Fund employees who preached the good news of political Zionism in North Africa (Laskier 1983:212). The head of AIU in Tunisia in the teens and twenties was hardly more sympathetic to Zionism. He argued that Zionist propaganda would never succeed in attracting North African and French Jews to Palestine, but might very well fuel anti-Semitism in countries that had long accused Jews of refusing and/or being unable to assimilate (Laskier 1994:49). In both countries, AIU officials called Zionists politically naïve, wondering whether they realized the backlash their position would provoke at home and among the Arab Muslims already living in Palestine.

51. Between 1948 and 1956, an estimated 70,000 Moroccan Jews and about 25,000 Tunisian Jews emigrated to Israel (Laskier 1994:126; Sebag 1991:274). Israeli immigration statistics are always somewhat political, since they intentionally exclude those who leave. A good many of these emigrants, facing dire economic conditions in Israel and notorious Ashkenazi racism, subsequently may have returned to their native lands.

52. As early as the 1930s, the largest Moroccan nationalist party began making overtures to Jews (Bensimon 1978:102). By the 1950s, a few Jewish leaders had heeded these calls, joining the Istiqlal and the Parti démocratique d'indépendence (Democratic Independence Party, PDI). Just after independence in 1956, Sultan Muhammed V told Jews that they would be considered citizens on equal footing with Muslims (Bensimon 1978:35). Tunisian independence advocates behaved similarly. Small numbers of Jewish intellectuals were involved in the first Tunisian nationalist party created after World War I, Destour, and its later reincarnation, Néo-Destour (Memmi 1974:53). Nationalist rallies were held to encourage Jews to break with the French and side with their fellow Tunisians in the anticolonial struggle. In 1952, Habib Bourghiba, Néo-Destour's leader who was at the time imprisoned by the French, noted: "The presence in this camp . . . of Jews and Muslims having fought and suffered side by side for the same national ideal of liberty and justice is an apt symbol of our movement. It will always be this way, as long as

Néo-Destour remains in existence" (cited in Sebag 1991:278). The first Moroccan and Tunisian postcolonial governments included Jewish ministers, and Jews voted in the first national elections like everyone else.

Chapter 2

1. Excerpt from the monthly newsletter *Observatoire du monde juif*, begun by Algieran-born French philosopher Shmuel Trigano in the wake of the Second Palestinian Intifada.

2. For a full account of the way that "decolonization" emerged as a historical and ideological project in Metropolitan France, see Shepard (2006).

3. For a rich and nuanced account of this shift as it pertains to French antiracist organizations, see Mandel forthcoming.

4. Women are the significant exception to this rule. In 2000 the French Parliament passed a law forcing political parties under threat of financial penalty to make women at least half of the candidates on their electoral lists. At the same time, those who lobbied for the legal change insisted, somewhat incomprehensibly from an American perspective, that it in "no way suggested that women would represent their sex" (Fassin n.d.:2; see Scott 2005).

5. The sociologist Eric Fassin has argued that this opposition started lessening in academic circles around 2005, a year that witnessed the creation of the Conseil représentatif des associations noires (CRAN) (see Fassin 2008).

6. André-Pierre Taguieff has written about this most extensively in the French context. For an equivalent analysis of the British context, see Gilroy (1992).

7. This was particularly true for the children of Algerian immigrants. Algeria was considered part of territorial France from 1848 until 1962. At the time, under a French law referred to as the *double jus soli*, anyone born on French territory to someone born on French territory (whether or not that person held French nationality him- or herself) automatically acquired French nationality (Weil 2005:58).

8. According to the historian Todd Shepard, Charles de Gaulle articulated precisely this kind of understanding of France in order to justify his support for the decolonization of Algeria. Shepard writes: "De Gaulle's conception of France was somewhat cosmopolitan. It was in this acceptance of visible and marked difference that he differed strikingly from the Charles Maurras/Maurice Barrès . . . brand of xenophobic nationalism. As he stated to [Alain] Peyrefitte [his minister of information in the late 1950s], 'It is all very well that there are yellow French, black French, brown French. They demonstrate that France is open to all races and that she has a universal mission.' In his view, however, the sine qua non of that vision was that 'they stay a small minority. If not, France will no longer be France. We are, in any case, above all a European people, racially white, culturally Greek and Latin, and religiously Christian'" (Shepard 2006:76). In other words, Shepard believes that the decolonization of Algeria required and entailed the reimagination of France in ethnicized or Europeanized terms (ibid.:167–168).

9. Historian Naomi Davidson (2012) has traced out the long colonial history

behind treating North Africans in the Metropole as Muslims, rather than as immigrants. This was part and parcel of the gradual 20th-century reification of Islam as an inescapable corporeal and then ethno-religious identity.

10. French street slang, called *verlan,* works through syllabic inversion. The word *verlan* is itself an inversion of *à l'envers,* the phrase meaning "backward." And generations of street slang can be marked by the number of times a word has been inverted. *Beur* is the first inversion of *Arabe.* Today, Arab Muslims are called *rebeu,* the inversion of *beur.*

11. This is also evident in the continued discomfort with collecting official information about ethnic or racial identities. In 2009, then President Sarkozy created a commission (Comité pour la mesure et l'évaluation de la diversité et des discriminations) to study the question of introducing ethnic statistics. Almost immediately, a group of academics created a shadow committee to denounce the (favorable) opinions of the official commission (Coroller 2009; Le Bras 2009; van Eeckhout 2009). The official commission released its recommendations in February 2010. As of the writing of this text, they have yet to be implemented; even the Sarkozy government backpedaled significantly on the question of ethnicized census information.

12. Douglas Holmes (2000) has argued that the logic of autochthony is at the heart of far-right politician Jean-Marie Le Pen's perennial regional and national political campaigns. In less detail, Peter Geschiere and Francis Nyamnjoh (2000) have made a similar argument.

13. This was particularly true for Algerian Jews, who after 1870 could serve in the French colonial administration in the same capacity as European colonists (Allouche-Benayoun and Bensimon 1998; Chouraqui 1998a; Stora 2003). Moroccan and Tunisian Jews remained a more marginal presence in the colonial administration (Abitbol 1998b; Cohen-Hadria 1980; Memmi 1991).

14. Like almost all pieds-noirs, Algerian Jews were hastily and unsystematically evacuated between 1961 and 1962, just prior to the transition to Algerian nationalist rule. Transport conditions as well as a desire for stealth reduced most evacuees to the clothes on their backs and a handful of suitcases. After 1961, but not before, Tunisian Jews who emigrated were restricted in the amount of wealth they could take out of the country (Bensimon 1971:31).

15. Among adults, 74% of Algerians, 85% of Tunisians, and 80% of Moroccans said they knew Arabic. Among young people, those numbers were considerably lower: 45% of Algerian, 77% of Tunisian, and 63% of Moroccan youth claimed to know Arabic (Bensimon 1971:24). Sizeable pluralities also claimed to speak Spanish and/or Italian (ibid.).

16. Doris Bensimon found that almost half of the Moroccan-born youth in her study still possessed Moroccan rather than French nationality (1971:17). Similarly, slightly less than half of the Tunisian-born youth in her sample continued to be Tunisian citizens (ibid.).

17. The Jewish press rarely highlighted these legal similarities. In the mid-1980s, the president of the Union des Etudiants Juifs de France (UEJF), Marc Bitton, was

one of the few Jewish leaders to acknowledge that proposed changes to immigration laws making nationality harder to obtain would impact North African Jews as well as Muslims. He noted: "What concerns us the most is the nationality law. Many Moroccan Jewish students will be impacted by the law, and we have asked for an audience with M. Pasqua [then Interior Minister] to make our concerns known" (Bitton 1986:10). Not insignificantly, he was quoted in the context of an article that stressed Jewish high school students' seemingly total disinterest in a political issue that might have been understood as impacting their friends and family members.

18. For a fuller account of Ghebali and the UEJF's influence on Jewish and interethnic antiracist efforts, see Mandel forthcoming.

19. Apparently even Joseph Sitruk, who became the chief French rabbi and thus the religious head of the Consistoire, opened a synagogue entirely independent of consistorial authority (Le Bars 2008:2).

20. By 1955, more than half of the funds raised by the Appeal Unifié des Juifs de France (AUJF, United Jewish Appeal in France) was dedicated to providing material and spiritual assistance to immigrants whose citizenship status prevented them from receiving state help (Poirier 1998:67). Between 1961 and 1968, the FSJU raised and distributed over 10 million francs, about 10.9 million in today's euros, in the form of no-interest housing loans (ibid.).

21. Previously, Loss had rather cryptically described part of this "new reality" as an attempt to rigorously circumscribe acceptable religious and political practices, including imposing a gag rule on any critique of Israel. He never specified who exactly was engaged in what he called this new "fundamentalism," but his complaints coincided with the beginning of the shift toward greater Sephardi representation in important institutions. He noted: "How can one not be shocked by the preemptory judgments, the condemnations without appeal, the exclusions justified by the flimsiest reasons, or rather pretexts, that have become commonplace? What is at stake is tolerance. . . . Most Jews do not recognize themselves in the forms of exclusivity people are trying to impose" (Loss 1979:17). By May 1985, Loss had resigned as head editor for *l'Arche*, a move that the Jewish press hinted had been prompted by "certain hard-line elements in the community" who considered his editorials "too liberal" (D.L. 1985).

22. Ironically, the conversion had been performed in Morocco. The supposed source of Sephardi religious excess and intolerance proved too liberal for the new French Sephardi establishment.

23. The head of FSJU's youth programs also indirectly attributed the growth of Sephardi religiosity to conditions in France. He characterized post-1980s Jewish religious practice as having lost all of the tolerance and openness inspired by an early generation of Sephardi sages like Leon Ashkenazi, Emmanuel Lévinas, and André Neher. "We no longer have this generation of spiritual guides with us, they have all died and not been replaced. And there is this new generation that is focused on orthodox practice to the exclusion of all else. When I was young [he

grew up in Algeria], it was possible to take your car to synagogue on Saturday morning, to go to services and then open your shop later in the afternoon for business. Today, that kind of thing has become totally unthinkable." He described this as a "less intelligent form of Judaism" that values "religious acts" above considerations of ethics and values.

24. There has since been a shift within the Consistoire. In June 2008 consistorial elections for chief rabbi, Joseph Sitruk, then the incumbent, was defeated by Gilles Bernheim, an Ashkenazi Jew. Although revered by many strictly observant (often Sephardi) Jews, Sitruk was widely described by Jews with a commitment to French Republican norms as a "fundamentalist" and/or an "idiot." One of the few Ashkenazi members of the UEJF board told me that he was "ashamed" that Sitruk "represented" French Jews, and even questioned his mental capacity for such a role. Bernheim, in contrast, was often described as a tolerant intellectual. A Moroccan-born woman married to a non-Jew described how happy she had been to find Bernheim for her son's bar mitzvah after a series of terrible experiences with rabbis she described as judgmental and unhelpful. "The Ashkenazim are really nice," she sighed. "They welcomed us warmly; they encouraged us; and above all they encouraged [Marc, her son]."

25. Cukierman was still a child during the war. He was hidden with a non-Jewish family and remained on French soil throughout Vichy and the Occupation.

26. The only Jewish institution that seems to have publicly defended Cukierman was *Actualité Juive*, whose editor Serge Benattar told the newspaper *Libération*: "The Jewish community is the first affected by insecurity. It is a fact that 95% of [anti-Semitic] incidents are perpetrated by individuals who belong to the Muslim community" (Laske 2002:7).

27. This was also true in the late 1970s and early 1980s, when Paris witnessed a number of deadly attacks against Jewish institutions. Despite the calls of Jewish elites for calm and faith in Republican authorities, a number of (often Sephardi) Jews organized self- and neighborhood-defense associations (Tribune Juive 1979:15; Haymann 1980:9).

28. When characterizing pieds-noirs in the period proceeding and following decolonization, Metropolitan French intellectuals like Pierre Nora used language that mirrors dominant Jewish characterizations of North African Jews; like Sephardim, pieds-noirs were accused of being irrational, overly emotional, and incapable of intellectual debate (Shepard 2006:197).

29. Even in the mid-1980s, there were vocal critics of the alliance between, for example, the UEJF and SOS-Racisme, an antiracist organization created by a multireligious, multiethnic coalition. In 1985, a university student wrote to *Actualité Juive* to condemn what he viewed as an unholy alliance between "feujs" and "beurs" that paid too little attention to respective positions on Israel. He even asked when the UEJF would get "judaized" (Levi 1985:n.p.).

30. The proximate cause of this schism was Valéry Giscard d'Estaing's March 7, 1980 announcement from Jordan that he supported Palestinian self-determination.

31. That political honeymoon did not last long. A few years into his mandate, Mitterrand had become a symbol of the impossibility of escaping France's "pro-Arab" politics. When Mitterrand invited Yasser Arafat to France in 1989, a former president of the UEFJ noted that he no longer believed in the "vote sanction"—ultimately Jews could not trust anyone but themselves (Bitton 1989:n.p.).

32. The alternative explanation, also widely circulated, was that neo-Nazis were responsible. In different ways, both explanations enabled Jews to knit themselves socially and politically into the French and European mainstream. While often "natives," neo-Nazis were (and still are) politically and culturally unpalatable.

33. See chapter 3. The commission condemned as "illegal" the fact that "certain private schools under contract accept only students who can prove that they belong to the same religion as the establishment. In addition, these schools do not teach the parts of the [national] curriculum that, in their eyes, do not conform to their vision of the world" (Stasi Commission 2004:91). Parents, teachers, administrators, and students involved in government-contracted Jewish schools know that this is common practice at virtually all such Parisian institutions.

34. According to John Bowen (2007:167), Alain Seksig, a school inspector and witness to the Stasi commission, came very close to explicitly equating the problems of observant Judaism and Islam in a televised news program called *Egalité, Laïcité, Anxiété* that aired on France 5 on December 7, 2003.

35. Apparently afraid for his life, Bensoussan used an alias ("Emmanuel Brenner") for publication purposes. This "secret" is a rather public one, at least among Jews affiliated with Jewish institutions.

36. The term's widespread postcolonial use may be linked to Israeli political concerns, particularly the desire to create as much distance as possible between "Arabs" and that country's very large population of Middle Eastern Jews (Shohat 1988).

37. At least for Algerian Jews, long accustomed to the centrality of European-ness as an identity narrative, this habit of conflating North African Jewishness with Spanishness predates the more widespread autochthony discourse I am highlighting. In her 1970s work with a small group of first- and second-generation Jewish Algerian immigrants living in Aix-en-Provence, Elizabeth Friedman found that the vast majority of her informants claimed Spanish ancestry (1988:13).

38. Moses Montefiore was born in Italy but worked, married, and was knighted in England. He visited Morocco once in the mid-19th century as part of a lengthy humanitarian trip for Jews in the Middle East and North Africa.

39. In a sense, he is right. North African or Turkish Jews living in France under the Nazi Occupation fared no better than Eastern European Jews. Algerian Jews suffered economically and psychologically under Vichy's anti-Jewish codes. And some Tunisian Jews were interned in work camps during the Nazi Occupation (Laskier 1994). But my informant also completely elided a fundamental historical reality: in almost all cases, living in North Africa and not in the Metropole meant the difference between life and death.

40. Tunisian-born chief rabbi Joseph Sitruk caused a scandal when he backed the Sephardi chief rabbi of Israel Ovadia Yossef's assertion that the Holocaust was divine punishment for those who had abandoned God's mitzvoth.

41. I would like to thank John Comaroff for pointing this out.

Chapter 3

1. There was another, less constraining possibility for elementary schools. Called a *contrat simple*, this option was a temporary arrangement that allowed the school to receive a state-trained and -paid teacher for a particular class without being subject to the other rules governing contracted education.

2. Inspectors have disciplinary and grade-level-specific competences and are given inspection assignments accordingly. So, for example, a given inspector may be responsible for all fifth- and sixth-grade French classes in a geographical area, regardless of whether those classes happen to be in private or public institutions.

3. The 1971 Habib-Deloncle law downgraded the 1959 requirements. Rather than insisting that contracted schools follow the exact content and structure of public education, they were required to observe the "general rules" created by the Department of Education (Bellengier 2004:44). In 1977, the Guermeur law turned the Debré provisions for hiring teachers on their head, allowing directors of contracted schools to pick their own teachers, who were then rubber-stamped by the state (ibid.:46). In addition, the law authorized the firing of teachers who failed to respect the school's "special character," leading to a series of court battles in which Catholic schools' right to apply illiberal standards to state employees were upheld. In one instance, a Catholic school was allowed to fire a state-paid teacher whose marital status did not conform to religious doctrine (Battut et al. 1995; Poucet 2005:12).

4. It also resulted in one of the worst political defeats for the Mitterrand government. In 1984, a long-negotiated comprehensive proposal for bringing private schooling even closer to public education brought hundreds of thousands of conservative demonstrators into the street. They were protesting the creation of a state education "monopoly" and supporting "free choice" in schooling, which meant continued government funding for private schools without increased state oversight (Battut et al. 1995). As Jacquot Grunewald noted at the time, it may have been the first time Jews protested with conservative Catholics to strengthen the position of religion in French public life (Grunewald 1984:4).

5. A court ruling on the 1985 Chevènement law that replaced the Guermeur law claimed that teachers were required, at the very least, to remain silent about issues touching on a school's special character. While they no longer had to support it overtly, they also could not challenge it—a move that the court imagined as reconciling state-paid teachers' rights with that of a parent to choose an educational environment that conformed with his or her values (Battut et al. 1995). In addition, although the Chevènement law intended to return the power of hiring and firing state-paid teachers to the state, a 1987 circular written by then Educa-

tion Minister Monory endorsed the 1977 revisions that gave that power to private school principals (Bellengier 2003:155).

6. According to an Ashkenazi college student who attended Catholic secondary school in Lille, this is more than just hype. The Catholic administration bent over backward to demonstrate its liberal tolerance. The student was exempt from catechism and mass; teachers asked if they could attend his bar mitzvah; he was even given permission to miss an obligatory field trip in order to attend a family wedding (permission that was denied to one of his post-Christian friends for a similar event).

7. Many Jewish communities in Western democracies experienced the same kinds of dramatically increased demand (see Miller 2001 for the United Kingdom; Zeldin 1983 for the United States). This may be tied to the general growth of identity politics beginning in the 1960s as well as to changing immigration and residency patterns (see below).

8. Many "traditionalist" Jews may maintain a strictly kosher kitchen but will eat some nonkosher food when outside the home. This can mean simply eating vegetarian or fish in a nonkosher restaurant; or it can mean eating nonkosher meat and even shellfish (there are licit and illicit fish under kashrut laws, but the manner of killing the fish, unlike the manner in which a mammal is slaughtered, is irrelevant to its ritual purity).

9. If students of Algerian origin were underrepresented, self-identified Ashkenazim were even more rare; in each school they could be counted on one hand. At Beit Sarah, I met four self-identified Ashkenazim. Consistent with the preponderance of children whose parents were recent immigrants, two of those students had mothers (who were also sisters) born in Russia. At Brith Abraham, I met two Ashkenazim. One hailed from a *haredi* family originally from Alsace; his Eastern European dress as well as his religiosity distinguished him profoundly from all other students, who often mocked him. Apparently, similarly observant Ashkenazi families tend to put their children in *heder* and then *yeshivot*, religious schools with no secular curriculum that are not under contract. The second was the son of recent Polish immigrants. Even the faculty in day schools was predominantly North African. Beit Sarah had 31 teachers on staff, 15 of whom were born in North Africa. Of those 15, 7 were from Tunisia, 4 from Morocco, and 3 from Algeria.

10. Many were convinced that students whose parents could pay full tuition were less likely to be expelled for academic or behavior problems than those whose parents paid reduced amounts. They also thought that students with wealthy parents were more likely to get off the school waiting list than those who would need financial assistance.

11. Being a doctor is a quintessential petit bourgeois occupation in France. Since medicine is socialized, it is not nearly as lucrative as in the United States. In addition, medicine is studied in public universities. And although students must pass a number of competitive examinations in order to graduate, it is not nearly as prestigious as studying engineering in a semipublic *grande école*.

12. This is true for parochial schooling in Western democracies in general. For

an account of the relationship between legal desegregation and the growth of non-Catholic parochial schooling in the United States, see James Ryan (2004) "Brown, School Choice, and the Suburban Veto."

13. Until 1985, with the passage of the Chevènement law, the creation of new classes in the public sector was determined by reaching a minimum number of students for the new class. In private education, it was determined by a maximum number of students in the existing class. As a result, new classes were created more quickly in private schools than in public schools, meaning class size as a whole remained somewhat lower (Battut et al. 1995). The Chevènement law tied private education funding to class expansion in public schools. If new classes were created in public schools, the same number of new classes could be added to private education globally. If not, private schools had to make due with existing contracts (Petit-Ohayon 2003).

14. Most recent figures are taken from the French Department of Education's website: http://www.education.gouv.fr/cid251/les-etablissements-d-enseignement -prives.html.

15. The mother of two children enrolled in different Catholic schools in the 7th arrondissement noted that there were few Jews and even fewer "foreigners" in either place. She clarified: "There are only one or two students of the Muslim religion."

16. In order of descending prestige, there were three different general studies baccalauréats: the scientific baccalauréat (Bac S), the social science baccalauréat (Bac ES), and the literary baccalauréat (Bac L). Only the best students were allowed to remain in the Bac S program, which is reputed to be the most difficult. To a great extent, the kind of baccalauréat a student pursues and his or her score on the exam determines what kind of university studies and therefore careers are possible. The most prestigious postsecondary training in France is in engineering, and only those with a Bac S could even be considered for the handful of semipublic engineering schools in France.

17. In 2007, for example, in one of the Jewish schools that had a 100% passing rate on the baccalauréat—and was classed among the 10 "best" Parisian schools— only 11% of those who enrolled in tenth grade made it to the exam in twelfth grade (Charpentier 2008:3). In an equally well-classed Catholic school, just over a quarter of those enrolled in tenth grade took the test (ibid.). So, in any private school setting, the "second chance" parents are seeking may be very short-lived.

18. A number of teachers described their fear of crossing student sensibilities for this very reason. At Brith Abraham, the only black male teacher at the school had to fight for months to keep his job after students told parents and administrators that he was a pedophile and an anti-Semite, a rumor that seems to have been fueled by racist stereotypes about Caribbean men. The principal ultimately sided with the teacher and against the students, but that is not always the case. Beit Sarah's principal reprimanded a non-Jewish history teacher after students denounced him for identifying Tel Aviv, and not Jerusalem, as the capital of Israel.

19. Virginie, a Moroccan-born hall monitor at Brith Abraham, told me that

Muslims did not share this commitment to education. "Muslims don't want to pay for their children's education. They want their children in public school because it's free. They don't care what kind of education their children get. They just want them out of their hair, and they don't want it to cost them anything. That's why there are no Muslim schools in France."

20. A Moroccan-born parent of three who had only a French baccalauréat degree told me virtually the same thing. "I've put off my dream of owning an apartment in order to finance my children's education. I spend 9,000 euros a year on my son's education plus 2,000 for each of my daughters [one of whom is still in high school and enrolled in Brith Abraham]. When they are finished, I would like to move on with my life and try to save to buy an apartment. But I don't regret for one second having tried to give them all the tools they need to succeed in life. That is the most important thing. I will never understand why people buy large, expensive cars but might not be willing to finance their children's education. There's nothing wrong with a big fancy car, as long as there is enough money for things that matter, like education."

21. One of the students I interviewed attended a Catholic school before enrolling in Brith Abraham in middle school. His story, however, was unique. Almost all the other students with whom I spoke who had spent some time outside Jewish institutions had been enrolled in local public schools.

22. The major exception is ORT, the network of Jewish technical schools founded at the turn of the 20th century in Russia to "regenerate" Jews by teaching them to perform "productive" labor. ORT schools are often a safety net for students who have been kicked-out of public school and/or private academic schools. The population thus includes a significant percentage of non-Jews (at least 10% according to one teacher's estimate). As a result, parents, administrators, teachers, and students do not view it as Jewish schooling. The principal of Brith Abraham told me that studying ORT schools would be a waste of my time because they were "not interested in Jewish identity." There is also a small "secular" Zionist elementary school in the center of Paris that accepts non-Halakhic Jews (i.e., children born to a Jewish father and a non-Jewish mother) and anyone else interested in their educational project. The principal of Brith Abraham also characterized this elementary school as "not interested in Jewish identity."

23. *Ketubboth* (plural; sing.: *ketubah*) issued by the handful of nonorthodox synagogues that conduct their own conversion and marriage ceremonies (e.g., the Conservative Massorti or the Liberal Mouvement Juif Libéral de France) may be refused on the grounds that those traditions do not comply with Halakhic law.

24. The Moroccan-born principal of Beit Sarah claimed that people from other religions did occasionally knock on his door. He told the story of a Moroccan Muslim family that sought admission for a daughter on the grounds that the school's sex segregation, strict dress code, and heavy doses of religious instruction were perfect for their child. But the director also noted that the largest pool of problematic candidates came from Jewish men married to "*goyot*" or non-Jewish

women who wanted a Jewish education for their children. His "worst nightmare," as he put it, was a Jewish lawyer married to a *goyot* who wanted to send his daughter to Beit Sarah. If presented with such a case, he feared he might end up with a serious legal problem on his hands.

25. See Petit-Ohayon 1989:23; ADEJF 1989:32; Azeroual, Yves 1989a; CFDT Teachers 1989:28;. *Actualité Juive* hinted that the one non-Jewish teacher involved and, by extension, the other three Jewish teachers were anti-Semites (Azeroual 1989b). The more centrist *Tribune Juive* acknowledged that the substance of the teachers' complaints raised important issues for consideration, but wondered about the decision to articulate their concerns outside the "community."

26. The mainstream media's deafness to such concerns was hardly a onetime affair. In his scathing critique of left- and right-wing French policies vis-à-vis public and private education, Jean Battut makes a similar point. He notes that in the early 1980s, during the debates over proposed legislation that would have dramatically increased regulations associated with public funds for private schools, reporters paid very little attention to Jewish schools. He writes:

> It is significant that during these debates we neither saw nor heard reports about Jewish schools. There are not many of them under contract, but their solidarity with those defending Catholic education created an appearance of ecumenicalism that completely undermined secular organizations' accusations that public funds were being misused for religious or clerical purposes. The absence of . . . coverage of Jewish schools, where the religious component is more important than elsewhere, was a result of reporters self-censuring. (Battut et al. 1995:191–192)

27. At the time of the Commission, there were no government-funded Islamic schools in France. There were a handful of private institutions, but they had yet to meet the contractual requirement of five years of continuous operation prior to applying for government funds. As of this writing, there is one government-contracted Muslim school in Metropolitan France, the high school Averroès in Lille (*Liberation* 2009).

28. I had already left the field when this conference took place. I am indebted to Naomi Davidson for this information. Even researchers who have worked in some capacity on Jewish schools either ignore the issue entirely (Cohen 1991) or imply that state law necessarily entails compliance (Benveniste 2002:67).

29. As on Shabbat, one cannot, for example, use any form of mechanized transportation, carry any object that is not typically worn, or write, making sitting for an exam all but impossible.

30. Although many of Sarah's classmates shared her anxieties, one was convinced that the government would have to change its position because of Jewish intellectual superiority. "If they want 80% of the candidates to pass [the baccalauréat], they cannot do it without the Jews." I asked her how she figured that, given that most statistics suggest that all French Jews, most of whom are probably not

strictly religiously observant, make up 1% of the population. "Look at the statistics," she responded, "only the Jews get their bac[calauréat]."

31. Some might see this as a question of demographics. Many Jews argue that they are too few in number and too well-behaved to create any alarm. They see this as particularly relevant given the relative size of the Muslim population, which is reputed to be ten times more numerous. But this is an ideological judgment rather than a simple "fact" of demography. In 1891, at the beginning of the Dreyfus Affair, Jews accounted for roughly 0.17% of the Metropolitan population, a number that hardly stopped many French nationalists from viewing Jews as an existential threat to French national integrity and identity (Benbassa 1997:215). For Metropolitan census information, see www.insee.fr/fr/ffc/chifcle_fiche.asp?ref_id=NATnon02145&tab_id=683.

32. The same might be said for other minority populations who are largely ignored by politicians and the French public, particularly first- and second-generation immigrants from Asia.

33. Perhaps as a way of dissuading me from pursuing my research within their walls, some of the schools I contacted claimed to teach almost entirely in Hebrew.

34. Students did not necessarily use the same Internet sources as other French adolescents. Those who took the trouble of looking for information on the Internet tended to frequent Zionist or Jewish websites, like procheorient.info.

35. Middle-school and younger high-school students were given more extensive exposure to Jewish instruction than older students, who are focused on preparing for the baccalauréat exams.

36. In many French public schools, students still have the option of going home for lunch. Thus, while the school day is still relatively long, it has a considerable break in the middle.

37. Very few students even belonged to the large number of thriving Jewish youth groups operating inside Paris. These include movements that run the political and religious gamut, from Hashomer Ha'atzair, a secular Zionist movement; to the Eclaireurs/Eclaireuses Israélite Français, the nominally religious scouting group; to the Betar, a Zionist and religious movement affiliated with the Israeli far-right.

38. For example, when public school students were on vacation for a week at the end of October for "Toussaint," Beit Sarah students were still in session, compensating for a week and a half of missed school during Tishri, the month of High Holy Day observances. Similarly, when public schools were on Spring Break in 2004-2005, Beit Sarah students still had two weeks of classes before the beginning of Passover break.

39. A large number of relatively well-off Sephardi families also travel over Passover, often to Israel.

40. The relationship between "style," physiognomy, and ethno-religious classification among Jewish adolescents is the subject of chapter 6.

41. Since 2000, the Service de Protection de la Communauté Juive (Protection

Service for the Jewish Community, SPCJ), has been creating lists of and investigating anti-Semitic acts in conjunction with the French police and the Consistoire, CRIF, and FSJU. Portions of these lists of acts, organized by date and type of aggression, have been published by the Observatoire du Monde Juif (2001), the CRIF at www.crif.org, and the UEJF and SOS Racisme (2002).

42. This absence of class motivation was also true for the horrific 2012 shooting of Jewish day school students in Toulouse.

43. Please note that my research did not address the objective realities of French anti-Semitism in the mid-2000s; rather, I was focused on how some Jews perceived and reacted to reported anti-Semitic acts and, much more rarely, to cases of actual violence.

44. French public schools have no busing system. Students either walk or take public transportation.

45. I have never seen a CRIF or SPCJ report of such an incident.

46. I am referring to the RER D incident. Although the police seem to have known that the accusations were manufactured, neither journalists nor politicians waited for any proof before denouncing the (fictitious) perpetrators. This reaction may have been prompted by the way in which the story played on common stereotypes: the aggressors were male blacks or Arabs; the victim was a helpless woman with a baby; she was accused of being rich and therefore Jewish; she was violently mauled; and no one on the crowded commuter train raised a finger to help her (see Agence France Presse 2004; Le Figaro 2004; Mouloud 2004; Portes 2004; Smolar 2004).

47. Brith Abraham, as mentioned above, had particularly visible and pronounced security measures.

48. Beit Sarah had a relatively unelaborated security system, which nonetheless included a high fence, single entry point, and an intercom.

49. This seems to be the case more generally as well. There are a number of incidents of verbal insults and even violence between Jewish school students and those in neighboring public institutions (see CRIF 2002b; Observatoire du Monde Juif 2001:4).

50. The UEJF program, called "Co-Exist," was a relatively recent creation that attempted to address adolescent stereotypes about commonsense French social groupings: women, blacks, Arabs, Jews, and the white post-Catholic majority. Although readily welcomed by semiurban public schools, the group coordinator told me that they were having trouble making inroads into Jewish schools, whose directors associated the problem with "others," not with Jewish children.

Chapter 4

1. For a discussion of the relationship between race and religion for Islam and Muslims, see Davidson (2012).

2. For examples of the conflation of these terms in academic circles, see Brenner et al. (2002), Taguieff (2005), and Trigano (2003).

3. See chapter 2 and Bowen (2007:164) for an account of how *Les territories perdus de la République* featured in public debates about and eventually legislation against veiling.

4. Similarly, the Dutch state now requires immigrants from Muslim countries—but not the Vatican!—to watch a film that shows bare-breasted women and amorous homosexual men.

5. Some contemporary forms of Jewish orthodoxy, many of which are heavily infused with "modern" conceptions of self, defy this characterization.

6. This, however, has not been historically true of Hasidism, which draws heavily on the mystical writings and conceptions of the kabbalah. This has become particularly apparent through the recent controversy in Israel over the integration of Sephardi girls into an ultraorthodox yeshiva attended primarily by Ashkenazi Hasidim called "Slonim" (Ettinger 2010).

7. This may be changing. Early in 2010, the Israeli rabbinate changed a standing ruling and declared that Jewishness was determined by the religious status of the gamete, not the womb. This is indeed a significant step toward racializing what it means to be Jewish (personal communication with Susan Kahn).

8. For an interesting ethnographic account of the difference between racial "authenticity" and "sincerity," see John Jackson Jr., *Real Black: Adventures in Racial Sincerity* (2005).

9. Emile Durkheim's (2002) *Moral Education* is a classic example. It is a manifesto for a particular kind of public school education in the interest of creating good Republican citizens. See Eugen Weber (1976) for an account of late 19th-century French nationalist investment in public schooling and a critique of the power of those institutions.

10. For a typical account of the role of Jewish schooling in producing French Jewishness, see Chvika (1984). For a critical account of the widespread ideological commitment to Jewish day schooling as a mode of identity production, see Sigal et al. (1981).

11. Here, "Jewish" biology, DNA, is imagined as the cause of cultural Jewishness. This is very different than the claims made in emerging Jewish genomics, where evidence of distinctively "Jewish" DNA is the result (rather than the cause) of fidelity to traditional cultural practices (Abu El-Haj 2007).

12. This is a partial presentation of Halakhic logic. Rashi, a renowned *tosafist*, who lived in twelfth-century Troyes in what is modern-day France, insisted that the priests had to articulate their improper intent for the sacrifice to be invalid. In other words, intent had to be enacted, not simply imagined (Linzer 2011).

13. As Adam Seligman reminded me, Jewish tradition holds that the priesthood is an entirely hereditary office; thus, even from a purely religious perspective, Mme. Benayoun's response made little sense.

14. These are just a few examples. Another religious instructor insisted that people chose very few things in their lives, not even their mates, who were preselected by God. Still another explained that "free will" was very complicated given

that God had already decided everything. Others explained history as a cyclical pattern of divine intervention: a barely avoided accident was God's post–Yom Kippur positive judgment about Jews; the Israeli-Palestinian conflict and the Holocaust were just the opposite.

15. Male non-Jewish slaves were circumcised and treated, for domestic and ritual purposes, as Jews. Upon manumission, these "half converts" became full Jews, with the exception that they were only allowed to marry *mamzer* or bastard Jews or other converts, not unmarked Jews (Katz 1961a:41–42).

16. In many ways, this reflects the priorities of rabbinic Judaism, which ties model (male) observance to continuous study and the imitation of those considered deeply learned, none of which necessarily translates into actual knowledge. Jacob Neusner writes: "The central *ritual* of the rabbinic tradition . . . is study. . . . When a disciple memorizes his master's traditions and actions, he participates in the rabbinic view of Torah as the organizing principle of reality. . . . Study loses its referent in intellectual attainment. The *act* of study itself becomes holy, so that its original purpose, which was mastery of particular information, ceases to matter as much. What matters is piety, piety expressed through the rites of studying" (1974:9, emphasis in the original).

17. To some extent, this may be a product of the French education system itself, which emphases rote memorization and word-for-word regurgitation of information on exams.

18. This comment alone captures the problematic I am trying to describe. Only someone unfamiliar with the extensive debates, disagreements, and paradigm shifts in Jewish law could imagine anything so frankly Protestant as the kind of biblical literalism Jennifer articulates.

19. Even for the most thoroughly observant Jews this is a process and not a state. Following Maimonides, orthodox Jews enumerate 613 divine injunctions that Jews are obligated to enact. While almost no one is expected to achieve regular performance of all 613, observant Jews engage in constant *teshouva*, or repentance and return, in order to eliminate sins and add Jewish acts to their daily lives.

20. For accounts of *yein nesekh*, or libation wine, see Katz (1961a) and Soloveitchik (1978; 2003).

21. By definition, idolaters do not conform to the seven noachide principles that make for "righteous" non-Jews.

22. Two major exceptions were, in the Spanish and then North African context, Moses Maimonides (12th century), and in the Halakhic tradition associated with *Ashkenaz*, what is now France and Germany, R. Menahem Ha-Me'iri (14th century) (Katz 1961a).

23. Commensality between Jews and non-Jews in some of these places had become so common that mystically influenced rabbis resorted to reinterpreting the Halakhah on racialized grounds, insisting on the innate and unchangeable differences between Jews and non-Jews (Katz 1961b).

Chapter 5

1. Belly button piercing, like ear piercing in men, would be considered a flagrant violation of tzniout in an orthodox or ultraorthodox setting.

2. Only the economics teacher at Brith Abraham refused to wear one on the grounds that it ran counter to his ideological convictions. Religious differences among married women, however, remained visible—those who were observant covered their heads (in a variety of different ways); those who were not, did not.

3. In fact, it seemed considerably more rigorous and less flexible: the rule presented as "Sephardi" was variable and therefore could conform more closely to a woman's cycle, while the "Ashkenazi" practice was standardized and considerably longer.

4. This is part of a general trend in increasingly observant Judaism; see Soloveitchik (1994) and Jacobson (2006).

5. All observant Jews buy kosher meat, but many buy vegetarian foodstuffs "off-list," i.e., mainstream brands from mainstream supermarkets whether or not they have Beit Din certification.

6. The baccalauréat is a national exam that marks the end of high school.

7. As an aside, during my two years of fieldwork I saw scores of black Jews in France. But I saw them in places that Jewish day school students tended not to be: at street protests against anti-Semitism and as part of the leadership of the UEJF, the reasonably progressive Jewish student union active in French universities.

8. When I asked a history teacher at Brith Abraham why there were no such visual aids, she told me that she was ashamed never to have noticed their absence. "But there should be maps of France!" she added as if scolding herself. "Creating a French identity requires knowing what France looks like!" The next week, she bought (with her own money) maps of the European Union for all the history teachers on her floor.

9. Before my arrival, the school apparently also had representatives from the Jewish Agency come and conduct "workshops" during Tou Bishvat with eighth-grade students. Tou Bishvat, which is an agricultural festival, celebrates the spring renewal of trees and plants. As such, the holiday lends itself to celebrating past and present links with the land of Israel. The Jewish Agency representatives taught the students to sing and dance to "Israeli folk songs." They also hosted a video-conference call that allowed students to pray with Israeli students and to "receive messages directly from the Kotel" (Lévy and Szwarc 2003).

10. While principals and FSJU officials were very forthcoming about the generalities of Jewish school funding, I was given almost no specifics.

11. Edict issued in 883 by Louis the Pious (cited in Philippe 1997:24). The same document might have been used to indicate the fluidity of medieval status laws.

12. She was equally frustrated with the way her students conflated France's Arab-Muslim population with the oil sheikhs courted by French foreign policy. After she described France's international policies as "a little bit pro-Arab," a student asked:

"But why do they [the French] love the Arabs? The Arabs have . . ." She cut him off: "What's the connection with the Arabs? They haven't done anything, the government. . . . [here the students break into laughter] No! The government needs oil from the Arabs. The Arabs from Saudi Arabia, not from the unhappy North African who has done nothing and cannot even find enough bread to eat. . . . Look how you conflate everything!"

13. M. Bensaïd also used a discussion of medieval trade restrictions and expulsions to explain Jewish behavior in the 20th century: "Ultimately we find [Jews] in entirely new domains [like cinema and high finance] because Jews were creating the world that they had been refused. For Jews, the fact that they were implicated in new domains, in domains that had never existed, was not so much because they liked risk as because of the desire to create a world with their own rules, precisely because the world in which they lived did not accept them. They wanted to create their own rules because the others rejected them, to create a universe that valued them because the universe in which they lived rejected them."

14. Among many Jews in France, being "Zionist" has come to simply mean supporting the (more or less) status quo existence of the State of Israel. The historian of French Jewry Esther Benbassa has famously called French Jews "Zionists without Zionism" (2004c). In other words, French Jews have offered continuous moral and/or material support for the Jewish state in the absence of any serious notion of "return." As one of the officers of the Union des Etudiants Juifs de France insisted, "In the strict sense of the term, being Zionist means desiring the creation of the State of Israel. After 1948, when that was done, there was technically no more reason for Zionism to exist. But the definition has shifted [and is now about supporting the existence of Israel]."

15. I asked why the larger religious network with which his school is affiliated did not operate schools in Israel. He told me that they only go where they are needed.

16. I had in fact done no such thing. The comment was inspired by an English teacher's account of a conversation I had with her class about Thanksgiving. During a short lecture, I explained that the English Puritans who landed on the North Atlantic Coast imagined their migration as the fulfillment of a divine promise and the New World as a "promised land." The Tunisian-born teacher sitting in the back of the class had almost immediately risen to interrupt me: "The difference," she angrily informed the class, "is that we [Jews] are not colonizing; we are returning to land that has always been ours." I had never mentioned Jews or Israel, but that is clearly not what she told the principal.

17. Students accused the principal of downplaying anti-Semitism. After two girls came running to tell me that they had just been called "dirty Jews" by a public school student in the neighborhood, I asked them whether they intended to report the incident to the school director. "No," I was told. "Why not?" I asked. "Because he will accuse us of provoking the incident," they replied.

18. Orthodox objections to Yom Ha'Shoah stem from the fact that it was not incorporated into one of the myriad days of fasting and mourning that already exist in the Jewish ritual calendar. Many haredim mourn for the Jewish lives lost during the Holocaust on Tish b'Av, the ninth day of the month of Av, the day rabbinical tradition associates with the destruction of both Temples.

19. The principal told me: "People misunderstand the way that [Beit Sarah] expresses its solidarity with Israel. We celebrate Yom Ha'atzmaout, but not by dancing and screaming in the streets like crazy people. We tell our students that there are special foods, special programs, special TV shows, everything for the week of Yom Ha'atzmaout. But because we are not out there in the streets, people think we do not support Israel."

20. There are at least two exceptions to this. The texts used in Beit Sarah's modern Hebrew classes are explicitly Zionist. According to one Israeli teacher, the workbook used in high school was designed for recent immigrants to Israel, and thus includes a series of explicitly nationalist texts. In one lesson that I attended, students read and attempted to translate an essay exposing the reasons for aliyah, including anti-Semitism. In addition, as at Brith Abraham, there was an annual Israel trip organized for eleventh-graders.

21. There was, however, an assumption that students either did or should *speak* Hebrew. When I asked a non-Jewish Spanish teacher why she thought so many students took Spanish rather than Hebrew she looked at me as if I were simpleminded. "Most of them are already fluent in Hebrew," she explained, "because they speak it at home." According to the students, however, many of them take Spanish because Hebrew is too hard, and they do not want to get bad grades that might cause them to be thrown out of their academic program of choice.

22. Even those with an Israeli parent sometimes struggled. In one of the advanced Hebrew classes that I attended, the Israeli teacher spent most of her time asking questions of and upbraiding the one student in the class with a fluent parent. The teacher repeated over and over again how "disappointed" and "shocked" the girl's father would be when he found out how poor her performance was.

23. Some teachers seemed interested in making spoken Hebrew one of the school's operational languages. Mlle. Chicheportiche tried to speak Hebrew with her colleagues in the teachers' lounge, prompting ridicule from the handful of teachers who knew that she spoke terribly. She also sprinkled her lessons with Hebrew instructions that she forced students to memorize. A typical lesson thus often included students reciting the phrase "all together" in Hebrew as many times as they repeated the text from the Mishnah or the Torah.

24. The gap between lived and taught practice is far less pronounced at Brith Abraham in part because what is practiced as "orthodoxy" is much more limited. But, nonetheless, a few students talked about the gap between what they learned in kodesh classes and parental practices. Some even described being frustrated

about their inability to convince parents and/or grandparents that they were in the wrong. Joshua, a Brith Abraham junior, described his parents' unfortunate habit of saying the Kiddush, the blessing over the wine that ushers in Shabbat, over sugar water. "That's part of the bad habits they have, but whatever. . . . I say to my mother, I'm in a Jewish school, you put me in a Jewish school to learn the religion. But when I want to teach you the religion, you don't want to learn!"

25. This, however, may have been changing. The principal told me that he was in negotiations with the Jewish Agency over the funding and content of a Jewish history program. When I asked him to describe the content of the curriculum, he outlined a program that sounded very similar to the one already taught at Brith Abraham.

26. There is also a preordained end-point to this continuously repeating present. Mme. Benayoun gave her tenth-graders a timeline that included all the major events in Jewish, and thus seemingly human, history from the creation of the world to the year 6000, which she identified as the end of time. (At the time, 5765 was the Jewish calendar year.) She then asked students to calculate how much time was left until the Messiah came, and how much time was left until the end of the world. "Not much time left!" she said cheerfully, "only a couple of generations!" Although one student questioned her dates, wondering how she figured out the year of Abraham's birth using a modern system of time reckoning, no one seemed surprised by the assertion that the end of the world was imminent.

27. Rosenak (1993) recounts a similar story that circulated in a newsletter distributed by the Society for the Implementation of Jewish Values. The biblical passage describing the exile of Hagar and Ishmael from Abraham's house is used to illustrate that the "transfer" of Palestinians out of Israel (meaning Israel and the occupied territories) is the most "humane" solution to the Intifada (cited in Rosenak 1993:397).

28. This is a very different conception of the Israeli-Palestinian conflict than the one that typically circulates in secular Zionist circles. In many of those accounts, which are common in the United States as well, the "Palestinians" have no historical or cultural identity. In other words, they are not a legitimate "people" with any kind of right to claim self-determination or a homeland. In contrast, religion teachers at Beit Sarah seem to view the Israeli-Palestinian conflict as a continuation of the divinely ordained battles described in the Torah. For those very much enmeshed in this worldview, Jewish setbacks stem from God's displeasure with Jewish actions. The director of a *haredi* boys' school told me that the only way to end the Palestinian-Israeli conflict would be through massive Jewish *teshouva*, or return to orthodoxy. Israelis needed to embrace religious principles in public, civic, and private life. "Even the American president says 'God Bless America' at the end of every speech. Why can't Israeli Prime Ministers do the same?" he asked.

29. A number of students claimed that they disliked Mme. Benayoun, and one even found the lesson about Arafat "racist." When I asked her why that was, she said that she thought the teacher's happiness about Arafat's death was misplaced because

"Arafat had never done anything to her and therefore she had no right to judge him. Only God could judge him." Another student disagreed, insisting that as an Israeli—she had been born in Israel—she might very well have reason to judge him. And in any case, she too was happy that Arafat would soon be dead. The debate between the students over the teacher's merits and failings continued for a while. But at no point did anyone object to the conflation of Israelites and Israelis or Philistines and Palestinians, or to the use of scripture to understand current events.

30. Mme. Amsallem also insisted that present-day ethno-cultural groups existed in biblical times. In her explanation of the changes Nehemiah introduced after becoming governor of Jerusalem, she noted: "Nehemiah wants Jerusalem to be Jewish. Others have come and settled here, but they are not in the land legitimately. And he already talks about the Arabs. He says to them: You are here, but you are not at home. You are not concerned by what happens here. Jerusalem and Judea are for. . . . [Student interrupts: the Jews.] Obviously! God didn't give them [Jerusalem and Judea] to everyone."

31. In fact, students and parents who seemed to have the least financial resources were often those who insisted most forcefully on universal Jewish economic success. An unemployed Beit Ya'acov parent told me that it was no accident that all the people living in the 16th arrondissement, a very chic and historically bourgeois Parisian neighborhood, had Jewish last names.

Chapter 6

1. There is a parallel story that has been told about Jewishness in Europe, and more particularly Central and Eastern Europe. In this story, the status of Jews as national subjects/citizens who were not quite like other subjects/citizens created the conditions of possibility for brilliant Jewish social commentators like Simmel, Kafka, and Benjamin, who were capable of viewing the social order as an artificial and thus malleable form. See Bauman (1991; 2000).

2. A handful of students mentioned that they thought Jews spoke differently from other people. When I asked what this was tied to—accent, vocabulary, syntax, intonation—no one was sure. One girl told me rather vaguely that she thought it was about the way Jews used their hands. For an analysis of "Jewish language" and Christian anti-Semitism see Gilman (1991).

3. I am particularly thinking about an attack led by members of the Ligue de défense juive (Jewish Defense League, LDJ) against a pro-Palestinian student group in front of a university tribunal in December 2003. One of the LDJ attackers, Anthony Attal, was given a prison sentence for his involvement in the affair. Not a single major newspaper carried the story when it occurred, when Attal was initially found guilty, or when the conviction was upheld on appeal. I found out about the trial from posters on a university campus.

4. Cosgrove (2005) has made a similar claim for Puerto Rican zoot-suiters in World War II–era America. He notes: "Rather than disguise their alienation or efface their hostility to the dominant society, the *pachucos* [slang for poor Puerto

Rican males] adopted an arrogant posture. They flaunted their difference, and the zoot-suit became the means by which that difference was announced" (2005:267). That announcement was often accompanied by a violent reaction: "To wear a zoot-suit was to risk the repressive intolerance of wartime society and to invite the attention of the police, the parent generation and the uniformed members of the armed forces" (ibid.:276).

5. The 2006 torture and execution of the young Jewish cell-phone merchant, Ilan Halimi, followed this pattern. Youssouf Fofana, the man convicted of masterminding the crime, claimed that he targeted Halimi because Jews are rich and clannish and thus would be willing to pay a hefty ransom.

6. This reflects Hasidic logic about the distinctive nature of the Jewish soul, which has sparks of divinity not present, or not present in the same way, in non-Jews (Goldschmidt 2006).

7. In response to this assumption, some light-skinned Sephardi teenage girls darkened their complexions with orange-tinted cosmetics, thus artificially acquiring a "Jewish" hue.

8. Robin Kelley (1998) has described the politics of "loud" and aggressive African American speech both in the context of Jim Crow laws and contemporary gangsta rap, suggesting that such practices are used as acts of rebellion against white assumptions about the rightful place and nature of black bodies. At the same time, such acts often reinforce racializing practices.

9. We have already seen (chapter 3) how some, often assimilated, Sephardim echo such racist comments.

Bibliography

Abitbol, Michel. 2005. Les amnésiques: juifs et arabes à l'ombre du conflit du proche-orient. Paris: Perrin.

———. 1998a. La Cinquième République et l'accueil des juifs d'Afrique du Nord. *In* Les Juifs de France: de la révolution française à nos jours, Jean-Jacques Becker and Annette Wieviorka, eds. Paris: Liana Levi.

———. 1998b. Colonialisme et relations judéo-musulmanes. *In* Pérception & réalitiés au Maroc: Relations judéo-musulmanes. Maroc: CRJM.

———. 1985. The Encounter Between French Jewry and the Jews of North Africa: Analysis of a Discourse (1830–1914). *In* The Jews in Modern France. Frances Malino and Bernard Wasserstein, eds. Hanover, NH: University Press of New England.

Abu El-Haj, Nadia. 2007. The Genetic Reinscription of Race. Annual Review of Anthropology 36:283–300.

———. 1998. Translating Truths: Nationalism, the Practice of Archaeology, and the Remaking of the Past and Present in Contemporary Jerusalem. American Ethnology 25(2):166–188.

Abu-Lughod, Lila. 2005. Dramas of Nationhood: The Politics of Television in Egypt. Chicago: University of Chicago Press.

Agence France Presse. 2008a. Agression contre un jeune juif: tollé dans le monde politique et associatif. June 22.

———. 2008b. Le jeune juif aggressé avait été interpellé par la police en 2007. Libération, June 23.

———. 2006. Collège musulman d'Aubervilliers: "tout l'argent qui entre est tracé." June 20.

———. 2004. La police enquête sur une aggression antisémite, la France sous le choc. July 12.

Albert, Phyllis Cohen. 1977. The Modernization of French Jewry: Consistory and Community in the Nineteenth Century. Waltham, MA: Brandeis University Press.

Allali, Jean-Pierre, et al. 1989. Les Juifs de Tunisie. Paris: Editions du Scribe.

Allouche-Benayoun, Joelle, and Doris Bensimon. 1998. Les juifs d'Algerie: Mémoires et identités plurielles. Paris: Stavit.

Alon, Gedaliah. 1977. The Levitical Uncleanness of Gentiles. *In* Jews, Judaism and the Classical World: Studies in Jewish History in the Time of the Second Temple and Talmud. Jerusalem: Magnes.

Amit-Talai, Vered, and Helena Wulff. 1995. Youth Cultures: A Cross-Cultural Perspective. New York: Routledge.

Anderson, Benedict. 1991. Imagined Communities: Reflections on the Origin and Spread of Nationalism. New York: Verso.

Appadurai, Arjun. 2006. Fear of Small Numbers: An Essay on the Geography of Anger. Durham, NC: Duke University Press.

———. 1998. Dead Certainty: Ethnic Violence in the Era of Globalization. Public Culture 10(2):225–247.

———. 1996. Modernity at Large: Cultural Dimensions of Globalization. Minneapolis: University of Minnesota Press.

l'Arche. 1979. Unsigned Letter to the Editor. September-October: 9.

Arkin, Kimberly. 2009. Rhinestone Aesthetics and Religious Essence: Looking Jewish in Paris. American Ethnologist 36(4):722–734.

Asad, Talal. 1993. Genealogies of Religion: Discipline and Reasons of Power in Christianity and Islam. Baltimore: Johns Hopkins University Press.

Association des Directeurs d'Ecoles Juives de France (ADEJF). 1989a. L'ADEJF indigné. 1989. Actualité Juive, June 28.

———. 1989b. Letter to the Editor. Tribune Juive, June 30–July 6:32.

Association Européenne des Directeurs d'Ecoles Juives (AEDEJ). 1978. Untitled. Hamoré 85(6):39–40.

Auslander, Leora. 2000. Bavarian Crucifixes and French Headscarves: Religious Signs and the Postmodern European State. *In* Cultural Dynamics, vol. 12. Vivek Dhareshwar et al., eds. London: Sage Publications.

———. 1996. The Gendering of Consumer Practices in Nineteenth Century France. *In* The Sex of Things: Gender and Consumption in Historical Perspective. Victoria De Grazia and Ellen Furlough, eds. Berkeley: University of California Press.

Axel, Brian. 2004. The Context of Diaspora. Cultural Anthropology 19(1):26–60.

———. 2002. The Diasporic Imaginary. Public Culture 14(2):411–428.

———. 2000. The Nation's Tortured Body: Violence, Representation, and the Formation of a Sikh "Diaspora." Durham, NC: Duke University Press.

Ayoun, Richard. 2003. Les juifs d'Algérie de l'antiquité a l'acquisition de la nationalité française. *In* L'identité des juifs d'Algérie. Shmuel Trigano, ed. Paris: Alliance Israelite Universelle.

Azeroual, Yves. 1990. Untitled interview with Marc Rochman [President of UEJF]. Actualité Juive, June 27:10–11.

———. 1989a. Réplique à mesdames et messieurs les enseignants CFDF d'Ozar Hatorah. Actualité Juive, June 28.

————. 1989b. Polemique autour d'une école juive. Actualité Juive, June 21.

————. 1983. Le culte de la table dressée: rites et traditions de la table juive algérienne. Paris: Editions A.M. Métailié.

Back, Les. 1996. New Ethnicities and Urban Culture: Racisms and Multiculture in Young Lives. New York: St Martins.

Bahloul, Joelle. 1996. The Architecture of Memory: a Jewish-Muslim household in colonial Algeria, 1937–1962. Catherine Du Peloux Menage, trans. New York: Cambridge University Press.

Balibar, Etienne, and Immanuel Wallerstein. 1991. Race, Nation, Class: Ambiguous Identities. Chris Turner, trans. New York: Verso.

Le Bars, Stéphanie. 2008. Qui représente les juifs et les musulmans? Le Monde, June 4:2.

Barth, Frederik. 1969. Ethnic Groups and Boundaries: The Social Organization of Cultural Difference. Boston: Little Brown.

Battut, Jean et al. 1995/1984. La guerre scolaire a bien eu lieu. Paris: Desclée de Brouwer.

Bauman, Zygmunt. 1991. Modernity and Ambivalence. Ithaca: Cornell University Press.

Beaud, Stephane, and Michel Pialoux. 2003. Violences urbaines, violence sociale: genèse des nouvelles classes dangereuses. Paris: Fayard.

Bellengier, Ferdinand. 2004. Le chef d'établissement privé et l'Etat. Paris: Berger-Levrault.

Benattar, Serge et al. 1989. Interview with Joseph Sitruk. Actualité Juive, November 1.

Benayoun, Chantal. 1993. L'esprit du temps: les définitions identitaires chez les Juifs et les Arabes en France. Revue Européenne des Migrations Internationales 9(3):95–117.

————. 1992. Entre l'exil assumé et l'exil réinventé: les juifs d'Afrique du Nord en France. Les Nouveaux Cahiers 110.

————. 1984. Les Juifs et la politique. Paris: Centre National de Recherche Scientifique.

Benbassa, Esther. 2010. Le CRIF, vrai lobby et faux pouvoir. Le Monde, February 17:20.

————. 2006. Non au boycott du Hamas; Le déni de légitimité dont le mouvement palestinien est l'objet freine la marche vers la paix. Libération, June 5:32.

————. 2004a. Pour une autre politique du CRIF: le président élu dimanche devra s'attacher à dissocier la lutte contre l'antisémitisme du soutien inconditionnel à Israel. Libération, May 13:40.

————. 2004b. L'urgence de la prudence: pour ne pas céder au sensationnalisme après des actes antisémite, il faut se doter d'une éthique de la réactivité. Libération, August 31, 201030:40–41.

————. 2004c. Les juifs de France, des sionistes sans sionisme. Le Monde, August 30.

———. 2003. La République face à ses minorités: les juifs hier, les musulmans aujourd'hui. Paris: Mille et Une Nuits.

———. 2002. Entre la honte et la rage; Notre éthique et notre soutien lucide à Israël nous imposent de mettre en cause les derniers agissements de son gouvernement. Libération, April 10:11.

———. 1997. Histoire des juifs de France. Paris: Editions du Seuil.

Benbassa, Esther and Jean-Christophe Attias. 2001. Nous ne sommes pas des victimes. Le Monde, December 18.

Benmergui, Eric. 1982. Untitled. Tribune Juive, May 14–20 (722):8.

Bensimon, Doris, and Sergio DellaPergola. 1984. La population juive de la France: socio-démographie et identité. Paris: Centre National de la Recherche Scientifique.

Bensimon, Doris. 1978. Relations entre juifs et musulmans au Maroc sous le Protectorat Français. In Les Relations entre juifs et musulmans en Afrique du Nord, XIX–XXème siècles. Marseilles: CNRS.

———. 1972 L'intégration des juifs nord-africains en France. La Haye: Mouton.

Bensoussan, Georges. 2004. Antisemitism in French Schools: Turmoil of a Republic. Jerusalem: Hebrew University.

Benveniste, Annie. 2002. Figures politiques de l'identité juive à Sarcelles. Paris: L'Harmattan.

Benzimra, Alain. 1982. Letter to the Editor. L'Arche, January:13.

Berg, Boas. 1982. Untitled. L'Arche, February:56–57.

Berger, David. 2002. Jacob Katz on Jews and Christians in the Middle Ages. In The Pride of Jacob: Essays on Jacob Katz and his work. Jay Harris, ed. Cambridge: Harvard University Press.

Berkowitz, Jay. 2010. Acculturation and Integration in Eighteenth-Century Metz. Jewish History 24:271–294.

Bhabha, Homi. 1994. Interrogating Identity: Franz Fanon and the Postcolonial Prerogative. In Locations of Culture. New York: Routledge.

———. 1993. Culture's In Between. Artforum International 32(1).

Birnbaum, Pierre. 2000. Jewish Destinies: Citizenship, State and Community in Modern France. Arthur Goldhammer, trans. New York: Hill and Wang.

———. 1998. Les juifs et l'affaire. In Les juifs de France. Jean-Jacques Becker and Annette Wieviorka, eds. Paris: Liana Levi.

———. 1996. The Jews of the Republic: The Political History of State Jews in France from Gambetta to Vichy. Jane Marie Todd, trans. Stanford: Stanford University Press.

———. 1995. Between Social and Political Assimilation: Remarks on the History of Jews in France. In Paths of Emancipation: Jews, States, and Citizenship Birnbaum. Pierre and Ira Katznelson, eds. Princeton: Princeton University Press.

———. 1988. Un mythe politique, "la République juive": de Léon Blum à Pierre Mendès France. Paris: Fayard.

Bitton, Marc. 1989. Untitled. Actualité Juive, June 7.

Blatt, David. 1997. Immigrant Politics in a Republican Nation. *In* Post-Colonial Cultures in France. Alec Hargreaves and Mark McKinney, eds. New York: Routledge.

Bloch, Maurice. 1977. The Past and the Present in the Present. Man 12(2):278–292.

Blommaert, Jan, and Jef Vershueren. 1996. European Concepts of Nation-Building. *In* The Politics of Difference: Ethnic Premises in a World of Power. Chicago: University of Chicago Press.

Bordenave, Yves, and Stéphanie Le Bars. 2008. La rue Petit, son ennui et ses bandes. Le Monde, June 24.

Bourdieu, Pierre. 1984. Distinction: A Social Critique of the Judgment of Taste. Richard Nice, trans. Cambridge: Harvard University Press.

Bourdieu, Pierre, and Jean-Claude Passeron. 1990. Reproduction in Education, Culture and Society. Richard Nice, trans. London: Sage.

Bourdrel, Philippe. 2004. Histoire des juifs de France: des origines à la Shoah. Tome 1. Paris: Albin Michel.

Bowen, John. 2010 Can Islam be French? Pluralism and Pragmatism in a Secularist State. Princeton: Princeton University Press.

———. 2007. Why the French Don't Like Headscarves: Islam, the State, and Public Space. Princeton: Princeton University Press.

Boyarin, Daniel. 2004. The Christian Invention of Judaism: The Theodosian Empire and the Rabbinic Refusal of Religion. Representations 85:21–57.

Boyzon-Fradet, Danielle and Serge Boulot. 1991. Le système scolaire français: aide ou obstacle à l'intégration. *In* Face au racisme. Pierre-André Taguieff, ed. Paris: Editions de la Découverte.

Brenner, Emmanuel. 2004. France, prends garde de perdre ton âme: fracture sociale et antisémitisme dans la République. Paris: Mille et Une Nuits.

Brenner, Emmanuel, et al. 2002. Les territoires perdus de la République: antisémitisme, racisme et sexisme en milieu scolaire. Paris: Mille et Une Nuits.

Bringa, Tone. 1995. Being Muslim the Bosnian Way: Identity and Community in a Central Bosnian Village. Princeton: Princeton University Press.

Brown, Wendy. 2006. Regulating Aversion: Tolerance in an Age of Identity and Empire. Princeton: Princeton University Press.

———. 2003. Neo-liberalism and the End of Liberal Democracy. Theory & Event 7(1):1–29.

Bucholtz, Mary. 2002. Youth and Cultural Practice. Annual Review of Anthropology 31:525–552.

Bunzl, Matti. 2003. Austrian Zionism and the Jews of the New Europe. Jewish Social Studies 9(2).

Cabourg, Céline, and Jessica Gourdon. 2004. La tribu chalala. Paris Observatoire, April 29–May 5:22–23.

Cesari, Jocelyne, et al. 2001. "Plus marseillais que moi, tu meurs!" Migrations, identités et territoires à Marseille. Paris: Harmattan.

Cesari, Jocelyne. 1998. Musulmans et républicains: les jeunes, l'islam et la France. Brussels: Editions Complexe.

Charpentier, David. 2008. Le privé truste les neuf premières places. Le Parisien, April 3:3.

Charrier, Chistiane. 1989. Letter to the editor. Tribune Juive, December 22–January 4, 1990:30.

Chatterjee, Partha. 1998. Secularism and Tolerance. *In* Secularism and Its Critics. Rajeev Bhargava, ed. New York: Oxford University Press.

Chombeau, Christiane. 2006. Philippe de Villiers tente de séduire l'électorat juif le plus à droite; Présidentielle stratégie du Mouvement pour la France. Le Monde, May 25.

Chouraqui, André. 1952. Les Juifs d'Afrique du Nord. Paris: Presses Universitaires de France.

———. 1998a. Histoire des juifs en Afrique du Nord: en éxil au Maghreb. Monaco: Editions du Rocher.

———. 1998b. Histoire des juifs en Afrique du Nord: le retour en Orient. Monaco: Editions du Rocher.

Chvika, Yossef. 1984. Ecole juive et communauté Israélite: leurs rapports en France et la situation à Lyon. Doctoral dissertation, Université Lumière (Lyon).

Clifford, James. 1988. The Predicament of Culture: Twentieth-Century Ethnography, Literature, and Art. Cambridge: Harvard University Press.

Conféderation française démocratique du travail, Teachers at Ozar Hatorah. 1989. Letter to the Editor. Tribune Juive, July 7–13:28.

Cohen, Erik. 2002. Les juifs de France: valeurs et identité. Paris: Fonds Social Juif Unifié.

———. 1991. L'étude et l'éducation juive en France: ou l'avenir d'une communauté. Paris: Les Editions du Cerf.

Cohen, Mark. 1996. Islam and the Jews: Myth, Counter-Myth, History. *In* Jews Among Muslims. Shlomo Deshen and Walter Zenner, eds. New York: New York University Press.

Cohen, Shaye. 1983. From the Bible to the Talmud: The Prohibition of Intermarriage. Hebrew Annual Review 7:23–39.

Cohen, Steven. 1974. The Impact of Jewish Education on Religious Identification and Practice. Jewish Social Studies 36(3/4):316–326.

Cohen-Hadria, Elie. 1980. Les juifs francophones dans la vie intellectuelle et politique de la Tunisie entre les deux guerres. *In* Judaïsme d'Afrique du Nord aux XIXe–XXe siècles. Michel Abitbol, ed. Jerusalem: Institut Ben-Zvi.

Cole, Joshua. 2010. Antisémitisme et situation coloniale pendant l'entre-deux-guerres en Algérie: les émeutes antijuives de Constantine. Vingtième Siècle 108, octobre–decembre:3–23.

Colonna, Fanny. 1997. Educating Conformity in French Colonial Algeria. *In* Tensions of Empire: Colonial Cultures in a Bourgeois World. Frederick Cooper and Ann Laura Stoler, eds. Berkeley: University of California Press.

Comaroff, Jean, and John Comaroff. 2007. Ethnicity Inc. Chicago: University of Chicago Press.

———. 2003. Reflections on Liberalism, Policulturalism, and ID-ology: Citizenship and Difference in South Africa. Social Identities 9(4).

———. 2000. Naturing the Nation: Aliens, Apocalypse, and the Postcolonial State. International Social Science Review 1(1):7–40.

———. 1992. Of Totemism and Ethnicity. *In* Ethnography and the Historical Imagination. Boulder, CO: Westview Press.

Comaroff, John. 1996. Ethnicity, Nationalism and the Politics of Difference in an Age of Revolution. *In* The Politics of Difference: Ethnic Premises in a World of Power. Chicago: University of Chicago Press.

Conan, Eric, and Henry Rousso. 1994. Vichy, un passé qui ne passe pas. Paris: Fayard.

Corcos, David. 1964. The Jews of Morocco under the Marinides. The Jewish Quarterly Review 54(4):271–287.

Coroller, Catherine. 2009. Statistiques ethniques: le duel des commissions. Libération, June 29:14.

Coroller, Catherine and Daniel Licht. 2003. "On ne modifiera pas la loi de 1905": Sarkozy revient sur la création d'un Conseil du culte musulman. Libération, February 21:14.

Cosgrove, Stuart. 2005. The Zoot Suit and Style Warfare. *In* Looking for America. Ardis Cameron, ed. Malden, MA: Blackwell Publishing

CRIF. 2008. Un jeune juif de 17 ans agressé à coups de barre de fer par une bande, dans le 19e arrondissement. June 23.

———. 2006. Incendie à une école juive de à Gagny. November 9. www.crif.org/index.php?page=articles_display/detail&aid=7843&returnto=searchadv/motor&artyd=9. Consulted June 16, 2008.

———. 2005. Aggréssion contre une école à Paris. July 24. http://www.crif.org/index.php?page=articles_display/detail&aid=5248&returnto=searchadv/motor&artyd=9. Consulted June 16, 2008.

———. 2002a. France/Antisémitisme. September 10. http://www.crif.org/index.php?page=articles_display/detail&aid=167&returnto=searchadv/motor&artyd=5. Consulted June 16, 2008.

———. 2002b. Antisémitisme. November 15. www.crif.org/index.php?page=articles_display/detail&aid=432&returnto=searchadv/motor&artyd=5. Consulted June 16, 2008.

———. 1982. Untitled. Tribune Juive, June 25–July 1 (729):19.

———. 1979. Untitled. Tribune Juive, December 29, 1978–January 5,1979 (548):26.

Ceuppens, Bambi, and Peter Geschiere. 2005. Autochthony: Local or Global? New Modes in the Struggle over Citizenship and Belonging in Africa and Europe. Annual Review of Anthropology 34:385–407.

Cukierman, Roger. 2001. Terrorisme: après le quadruple attentat aux Etats-Unis; Durban prémonitoire? Le Figaro, September 18.

Davidenkoff, Emmanuel. 2005. L'école catho veut un partage chrétien. Libération, September 21:18.

Davidson, Naomi. 2012. Only Muslim: Embodying Islam in Twentieth Century France. Ithaca: Cornell University Press.

———. 2007. Becoming Secular? Making Islam French, 1916–1982. Ph.D. dissertation, Department of History, University of Chicago.

Derai, Yves. 1991. Juifs-Arabes en France: Attention danger! Actualité Juive, January 31:1; 7.

Derai, Yves, and Yves Azeroual. 1990. Interview with Marc Bitton and Serge Malik. Actualité Juive, June 20:4–5.

Derai, Yves, and Alexandrine Cohen. 1993. Untitled interview with Joseph Sitruk. Tribune Juive, March 4:8–9.

Derczansky, A. P. 2000. Y-a-t-il une vie après l'école juive? Actualité Juive, June 15:n.p.

Dermenjian, Geneviève. 2003. Le Juif est-il français? Antisémitisme et idée républicaine en Algérie (1830–1939). In L'identité des juifs d'Algérie. Shmuel Trigano, ed. Paris: Alliance Israelite Universelle.

Dishon, Daniel. 1979. Le monde musulman: de réformisme à l'intégrisme. Tribune Juive, November 30–December 5 (596):18.

Dolby, Nadine. 2001. Constructing Race: Youth, Identity and Popular Culture in South Africa. Albany: SUNY Press.

Douglas, Mary. 1966. Purity and Danger: An Analysis of the Concepts of Pollution and Taboo. New York: Routledge.

Du Bois, W. E. B. 1989. The Souls of Black Folk. New York: Bantam Books.

Durkheim, Emile. 2002. Moral Education: A Study in the Theory and Application of the Sociology of Education. Everett Wilson, trans. New York: Free Press of Glencoe.

Eisenstadt, Shmuel, and Bernhard Giesen. 1995. The Construction of Collective Identity. Archives européenes de sociologie 36(1):72–102.

Elkouby, Prosper. 1979. Essor de l'éducation juive. L'Arche, June 1979:68–72.

Ellenson, David. 1985. Representative Orthodox Responsa on Conversion and Intermarriage in the Contemporary Era. Jewish Social Studies 47(3/4):209–220.

El-Or, Tamar. 1994. Educated and Ignorant: Ultraorthodox Jewish Women and Their World. Haim Watzman, trans. Boulder: Lynne Rienner Publishers

Escafré-Dublet, Angéline. 2008. L'Etat et la culture des immigrés, 1974–1984. Histoire@Politique: politique, culture, société 4 (January–April).

Ettinger, Yair. 2010. Slonim Grand Rabbi: Even a Firing Squad Won't Make Us Compromise on Immanuel School Row. Haaretz, June 23. Electronic resource (www.haaretz.com) consulted on August 23, 2010.

Evans, Grace. 1988. Those Loud Black Girls. In Learning to Lose: Sexism and Education. London: The Women's Press.

Eytan, Edwin. 1983. Untitled. Tribune Juive, January 7–13 (755):6.

———. 1981. Un ami d'Israél entre à l'Elysée. Tribune Juive, May 15–21 (672):4–6.

————. 1980. La grande colère des juifs de France. Tribune Juive, October 10–16:7–8.

————. 1979. Séries d'attentats antisémites. Tribune Juive, March 30-April 5 (561):11–12.

Fanon, Frantz. 1967. Black Skins White Masks. New York: Grove Press.

Fassin, Eric. 2008. Actualité de la "question noire." *In* Histoire politique des immigrations (post)coloniales: France, 1920–2008. Ahmed Boubeker and Abdellali Hajjat, eds. Paris: Editions Amsterdam.

————. n.d. Minorités: du "peril communautariste" à la dérive individualiste. Paris: Ecole Normale Supérieure.

Ferguson, Ann Arnett. 2000. Bad Boys: Public Schools and the Making of Black Masculinity. Ann Arbor: University of Michigan Press.

Fernando, Mayanthi. 2010. Reconfiguring Freedom: Muslim Piety and the Limits of Secular Law and Public Discourse in France. American Ethnologist 37(1):19–35.

————. 2009. Exceptional Citizens: Secular Muslim Women and the Politics of Difference in France. Social Anthropology 17(4):379–392.

————. 2006. "French Citizens of Muslim Faith": Islam, Secularism, and the Politics of Difference in Contemporary France. Ph.D. dissertation, Department of Anthropology, University of Chicago.

Le Figaro. 2004. Le train de la haine; a la lâcheté des voyous antisémites a répondu la lâcheté des passages du RER D. July 12 (18640):1; 7.

Finkielkraut, Alain. 2003. Au nom de l'autre: réflections sur l'antisémitisme qui vient. Paris: Gallimard.

Fourest, Caroline. 2005. La tentation obscurantiste. Paris: Grasset.

Friedman, Elizabeth. 1988. Colonialism and After: An Algerian Jewish Community. South Hadley, MA: Bergin & Garvey Publishers.

Friedman, Menachem. 1987. Life Tradition and Book Tradition in the Development of Ultraorthodox Judaism. *In* Judaism: Viewed from Within and From Without. Harvey Goldberg, ed. Albany: SUNY Press.

Foley, Douglas. 1990. Learning Capitalist Culture: Deep in the Heart of Tejas. Philadelphia: University of Pennsylvania Press.

Fordham, Signithia. 1993. 'Those Loud Black Girls': (Black) Women, Silence, and Gender "Passing" in the Academy. Anthropology and Education Quarterly 24(1):3–32.

Foster, Robert. 1991. Making National Cultures in the Global Ecumene. Annual Review of Anthropology 20:235–260.

Foucault, Michel. 1977. Discipline and Punish: the Birth of the Prison. New York: Vintage Books.

Gabizon, Cécilia. 2006. La droite progresse au sein de l'électorat juif. Le Figaro, June 19.

Garcia, Pierre-Louis. 2004. Délit d'écharpe rue des Rosiers. Libération, November 24.

Garson, Catherine. n.d. En souvenir du jour où on a brulé le Talmud. Actualité Juive.

Gaspard, Françoise, and Farhad Khosrokhavar. 1995. Le foulard et la République. Paris: Découverte.

Geertz, Clifford. 1973. The Integrative Revolution: Primordial Sentiments and Civil Politics in the New States. *In* The Interpretation of Cultures. New York: Basic Books.

Georgel, Jacques, and Anne-Marie Thorel. 1995. L'enseignement privé en France, du VIIIe au XXe siècle. Paris: Dalloz.

Geschiere, Peter, and Francis Nyamnjoh. 2000. Capitalism and Autochthony: The Seesaw of Mobility and Belonging. Public Culture 12(2):423–452.

Ghariani, Gerard. 1986. Sur le sort de nos frères en Tunisie. Actualité Juive, February 14:8.

Ghebali, Eric. 1983. Untitled. Tribune Juive, February 25–March 3 (762):16–17.

Gibson, James. 2004. Overcoming Apartheid: Can Truth Reconcile a Divided Nation? New York: Russell Sage Foundation.

Gilman, Sander. 1991. The Jew's Body. London: Routledge.

Gilroy, Paul. 1993. The Black Atlantic: Modernity and Double Consciousness. Cambridge: Harvard University Press.

———. 1992. The End of Antiracism. *In* "Race," Culture and Difference. J. Donald and A. Rattansi, eds. Newbury Park, CA: Sage Publications.

———. 1991. There Ain't No Black in the Union Jack: the Cultural Politics of Race and Nation. Chicago: University of Chicago Press.

———. 1990. Nationalism, History, and Ethnic Absolutism. History Workshop Journal 30:114–120.

Goldberg, Harvey. 1978. The Mimuna and the Minority Status of Moroccan Jews. Ethnology 17(1):75–87.

Goldschmidt, Henry. 2006. Race and Religion Among the Chosen Peoples of Crown Heights. Rutgers: Rutgers University Press.

Goldstein, Richard. 1994. The New Anti-Semitism. *In* Blacks and Jews: Alliances and Arguments. Paul Berman, ed. New York: Delacorte Press.

Gopinath, Gayatri. 1995. Bombay, UK, Yuba City: Bhangara Music and the Engendering of Diaspora. Diaspora 4(3):303–321.

Gottleib, Eric. 1982. Untitled. Tribune Juive, March 26–April 1 (715):14.

Graetz, Michael. 1996. The Jews in Nineteenth-Century France: From the French Revolution to the Alliance Israélite Universelle. Stanford: Stanford University Press.

Green, Nancy. 1986. The Pletzl of Paris: Jewish Immigrant Workers in the Belle Epoque. New York: Holmes and Meier.

Grossman, Willy. 1980. Letter to the editor. Tribune Juive, March 21–27 (612):5.

Grunewald, Jacquot. 1986. L'amitié retrouvée entre la France et Israél. Tribune Juive, March 7–13:14–19.

———. 1985a. Editorial. Tribune Juive, October 25–31:8.

———. 1985b. De la rue Copérnic en 1980 à la rue de Rivoli en 1985: les étapes de l'espoir. Tribune Juive, April 5–11:17.

———. 1984. L'école juive à Versailles. Tribune Juive, March 9-15:4–5.

———. 1983. Untitled interview with Israeli Ambassador Meir Rosenne. Tribune Juive, March 18–24 (765):14.

———. 1982. L'école juive dans l'environnement chrétien de l'école laïque. Tribune Juive, June 11–17 (726):17–18.

———. 1980a. L'antisémitisme de papa n'est pas mort. Tribune Juive, October 10-16 (641):5–6.

———. 1980b. Editorial. Tribune Juive, March 21–27 (612):8.

———. 1980c. La nécessaire de solidarité avec les travailleurs immigrés. Tribune Juive, March 6–12 (662):4.

———. 1979. La chance des juifs de France. Tribune Juive, May 18–24 (586):14–15.

Gupta, Akhil, and James Ferguson. 1992. Beyond 'Culture': Space, Identity, and the Politics of Difference. Cultural Anthropology 7(1):6–23.

Hajdenberg, Henri. 1985. Untitled. Tribune Juive, May 3–9:n.p.

———. 1980a. 12 Heures pour Israel. Tribune Juive, May 23–June 5(621–622):viii–xiv.

———. 1980b. Letter to the Editor. Tribune Juive, March 21–27 (612):2–3.

Halbwachs, Maurice. 1992. On Collective Memory. Chicago: University of Chicago Press.

Halkin, Abraham, and David Hartman. 1985. Crisis and Leadership: Epistles of Maimonides. Philadelphia: Jewish Publication Society of America.

Hall, Kathleen. 2002. Lives in Translation: Sikh Youth as British Citizens. Philadelphia: University of Pennsylvania Press.

Hall, Stuart. 1990. Cultural Identity and Diaspora. *In* Identity: Community, Culture, Difference. Jonathan Rutherford, ed. London: Lawrence and Wishart.

Hall, Stuart, and Tony Jefferson. 1976. Resistance Through Rituals: Youth Subcultures in Post-War Britain. London: Hutchinson.

Hamon, Hervé. 2004. Tant qu'il y aura des élèves. Paris: Seuil.

Hannerz, Ulf. 1989. Notes on the Global Ecumene. Public Culture 1(2):66–75.

———. 1987. The World in Creolization. Africa 57(4):546–559.

Hargreaves, Alec. 1995. Immigration, "Race," and Ethnicity in Contemporary France. New York: Routledge.

Harris, Jay. 1994. 'Fundamentalism:' Objections from a Modern Jewish Historian. *In* Fundamentalism and Gender. Hawley, John Stratton, ed. New York: Oxford University Press.

Harvey, David. 1989. The Condition of Post-Modernity: An Inquiry into the Origins of Cultural Change. New York: Blackwell.

Hasson, Maurice. 1992. Letter to the Editor. Actualité Juive, April 30:2.

Haus, Jeffrey. 2002. Liberté, Egalité, Utilité: Jewish Education and State in Nineteenth Century France. Modern Judaism 22:1–27.

———. 1997. The Practical Dimensions of Ideology: French Judaism, Jewish Education and State in the Nineteenth Century. Ph.D. dissertation, Near Eastern and Judaic Studies, Brandeis University.

Haymann, Emmanuel. 1985. SOS Nazis. Tribune Juive, April 5–11:11–12.

———. 1980. La psyschose des nazillons. Tribune Juive, June 20–26(625):9.

———. 1978. Untitled. Tribune Juive, November 10–16 (541):15.

Hayes, Christine. 1999. Intermarriage and Impurity in Ancient Jewish Sources. Harvard Theological Review 92(1):3–36.

Hebdige, Dick. 1979. Subculture: The Meaning of Style. New York: Methuen.

Hefner, Robert. 2007. School for Zealots? Islamic Education in Southeast Asia. Talk given at the Boston University Institute on Culture, Religion and World Affairs, November 17.

Hefner, Robert, and Muhammad Qasin Zaman. 2007. Schooling Islam: The Culture and Politics of Modern Muslim Education. Princeton: Princeton University Press.

Heilman, Samuel. 1994. Quiescent and Active Fundamentalisms: The Jewish Cases. *In* Accounting for Fundamentalisms. Martin Marty and R. Scott Appleby, eds. Chicago: University of Chicago Press.

Hertzberg, Arthur. 1990. The French Enlightenment and the Jews: The Origins of Modern Anti-Semitism. New York: Columbia University Press.

Herzfeld, Michael. 1997. Cultural Intimacy: Social Poetics in the Nation-State. New York: Routledge.

Hirsi Ali, Ayaan. 2007. Infidel. New York: New York Free Books.

Holmes, Douglas. 2000. Integral Europe: Fast-Capitalism, Multiculturalism, Neofascism. Princeton: Princeton University Press.

Huntington, Samuel. 1996. The Clash of Civilization and the Remaking of the World Order. New York: Simon & Schuster.

Hyman, Paula. 1998. The Jews of Modern France. Berkeley: University of California Press.

———. 1991. The Emancipation of the Jews of Alsace: Acculturation and Tradition in the Nineteenth Century. New Haven: Yale University Press.

———. 1979. From Dreyfus to Vichy: The Remaking of French Jewry, 1906–1939. New York: Columbia University Press.

Jackson, John Jr. 2008. Real Black: Adventures in Racial Sincerity. Chicago: University of Chicago Press.

Jacobson, Jessica. 1998. Islam in Transition: Religion and Identity among British-Pakistani Youth. New York: Routledge.

Jacobson, Matthew Frye. 2005. Looking Jewish, Seeing Jews. *In* Looking for America. Ardis Cameron, ed. Malden, MA: Blackwell Publishing.

Jacobson, Shari. 2006. Modernity, Conservative Religious Movements, and the Female Subject: Newly Ultraorthodox Sephardi Women in Buenos Aires. American Anthropologist 108(2):336–346.

Jarville, Eric. 2000. Untitled letter to the editor. Actualité Juive, September 7:4.

Journal Officiel. 1959. Compte rendu intégral des débats parlementairs, 1ᵉ séance, Wednesday December 23:3595–3614.

Kahn, Jean-François. 1980. Les juifs de France: ce qui change. L'Arche, November:105–106.

Kahn, Susan. 2005. The Multiple Meanings of Jewish Genes. Culture, Medicine and Psychiatry 29(2):179–192.

Katz, Ethan. 2010. Constantine Riots (1934). *In* Encyclopedia of Jews in the Islamic World. Norman Stillman, ed. Boston: Brill.

Katz, Jacob. 1961a. Exclusiveness and Tolerance: Studies in Jewish–Gentile Relations in Medieval and Modern Times. Westport, CT: Greenwood Press.

———. 1961b. Tradition and Crisis: Jewish Society at the End of the Middle Ages. Jerusalem: Hebrew University.

Kelley, Robin. 1998. The Riddle of the Zoot: Malcolm Little and Black Cultural Politics During World War II. *In* Generations of Youth: Youth Cultures and History in 20th Century America. New York: New York University Press.

Kepel, Gilles. 1987. Les banlieues de l'Islam: naissance d'une religion en France. Paris: Seuil.

Knoll, E. 1982. Letter to the editor. Tribune Juive, December 3–9 (750):24–25.

Kramer, Ne'hama. 199?. Un cri sans réponse: une bouleversante histoire vécue. Jerusalem: Kol Hatechouvah.

Kriegel, Annie. 1979. Repli-sur-soi. L'Arche, March: 24–26.

Kroeber, Afred. 1948. Anthropology. New York: Harcourt Brace.

Kuchta, David. 1996. The Making of the Self-Made Man: Class, Clothing, and English Masculinity, 1688–1832. *In* The Sex of Things: Gender and Consumption in Historical Perspective. Victoria de Grazia and Ellen Furlough, eds. Berkeley: University of California Press.

Kurtz, David. 2007. Esther Benbassa: hazard et nécessité médiatique. Controverses 4:272–280.

Ladurie, Emmanuel Leroy. 1982. Untitled. Tribune Juive, November 5–11 (746):18–19.

Landau, Philippe. 1990. La patrie en danger: d'une guerre à l'autre. *In* Histoire politique des juifs de France: entre universalisme et particularisme. Pierre Birnbaum, ed. Paris: Presses de la Fondation Nationale des Sciences Politiques.

Landrin, Sophie. 2006. Une décision du rectorat de Lyon; le collège-lycée musulman de Décines ne sera pas autorisé à ouvrir. Le Monde, August 31:12.

Laronche, Martine. 2006. La classe devient un lieu de plus en plus violent; Eric Debarbieux, directeur de l'Observatoire international de la violence à l'école. Le Monde, January 5.

Laske, Karl. 2002. Le président du CRIF dérape sur le vote FN; L'électrochoc. Libération, April 23:7.

Laskier, Michael. 1994. North African Jewry in the Twentieth Century: The Jews of Morocco, Tunisia and Algeria. New York: New York University Press.

———. 1983a. The Alliance Israélite Universelle and the Jewish Communities of Morocco: 1862–1962. Albany: SUNY Press.

———. 1983b. Aspects of the Activities of the Alliance Israélite Universelle in the Jewish Communities of the Middle East and North Africa, 1860–1918. Modern Judaism 3(2):147–171.

Le Bras, Hervé. 2009. Inutiles statistiques ethniques. Le Monde, July 15:13.

Lecat, Yvonne. 1982. Letter to the Editor. L'Arche, September-October:25.

Lefebvre, Barbara, and Ève Bonnivard. 2005. Élèves sous influence. Paris: Audibert.

Lellouche, Charles. 1986a. Untitled interview with André Rossinot (UDF). Actualité Juive, February 14:5.

———. 1986b. Untitled interview with Giselle Moreau (PC) and Didier Bariani (UDF). Actualité Juive, February 28:7.

Levi, Jean-Marc. 1985. Liaisons Dangereuses. L'Actualité Juive, September 4:n.p.

Lévy, Bernard-Henri. 2001. Etre juif aujourd'hui: une fausse erudition, un livre choquant. Le Point, October 19 (Société).

Lévy, Charles, and Sandrine Szwarc. 2003. Un mois de festivités en janvier. Actualité Juive, February 6.

Lewer, Dan. 1985. Les étudiants juifs fer de lance de SOS Racisme. Tribune Juive, May 17–23:17.

———. 1981. Untitled. Tribune Juive, February 13–19 (659):13.

Libération. 2009. Repères. December 28:10.

Lindon, Raymond. 1979. Le 'détachement' discret des juifs de France. Tribune Juive, November 9-15 (593):14–16.

Linzer, Dov. 2011. Siyyum on Zevachim—Action and Thought in Korbanot. The Daily Daf. http://www.the-daf.com/talmud-general-interest/siyyum-on-zevachim-action-and-thought-in-korbanot/. Accessed July 31, 2012.

Liscia, Richard. 1980. Untitled. L'Arche, November:36–37.

Lorcerie, Françoise. 2003. L'école et le défi ethnique: éducation et intégration. Paris: Institut National de la Recherche Pédagogique.

Lorcin, Patricia. 1995. Imperial Identities: Stereotyping, Prejudice and Race in Colonial Algeria. New York: IB Tauris.

Loss, Adam. 1980a. Ce qui bouge en profondeur. L'Arche, July:17.

———. 1980b. La communauté juive et le pouvoir. L'Arche, April:17.

———. 1979. Untitled editorial. L'Arche, May:17.

Luykx, Aurolyn. 1999. The Citizen Factory: Schooling and Cultural Production in Bolivia. Albany: State University of New York Press.

L., D. 1985. Untitled article. Tribune Juive, May 3–9.

M., C. 1990. Agréssion: elle avait parlé du racisme. Actualité Juive, May 23:5.

MacDonald, Maryon. 1989, "We are not French!" Language, Culture, and Identity in Brittany. London: Routledge.

Mahmood, Saba. 2005. Politics of Piety: The Feminist Subject and the Islamic Revival. Princeton: Princeton University Press.

Malka, Victor and Roger Ascot. 1982. Interview with Lionel Jospin. L'Arche, September–October:69.

Malkki, Liisa. 1995. Purity and Exile. Chicago: University of Chicago Press.

Mandel, Maud. Forthcoming. Muslims and Jews in France: The Genealogy of a Conflict. Princeton: Princeton University Press.

Marrus, Michael. 1971. Politics of Assimilation: A Study of the French Jewish Community at the Time of the Dreyfus Affair. Oxford: Clarendon Press.

Marrus, Michael, and Robert Paxton. 1981. Vichy France and the Jews. Stanford: Stanford University Press.

Mayer, David. 1980. Untitled. L'Arche, November:32.

McKesson, John. 1994. Concepts and Realities in a Multiethnic France. French Politics and Society 12(1):16–38.

Memmi, Albert. 1991 [1965]. The Colonizer and the Colonized. Howard Greenfeld, trans. Boston: Beacon Press.

———. 1974. Les Juifs et les Arabes. Paris: Gallimard.

Midi Libre. 2008. Rudi, jeune juif de 17 ans, tabassé par une bande à Paris. Côtes casés, fractures au crâne, coma artificiel et troubles neurologiques. June 23.

Miller, Helena. 2001. Meeting the Challenge: The Jewish Schooling Phenomenon in the UK. Oxford Review of Education 27(4):501–513.

Le Monde. 2002a. Judaisme: Michel Dreyfus-Schmidt a demandé la démission de Roger Cukierman de la présidence du CRIF. April 25.

———. 2002b. Pour le president du CRIF, c'est un message aux musulmans leur indiquant de se tenir tranquille. April 23.

de Montvalon, Jean-Baptiste, and Laetitia Van Eeckhout. 2006. La France résiste au comptage ethnique; discrimination positive. Le Monde, July 2.

Mouloud, Laurent. 2004. La dignité humaine assassinée; antisémitisme. L'Humanité, July 12:4.

Munholland, Kim. 1994. Wartime France: Remembering Vichy. French Historical Studies 18(3):801–820.

Natanson-Mosbah, Elizabeth. 1982. Letter to the Editor. L'Arche, August:11.

Neusner, Jacob. 1996. Religion and Law: How through Halakhah Judaism Sets Forth Its Theology and Philosophy. Atlanta: Scholars Press.

———. 1974. Introduction. In Understanding Rabbinic Judaism: From Talmudic to Modern Times. New York: Ktav.

Nicault, Catherine. 1990. La réceptivité au sionisme, de la fin du 19e siècle à l'aube de la seconde guerre mondiale. In Histoire politique des juifs de France: entre universalisme et particularisme. Pierre Birnbaum, ed. Paris: Presses de la fondation nationale des sciences politiques.

Noiriel, Gérard. 2007. Immigration, antisémitisme et racisme en France (xixe–xxe siècles): Discours publics, humiliations privées. Paris: Fayard.

———. 1999. Les origines républicaines de Vichy. Paris: Hachette.

———. 1996. The French Melting Pot: Immigration, Citizenship, and National

Identity. Geoffroy De Laforcade, trans. Minneapolis: University of Minnesota Press.

Observatoire du Monde Juif. 2001. Une atmosphère d'insécurité: liste des incidents dont les communautés juives ont été victimes depuis le début de la deuxième Intifada. November (1):2–9.

Ong, Aihwa. 1999. Flexible Citizenship: the Cultural Logics of Transnationality. Durham, NC: Duke University Press.

Ozouf, Mona. 1988. Festivals and the French Revolution. Alan Sheridan, trans. Cambridge: Harvard University Press.

Park, Robert. 1928. Human Migration and the Marginal Man. The American Journal of Sociology 33(6):881–893.

Petit-Ohayon, Patrick. 2004. Un tableau de l'école juive en France. L'Arche, May(555):51–53.

———. 1989. Les écoles religieuse interdites d'intégrisme? Tribune Juive, June 23–29:23.

Petit-Ohayon, Patrick, ed. 2003. L'école juive en France 1945–2003; état des lieux. Paris: Fonds Social Juif Unifié, Department de l'enseignement.

Philippe, Béatrice. 1997. Être juif dans la société française du Moyen Âge à nos jours. Paris: Éditions Complexe.

Podselver, Laurence. 2002. La techouva: Nouvelle orthodoxie juive et conversion interne. Annales: Histoire, Sciences sociales 57(2):275–296.

———. 1996. Sarcelles, une communauté bien dans sa ville. Urbanisme 291:77–81.

———. 1994. La communauté juive ou la singularité sarcelloise. Hommes et Migrations 1181:37–40.

———. 1992. La tradition réinventée: les hassidim de Loubavitch en France. Revue des Etudes Juives, July–December.

———. 1986. Le mouvement Lubavitch: déracinement et réinsertion des Sepharades. Pardès 3:54–68.

Poirier, Véronique. 1998. Ashkénazes et Séfarades: une étude comparée de leurs relations en France et en Israël (1950–1990). Paris: Le Cert.

Portes, Thierry. 2004. RER D: la police à la recherché des témoins. Le Figaro, July 12 (18640):7.

———. 2003. Faut-il craindre l'émergence des écoles musulmanes? Seuls trois établissements islamiques fonctionnent actuellement, avec un nombre limité d'élèves. Le Figaro, December 13 (18460):7.

Porton, Gary. 1988. Goyim: Gentiles and Israelites in Mishnah-Tosefta. Atlanta: Scholars Press.

Poucet, Bruno. 2005. L'application de la loi Debré. Paper presented at Nouvelles approches de l'histoire de la laïcité au XXᵉ siècle, Paris I, November 18–19.

Povinelli, Elizabeth. 2002. The Cunning of Recognition: Indigenous Alterities and the Making of Australian Multiculturalism. Durham, NC: Duke University Press.

Rampton, Ben. 1999. Sociolinguistics and Cultural Studies: New Ethnicities, Liminality and Interaction. Social Semiotics 9(3):355–373.

Rancière, Jacques. 1999. Disagreement: Politics and Philosophy. Julie Rose, trans. Minneapolis: University of Minnesota Press.

Ribert, Evelyne. 2006. Liberté, égalité, carte d'identité: les jeunes issus de l'immigration et l'appartenance nationale. Paris: Editions la Découverte.

Rodrigue, Aron. 1990. L'Exportation du paradigme révolutionnaire: son influence sur le judaïsme sépharade et oriental. In Histoire politique des juifs de France: entre universalisme et particularisme. Pierre Birnbaum, ed. Paris: Presses de la Fondation Nationale des Sciences Politiques.

Rollot, Catherine. 2007. La violence à l'école progressé de 7% dans les ZEP en 2005-2006. Le Monde, January 3:10.

Rosenak, Michael. 1993. Jewish Fundamentalism in Israeli Education. In Fundamentalisms and Society: Reclaiming the Sciences, the Family, and Education. Martin Marty and R. Scott Appleby, eds. Chicago: University of Chicago Press.

Rothschild, Alain. 1979. Untitled. Tribune Juive, April 6–12 (562):15.

de Rothschild, Guy. 1980. Untitled article. L'Arche, November:67.

Roos, Gilbert. 1982. Untitled. Tribune Juive, July 23–29 (732):22.

Rousso, Henry. 1991. The Vichy Syndrome: History and Memory in France Since 1944. Cambridge, MA: Harvard University Press.

Roy, Olivier le. 2004. Globalized Islam: The Search for a New Ummah. New York: Columbia University Press.

Rufin, Jean-Christophe. 2004. Chantier sur la lutte contre le racisme et l'antisémitisme. Report for the French Ministry of the Interior. Accessed through lesrapports.ladocumentationfrancaise.fr on July 8, 2008.

Ryan, Donna. 1996. The Holocaust and the Jews of Marseille: The Enforcement of Anti-Semitic Politics in Vichy. Champaign: University of Illinois Press.

Ryan, James. 2004. "Brown," School Choice, and the Suburban Veto. Virginia Law Review 90(6):1635–1647.

Sabbath, Jacques, and Victor Malka. 1980. Interview with Raymond Barre. L'Arche, November:22–23.

Safran, William. 1985. The Mitterrand Regime and Its Policies of Ethnocultural Accommodation. Comparative Politics 18(1):41–63.

Sahlins, Peter. 1990. Natural Frontiers Revisited: France's Boundaries Since the Seventeenth Century. American Historical Review 95(5):1423–1451.

Said, Edward. 1978. Orientalism. New York: Pantheon Books.

Sartre, Jean-Paul. 1946. Réflexions sur la question juive. Paris: P. Moirhien.

Schnapper, Dominique. 1983. Jewish Identities in France: An Analysis of Contemporary French Jewry. Arthur Goldhammer, trans. Chicago: University of Chicago Press.

Schnapper, Dominique, and Sylvie Strudel. 1983. Le 'vote juif' en France. Revue Française de Science Politique, December.

Schneider, William. 1990. Quality and Quantity: The Quest for Biological Regeneration in Twentieth-Century France. New York: Cambridge University Press.

Schuker, Stephen A. 1985. Origins of the "Jewish Problem" in the Later Third

Republic. *In* The Jews in Modern France. Frances Malino and Bernard Wasserstein, eds. Hanover, NH: Brandeis University Press.

Schwarzfuchs, Simon. 1989. Du juif à l'israélite: Histoire d'une mutation, 1770–1870. Paris: Fayard.

———. 1980. Colonialisme français et colonialisme juif. *In* Judaïsme d'Afrique du Nord aux XIXᵉ–XXᵉ siècles. Michael Abitbol, ed. Jerusalem Institut Ben-Zvi.

———. 1979. Napoleon, the Jews, and the Sanhedrin. Boston: Routledge.

———. 1975. Les juifs de France. Paris: A. Michel.

Scott, Joan Wallach. 2005. Parité: Sexual Equality and the Crisis of French Universalism. Chicago: University of Chicago Press.

———. 1996. Only Paradoxes to Offer: French Feminists and the Rights of Man. Cambridge: Harvard University Press.

Sebag, Paul. 1991. Histoire des juifs de Tunisie: des origines à nos jours. Paris: l'Harmattan.

Seeman, Don. 1999. "One People, One Blood": Public Health, Political Violence, and HIV in an Ethiopian-Israeli Setting. Culture, Medicine and Psychiatry 23(2):159–195.

Seligman, Adam. 2004. Modest Claims: Dialogues and Essays on Tolerance and Tradition. Notre Dame: University of Notre Dame Press.

———. 2000. Modernity's Wager: Authority, the Self, and Transcendence. Princeton: Princeton University Press.

Seligman, Adam et al. 2008. Ritual and Its Consequences: An Essay on the Limits of Sincerity. New York: Oxford University Press.

Seligman, Adam, and Robert Weller. 2012. Rethinking Pluralism: Ritual, Experience and Ambiguity. New York: Oxford University Press.

Serafini, Tonino. 2008. Un jeune juif entre la vie et la mort après avoir été lynché. Libération, June 23.

Shapiro, Howard, and Arnold Dashefsky. 1974. Religious Education and Ethnic Identification: Implications for Ethnic Pluralism. Review of Religious Research 15(2):93–102.

Sheva, Arutz. 2004. Untitled. Connec'sion, electronic newsletter, July 14, www.connec-sion.com/cgi-bin/gce/gce.cgi?id=4011.

Shepard, Todd. 2006. The Invention of Decolonization: The Algerian War and the Remaking of France. Ithaca: Cornell University Press.

Shohat, Ella. 1988. Zionism from the Standpoint of its Jewish Victims. Social Text 19/20:1–35.

Sigal, John et al. 1981. Impact of Jewish Education on Jewish Identification in a Group of Adolescents. Jewish Social Studies 43(3/4):229–236.

Silbert, Reine. 1986. Face aux échéances du 16 mars le vote juif: un je ne sais quoi et un presque rien qui pourraient faire la différence pour les candidats en bas de liste. Tribune Juive, March 14-20:14–18.

———. 1985 Voyage au bout du racisme. Tribune Juive, June 28–July 4:14–15.

Silverman, Maxim. 1992. Deconstructing the Nation: Immigration, Racism, and Citizenship in Modern France. London: Routledge.

Silverstein, Paul. 2004. Algeria in France: Transpolitics, Race and Nation. Bloomington: Indiana University Press.

Skelton, Trace, and Gill Valentine. 1998. Cool Places: Geographies of Youth Cultures. New York: Routledge.

Smolar, Piotr. 2004. Stupeur après l'agréssion antisémite d'une femme dans le RER. Le Monde, July 13.

Smolarski, Henri. 1986. Car vous avez été des étrangers. Tribune Juive, July 4–10:4.

Soloveitchik, Hayim. 1978. Can Halakhic Texts Talk History? AJS Review 3:153–196.

———. 1994. Rupture and Reconstruction: The Transformation of Contemporary Orthodoxy. Tradition 28(4). www.lookstein.org/links/orthodoxy

———. 2003. Principles and Pressure: Jewish Trade in Gentile Wine in the Middle Ages. Tel Aviv: Am Oved [Hebrew].

Stasi Commission. 2004. Rapport de la commission de réflexion sur l'application du principe de laïcité dans la République remis au Président de la République le 11 décembre 2003. Paris: La Documentation Française.

Sternhell, Zeev. 1985. The Roots of Popular Anti-Semitism in the Third Republic. In The Jews in Modern France Frances Malino and Bernard Wasserstein, eds. Hanover, NH: Brandeis University Press.

Stillman, Norman. 1991. The Jews of Arab Lands in Modern Times. New York: Jewish Publication Society.

———. 1980. L'expérience Judéo-Marocaine: Un point de vue révisionniste. In Judaïsme d'Afrique du Nord aux XIXe-XXe siècles. Michel Abitbol, ed. Jerusalem: Institut Ben-Zvi.

Stock-Morton, Phyllis. 1988. Moral Education for a Secular Society: The Development of Morale Laïque in Nineteenth Century France. Albany: State University of New York Press.

Stoler, Ann Laura. 1997. Sexual Affronts and Racial Frontiers: European Identities and the Cultural Politics of Exclusion in Colonial Southeast Asia. In Tensions of Empire: Colonial Cultures in a Bourgeois World. Frederick Cooper and Ann Laura Stolers, eds. Berkeley: University of California Press.

Stora, Benjamin. 2003. Exils multiples des juifs d'Algérie. In L'identité des juifs d'Algérie. Shmuel Trigano, ed. Paris: Alliance Israelite Universelle.

———. 1992. La gangrène et l'oubli: la mémoire de la guerre d'Algérie. Paris: Editions de la Découverte.

Strouf, Jean-François. 1990. Du tchador à la kippa. Tribune Juive, January 19–25:25.

Strudel, Sylvie. 1996. Votes juifs: itinéraires migratoires, religieux et politiques. Paris: Presses de la Fondation Nationale des Sciences Politiques.

Sussman, Sarah. 2002. Changing Lands, Changing Identities: The Migration of Algerian Jewry to France, 1954–1967. Ph.D. dissertation, Department of History, Stanford University.

Sweets, John. 1988. Hold That Pendulum! Redefining Fascism, Collaborationism and Resistance in France. French Historical Studies 15(4):731–758.

Szlakmann, Charles. 1990. Untitled. Actualité Juive, April 25:11.

Taguieff, Pierre-André. 2005. La République enlisée: pluralisme, communautarisme et citoyenneté. Paris: Syrtes.

———. 2002. La nouvelle judéophobie. Paris: Mille et Une Nuits.

———. 2001. The Force of Prejudice: Racism and Its Doubles. Minneapolis: University of Minneapolis Press.

Taieb, Jacques. 1989. Les temps nouveaux. *In* Les juifs de Tunisie. Jean-Pierre Allali, ed. Paris: Editions du Scribe.

Tambiah, Stanley. 1990. Presidential Address: Reflections on Communal Violence in South Asia. Journal of Asian Studies 49(4):741–760.

Tapia, Claude. 1986. Les juifs sépharades en France (1965–1985): Etudes psycho-sociologiques et historiques. Paris: Editions l'Hartmattan.

Tarnero, Jacques. 2001. De Jérusalem à Durban: les jouisseurs de haine. Le Monde, September 11.

———. 1983. Les nouveaux drapeaux de l'antisionisme. Tribune Juive, April 1–14 (767):12–13.

Taussig, Michael. 1999. Defacement: Public Secrecy and the Labor of the Negative. Stanford: Stanford University Press.

Taylor, Charles. 1994. The Politics of Recognition. *In* Multiculturalism: Examining the Politics of Recognition. Amy Gutman, ed. Princeton: Princeton University Press.

Le Temps. 2007. Un deuxième lycée musulman a ouvert ses portes en France. March 6.

Ternsien, Xavier. 2005. Le discours musclé de Roger Cukierman au diner annuel du CRIF est critiqué par des juifs de France. Le Monde, March 4.

Touaty, Gerard. 1982a. Politique Tac. Actualité Juive, November 10.

———. 1982b. Petit plaidoyer pour un doux fanatisme. Actualité Juive, December 2.

Tribalat, Michèle. 1995. Faire France: Une enquête sur les immigrés et leurs enfants. Paris: La Découverte.

Tribune Juive. 1986. Le calme dans les lycées juifs. December 12–18:10.

———. 1983. Le 1ᵉʳᵉ mai antisioniste de la CGT. May 5–12 (771):22.

———. 1980. Un tract musulman. September 1–8(635):19.

———. 1979. Retour en Egypte. April 6–12 (562):15.

Trigano, Shmuel, ed. 2003. L'identité des juifs d'Algérie: une expérience originale de la modernité. Paris: Alliance Israélite Universelle.

Trigano, Shmuel. 2007. Une enterprise de déligitimation de l'état d'Israël. Published on desinfo.com, May 25.

———. 2003 La démission de la République. Paris: Presses Universitaires de France.

———. 2001. Les juifs de France visés par l'Intifada? Observatoire du monde juif 1:1–17.

———. 2000. Les logiques perverses de la politique française. Observatoire du monde juif, November (1):22–28.

———. 1994. The Notion of a 'Jewish Community' in France, a Special Case of Jewish Identity. *In* Jewish Identities in the New Europe. Jonathan Webber, ed. Washington, DC: Oxford Center for Postgraduate Hebrew Studies.

———. 1980a. Les sépharades comme question. Tribune Juive, June 20–26 (625):20–21.

———. 1980b. La conscience sépharade. Tribune Juive, May 23–June 5(621–622):14–16.

———. 1979a. Les fils sont sur le point de naître et point de force pour accoucher. L'Arche, March:38–39.

———. 1979b. Vers un renouveau de la question juive. L'Arche, February:36–37.

UEJF-SOS Racisme. 2002. Les Antifeujs: le livre blanc des violences antisémites en France depuis septembre 2000. Paris: Calmann-Lévy.

Van der Veer, Peter. 2006. Pim Fortuyn, Theo van Gogh and the Politics of Tolerance in the Netherlands. Public Culture 18(1):111–124.

Van Eeckhout, Laetitia. 2009. Des chercheurs s'alarment du 'retour de la race.' Le Monde, July 1:11.

———. 2005. Un appel est lancé contre les "ratonnades anti-blancs." Le Monde, March 26.

Vichniac, Judith. 1991. French Socialists and Droit à la Différence: a changing dynamic. French Politics and Society 9(1):41–56.

Vidaline, Anne. 2007. Décline: la foi des pionniers. L'Express, March 15 (2906):15.

Wahl, Roger. 1982. Letter to the Editor. Tribune Juive, September 3–9 (734–737):n.p.

Waintrop, Bertrand. 1993. Une circulaire contre l'intégration. Tribune Juive, March 11:23.

Warner, Michael. 1992. The Mass Public and the Mass Subject. *In* Habermas and the Public Sphere. Craig Calhoun, ed. Cambridge: MIT Press.

Weber, Eugen. 1985. Reflections on Jews in France. *In* The Jews in Modern France. Frances Malino and Bernard Wasserstein, eds. Hanover, NH: Brandeis University Press.

———. 1976. Peasants into Frenchmen: The Modernization of Rural France. Stanford: Stanford University Press.

Weil, Patrick. 2005. La République et sa diversité: Immigration, intégration, discriminations. Paris: Seuil.

———. 1998. De l'Affaire Dreyfus à l'Occupation. *In* Les juifs de France. Jean-Jacques Becker and Annette Wieviorka, eds. Paris: Liana Levi.

Weill-Raynal, Aude, and Gilles-William Goldnadel. 1982. Untitled. Tribune Juive, June 25–July 1 (729):18.

Weinstock, Nathan. 2004. Histoire de chiens: la dhimmitude dans le conflit Israelo-Palestinien. Paris: Mille et Une Nuits.

Weisberg, Richard. 1996. Vichy Law and the Holocaust in France. New York: New York University Press.

Werbner, Pnina. 2002. Imagined Diasporas Among Manchester Muslims: The Public Performance of Pakistani Transnational Identity Politics. Santa Fe: School of American Research Press.

Wieviorka, Annette. 1992. Déportation et génocide: entre la mémoire et l'oubli. Paris: Plon.

Wieviorka, Michel. 2005. La tentation antisémite: la haine des juifs en France aujourd'hui. Paris: Laffont.

———. 1992. La France Raciste. Paris: Editions du Seuil.

Wihtol de Wenden, Catherine. 1999. Les "jeunes issus de immigration," entre integration culturelle et exclusion sociale. In Immigration et inégration: l'état des saviors. Philippe Dewitte, ed. Paris: Editions de la Découverte.

Wikan, Unni. 2002. Generous Betrayal: Politics of Culture in the New Europe. Chicago: University of Chicago Press.

Wilder, Gary. 2005. The French Imperial Nation-State: Negritude and Colonial Humanism between the Two World Wars. Chicago: University of Chicago Press.

Willis, Paul. 1977. Learning to Labor: How Working Class Kids Get Working Class Jobs. New York: Columbia University Press.

Winock, Michel. 2004. La France et les juifs: de 1789 à nos jours. Paris: Seuil.

Wulff, Helena. 1995. Inter-racial Friendship: Consuming Youth Styles, Ethnicity and Teenage Femininity in South London. In Youth Cultures: A Cross-Culture Perspective. Vered Amit-Talai and Helena Wulff, eds. New York: Routledge.

Ya'ari, Pinhas. 1982. L'école juive: problèmes de survie. Tribune Juive, June 11–17 (726):26–30.

———. 1983. Untitled. Tribune Juive, March 25–31:4–5.

Ye'or, Bat. 2005. Eurabia: The Euro-Arab Axis. Rutherford, NJ: Fairleigh Dickinson University Press.

———. 1999. The Dhimmi Factor in the Exodus of Jews from Arab Countries. In The Modern Jewish Exodus from Arab Lands. Malka Hillel Shulewitz, ed. New York: Cassel.

———. 1985. The Dhimmi: Christians and Jews under Islam. Maisel, David, trans. Rutherford, NJ: Farleigh Dickinson University Press.

———. 1980. Le dhimmi: profil de l'opprimé en Orient et en Afrique du nord depuis la conquête Arabe. Paris: Anthropolos.

Yerushalmi, Yosef. 1996. Zakhor: Jewish History and Jewish Memory. Seattle: University of Washington Press.

Zafrani, Haim. 2005. Two Thousand Years of Jewish Life in Morocco. New York: Sephardic House.

Zeitlin, Solomon. 1960. The Offspring of intermarriage. Jewish Quarterly Review 51(2):135–140.

Zeldin, M. 1983. Jewish schools and American Society: Patterns of Action and Reaction. Religious Education 2(2).